STUDIES ON MODERN ASIA AND AFRICA

Volume 6

INDIA AND THE COMMONWEALTH 1885–1929

INDIA AND THE
COMMONWEALTH 1885–1929

S. R. MEHROTRA

LONDON AND NEW YORK

First published in 1965 by George Allen & Unwin Ltd

This edition first published in 2022
by Routledge
2 Park Square, Milton Park, Abingdon, Oxon OX14 4RN

and by Routledge
605 Third Avenue, New York, NY 10158

Routledge is an imprint of the Taylor & Francis Group, an informa business

© 1965 George Allen & Unwin Ltd

All rights reserved. No part of this book may be reprinted or reproduced or utilised in any form or by any electronic, mechanical, or other means, now known or hereafter invented, including photocopying and recording, or in any information storage or retrieval system, without permission in writing from the publishers.

Trademark notice: Product or corporate names may be trademarks or registered trademarks, and are used only for identification and explanation without intent to infringe.

British Library Cataloguing in Publication Data
A catalogue record for this book is available from the British Library

ISBN: 978-1-03-215171-7 (Set)
ISBN: 978-1-00-324754-8 (Set) (ebk)
ISBN: 978-1-03-215369-8 (Volume 6) (hbk)
ISBN: 978-1-03-215374-2 (Volume 6) (pbk)
ISBN: 978-1-00-324383-0 (Volume 6) (ebk)

DOI: 10.4324/9781003243830

Publisher's Note
The publisher has gone to great lengths to ensure the quality of this reprint but points out that some imperfections in the original copies may be apparent.

Disclaimer
The publisher has made every effort to trace copyright holders and would welcome correspondence from those they have been unable to trace.

INDIA AND THE COMMONWEALTH
1885-1929

BY

S. R. MEHROTRA

*Lecturer in South Asian Politics, School
of Oriental and African Studies,
University of London*

London
GEORGE ALLEN & UNWIN LTD
RUSKIN HOUSE MUSEUM STREET

FIRST PUBLISHED IN 1965

This book is copyright under the Berne Convention. Apart from any fair dealing for the purpose of private study, research, criticism or review, as permitted under the Copyright Act, 1956, no portion may be reproduced by any process without written permission. Enquiries should be addressed to the Publishers.

© *George Allen & Unwin Ltd, 1965*

PRINTED IN GREAT BRITAIN
in 11 on 12 point Fournier type
BY SIMSON SHAND LTD
LONDON, HERTFORD AND HARLOW

FOREWORD

The decision of newly independent India and Pakistan in 1947 to remain within the Commonwealth came as a surprise to many well-informed observers. In the light of nationalist statements made during the years of war, it had been expected that India, if not Pakistan, would quit the Commonwealth; and in the final headlong rush to independence little discussion was directed to clarifying this particular issue. A full explanation of what happened and why it happened must be sought in the history of the subject.

Despite its great importance, the subject of India's place in the Commonwealth in the nineteenth and early twentieth centuries has received little attention from scholars, and particularly from Indian scholars. Dr Mehrotra's crystal-clear, incisive, well-balanced and thorough study is therefore to be warmly welcomed. It reveals the main phases through which Indian consideration of the subject passed, and also gives a new dimension to our understanding of the part which India played in defining and re-defining the Commonwealth idea. His book therefore forms a contribution both to Commonwealth and modern Indian history.

Dr Mehrotra first analyses the acceptance of the view in the nineteenth century both in India and Britain that India was to follow the model of colonial government leading to dominion status. This leads to a discussion of the nature of the transition in thought which took place in the first quarter of the twentieth century culminating in the view that complete independence, which it is important to note did not mean secession, must be India's aim. Naturally this inquiry is conducted with major reference to the Indian National Congress, but Dr Mehrotra also examines the attitudes of the Muslim League, and in a particularly valuable chapter draws fresh attention to the contribution of the Liberals and the Liberal Federation, whose activities have tended to be obscured by the failure of the system of dyarchy which they tried to work after 1919.

Dr Mehrotra succeeds in showing that it was the simultaneous growth and enlargement of the idea of Commonwealth in India and of the concept of dominion status in the Commonwealth at large which made it feasible in 1947 for India and Pakistan to become Commonwealth members in the fullest sense.

C. H. PHILIPS

School of Oriental and African Studies

CONTENTS

FOREWORD by Professor C. H. Philips		7
INTRODUCTION		11
I	The Growth of Indian Nationalism and British Policy in India, 1885–1910	15
II	War and a New Angle of Vision	56
III	The Indian National Congress and the Commonwealth	107
IV	The National Liberal Federation of India and the Commonwealth	148
V	The All-India Muslim League and the Commonwealth	179
VI	India, Britain and the Commonwealth, 1917–29	208
	Some Concluding Reflections	254
	Select Bibliography	258
	Index	280

INTRODUCTION

The transformation of the British Empire into the modern Commonwealth has been one of the most remarkable events of our age and provides a perennial source of interest to the students of history. The subject has a special significance for students from those parts of the Empire which have grown or are growing into the sphere of the Commonwealth. It is a record of life which is their own. And even where it is not directly and immediately so, it affords a wider perspective which is essential to the proper understanding of the histories of their own individual countries. It would, for example, be a mistake to examine the history of India under British rule merely as the outcome of her relationship with Great Britain without taking into account the developments, both past and contemporaneous, in other parts of the Empire, for it would mean ignoring some of the deepest, most essential and most fruitful factors that have gone into its making. Neither logic nor accident but historical experience has been the mainspring of British Imperial policy. Nor can it be denied that the history of the British Empire has a certain unity and rhythm of its own.

The study of the growth of the idea of Commonwealth in India is full of interest not only with reference to Indian history, but to Commonwealth history as a whole. The modern Commonwealth is a living monument to the constructive genius of the British people, but it has been made as much by nationalism in the distant parts of the Empire as by British statesmanship. Enthusiasts and heretics, imperialists and nationalists—all have contributed to its shaping. It has been truly a work of challenge and response. If Canadians are proud of the fact that their country has played a major part in the long, peaceful evolution through the nineteenth and twentieth centuries which has transformed the British Empire into the British Commonwealth, Indians may take pride in the fact that in the evolution of the modern multi-racial Commonwealth their country has played a significant and often a decisive role.

The contribution which the older Dominions made to the evolution of the Commonwealth and their individual conceptions of the latter have been examined by many eminent scholars. The story has not been told from the Indian point of view. The present study is a modest attempt to fill this gap. It concerns itself with a neglected aspect of both Commonwealth and Indian history.

This book is a study of the attitudes of the three major political parties in India—the Indian National Congress, the National Liberal

Federation of India, and the All-India Muslim League—towards the Empire-Commonwealth during the years 1885–1929. The reasons why the present inquiry has been confined to these three political parties may be stated at once: they alone were all-India organizations worth the name; they alone did any conscious thinking on the subject; and between them they could well claim to represent the main currents of organized public opinion in the country. Our starting point is the year 1885, when the Indian National Congress—the party which was to lead the Indian freedom movement—was organized. We bring our inquiry to a close in 1929, the year in which the British Government clearly affirmed their intention of granting India Dominion Status in the fullness of time and in which also the Congress rejected that goal in favour of 'Complete Independence'. The period covered in this book is momentous in Indian history and far more so in Commonwealth history as anyone who tries to recall the developments from, say, Gladstone's unsuccessful attempt in 1886 to give 'Home Rule' to Ireland to the passing of the Statute of Westminster in 1931, will realize.

The main theme of this study is the growth of the Commonwealth idea in India. It is not a political or constitutional history of the period. As internal politics dominated the scene and exercised a direct and immediate influence on the attitudes of the various parties towards the Empire-Commonwealth, they have been closely examined. An attempt has, however, been made to confine the study of domestic issues to what is strictly relevant to an analysis of the principal theme.

The realm of intellect offers great opportunities for more systematic and intensive cultivation but rarely a virgin field. Intellectual discoverers and explorers seem to have been everywhere. There is no dearth of books dealing with the history of the Indian national movement or with the constitutional and political issues of the period. Stray references in such general works to the attitude of Indians towards the Empire-Commonwealth are not hard to find. Intra-Commonwealth affairs have found able historians, but there have been only a few scholars such as Professors W. K. Hancock, A. B. Keith and P. N. S. Mansergh, who have really attempted to bring the light of Commonwealth history to bear on the study of Indian problems. Writers on Indian history, even when they have been British, have generally lacked the necessary Commonwealth perspective. The two notable exceptions have been Professor John Coatman and Sir Reginald Coupland. No attempt has, however, been made so far to examine closely how politically-minded Indians thought about the

INTRODUCTION

Empire-Commonwealth. What did the British Empire mean to the early Indian nationalists? What was their idea of India's place therein? How did the ideal of self-government for India on the Dominion model grow? How did the concept of Dominion Status come to be applied to India? What did it signify to Indian nationalists? What part did India play in the evolution of the modern Commonwealth? Why was India's continued association with the Commonwealth valued by people in India and in England? These are some of the questions to which answers have been attempted in the following pages.

This book has grown out of a thesis I submitted on the same subject for the degree of Doctor of Philosophy in the University of London in 1960. I am grateful to the British Council for the award of a scholarship for two years (1958–60) and to the University of Saugor for granting me study leave for the period, which enabled me to pursue my studies at the School of Oriental and African Studies, University of London. I should like to thank the staff of the Public Record Office, London, the India Office Library, the British Museum, the National Library of Scotland, Edinburgh, and the University of Birmingham Library for their courtesy and helpfulness. I am indebted to Mr Dermot Morrah for permission to use the Curtis Papers and to the Librarian of the University of Birmingham for allowing me leave to use the Austen Chamberlain Papers. Professor Nicholas Mansergh of St John's College, Cambridge, Professor Kenneth Robinson, Director of the Institute of Commonwealth Studies, London, Professor Gerald S. Graham of King's College and Dr Mary Cumpston of Birkbeck College, London, have read this book in typescript and I am grateful to them for their many criticisms and suggestions. My greatest debt is to Professor C. H. Philips, Director of the School of Oriental and African Studies, who, amidst his numerous preoccupations, found time to guide me in my research and has very kindly written a Foreword to this book. I must record my grateful thanks to the Publications Committee of the School of Oriental and African Studies, particularly to its Secretary, Mr J. R. Bracken, for including this book for publication in their series of Studies on Modern Asia and Africa. My thanks are due also to Mrs Margaret Morris, Mr R. A. Hasson and my wife for assisting me in preparing the work for press.

1

THE GROWTH OF INDIAN NATIONALISM AND BRITISH POLICY IN INDIA, 1885-1910

In 1884 a distinguished ex-Indian civil servant, Sir John Strachey,[1] delivered a series of lectures on India at the University of Cambridge. He began by telling his audience: 'This is the first and most essential thing to learn about India—that there is not, and never was an India....'[2] Nor need it be feared, Strachey added, that the bonds of union fashioned by British rule could ever 'in any way lead towards the growth of a single Indian nationality'.[3] 'However long may be the duration of our dominion,' he remarked, 'however powerful may be the centralizing attraction of our government, or the influence of the common interests which grow up, no such issue can follow.'[4] To Strachey it seemed 'impossible' 'that men of Bombay, the Punjab, Bengal and Madras should ever feel that they belong to one great Indian nation'.[5]

Next year, in 1885, another Indian civil servant, Henry Cotton,[6] published a book entitled *New India or India in Transition*, in which he pointed out that significant changes were taking place in India and a new nation was rising before their eyes. Mainly as a result of British rule, wrote Cotton, and especially because of the growth of English education, a feeling of nationality was fast developing in the country which needed only an organization to crystallize.[7]

In the event, it was not Strachey's but Cotton's judgement which proved to be correct. Before the year 1885 ran out, the spirit of nationality in India had found a body in the Indian National Congress.

[1] B. 1823; entered Bengal Civil Service 1842; Lieutenant-Governor of the North-West Provinces 1874–6; member of Viceroy's council 1876–80; returned to England 1880; member of Secretary of State's council 1885–95; d. 1907.
[2] Strachey, *India* (1888), p. 5.
[3] Ibid., p. 8. [4] Ibid. [5] Ibid.
[6] Henry John Stedman Cotton, b. 1845; entered Indian Civil Service 1867; Chief Commissioner of Assam 1896–1902; KCSI 1902; retired 1902; President of the Indian National Congress 1904; MP 1906–10; d. 1915.
[7] Cotton, *New India or India in Transition* (1885), pp. 3 ff. Charles Dilke had noted these developments as early as 1867 on a visit to India. See *Greater Britain* (1868), vol. ii, p. 388.

The factors which contributed towards the growth of a national movement in India may be noted briefly. The British *Raj*, which united and held together the vast sub-continent and ensured its peace and security, made a pan-Indian political consciousness possible. The increasing influence of a free press and the progress of railways, posts and telegraphs broke down barriers which separated different sections of the communities in India and facilitated their union for a common purpose. The spread of English education and of Western ideas of liberty, equality and nationality provided the motive force. It was encouraged by the growth of self-government in the Colonies[1] and the national movements in Europe—the unification of Italy and Germany, and, more especially, the Home Rule agitation in Ireland. Economic and social discontent, racial bitterness, and cultural revivalism, all played an important part.

The Congress, however, did not begin as an organization in opposition to British rule. It owed its origin largely to the initiative of a retired British civil servant, Allan Octavian Hume;[2] it was blessed by the Viceroy of the day, Lord Dufferin.[3] Hume had the sympathy and wisdom to understand that 'the broadcast dissemination of Western education and Western ideas of liberty, the rights of subjects, public spirit and patriotism' had let loose forces in India which needed control and direction into channels through which they might 'flow, not to ravage and destroy but to fertilize and regenerate'.[4] The Congress was to serve the purpose of 'a safety-valve', an 'overt and constitutional channel' for the discharge of the Indian ferment.[5] Its fundamental objectives were laid down to be the promotion of Indian nationality, the social, moral and political advancement of the Indian people, and 'the consolidation of the union between England and India, by securing the modification of such of its conditions as may be unjust or injurious'.[6]

[1] The term 'Colonies' is used here and in the following pages in the sense of the self-governing Colonies, which later came to be called the Dominions.

[2] B. 1829; son of the Radical politician Joseph Hume (1777–1855); entered Bengal Civil Service 1849; awarded CB for services in Mutiny 1860; Secretary in the Revenue and Agricultural Department, Government of India 1870–9; retired 1882; General Secretary of the Indian National Congress 1885–1906; left India 1892; d. 1912.

[3] Frederick Temple Hamilton-Temple Blackwood, first Marquis of Dufferin and Ava (1826–1902). Under-Secretary for India 1864–6; Governor-General of Canada 1872–8; Ambassador at St Petersburg 1879–81 and at Constantinople 1881–2; Special Commissioner to Egypt 1882–3; Viceroy of India 1884–8; Ambassador at Rome 1889–91 and at Paris 1891–6.

[4] W. Wedderburn, *Allan Octavian Hume* (1913), p. 66.

[5] Ibid., p. 77.   [6] Ibid., p. 47.

'Unswerving loyalty to the British Crown' was to be 'the keynote of the institution'.[1] 'The continued affiliation of India to Great Britain, at any rate for a period, far exceeding the range of any practical forecast,' was considered 'to be *absolutely essential* to the interests of our own National Development'.[2] The Congress was to work not to supplant the British Government in India, but to supplement it. It was to acknowledge frankly and gratefully the many blessings of British rule and to seek their extension. Real grievances were to be voiced and reasonable concessions demanded in a loyal and temperate manner. The people of India were to be educated into 'a genuine parliamentary frame of mind'[3] and the virtues of united, patient, constitutional agitation. The authorities in India and England were to be acquainted with the needs and aspirations of their Indian fellow-subjects. Official acts and omissions were to be subjected to fair criticism. Suggestions and modifications were to be offered in order to make the British administration in India more beneficent. The Congress was to insist that British policy in India be guided by the noble spirit which inspired the Act of 1833[4] and the Queen's proclamation of 1858[5]. It was to demand that the rights and privileges of British citizenship be gradually extended to Indians.

For at least twenty years the Indian National Congress retained the spirit and temper of its founders. No less than four Britons[6] presided over its annual sessions during these years; its strategy and tactics continued to be determined by men like Hume and William Wedderburn.[7] This close association of Britons imparted to the Congress a liberal and moderate character. By precept and example these devoted

---

[1] *Allan Octavian Hume*, p. 53.   [2] Ibid.   [3] Ibid., p. 65.

[4] The Charter Act of 1833 (3 & 4 Will. 4, c. 85) laid down that no native of India 'shall by reason only of his religion, place of birth, descent, colour, or any of them, be disabled from holding any place, or employment' under the East India Company. For the full text see A. B. Keith, *Speeches and Documents on Indian Policy* (1922), vol. i, pp. 266–74.

[5] The Queen's proclamation of November 1, 1858, said, among other things, that, 'so far as may be, our subjects, of whatever race or creed, be freely and impartially admitted to office in our service, the duties of which they may be qualified by their education, ability, and integrity duly to discharge'. For the full text see ibid., pp. 382–6.

[6] George Yule, 1888; William Wedderburn, 1889; Alfred Webb, 1894; Henry Cotton, 1904.

[7] B. 1838; entered Indian Civil Service 1860; Judge of the Bombay High Court 1885; Officiating Chief Secretary to Bombay Government 1886–7; retired 1887; MP 1893–1900; Chairman of the Indian Parliamentary Committee; President of the Indian National Congress 1889 and 1910; d. 1918.

British friends impressed upon the Congress strict constitutionalism in its methods, firm loyalty to the British Government, and faith in the sense of freedom and justice of the British people.

The early Congress was a dignified debating society. Every year at Christmas time a few hundred educated and intelligent Indians from all parts of the country met in some big town for three or four days, reviewed the events of the year, passed a number of academic resolutions and dispersed to meet again. They gave voice to the public opinion of the country taking shape, presented their demands, criticized the shortcomings of the administration and offered their suggestions. Their tone was loyal and moderate; their criticism lacked bitterness. They were no professional politicians or agitators. Nor were they rainbow-chasers or whistlers for the moon. They urged redress of acknowledged grievances and demanded practical reforms.[1] They never desired to subvert British rule or substitute another in its place.

Official testimony on this score is overwhelming. Dufferin wrote to the Secretary of State in 1886: 'Amongst the natives I have met there are a considerable number who are both able and sensible, and upon whose loyal co-operation one could undoubtedly rely.'[2] He admitted that 'the objects even of the more advanced party are neither very dangerous nor very extravagant'.[3] Lord Lansdowne[4] wrote in 1891 that the Congress was 'reasonable and moderate in its tone' and that 'most of its proposals have reference to questions which have at one time or another been treated by the Government of India as subjects open to discussion'.[5] 'With a free Press and the right of public meeting', he added, 'we shall always have some organization of this kind to deal

---

[1] The main demands of the Congress during this period were: the holding of simultaneous examinations for the Indian Civil Service in India and in England; the reform of the legislative councils; the increased employment of Indians in the public services; the separation of the executive and the judicial functions; the fixity and permanence in land revenue; increased grants for education; the reduction in military expenditure; commissions for Indians in the army; the reform of the Secretary of State's council; periodical inquiry into the administration of India; and the appointment of Indians to the executive councils of the Governors and the Viceroy.

[2] Dufferin to Kimberley, April 26, 1886, Dufferin Papers, vol. 19, No 17.

[3] Ibid.

[4] Henry Charles Keith Petty-Fitzmaurice, fifth Marquis of Lansdowne (1845–1927). Under-Secretary for War 1872–4; Under-Secretary for India 1880; Governor-General of Canada 1883–8; Viceroy of India 1888–94; Secretary of State for War 1895–1900; Foreign Secretary 1900–5.

[5] Lansdowne to Cross, January 28, 1891, Lansdowne Papers, MSS. Eur. D.558/IX/III, No 5.

with. I doubt whether it could, upon the whole, assume a more innocuous shape than that which it now takes.'[1] Lord Elgin,[2] whose viceroyalty (1894–8) is said to mark the beginning of Indian unrest, did not agree with the opinion of the Secretary of State that Congressmen were disloyal. 'Remember, I do not myself admit', he wrote, 'that these men are disloyal. Some of them are discontented men, and discontent may of course verge on disloyalty; but I do not believe that a man like Mr [Pherozeshah] Mehta[3] wishes to overthrow the British Government.'[4] Elgin believed that they were 'men of intelligence' whose proper place was in the legislative councils.[5] His own experience was 'that the leading men . . . of the Congress party, when brought face to face with practical administration, whether in the form of legislation or otherwise, are more disposed to deal with it reasonably than demagogues further west'.[6] Even the Conservative Secretary of State, Lord George Hamilton,[7] who often complained of the lack of active loyalty in India and despaired of the future of the British *Raj*, remarked in 1899: 'I look upon the Congress movement as an uprising of Indian Native opinion against, not British rule, but Anglo-Indian bureaucracy.'[8]

The truth of Hamilton's remark was vindicated almost immediately afterwards. When the South African War broke out in October 1899, Indian nationalists displayed what Lord Curzon[9] described as 'a most exemplary and gratifying loyalty'.[10] 'There is considerable annoyance', the Viceroy wrote to the Secretary of State, 'that no Native troops are sent [to South Africa], on the ground that it implies a distrust of their

[1] Lansdowne Papers, MSS. Eur. D.558/IX/III, No. 5.
[2] Victor Alexander Bruce, ninth Earl of Elgin and thirteenth Earl of Kincardine (1849–1917). Viceroy of India 1894–8; Colonial Secretary 1905–8.
[3] B. 1845; barrister of the Bombay High Court; President of the Indian National Congress 1890; d. 1915.
[4] Elgin to Hamilton, August 25, 1896, Elgin Papers, MSS. Eur. F.84/14, No. 34.
[5] Elgin to Hamilton, April 21, 1897, ibid., MSS. Eur. F.84/15, No. 16.
[6] Elgin to Hamilton, December 23, 1897, ibid., MSS. Eur. F.84/15, No XLVI.
[7] Lord George Francis Hamilton (1845–1927), Under-Secretary for India 1874–80; First Lord of the Admiralty 1885–6 and 1886–92; Secretary of State for India 1895–1903.
[8] Hamilton to Curzon, October 20, 1899, Curzon Papers, MSS. Eur. F.111/158, No. 54.
[9] George Nathaniel, first Marquis Curzon of Kedleston (1859–1925). Under-Secretary for India 1891–2; Viceroy of India 1898–1905; Lord President of the Council and member of the War Cabinet 1916–18; Foreign Secretary 1919–24.
[10] Curzon to Hamilton, December 28, 1899, Curzon Papers, MSS. Eur. F.111/158, No. 64. A similar phenomenon had been witnessed in 1885 when a war with Russia seemed imminent.

loyalty and a derogation of the great position that India holds in the Empire.'[1]

The antipathy of early Indian nationalists to the bureaucracy did not imply any want of loyalty to the Throne or the Empire. They always spoke of the Sovereign in most respectful terms and were effusive in their professions of loyalty, which at times even irritated some of their ultra-radical friends in England. Queen Victoria was almost venerated in India and usually referred to as the 'Mother'. Sidney Low,[2] who accompanied the Prince of Wales during the latter's visit to India in the winter of 1905–6, noted that there was not much disloyalty even among the agitators of the platform and the press, still less among those who listened to their exhortations. 'The journey of the Prince of Wales showed', he wrote, 'that there is a deep and widespread attachment to the Imperial House among the Indian people, and that even where there is discontent with the mode of government there is no feeling against the Throne. Nor, I imagine, is there any hostility to the Empire and the Flag, so far as the meaning of these terms is understood.'[3] Low cited the instance of Calcutta in support of his conclusion. The city was, he wrote, in the trough of a furious agitation against the partition of Bengal, but when the Prince visited it, he was received by its 'angry population' 'not only with cordiality and good humour but even with demonstrative enthusiasm'.[4] The death of King Edward in May 1910 was universally mourned in India. The Viceroy, Lord Minto,[5] informed the Secretary of State of a condolence meeting held on the Calcutta Maidan at which prominent Congress leaders like Surendranath Banerjea,[6] Motilal Ghose[7] and Bhupendranath Basu[8] joined a crowd of 'at least 100,000 people' in paying obeisance to a huge portrait of the deceased Emperor.[9] King George V and Queen Mary received a warm and enthusiastic reception on their visit to India in 1911 and the Coronation Durbar in Delhi was on all accounts a

[1] Curzon Papers, MSS. Eur. F.111/158, No. 64.
[2] Sir Sidney James Mark Low (1857–1932), author and journalist.
[3] Sidney Low, *A Vision of India* (1906), p. 362.   [4] Ibid., pp. 362–3.
[5] Gilbert John Murray Kynymond Elliott, fourth Earl of Minto (1845–1914). Governor-General of Canada 1898–1904; Viceroy of India 1905–10.
[6] B. 1848; entered Indian Civil Service 1871; dismissed from Indian Civil Service 1874; teacher and journalist at Calcutta; President of the Indian National Congress 1895 and 1902; Minister in the Bengal Government 1921–3; d. 1925.
[7] B. 1847; editor of the Calcutta *Amrita Bazar Patrika* and a prominent radical nationalist; d. 1922.
[8] B. 1859; attorney of the Calcutta High Court; President of the Indian National Congress 1914; member of Secretary of State's council 1917–24; d. 1924.
[9] Mary, Countess of Minto, *India: Minto and Morley* (1934), p. 402.

great success. It was the great popularity of British Royalty in India which encouraged some people to advocate the appointment of a 'Royal Viceroy' to counteract the growing unpopularity of the British administration in that country.

Early Indian nationalists took pride in their membership of an Empire on which the sun never set. They were fond of recalling that India was the brightest jewel in the British Crown and that she alone made the British Empire truly 'Imperial'. When in 1902 Curzon asked Indians to feel for the Empire with Englishmen a 'composite patriotism' and to accept the union of England and India, which was 'so mysterious as to have in it something of the divine',[1] his words struck a responsive chord in the hearts of his listeners. 'Now that is an aspiration', commented Gopal Krishna Gokhale,[2] the leader of the moderate Indian nationalists, 'which is dear to the heart of many of us also. But the fusion of interest between the two races will have to be much greater and the people of India allowed a more definite and a more intelligible place in the Empire before that inspiration is realized.'[3] Even Bal Gangadhar Tilak,[4] the leader of the radical Indian nationalists, expressed his approval of Curzon's views, only adding that Indians should be 'living' and 'worthy' partners in the Empire.[5] And though, taking a cue from British radicals, Indian nationalists began to denounce 'insane imperialism' and 'Birmingham imperialism' at the turn of the century, it was as yet not 'imperialism' as such but a particular, depraved variant of it which came in for denunciation. Similarly, the racial policies pursued by Australia and South Africa were condemned as lapses from the high ideals and noble traditions of the Empire.

Educated Indians in the later half of the nineteenth century were full of admiration—almost adulation—for British history and culture. They gratefully acknowledged the manifold advantages derived by their country from the British connection. They frankly and loyally accepted British rule because they were convinced that 'that rule alone could secure to the country the peace and order which were necessary for slowly evolving a nation out of the heterogeneous elements of which it

[1] *Speeches by Lord Curzon of Kedleston* (1902), vol. ii, pp. 434–5.
[2] B. 1866; teacher and journalist at Poona; member of the Bombay Legislative Council 1899–1901 and of the Imperial Legislative Council 1901–15; President of the Indian National Congress 1905; d. 1915.
[3] *Abstract of the Proceedings of the Council of the Governor-General of India*, 1902, vol. xli, p. 141.
[4] B. 1856; teacher and journalist at Poona; jailed for sedition 1897–8 and 1908–14; d. 1920.
[5] *Speeches of Srj B. G. Tilak delivered at Bellary* (1905), pp. 12–13, 17.

was composed, and ensuring to it a steady advance in different directions'.[1] They had a strong belief that 'the great English people' would prove to be their deliverers, and that slowly but surely they would admit Indians as equal sharers in 'their noble inheritance of freedom'. It was this gratitude for the past and hope for the future which made men like Mahadev Govind Ranade,[2] Pherozeshah Mehta and Gopal Krishna Gokhale speak of the British connection as 'providential'. The Indian leaders of the early Congress were no 'failed BAs' or 'Macaulay's Frankenstein'. They were men who devoted the best part of their lives to the study of the mighty English literature, who found solace in English poetry, and whose minds were nurtured on English history, law and political thought. They valued English political institutions as the acme of human genius and were inspired by 'the large-hearted liberalism of the nineteenth century English politics'.[3] It was not their fault that they desired to put into practice the principles they had learnt and to imitate the model held out to them. 'Just look for a moment', said Sankaran Nair[4] in 1897, 'at the training we are receiving. From our earliest school-days the great English writers have been our classics. Englishmen have been our professors in colleges. English history is taught us in our schools. The books we generally read are English books.... It is impossible under this training not to be penetrated with English ideas, not to acquire English conceptions of duty, of rights, of brotherhood.... Imbued with these ideas and principles, we naturally desire to acquire the full rights and to share the responsibilities of British citizenship.'[5]

The early leaders of the Congress knew by heart the Charter Act of 1833, the Queen's proclamation of 1858, and all that Burke or Bright, Macaulay or Munro, Elphinstone or Malcolm had said about the purpose of British rule in India. They shared the belief in England's mission in their country. A disillusioned and faithless generation may well dismiss them today as the greatest dupes of Whig history and oratory. But those who lived in that age of faith and hope and innocence were convinced that the British people were essentially just, righteous and

---

[1] *Speeches of Gopal Krishna Gokhale* (1920 ed.), p. 1006.
[2] B. 1842; Judge of the Bombay High Court 1893–1901; social reformer; d. 1901.
[3] R. Tagore, *Crisis in Civilization* (1942), p. 2.
[4] B. 1857; vakil of the Madras High Court; President of the Indian National Congress 1897; Judge of the Madras High Court 1908–15; member of Viceroy's council 1915–19 and of Secretary of State's council 1920–1; d. 1934.
[5] *Report of the Thirteenth Indian National Congress*, 1897, p. 15.

freedom-loving. Dadabhai Naoroji,[1] the greatest figure in early Indian nationalism, was never tired of recalling how, at a time when Indians did not fully understand their rights and were too unenlightened even to ask for them, the statesmen of England had themselves declared that their policy in India was to be one of justice and equality, that the possession of India was a solemn trust with them, that the material and moral welfare of her people was the prime object of British rule, that Englishmen were not to form a governing caste in the country, and that Indians were to be helped to advance steadily to a position of equality, so that they might in due course acquire the capacity to govern themselves in accordance with the higher standards of the West. And his advice to his countrymen regarding their course of action was very simple: Remind the Government and the British people of their pledges and demand their fulfilment. Take your stand upon British charters and proclamations and insist that the rights of British citizenship be granted to you. If the bureaucracy in India refuse to listen, approach the British Demos. 'Nothing is more dear', he assured his people, 'to the heart of England—and I speak from actual knowledge—than India's welfare; and if we only speak out loud enough, and persistently enough, to reach that busy heart, we shall not speak in vain.'[2] To the people of Britain he said: Indians are either 'British citizens or British helots'. Tell us frankly how you mean to treat us. Speak out 'with your English manliness' whether 'you really mean to fulfil the pledges given before the world and in the name of God . . . or to get out of them'.[3]

'This springtime of Indian nationalism', writes Guy Wint about the last two decades of the nineteenth century, 'was perhaps its fairest period. The public mind if ardent was yet generous; if naïve it was also appealing; if unpractical it was responsive to reason. It was a tragedy that the government allowed so early a breach to come between itself and this Indian patriotism which did no more than repeat the commonplaces of English political platforms and desired no more than to be accepted by the British as partners in the administration of their country.'[4]

The story of this tragic breach has often been told. In part, it was a natural and inevitable process caused by the growth of education, of

---

[1] B. 1825; journalist and businessman; first Indian Member of British Parliament 1892–5; President of the Indian National Congress 1886, 1893 and 1906; d. 1917.
[2] *Speeches and Writings of Dababhai Naoroji* (1910), p. 18.
[3] Ibid., p. 210.
[4] G. Schuster and G. Wint, *India and Democracy* (1941), pp. 93–4.

racial and national consciousness, and of a hypercritical attitude towards an alien administration which, however benevolent, could never be really popular. The British civil service in India is often blamed for widening the gulf between the governors and the governed. It became, it is said, a huge lifeless machine, an indoor-bureaucracy, an army of note-manufacturers, losing contact with both the old India and the new. Its mind was 'tempted to stand still'; its arteries hardened; and even its general intellectual calibre declined. Lansdowne was persuaded that half the troubles in India could be avoided if the officials manifested 'a little more gentleness and consideration' towards the people.[1] Curzon complained bitterly of the 'mediocrity' of the civil servant of his day, his lack of 'interest in India as India and in the Indian people', and his tendency to 'regard himself as an unfortunate exile in a land of regrets'.[2] Hamilton believed that 'the main cause of the unpopularity' which attached to British rule in India was 'the angularity and rigidity of officialdom'.[3] There is a good deal of truth in these accusations, but it would only be just to recognize the difficulties facing the officialdom. An orderly, regularized, and symmetrical administration left no room for a spirit of adventure and enterprise. Not even the highest-placed official could dare to interfere with the stupendous and extremely artificial structure of the *Raj*. The natural temptation, therefore, was to govern and change nothing. The Indian Civil Service looked upon itself as the guardian of the people and hated the pretensions of educated Indians to pose as the representatives of the latter while, as it believed, in fact engaged in seeking jobs and distinctions for themselves. The most literary service in the world, it was prone to look down with contempt upon the educated and half-educated *Babus*. Severely practical by nature, it scorned the theories of arm-chair politicians. Trained to be dictatorial, it never cared to cultivate the confidence and co-operation of the governed. Conscientious, efficient, industrious, impartial and incorruptible, it judged educated Indians by its high standards and found them wanting. It was soured and embittered by what it considered to be the growing ingratitude and insolence displayed by the vocal sections in India. For the negative functions of administration it was well equipped, but it had no conception of the positive recon-

[1] Lansdowne to Cross, October 8, 1890, Lansdowne Papers, MSS. Eur. D.558/IX/II, No. 44.
[2] Curzon to Hamilton, March 11, 1900, and May 21, 1902, Curzon Papers, MSS. Eur. F.111/159, No. 12 and 111/161, No. 39.
[3] Hamilton to Curzon, March 3, 1899, Curzon Papers, MSS. Eur. F.111/158, No. 8.

struction of the political, social and economic life of the country. It was convinced that any attempt 'to hustle the East' was a folly and that political concessions were a sin against the Holy Ghost. To rob the administration of its autocracy, it felt, was to rob it of its benevolence. The conditions of its existence in India and those of Indian social life had always imposed an almost insuperable barrier to real intimacy and understanding between the rulers and the ruled. The suspicion and hostility engendered by politics enormously complicated the situation.

The non-official British community in India took little interest in the affairs of the country. Its manners were far from being desirable. The isolated but frequent cases of cuffing, kicking and even killing of Indians were a constant source of infinite mischief. Nothing so shook the confidence of Indians in English justice as the fact that no Englishman accused of killing an Indian ever got capital punishment. Nor was the Anglo-Indian press a model of sobriety and good manners. Its slighting and supercilious tone towards educated Indians wounded and alienated a sensitive people.

But when all is said of the shortcomings of Englishmen in India, the fact remains that the evil was caused mainly by the failure of the British Government and Parliament to give guidance. Fearing the possible evil effects of the democracy at home on the Indian Empire or those of an 'utterly un-English', autocratic, 'Oriental Enpire' upon that democracy itself, India was 'held at an arm's length'.[1] British Governments—Conservative and Liberal alike—dreaded lest India be lost on the floor of Parliament. They tried their best to keep India away from the House of Commons and resented even the occasional questions asked in that chamber by a few radicals. Parliament lost its grip of Indian affairs. Even the periodic inquiries held in the time of John Company were allowed to lapse. The rare debates at Westminster on Indian questions, with hardly a dozen members in attendance, made a mockery of Parliamentary control. Indian nationalists appealed to the busy heart of England in vain. In the matter of the 'home charges',[2] the British army in India[3] and the 'cotton duties',[4] the British Government behaved in a

[1] The quotations are from John Seeley, *The Expansion of England* (1883), pp. 190, 304.
[2] The payments made by India to the British Government towards the cost of the establishment of the Secretary of State, including his salary, and the British army in India, civil and military pensions, and the interest on loans, etc.
[3] The total strength of the British army in India was about 60,000.
[4] Acting on the free-trade principle, but not without pressure from the Lancashire interests, the British Government forced the Government of India to gradually remove all import duties on cotton goods between 1878 and 1882. When

manner which successive Viceroys denounced as unjust and unfair. Not only did they provide Indian nationalists with permanent grievances, they shook, as Curzon warned,[1] the moral bases of British dominion in India. Indians were increasingly convinced that the primary aim of British rule in India was to serve British interests, that John Bull at home was no better than John Bull abroad, and that neither the Conservative nor the Liberal Party could be relied upon to do justice to India.

The gravamen of the charge against the British Government and Parliament, however, would be that they failed in their primary duty of determining—what they alone could determine—the policy of the Government of India. Certainly the Government of India was to be in India, but Parliament was to lay down the lines on which the former was to run. Parliament and the Home Government had no sense of direction, no definite conception of the goal towards which the Government of India was to travel. A double-headed machine like the Indian Government could only work satisfactorily if both its ends were inspired by a clear, consistent and definite purpose. Any such purpose was wholly lacking. An examination of the history of the passing of the Act of 1892 reveals that there was often more imagination on the hilltops of Simla than at Whitehall.

In December 1881 Lord Ripon[2] had suggested the introduction of an elected element into the legislative councils—something that Indians had been demanding for thirty years. The reform would, the Viceroy had argued, be appreciated by the people of India and promote their 'political education'; it would prevent the councils from becoming shams and subject Government bills to real discussion; it would be 'a substantial assistance to the Government', for it would enable them to ascertain the views of the public and give them an opportunity of explaining their real intentions and removing misunderstandings.[3] The

---

in 1894, due to financial stringency, the Government of India found it necessary to restore the old 5 per cent tariff, the British Government compelled it to levy a countervailing excise of the same amount on cotton goods manufactured in Indian mills.

[1] Curzon to Hamilton, July 22, 1903, Curzon Papers, MSS. Eur. F.111/162, No. 51.
[2] George Frederick Samuel Robinson, second Earl and first Marquis of Ripon (1827–1909). Secretary of State for India 1866; Viceroy of India 1880–4; Colonial Secretary 1892–5; Lord Privy Seal 1905–8.
[3] Ripon to Hartington, December 31, 1881, Ripon Papers, I.S. 290/5, No. 70.

Secretary of State, Lord Hartington,[1] had thought the suggestion premature and risky and ignored it.[2] Ripon's successor to the viceroyalty, Dufferin, was impressed with the rapid growth of political aspirations in India and the need to satisfy them. He felt that it would be both prudent and profitable from the point of view of the administration to associate qualified Indians with itself and to provide them with regular, constitutional channels for the expression of their wants and feelings.[3] The Liberal Secretary of State for India, Lord Kimberley,[4] to whom Dufferin communicated his proposals for the reform of the legislative councils in March-April 1886, was not opposed to 'some very cautious step in this direction',[5] but unfortunately before any step could be taken the Government of which he was a member had gone out of office in July 1886. Dufferin had to waste about two years more in persuading the new Tory Secretary of State, Lord Cross,[6] to permit him to submit his recommendations for the reform of the provincial legislative councils. And when in November 1888 Dufferin submitted his recommendations[7] for the introduction of the elective principle, the increase in the non-official element of the councils, and the grant to the latter of the right of interpellation and partial control of the finances, they did not commend themselves to the Secretary of State.[8] It required yet another Viceroy—Lansdowne—and three more years of persistent pressure on his part to compel a rather reluctant ministry at home to go to Parliament with a half-hearted measure[9] which did not even go as

[1] Spencer Compton Cavendish, Marquis of Hartington and eighth Duke of Devonshire (1833-1908). Chief Secretary for Ireland 1870-4; Secretary of State for India 1880-2; Secretary of State for War 1882-5; Lord President of the Council 1895-1903.
[2] Hartington to Ripon, December 26, 1882, Ripon Papers, I.S. 290/7, No. 156.
[3] Dufferin to Kimberley, March 21, April 6, and April 26, 1886, Dufferin Papers, vol. 19, Nos. 12, 14 and 17.
[4] John Wodehouse, first Earl of Kimberley (1826-1902). Lord Privy Seal 1868-70; Colonial Secretary 1870-4 and 1880-2; Secretary of State for India 1882-5, 1886 and 1892-4; Foreign Secretary 1894-5.
[5] Kimberley to Dufferin, April 22, 1886, Dufferin Papers, vol. 19, No. 20.
[6] Richard Assheton, first Viscount Cross (1823-1914). Home Secretary 1874-80; Secretary of State for India 1886-92; Lord Privy Seal 1895-1900.
[7] Dispatch of the Government of India, Home Department, Public, No. 67 of 1888, dated November 6, 1888, Public Letters from India, 1888, vol. 9, pp. 171-203, India Office Library. See also Dufferin to Cross, October 20 and November 11, 1888, Cross Papers, MSS. Eur. E.243/25, Nos. 115 and 118.
[8] Cross to Dufferin, Cross Papers, MSS. Eur. E.243/18, pp. 224-6.
[9] The Indian Councils Act of 1892 (55 & 56 Vict. c. 14) increased the number of additional members in the Governor-General's council, that is to say, the number of members added to the executive council when it went into legislative

far as the Government of India desired and could hardly be expected to satisfy Indian public opinion.

The alienation of Indian nationalists from their rulers was made inevitable by a yet more fundamental fact. The two main demands of the Congress were: first, the more extensive employment of Indians in the higher administrative posts—and for achieving this it urged that the examination for the Indian Civil Service, then held only in England, should be held in India also; and second, the steady development of representative institutions in India. British statesmen—of both parties —were convinced that to concede any one of these demands would be to endanger the continuance of British supremacy in India. Kimberley, the Liberal Secretary of State, was as emphatic as Lansdowne, the Unionist Viceroy, that come what may the predominance of the European element in the civil service must be maintained, and as the holding of examinations in India would imperil that predominance, it could not be allowed.[1] Curzon believed that there were already too many Indians in the civil service.[2] He warned the Secretary of State of 'the extreme danger of the system under which every year an increasing number of 900 and odd higher posts that were meant, and ought to have been exclusively and specifically reserved for Europeans, are being filched away by the superior wits of the Native in the English examinations'. 'I believe it to be', he added, 'the greatest peril with which our administration is confronted.'[3] The Secretary of State, Hamilton, was equally filled with apprehension and remarked: 'One of the greatest mistakes that ever was made was the issue in the Proclamation annexing India of the principle that perfect equality was to exist, so far as all appointments were concerned, between European and Native.'[4]

---

session, from a maximum of twelve to a maximum of sixteen, and that in the Governors' councils from a maximum of eight to a maximum of twenty. All the additional members were still nominated, but the regulations framed under the Act allowed the non-official members of the provincial councils to make recommendations for four seats in the Governor-General's councils, and the municipalities, district boards, chambers of commerce and universities to make recommendations for eight seats in the provincial councils. The provincial councils, though not the Governor-General's council, were empowered to discuss the budget and raise administrative questions, though not to vote on them.

[1] Kimberley to Lansdowne, June 9, 1893, Lansdowne Papers, MSS. Eur. D.55/8IX/V, No. 31; Lansdowne to Kimberley, June 13, 1893, ibid., MSS. Eur. D.558/IX/V, No. 37.

[2] There were not more than 20 Indians in the Indian Civil Service in 1900.

[3] Curzon to Hamilton, April 23, 1900, Curzon Papers, MSS. Eur. F.111/159. No. 24.

[4] Hamilton to Curzon, May 17, 1900, ibid,, MSS. Eur. F.111/159, No. 33.

The difficulties in the way of introducing representative institutions in India were many and obvious. The rooted fear in the minds of British statesmen, however, that free institutions would ultimately be fatal to the continuance of British rule in India, enfeebled, if it did not altogether kill, the will to make a sound beginning on proper lines.'You cannot apply constitutional principles', wrote Dufferin, 'to a conquered country, inasmuch as self-government and submission to a foreign Sovereign are incompatible terms. . . .'[1] Cross believed that the adoption of the principle of election in India would mean the beginning of the end of the British *Raj* and he had a mortal dread of even uttering the word 'election'.[2] Hamilton was clear and emphatic: 'We cannot give the Natives what they want: representative institutions or the diminution of the existing establishment of Europeans is impossible.'[3] And so, concerned primarily with the maintenance of British rule in India, unable or unwilling to visualize that it could develop into something else, with their highest ideal a benevolent despotism in India, blind to the inevitable tendency of their own work in that country, British statesmen in the last quarter of the nineteenth century—with a few noble exceptions such as Bright, Gladstone and Ripon—almost lost the sense of a mission or purpose. Things in which British rule ought to have gloried became the objects of secret derision. Macaulay and Metcalfe were referred to as the villains of the piece. The introduction of 'free press, civil courts, literary education, competitive examination as the test of a man's ability for higher office . . . and sundry other evils'[4] in India came to be regretted. Concessions to Indian public opinion were made grudgingly and without any conception of a larger purpose.

It was the realization that English statesmen were opposed to their most reasonable demands and had imposed a veto on their political future, which, more than anything else, shook the faith of Indian nationalists in the character and purpose of British rule and alienated them from their rulers. Gokhale and Mehta, with their deep knowledge of English character and history, might still refuse to lose 'faith in the ultimate wisdom, beneficence, and righteousness of the English

---

[1] Dufferin to Cross, October 20, 1888, Cross Papers, MSS. Eur. E.243/25, No. 115.
[2] See Cross to Lansdowne, January 23, 1890, and May 6, 1892, Lansdowne Papers, MSS. Eur. D.558/IX/I, No. 4 and 558/IX/IV, No. 20.
[3] Hamilton to Curzon, April 14, 1899, Curzon Papers, MSS. Eur. F.111/158, No. 14.
[4] Hamilton to Curzon, January 9, 1901, ibid., MSS. Eur. F.111/160, No. 3.

people',[1] but the minds of the vast majority of educated Indians came to be filled with disappointment, anger, and even hostility. And while this unhappy development was taking place, Viceroys and Secretaries of State were drawing comfort from the thought that, as a result of their 'indifference and unconcern' towards its proceedings, the Congress was dying.[2] 'My own belief is', Curzon wrote home in November 1900, 'that the Congress is tottering to its fall, and one of my greatest ambitions while in India is to assist it to a peaceful demise.'[3]

It was natural of Indians, who studied British history and watched the progress of self-government in the Colonies, to desire that their country, too, should become a self-governing member of the British Empire. Long before the Congress was founded the British Indian Association of Bengal had petitioned Parliament in 1852 'that the legislature of British India be placed on the footing of those enjoyed by most of the Colonies of Her Majesty'.[4] In 1867 W. C. Bonnerjee[5] had demanded a 'Representative and Responsible Government for India'.[6] In 1870 the *Amrita Bazar Patrika* had raised the cry of 'A Parliament for India'.[7] In 1874 Kristodas Pal[8] had written in the *Hindoo Patriot:* 'Our attention should ... be directed to Home Rule for India, to the introduction of constitutional Government for India in India. ... If the Canadas could have a Parliament, if such small and little advanced Colonies as Prince Edward Island, Newfoundland, New South Wales, New Zealand, St Christopher's Island and Barbadoes could have elected Councils, surely British India has a fair claim to similar representation. If taxation and representation go hand in hand in all British Colonies, why should this principle be ignored in British

---

[1] The phrase quoted is Mehta's. See *Report of the Twentieth Indian National Congress*, 1904, p. 13.

[2] Hamilton to Elgin, December 11, 1896, Elgin Papers, MSS. Eur. F.84/14, No. 51.

[3] Curzon to Hamilton, November 18, 1900, Curzon Papers, MSS. Eur. F.111/159, No. 72

[4] *Petition to Parliament from the Members of the British Indian Association, and other Native Inhabitants of the Bengal Presidency, relative to the East India Company's Charter* (1852), p. 15.

[5] B. 1844; barrister of the Calcutta High Court; President of the Indian National Congress 1885 and 1892; d. 1906.

[6] W. C. Bonnerjee, 'Representative and Responsible Government for India', *Journal of the East India Association*, September 1867, pp. 157–78.

[7] *Amrita Bazar Patrika*, September 1 and 8, November 10, 1870.

[8] B. 1838; editor of the *Hindoo Patriot;* Secretary of the British Indian Association; member of the Bengal Legislative Council 1872–82 and of the Imperial Legislative Council 1883–4; d. 1884.

India... Home Rule for India ought to be our cry, and it ought to be based upon the same constitutional basis that is recognized in the Colonies.'[1] In 1880 Surendranath Banerjea had remarked: 'The question of representative government looms in the not-far-off distance. Educated India is beginning to feel that the time has come when some measure of self-government must be conceded to the people of this country. Canada governs itself. Australia governs itself. And surely it is anomalous that the grandest dependency of England should continue to be governed upon wholly different principles.'[2] Ripon's extension of local self-government in India in 1883 was hailed by politically-alert Indians as the first step on the road to national self-government. Henry Cotton's book *New India*, which was published in 1885 and read avidly by educated Indians, had advocated the ideal of a self-governing India organized on federal lines and placed 'on a fraternal footing with the colonies of England'.[3] Cotton did not think that this ideal was capable of immediate realization, but he wanted the British Government always to keep it before their eyes and direct all their efforts to that end. 'The emancipation of India', he wrote, 'has become inevitable ever since a system of English education was established, and the principle of political equality accepted. It is now merely a matter of time.'[4] In the interval left to her, Cotton insisted, Britain should devote herself to the sublimer task of facilitating India's progress towards national unity and freedom.

But the Congress in its early years did not concern itself with the remote ideal of self-government. Whether it was due to the advice and influence of their English mentors or their own realism and timidity, early Congressmen contented themselves with demanding isolated reforms, such as the increased employment of Indians in the public services, the liberalization of the legislative councils, the separation of the executive and judicial functions, the extension of trial by jury, the reduction in military expenditure, and commissions for Indians in the army, etc. This does not, however, mean that the ideal of a self-governing India was not at the back of many minds. As we have already noted,[5] educated Indians were loyal because they were patriotic. Their faith in British justice, their avowals of loyalty to British rule and their

---

[1] *Hindoo Patriot*, August 24, 1874.
[2] R. C. Palit (ed.), *Speeches by Babu Surendranath Banerjea, 1876–80* (1894), vol. i, p. 224.
[3] Cotton, op. cit., pp. 117, 121, 130.
[4] Ibid., p. 108.
[5] See above, pp. 21–2.

perfervid orations about perpetuating it were inspired largely by the belief that their British rulers would train and enable them to govern themselves. 'I am loyal to the British Government,' said Bipin Chandra Pal[1] in 1887, 'because with me loyalty to the British Government is identical with loyalty to my own people and my own country; because I believe that God has placed this Government over us for our salvation; because I know that without the help and tuition of this Government my people shall never be able to rise to their legitimate place in the commonwealth of civilized nations; because I am convinced that there is no other government on the face of the earth which so much favours the growth of infant nationalities, and under which the germs of popular Government can so vigorously grow as under the British Government. ... I am loyal to the British Government, because I love self-government.'[2] Sankaran Nair emphasized the same point in 1897 when he remarked: ' ... it should not be forgotten for a moment that the real link that binds us indissolubly to England is the hope, the well-founded hope and belief, that with England's help we shall and, under her guidance alone, we can attain national unity and national freedom.'[3] The progress of self-government in the Colonies, more than anything else, gave Indian nationalists cause for hope and confidence. Will England refuse to her brown children what she gave to her white ones? Surendranath Banerjea remarked in 1895 that England was 'the august mother of free nations' and appealed to her 'gradually to change the character of her rule in India, to liberalize it, to shift its foundations, to adapt it to the newly-developed environments of the country and the people, so that, in the fullness of time, India may find its place in the great confederacy of free States, English in their origin, English in their character, English in their institutions, rejoicing in their permanent and indissoluble union with England, a glory to the mother-country, and an honour to the human race'.[4]

Though deep down in the heart of every Indian nationalist there was the fervent aspiration that his country would some day become self-governing and individual Congressmen often gave expression to that aspiration, yet for many a long year after its inception, the Congress as an organization did not explicitly commit itself to the objective of attaining self-government for India. Even as late as 1899 when the Congress gave to itself a written constitution for the first time, it did

---

[1] Author and journalist; b. 1858; d. 1932.
[2] B. C. Pal, *The National Congress* (1887), p. 9.
[3] *Report of the Thirteenth Indian National Congress*, 1897, pp. 14-15.
[4] *Report of the Eleventh Indian National Congress*, 1895, p. 51.

not consider it worth while to declare in set terms what its ultimate aim was. The constitution merely said: 'The object of the Indian National Congress shall be to promote by constitutional means the interests and the well-being of the people of the Indian Empire.'[1] The founders of the Congress were practical-minded enough to realize that India could not be fit for parliamentary self-government in their own lifetime. 'So far as I know', Hume had written in 1888, 'no leading member of the National Congress thinks that for the next twenty years at any rate the country will require or be fit for anything more than the mixed Councils that have been advocated at the Congresses. But we, one and all, look forward to a time, say 50, say 70 years hence, when the Government of India will be precisely similar to that of the Dominion of Canada; when, as there, each province and presidency will have its local Parliament for provincial affairs, and the whole country will have its Dominion Parliament for national affairs, and when the only officials *sent out to India* from England will be the Viceroy and Governor-General.... To such a system we all look forward.... But the country is not nearly fit for this yet. No one expects that a full Parliamentary system can possibly be introduced here under fifty years....'[2] Convinced that their ultimate objective lay in the distant future and that it could only be achieved through the goodwill and co-operation of Englishmen, the founders of the Congress saw no need to inscribe self-government on their banner. They did not wish to encourage impatient idealism in their followers or to scare their rulers. Moreover, the rejection of the Irish Home Rule Bill by the British Parliament in June 1886—within a few months of the launching of the Congress movement—must have served its leaders as a warning against putting forward a similar demand for India. Nor were the long years of Tory dominance and jingo imperialism which followed in England a favourable time for raising the cry of self-government.

By 1904, however, the situation had begun to change. The fever of jingoism had abated in England and there were signs of a Liberal revival. Indian nationalists could now expect to get a better hearing in England. The victories of Japan over Russia had aroused new hopes and aspirations throughout Asia. The avowed policy of the United States to prepare the Filipinos for self-government and that of Britain to grant representative government to its erstwhile enemies, the Boers, in South Africa was jealously noted by the Indians. Twenty years of

[1] *Report of the Fifteenth Indian National Congress*, 1899, p. 29.
[2] Letter, dated May 17, 1888, to the editor of the *Morning Post* (Allahabad) reproduced in the *Indian Mirror* (Calcutta), May 23, 1888.

fruitless agitation had demoralized the Congress. Its policy of loyalty, moderation and reasonableness had obviously not paid off. The need for an ennobling ideal and more vigorous methods of agitation was being widely discussed in India. It was at this time that William Digby[1] and Dadabhai Naoroji advised the Congress to unfurl the banner of self-government for India. Speaking before the London India Society on June 1, 1904, Digby referred to the new Asia being called into existence by the marvellous achievements of Japan, to the noble policy being pursued by the United States in the Philippines and to the inability of the average Englishman to appreciate the numerous individual and local grievances voiced by the Congress, and suggested that the forthcoming session of the Congress at Bombay 'should concentrate on one subject only'—'the need for Indian self-government'.[2] Naoroji, who followed Digby, spoke in a similar vein. He emphasized that there was only 'one remedy for the present dishonourable, hypocritical, and destructive system' of British rule in India and that was 'self-government under British paramountcy'. He urged the Indian people 'to claim unceasingly their birthright, and pledged rights of British citizenship, of self-government'. 'When this fundamental remedy would be accomplished', he remarked, 'every other evil or defect of the present system—all material and moral evils and administrative defects—would right themselves.' He revealed how at the very first Congress he had indicated 'this great and absolute necessity of the situation as the chief object and mission of the Congress' and remarked that 'it was high time—as matters had gone from bad to worse under such rulers as Lord George Hamilton and Lord Curzon—that Indians took up this demand as the front and foreground of their work'.[3]

The suggestion of Digby and Naoroji was at once approved of by the nationalist press in India and in December 1904 the President of the Bombay session of the Congress, Sir Henry Cotton, acting probably upon their suggestion, declared self-government within the British Empire to be the objective of the Indian people. 'The ideal of the Indian patriot', remarked Cotton on the occasion, 'is the establishment of a federation of free and separate States, the United States of India, placed on a fraternal footing with the self-governing Colonies ... under the aegis of Great Britain.'[4]

[1] B. 1849; editor of the *Madras Times* 1877–9; journalist and politician; founded and directed the Indian Political Agency in London 1887–92; d. 1904.
[2] *India*, June 10, 1904, pp. 281–2.   [3] Ibid., p. 282.
[4] *Report of the Twentieth Indian National Congress*, 1904, p. 37.

There was nothing new or revolutionary about this ideal, but it had never before been put forward in such unmistakable terms from the Congress platform. And in the circumstances of the time it acquired a peculiar significance and was taken up by others. Gokhale incorporated the ideal of Colonial self-government in the preamble to the rules of his Servants of India Society founded in June 1905.[1] In the autumn of 1905, while on a visit to England, he advanced it as the ultimate goal of the educated classes in India from numerous platforms.[2] In his message to the Indian people in November 1905, Naoroji re-emphasized 'the absolute necessity of freedom and self-government like that of the Colonies' as the only remedy for India's woes and wrongs.[3] Presiding over the 1905 session of the Congress at Benares, Gokhale declared: 'The goal of the Congress is that India should be governed in the interests of the Indians themselves, and that in course of time a form of Government should be attained in this country similar to what exists in the self-governing Colonies of the British Empire.'[4] In an interview with John Morley[5], August 1, 1906, Gokhale acquainted the Liberal Secretary of State with the ultimate hope and design of the Congress—'India to be on the footing of a self-governing colony'— and was met with the rejoinder that 'for many a day to come—long beyond the short span of time that may be left to me—this was a mere dream'.[6] But Gokhale could not afford to be discouraged. Curzon had raised a storm in India by his words and deeds. He had bred a spirit of resentment amongst the educated classes and brought them face to face with their rulers. As a combative response to his partition of Bengal, a boycott movement had been launched in that province. A new school of thought had developed within the Congress which began to preach the ideal of 'absolute autonomy' and 'freedom' from British rule. A 'new patriotism' had grown up as opposed to the 'old', 'loyal patriotism' of the founders of the Congress.

The rise of radical nationalism in India, which became marked after 1904, was at once a conservative and a revolutionary phenomenon. It drew its inspiration, on the one hand, from the reaction towards Indian religion and Indian ways of life of which the chief exponents had

[1] 'Constitution of the Servants of India Society' in *Speeches of Gopal Krishna Gokhale* (1920 ed.), p. 915.
[2] See *India*, October 6—November 24, 1905.
[3] *Speeches and Writings of Dadabhai Naoroji* (1910), p. 652.
[4] *Report of the Twenty-First Indian National Congress*, 1905, p. 13.
[5] Statesman and man of letters; b. 1838; Chief Secretary for Ireland 1886 and 1892–5; Secretary of State for India 1905–10; created Viscount 1908; d. 1923.
[6] Morley to Minto, August 2, 1906, Minto Papers, M.1006, No. 8.

been Dayanand[1] and Vivekanand[2] in the last quarter of the nineteenth century. On the other hand, it tried to apply to the Indian situation methods of mass agitation and even terrorism borrowed from the West. As early as 1893-4, in a series of articles published in the *Indu Prakash*, entitled 'New Lamps for Old',[3] Aurobindo Ghose[4] had made a scathing attack on the Indian National Congress. He had denounced its suppliant ways, accused its leaders of timidity, lack of vision and earnestness, and pronounced it to be an utter failure. This fierce onslaught was symptomatic of the rebellious feelings which were animating the younger generation. The latter soon found a leader in the formidable personality of Bal Gangadhar Tilak, with his emphasis on Hindu conservatism, mass appeal and direct action. The tide of Western liberalism began to recede in India by the end of the nineteenth century. Men searched for the moral basis of nationalism and found it in native history, religion and institutions. The past became glorified and transfigured. Old gods and heroes were invoked to drive away alien rulers. The young did not know about the century of anarchy that had preceded the establishment of British rule in India. They ridiculed the talk of their elders about the blessings of the *Raj*. 'New generations are rising up,' Gokhale remarked in the Imperial Legislative Council early in 1906, 'whose notions of the character and ideals of British rule are derived only from their experience of the last few years and whose minds are not restrained by the thought of the great work which England has on the whole accomplished in the past in this land.'[5] The young were bitter against their elder leaders at their inability to wrest concessions from the Government, and against their rulers for their attitude of indifference and hostility towards the demands of moderate men. The carrying out of the partition of Bengal in 1905, in spite of determined local protests, finally discredited the Congress methods of remonstrance and petition. The hopes aroused by the coming into power of a Liberal Government in England towards the end of 1905 were disappointed when Morley, the new Secretary of

[1] Founder of the Arya Samaj; b. 1824; d. 1883.
[2] Hindu missionary; b. 1863; d. 1902.
[3] The articles are reproduced in Haridas and Uma Mukherjee, *Sri Aurobindo's Political Thought* (1958), pp. 63-123.
[4] B. 1872; passed the written examination for the Indian Civil Service but failed in the riding test 1890; teacher at Baroda 1893-1906; leader of the Bengali Extremists 1906-10; retired to Pondichery in 1910 and devoted himself to spiritualism; d. 1950.
[5] *Abstract of the Proceedings of the Council of the Governor-General of India*, 1905-6, vol. xliv, p. 309.

State, declared partition to be 'a settled fact'[1] and remarked that the transplantation of English institutions in India was 'a fantastic and ludicrous dream'.[2] The need for more vigorous and self-reliant methods of agitation came to be widely felt.[3] It was encouraged by the spirit of the times. Those who watched the triumphs of Japan, the revolutionary rumblings in Russia, the rise of the Sinn Féin movement in Ireland, the Egyptian struggle for freedom, the Young Turk revolt, the adoption of a constitution in Persia, the introduction of representative institutions in the Philippines, and the grant of responsible self-government to the Transvaal and the Orange River Colony could not but be filled with new-born aspirations for their country and prompted to more energetic action.

The rebels within the Congress styled themselves the 'New Party' to distinguish themselves from the old organization. They called themselves 'Nationalists' as opposed to the old loyalist Congressmen. Their critics nicknamed them 'Extremists'. They began by denouncing the Congress method of agitation as futile and unbecoming. They called it 'mendicancy'. They dismissed the faith of older Congressmen in British justice and liberality as a snare and a delusion. Philanthropy, they said, had no place in politics; and appeals to the good feelings of rulers were vain. The Congress had so far devoted itself to demanding isolated reforms and the removal of particular grievances. The Nationalists did not believe in these palliatives and tinkerings. They demanded a radical change in the system of government itself—'the substitution for the autocratic bureaucracy, which at present misgoverns us, of a free and democratic system of Government and the entire removal of foreign control in order to make way for perfect national liberty'.[4] The older Congressmen believed that the continuance of British rule was the indispensable condition of India's progress and prosperity. The Nationalists argued that political freedom was the essential preliminary to all national progress. As Aurobindo Ghose put it: 'Political freedom is the life-breath of a nation; to attempt social reform, educational reform, industrial expansion, the moral improvement of the race without aiming first and foremost at political freedom, is the very height of ignorance and futility.'[5] The Nationalists were eager to foreshorten

[1] 152 H.C. Deb. 4s., col. 844.
[2] 161 H.C. Deb. 4s., col. 587.
[3] On this point see C. J. O'Donnell, *The Causes of Present Discontent in India* (1908), pp. 6–7, 30. It is significant that dissatisfaction at the behaviour of the Liberal Party encouraged extra-constitutional agitation in both India and Ireland.
[4] Aurobindo Ghose, *The Doctrine of Passive Resistance* (1952 ed.), p. 16.
[5] Ibid., p. 3.

history. England had hitherto been the model for the politically-minded classes in India. Their teachers had been English books and English politicians. They could not conceive of a truly popular and democratic government in India except by a process of gradual and slow evolution, of progress broadening from precedent to precedent. The Nationalists dismissed the English model as unsuited to India. How could the experience of an independent nation, they asked, be a valid guide to a subject people? They appealed instead to the revolutionary traditions of France, America, Italy and Ireland. Constitutional agitation, they said, in a country where there was no constitution and the people had no control over the administration, was futile. Borrowing the methods of the Irish Sinn Féin, they preached the need for organized passive resistance and self-reliance. The British Government in India was, they argued, based upon the help of the few and the acquiescence of the many. It was *maya*, a hypnotic illusion, which had to be destroyed. They hoped to make the administration impossible by an organized refusal to do anything which might help the rulers. They advocated a boycott of British goods, Government-controlled schools and colleges, law courts and executive authority in general. Along with this boycott, a campaign of self-development was to be inaugurated, aiming at the promotion of *swadeshi* (indigenous) goods, national education, arbitration courts, and the organization of public life independent of the Government—building up from the villages to a central national polity. For the time being their movement was to be confined to abstention from any co-operation with the Government, but if the latter did not pay heed to their demands, recourse was to be taken to such measures as the non-payment of taxes. They were to begin with the principle 'no control, no assistance', but when they had developed strength and a parallel government of their own, they could present an ultimatum to their alien rulers. The Nationalists hoped to achieve their objectives by peaceful and legal methods, but they did not rule out the possibility of resistance to 'unjust laws', or of resorting to force in self-defence, for after all, as they said, boycott was a war.

With such ideas and such a programme, it was but natural that the New Party should have fallen foul of the Congress ideal of self-government on the Colonial model. Aurobindo Ghose wrote in 1907: 'The Congress has contented itself with demanding self-government as it exists in the Colonies. We of the new school would not pitch our ideal one inch lower than absolute *Swaraj*—self-government as it exists in the United Kingdom. We believe that no smaller ideal can inspire national revival or nerve the people of India for the fierce, stubborn and formidable struggle by which alone they can again become a nation. We believe that this newly awakened people, when it has gathered its strength together, neither can nor ought to consent to any relations with England less than that of equals in a confederacy. To be content with the relations of master and servant or superior and subordinate, would be a mean and pitiful aspiration unworthy of manhood; to strive for anything less than a strong and glorious freedom would be to insult the greatness of our past and the magnificent possibilities of our future.'[1] It is noteworthy that Aurobindo Ghose and his associates were not opposed to having friendly relations with Great Britain on a footing of equality. In fact, the new religion of patriotism which they preached was permeated with a vague universal ideal of the ultimate unity of mankind. But they insisted that the nation must first realize its destiny to the full—unhampered in the least degree by foreign control. If India was to retain her individuality, said Aurobindo Ghose, as a political and cultural unit and fulfil her mission in the world, she could not do so 'overshadowed by a foreign power and a foreign civilization'.[2] 'The world needs India', he wrote, 'and needs her free. . . . She must live her own life and not the life of a part or subordinate in a foreign Empire.'[3] To Aurobindo Ghose the ideal of Colonial self-government for India was 'the very negation of patriotism' and a 'political monstrosity'.[4] He, instead, propagated the ideal of 'absolute autonomy' and 'unqualified *Swaraj*'.

One of Aurobindo Ghose's closest political associates, Bipin Chandra Pal, discussed at length the impracticability and impossibility of 'self-government under British paramountcy' in his famous speeches at Madras in May 1907.[5] If Britain controlled Indian foreign policy, he said, she could not do so without controlling India's armed forces and this would entail control of the purse, which would be a negation of India's right of self-taxation and self-government. The argument that Britain protected her Colonies without demanding the expenses thereof and could treat India similarly was, in his view, invalid, for the Colonies stood on a different footing. They were white and inhabited by the kith and kin of the British people. They received Britain's surplus population and her help in developing their resources. Britain was

---

[1] Aurobindo Ghose, *The Doctrine of Passive Resistance* (1952 ed.), pp. 69–70.
[2] H. and U. Mukherjee, *'Bande Mataram' and Indian Nationalism* (1957), p. 85.
[3] Ibid.
[4] H. and U. Mukherjee, *Sri Aurobindo's Political Thought* (1958), pp. 175, 181.
[5] B. C. Pal, *Swadeshi and Swaraj* (1954 ed.), pp. 149–67.

interested in their safety and well-being both for their sakes and her own. What Britain did for her Colonies, Pal argued, she would not do for India. He then tried to prove how self-government within the Empire would either be no self-government for India or no real overlordship for Britain. Indians would not be satisfied with 'a shadow of self-government' nor would Britain be satisfied with 'a shadowy overlordship'.[1] If India became self-governing like the Colonies, he said, she would impose protective tariffs in order to encourage her industries and do away with the privileges enjoyed by British capital in the country at present, and this could never be tolerated by Britain. Moreover, if a country as big and populous as India obtained self-government, 'the [British] Empire would cease to be British', for India would soon become 'the predominant partner in this imperial firm'.[2] Pal, therefore, believed that Britain would herself prefer to have a self-governing India as an ally, like Japan, rather than as a partner in the Empire.

This frank and open repudiation of the ideal of Colonial self-government for India by Aurobindo Ghose and Bipin Chandra Pal was not much to the taste of the acknowledged leader of the Extremists, Tilak, who, for all his active and militant politics, was a great realist. He wrote in his paper, the *Kesari*, early in 1907 that self-government on the Colonial model sufficed for him as an ideal to work for.[3] His difference with the Moderates, he repeatedly pointed out, was not with regard to the objective but only with regard to the methods of agitation to be pursued by the Congress.[4] The young, impatient idealists in India, who looked up to Tilak as 'the one possible leader for a revolutionary party',[5] were disappointed to discover in their hero an old-world politician, cautious and conservative, who would not inscribe an academic and dangerous ideal on his banner.

The rapid growth of the New Party alarmed the Moderates. It threatened to destroy them, the Congress, and the reforms which they expected the Liberal Government to introduce in India. Already in the summer of 1906 Morley had assured Gokhale that the British Government were in earnest to make an effective move in the way of 'reasonable reforms' in India and warned him that the surest way to spoil their chances was the 'perversity and unreason' of his friends and their 'clamour for the impossible'.[6] Would the old leaders of the Congress

[1] *Swadeshi and Swaraj*, p. 162.
[2] Ibid., pp. 165–6.   [3] *Kesari*, January 22, 1907.
[4] See H. W. Nevinson, *The New Spirit in India* (1908), pp. 72, 75.
[5] H. and U. Mukherjee, *Sri Aurobindo's Political Thought* (1958), p 37.
[6] Morley to Minto, July 27 and August 2, 1906, Minto Papers, M.1006, Nos. 6 and 8.

throw overboard their rebellious followers and thus save the Congress and the reforms? *The Times* in a special article on October 16, 1906, frankly recommended such a course of action. It suggested to the Moderates 'a public repudiation' of the Extremists both as a matter of public honesty, for men holding such divergent views as Gokhale and Tilak should not continue the pretence of working together, and in order to strengthen their own position. 'If the idea of separation from England were explicitly disavowed and condemned' and the Extremists formally repudiated, the writer of the special article in *The Times* said, the Congress would secure the support of Englishmen and Muslims who sympathized with its aspirations for moderate progress; it would be able to exert greater influence upon public affairs and 'the bulk of the other reforms demanded by the Congress would probably be realized'.[1] The Moderates still hesitated to take such a course. They were anxious to avoid an open split in the Congress and thereby weaken it. Nor were they without hope to win over the Extremists by means of persuasion. In order to counteract the election of Tilak as President of the Congress, for which the Bengali Extremists were working and which would have been a signal that the Congress had been captured by the radicals, the Moderate leaders persuaded Dadabhai Naoroji to come over from England to preside over the 1906 session to be held at Calcutta. The great personal influence of 'the Grand Old Man of India' sufficed to maintain the unity of the Congress for some time, but it was not without making large concessions to the wishes of the Extremists.

There was a curious mingling of old ways and new at the 1906 session of the Congress. Naoroji proclaimed the Congress ideal to be 'Self-government or *Swaraj* like that of the United Kingdom or the Colonies'.[2] The ideal of *Swaraj* emerged as the one main and comprehensive objective. Naoroji demanded it as the birthright of Indians as British citizens: 'I say we are British citizens and are entitled to and claim all British citizens' rights. . . . This birthright to be "free" or to have freedom is our right from the very beginning of our connection with England when we came under the British flag. When Bombay was acquired as the very first territorial possession, the government of the day in the very first grant of territorial rights to the East India Company [March 24, 1669] declared thus: "And it is declared that all persons being His Majesty's subjects inhabiting within the said Island and their children and their posterity born within the limits thereof shall be deemed free denizens and natural subjects as if living and born in

[1] 'Divided Counsels in the Congress', *The Times*, October 16, 1906.
[2] *Report of the Twenty-Second Indian National Congress*, 1906, p. 21.

England".'¹ This declaration of the rights of Indians as British citizens, Naoroji added, had been reinforced by latter-day pledges, chief amongst which was the Queen's proclamation of 1858 which read: 'We hold ourselves bound to the natives of our Indian territories by the same obligations of duty which bind us to all our other subjects, and these obligations, by the blessing of Almighty God, we shall faithfully and conscientiously fulfil.'² Naoroji was basing his claim on documents which had no legal validity, but what is significant is the fact that he claimed a British constitutional right instead of appealing to the French revolutionary doctrine of the inherent and inalienable right of all men to be free.³

By a formal resolution the Calcutta Congress expressed its opinion 'that the system of Government obtaining in the self-governing British Colonies should be extended to India' and urged the immediate adoption of certain reforms as 'steps leading to it'.⁴

Soon after the Calcutta session of the Congress Gokhale undertook a tour of northern India to combat the influence of the dangerous doctrines preached by the Extremists. In a speech at Allahabad, February 4, 1907⁵, he stated frankly and fully the creed of the Moderates. He recognized, he said on the occasion, no limits to his aspirations for his motherland. He wanted his people to rise to the full stature of their manhood and be in their country what other people were in theirs. He aspired to see his country take her proper place among the great nations of the world. But he felt convinced that the whole of this aspiration, in its essence and in its reality, could be realized within the Empire. 'The cases of the French in Canada and the Boers in South Africa showed', Gokhale remarked, 'that there was room in the Empire for a self-

---

[1] *Report of the Twenty-Second Indian National Congress*, 1906, pp. 17–18.
[2] Ibid., p. 19.
[3] The cruel comment of *The Times* (January 2, 1907) on Naoroji's speech was: 'Mr Naoroji contends that, because the inhabitants of India are British citizens, they are entitled to all the political rights, privileges, and franchises which the inhabitants of England enjoy. . . . But the contention has no more root in history or in law than it has in common sense. We have won India by the sword, and in the last resort we hold it by the sword. . . .'
[4] *Report of the Twenty-Second Indian National Congress*, 1906, pp. ii–iii. The reforms demanded were: simultaneous examinations for higher services in England and in India; adequate representation of Indians in the council of the Secretary of State and in the executive councils of the Viceroy and the Governors; expansion of the legislative councils; increased representation of Indians thereon and larger control over administration and finances; and the extension and liberalization of local self-government.
[5] *Speeches of Gopal Krishna Gokhale* (1920 ed.), pp. 947–57.

respecting India.'[1] It was not a question, he said, 'of what was theoretically perfect, but of what was practically attainable'.[2] While working for the achievement of self-government within the Empire, they were trying to advance along lines which were well understood and which involved 'a minimum disturbance of existing ideas'.[3] They would have in such an advance the sympathy and support of much that was high-minded, freedom-loving and honourable in England. Gokhale asserted that, despite occasional lapses and reactions, 'the genius of the British people, as revealed in history, on the whole, made for political freedom, for constitutional liberty',[4] and that it would be folly and madness on the part of Indians to throw away this great asset in the struggle that lay before them. He deprecated the cry that constitutional agitation had failed while they had not yet exhausted a thousandth part of its possibilities. While he recognized that nine-tenths of their work had to be done by them in India, Gokhale insisted on keeping in touch with 'British democracy', for it could be of valuable assistance to them in checking official retrogression and promoting nation-building. He condemned the doctrine of passive resistance and all-round boycott preached by the Extremists not only because he thought it to be impracticable and injurious, but also because he saw in it an 'attempt to shift the foundations of their public life'.[5] He pointed out that nation-building was nowhere an easy task and that in India it was beset with difficulties which were truly formidable. He warned his countrymen of the long and weary struggle that lay before them and of the dangers of undue impatience. Gokhale concluded on a note which, for all its wisdom and sincerity, showed that the Moderates were fighting a losing battle. 'Let us not forget', he said, 'that we are at a stage of the country's progress when our achievements are bound to be small, and our disappointments frequent and trying. . . . It will, no doubt, be given to our countrymen of future generations to serve India by their successes; we of the present generation, must be content to serve her mainly by our failures.'[6]

But the young were impatient, heedless of obstacles and careless as to methods. They were no longer in a mood to serve India by their failures. Their attacks on the Moderate leaders and the authorities grew increasingly bitter and strident. The Moderates judged correctly that the Extremist heresy was not as yet widespread. They decided to coerce the Extremists into submission or to eject them out of the Congress. They shifted the venue of the forthcoming session of the

---

[1] *Speeches of Gopal Krishna Gokhale* (1920 ed.), p. 949. [2] Ibid.
[3] Ibid., p. 950. [4] Ibid. [5] Ibid., p. 956. [6] Ibid., p. 957.

Congress in December 1907 from Nagpur, where it was likely to be flooded with the followers of Tilak, to Surat, which was Pherozeshah Mehta's pocket borough. They managed to get a Moderate Bengali, Dr Rashbehary Ghose,[1] elected as the President of the session. And finally, to force a few Extremists, who had openly preached the doctrines of complete independence and all-round boycott, out of the Congress, they decided to impose a new constitution on the organization which required every delegate to the Congress session to subscribe to the ideal of self-government similar to that enjoyed by the self-governing members of the British Empire, to be attained by strictly constitutional means.

Amidst all the dust and the din of the controversy about the Surat split—the clash of personalities, the charges and countercharges of irregularities and backslidings, of obduracy and responsibility for hurling the 'Mahratta shoe'—it is easy to discern two points of cardinal importance which divided the two sections in the Congress. Some of the Extremists, led by Aurobindo Ghose, already stood committed to the ideal of absolute autonomy and complete self-government. The attempt to confine the membership of the Congress only to those who definitely and openly subscribed to the ideal of self-government within the Empire was interpreted by them as a clever move designed to eliminate them from the organization. The second major difference was over the methods. The Congress at its Calcutta session in 1906 had given its approval to the campaign for the boycott of British goods as a temporary measure intended to put pressure on the British Government and draw their attention to the grievance about the partition of Bengal. The Extremists interpreted boycott in the widest possible sense. To them it was complete Irish Sinn Féin—a boycott not only of British goods, but of everything connected with the British administration. To yield to the Extremists on these two points—the creed and the methods—would have meant handing over the Congress to them. If the Congress were to remain a loyal, moderate and respectable organization, it could not shelter under its wings those who stood for 'absolute *Swaraj*' outside the British Empire and preached non-co-operation with the Government. The Congress had so far endeavoured to work for national advance in association with the British rulers. It was convinced that there was no other alternative to the British *Raj* in India, except chaos. Though disappointed of the bureaucracy, it still retained its faith in British democracy. The Moderates felt that the Extremists

[1] B. 1845; vakil of the Calcutta High Court; jurist and scholar; President of the Indian National Congress 1907 and 1908; d. 1921.

were not only challenging the very bases of older thought and belief, but endangering national progress itself. They decided, therefore, either to bridle the Extremists, or, if they proved recalcitrant, to disown them. Some youthful Extremists, headed by Aurobindo Ghose, decided to wreck the organization instead of being driven out of it.[1] The result was the Surat episode.

The Congress, however, did not dissolve in chaos at Surat. Soon after the disorderly scenes of the second day of the session, December 27, 1907, the older Moderate leaders, P. Mehta, D. E. Wacha,[2] G. K. Gokhale, R. B. Ghose, M. M. Malaviya[3] and others, met in private and drew up a notice calling a National Convention to meet the next day, December 28th, of all those delegates who subscribed to the ideal of self-government on the Colonial model and its attainment by strictly constitutional means. Over 900 delegates, out of the 1,600 who had come to Surat, attended the Convention, which appointed a committee to draw up a constitution for the Congress.[4] This 'Convention Committee' met at Allahabad, April 18th and 19th, and framed a constitution for the Congress, as also a set of rules for the conduct of its meetings. Article I of the constitution enunciated the creed of the Congress. It read: 'The Objects of the Indian National Congress are the attainment by the people of India of a system of government similar to that enjoyed by the self-governing Members of the British Empire, and a participation by them in the rights and responsibilities of the Empire on equal terms with those Members. These Objects are to be achieved by constitutional means by bringing about a steady reform of the existing system of administration and by promoting national unity, fostering public spirit and developing and organizing the intellectual, moral, economic and industrial resources of the country.'[5] Article II required every delegate to the Congress to express in writing his acceptance of this creed.[6]

The *Bande Mataram*, the organ of the Bengali Extremists, in its issue of April 23, 1908, accused the Convention of having betrayed 'the mandate of their country and the future of their people'. It condemned the Moderates as 'advocates of contradiction', 'servants of the alien

---

[1] See *Aurobindo on Himself and on the Mother* (1953), pp. 78–82.

[2] Businessman, journalist and politician; b. 1844; Joint General Secretary of the Indian National Congress 1895–1907; General Secretary of the Congress 1908–13; President of the Congress 1901; d. 1936.

[3] B. 1861; President of the Indian National Congress 1909 and 1918; Vice-Chancellor of Benares Hindu University 1919–40; d. 1946.

[4] *Report of the Twenty-Third Indian National Congress*, 1908, p. 17.

[5] Ibid., Appendix B., p. xix. [6] Ibid.

bureaucrat disguised as patriots', 'foes of Indian independence', timid men who had 'refused to serve the Mother with an undivided heart' and 'placed the alien on the throne of her future and dared to think that she would accept a left hand and inferior chair at the side of his seat of empire'.¹ Again on May 3rd it denounced the ideal adopted by the Convention as a denial of India's birthright, her individuality, her past and her independent future, an attempt to maintain India in 'the position of a subordinate satellite in a foreign system'.²

Morley was the Secretary of State and Minto the Viceroy when the first great wave of political unrest swept over India during the years 1905–10. The Secretary of State and the Viceroy differed widely in their political training, experience and general outlook. And as was to be expected, these differences were often reflected in their views regarding the manner in which the Indian problem should be tackled. Minto recognized that a new spirit was abroad in India, but he proposed to meet it by encouraging the more conservative and loyal elements in Indian society as 'a possible counterpoise to Congress aims'.³ Being the man on the spot and pressed by immediate anxieties, he was naturally more inclined to emphasize the subversive and disloyal character of the Congress movement. He often complained to Morley that the Congress agitation received mistaken sympathy and exaggerated importance at home and was aided by questions in the House of Commons. He considered the House of Commons to be 'perhaps the greatest danger to the continuance of our rule in the country'.⁴ Minto was a man with a wide outlook and fairly liberal sympathies, but he was too often tempted to emphasize the virtues of the strong hand, for he was convinced that India was held by the sword. He even demanded that the Government of India should be 'given a free hand to rule the country'.⁵ Minto, however, did not fail to realize that the growth of education and political consciousness had created aspirations in India which could not be ignored, and that it was urgently necessary to associate Indians with 'an administration which our military strength alone guarantees'.⁶ In this he was far in advance of the general official opinion in India.

Morley was nearing his seventieth year when he came to the India

---

[1] H. and U. Mukherjee, *'Bande Mataram' and Indian Nationalism* (1957), pp. 77–80.   [2] Ibid., pp. 80–8.
[3] Minto to Morley, May 28, 1906, Minto Papers, M.1005, No. 46.
[4] Minto to Morley, May 28, 1908, ibid., M.1008, No. 28.
[5] Ibid.   [6] Minto to Morley, May 29, 1907, ibid., M.1007, No. 27.

Office. He was, to quote his own words, 'as cautious a Whig as any Elliott, Russell, or Grey, that was ever born',[1] and he had 'no sort of ambition ... to take part in any grand revolution'[2] during his time of responsibility. He was, however, determined to adjust the machinery of Indian Government to the changed circumstances in India and growing democratic opinion at home. His liberal sympathies and his wide experience and study of European national and revolutionary movements gave him a better insight into the Indian problem. In Morley's view it was not the democracy in England, but the cast-iron bureaucracy in India with its outmoded ideas and methods, which was the real menace to the Empire. With the object-lesson of the Russian revolution before him, he was unrelenting in his belief that the British Demos must keep a strict watch over the 'Tchinovniks'[3] in India.[4] He also hoped that the reformed legislative councils in India would serve the latter as a whetstone. Morley was convinced that conciliation, not repression, was the right policy. 'Reforms', he wrote to Minto, 'may not save the *Raj*, but if they don't, nothing else will.'[5] The fundamental difference between the outlook of a liberal statesman and that of a soldier-administrator is nowhere more clearly revealed than in the reply which Minto made to the above remark. 'You say', he wrote back, 'that reforms may not "save the *Raj*"; they certainly will not, though if they are thoughtfully introduced they may help to render its administration happy. But when you say that "if reforms do not save the *Raj* nothing else will" I am afraid I must utterly disagree. The *Raj* will not disappear in India as long as the British race remains what it is, because we shall fight for the *Raj* as hard as we have ever fought, if it comes to fighting, and we shall win as we have always won.'[6]

But with all their differences, Morley and Minto were agreed on certain essentials of Indian policy. They were both convinced that the safety and welfare of India depended on the permanence of the British administration, that the Government of India was always to remain autocratic, and that the sovereignty must be vested in British hands and could not be delegated to any kind of representative assembly. Besides being incompatible with British supremacy, representative govern-

[1] Morley to Minto, November 30, 1906, Minto Papers, M.1006, No. 36.
[2] Morley to Minto, June 6, 1906, ibid., M.1005, No. 65.
[3] This was Morley's favourite appellation for the civil servants.
[4] Morley set forth his views in detail on this subject after relinquishing charge of the India Office. See 'British Democracy and Indian Government', *Nineteenth Century and After*, February 1911, pp. 189–209.
[5] Morley to Minto, May 7, 1908, Minto Papers, M.1008, No. 25.
[6] Minto to Morley, May 28, 1908, ibid., M.1008, No. 28.

ment was, in their view, wholly unsuited to Indian conditions; the only representation for which the country was fit was one by classes and communities, and that, too, to a very limited extent. What they aimed at was, in the main, a 'scheme of administrative improvement',[1] designed to win over the loyal and moderate elements in India and with their help to 'strengthen English government, and place it in a better position both for doing its work and for defending what it does'.[2] The Government of India stood exposed, isolated and ignorant. 'As it is,' Morley wrote to Minto, 'we are all in a cleft stick: we don't know the minds of the Natives, and the Natives don't know what is in our minds. How to find some sort of bridge? That's the question.'[3] Their reforms were intended to provide this bridge.

The two main features of the Morley-Minto reforms were: first, the admission of two Indians to the council of the Secretary of State and one Indian each to the executive councils of the Governor-General and the Governors; and second, the expansion and liberalization of the legislative councils. The first was a gesture intended to give concrete proof that the Government honestly meant to fulfil the promises contained in the Charter Act of 1833 and the Queen's proclamation of 1858, that race was to be no disqualification to the high offices in the state. The appointment of an Indian to the executive council of the Governor-General proved to be an extremely controversial issue. Morley and Minto were convinced of the utility of the step. The former considered it to be 'the *cheapest* concession'[4] that could be made, for it would leave the British executive authority unimpaired which, in his view, was the cardinal requirement of any reforming operations to be undertaken. The Viceroy thought that it would be 'by far the best answer to Congress agitation'.[5] Morley remarked: 'He [the Indian member] would tell you how things strike that queer article, the Native mind.'[6] And Minto expressed approval, saying: 'This is exactly the information we want.'[7] But a veritable storm raged for about two years over the question. Every member of Minto's executive council, except one, was opposed to the proposal. Morley's council was equally hostile. The local governments in India expressed their disapproval. The ex-Viceroys, Curzon, Lansdowne and Elgin, pronounced against it. The

[1] Morley to Minto, March 26, 1908, Minto Papers, M.1008, No. 18.
[2] Morley to Minto, November 5, 1908, ibid., M.1008, No. 57.
[3] Morley to Minto, May 16, 1907, ibid., M.1007, No. 29.
[4] Morley to Minto, November 23, 1906, ibid., M.1006, No. 34.
[5] Minto to Morley, October 28, 1906, ibid., M.1006, No. 26.
[6] Morley to Minto, March 14, 1907, ibid., M.1007, No. 16.
[7] Minto to Morley, April 2, 1907, ibid., M.1007, No. 17.

English press was almost universally opposed to the reform. Most Tories frankly detested the suggestion and even many Liberals were dubious. The Prince of Wales did not conceal his dislike and the King-Emperor administered an earnest remonstrance. The British community in India talked of organizing in self-defence. Morley and Minto feared a recrudescence of the clamour of the Ilbert Bill[1] days and at times well-nigh decided to abandon the idea. Morley admitted that had Parliamentary legislation been necessary for the appointment, the Lords would have thrown out the bill.[2] The Lords took their revenge none the less by vetoing a clause in the Indian Councils Bill of 1909 providing for executive councils to the Lieutenant-Governors. All this may give us some idea of the forces against which the Secretary of State and the Viceroy had to contend. The principle of election, implicit in the Act of 1892, was now frankly recognized. The legislative councils were allowed more time to discuss the budget, to move resolutions and to call for a division. The right of interpellation was extended and members could ask supplementary questions. Morley and Minto, however, stoutly repudiated the suggestion that these enlarged legislative councils were intended to pave the way for anything resembling parliamentary institutions in India.[3] The councils being already in existence, they attempted to make representation thereon more real and living with a view to making them better vehicles for expressing the opinions of the differing classes and communities in India. The liberalization of their procedure was intended to afford the Government 'additional opportunities both of becoming acquainted with the drift of public opinion, and of explaining their own actions'.[4] Indians were to be more closely associated with the tasks of administration and legislation, they

[1] In 1883, the Law Member, Sir Courtenay Ilbert, introduced a bill to remove judicial disqualifications based on race distinctions. It was vehemently opposed by the British community in India and had substantially to be withdrawn.

[2] Morley to Minto, February 4, 1909, Minto Papers, M.1009, No. 9.

[3] Morley's oft-quoted remark: 'If I were attempting to set up a Parliamentary system in India, or if it could be said that this chapter of reforms led directly or necessarily up to the establishment of a Parliamentary system in India, I, for one, would have nothing at all to do with it. . . . If my existence, either officially or corporeally, were prolonged twenty times longer than either of them is likely to be, a Parliamentary system in India is not the goal to which I for one moment would aspire.' 198 H.L. Deb. 5s., col. 1985. Minto was equally emphatic: 'We have aimed at the reform and enlargement of our councils, but not at the creation of parliaments.' *Proceedings of the Council of the Governor-General of India*, 1909–10, vol. xlviii, p. 51.

[4] *Proposals of the Government of India and Dispatch of the Secretary of State*, Cd. 4426 (1908), p. 47.

were to be given better opportunities of influencing the Government, but they were not yet to govern themselves or to be trained for doing so. The two-fold purpose of the legislative reforms was emphasized by Morley in his final dispatch to Minto, November 27, 1908. It was 'to enable Government the better to realize the wants, interests, and sentiment of the governed, and, on the other hand, to give the governed a better chance of understanding, as occasion arises, the case for the Government, against the misrepresentations of ignorance and malice'.[1] The elections to the legislative councils were indirect,[2] except in the case of the landlords and the Muslims; the electorate was indefinite and severely restricted.[3] The non-official majorities in the provincial legislative councils were unreal and an attempt was made to counteract the influence of the advanced political classes by special electorates created and weighted in favour of the landed gentry and the Muslims.

The Indian Councils Act of 1909 was, in the main, an extension of the Act of 1892. It doubled the number of Indians in the provincial legislative councils and gave the latter non-official (nominated + elected) majorities.[4] The Imperial Legislative Council also received an addition of Indian members, but here an official majority was retained.[5]

[1] *Proposals of the Government of India and Dispatch of the Secretary of State*, Cd. 4426 (1908), p. 50.

[2] The constituencies for the Imperial Legislative Council were the provincial legislative councils, landholders, Muslims and chambers of commerce. For the provincial legislative councils, the electors were municipal and district boards, landholders, planters, universities, Muslims and the trading community.

[3] For example, there were 4,818 electors for the 27 elective seats on the Imperial Legislative Council. Of these 2,406 were directly landlords and 1901 Muslims. Thirteen of the twenty-seven elected members were elected by the non-official members of the provincial legislative councils, six by landlords, six by Muslims, and two by the chambers of commerce. Eight electors chose the representative from Bombay. Nine electors chose the representative from Burma, fourteen the one from the Central Provinces, and fifteen the one from the Punjab. See *Report of the Committee appointed by the Secretary of State for India to inquire into questions connected with the Franchise and other matters relating to Constitutional Reforms* (Chairman: Lord Southborough), vol. i, Cmd. 141 (1919), pp. 81–2.

[4] The number of additional members was increased to a maximum of fifty in the larger and thirty in the smaller provinces. In Bombay, for example, of the total membership of forty-seven, five were ex-officio members, twenty-one were nominated (of which not more than fourteen could be officials) and twenty-one were elected. In Bengal alone there was a clear elected majority, but there the European representatives held the balance.

[5] Out of the total membership of sixty-eight, there were thirty-six officials and thirty-two non-officials; forty-one seats were filled by nomination and twenty-seven by election.

Morley and Minto often gave expression to their vague disquiet about the future of the British *Raj* in India. 'The question is the Future',[1] they repeatedly told each other, without indicating how it was to be met. In fact, the question was posed only to be dismissed as unreal. 'I lay down as an "axiom" ', wrote Minto to Morley in June 1909, 'that our considerations as to the future must be based on the recognition of our bounden duty to secure British administration in India and the welfare of the populations over whom we rule. As far as we can look ahead the existence of India must depend upon British supremacy.'[2] Proceeding on this 'axiom', it was but natural that the authors of the 1909 reforms should have refused to give serious thought to the pregnant question, 'Whither?' They dismissed the ideal of self-government for India like that of the Colonies, entertained by the vast majority of Indian nationalists at the time, as 'a mere dream'[3] and 'an impossibility'.[4] They could not conceive of the Government of India as anything but a benevolent despotism or a constitutional autocracy. Morley was all in favour of infusing the spirit of English institutions into the Government of India and of making the latter as just, constitutional and legal as possible, but he did not think it 'desirable, or possible, or even conceivable, to adapt English political institutions to the Nations who inhabit India'.[5] He repeatedly denounced the suggestion to do so as a 'gross and dangerous sophism'.[6] Minto considered the increased representation of Indians on the legislative councils to be 'a sop to impossible ambitions'.[7] Morley and Minto did not concern themselves with the distant scene. All that they attempted to do was to 'hatch some plan and policy for half a generation' or so.[8] Morley wrote to Minto: 'Do you know something said by Deák, the Hungarian statesman? "I can answer for today, I can do pretty well for tomorrow, the day after tomorrow I leave to Providence". So do I.'[9] Minto thought he could not afford 'to speculate on the problems of coming genera-

---

[1] Morley to Minto, May 9, 1907, Minto Papers, M.1007, No. 27.
[2] Minto to Morley, June 17, 1909, ibid., M.1009, No. 31.
[3] Morley to Minto, August 2, 1906, ibid., M.1006, No. 8.
[4] Minto to Morley, May 13, 1909, ibid., M.1009, No. 25.
[5] Morley to Minto, June 6, 1906, ibid., M.1005, No. 65.
[6] Morley, *Indian Speeches* (1909), p. 36.
[7] Minto to Morley, May 16, 1907, Minto Papers, M.1007, No. 24.
[8] 'If we can hatch some plan and policy for half a generation that will be something; and if for a whole generation, that would be better. Only I am bent, as you assuredly are, on doing nothing to loosen the bolts.' Morley to Minto, April 17, 1907, ibid., M.1007, No. 23.
[9] Morley to Minto, July 15, 1909, ibid., M.1009, No. 44.

tions'.[1] Parliament was equally disinclined to take long views.[2] But 'the day after tomorrow' came sooner than expected, hastened by the reforms themselves and the war, and those who had to attend to its tasks accused the authors of the 1909 reforms of lack of faith and foresight.

Early in 1906 Morley had warned Gokhale that if he and his friends attempted to belittle the reforms which he contemplated to inaugurate, its only effect would be 'to set the clock back'.[3] Gokhale and his friends tried their best to create an atmosphere favourable to the reception of the reforms in India and in the attempt even split the Congress. When the reform proposals were announced towards the end of 1908, the Moderates deliberately avoided voicing their dissatisfaction with them. They did so for two main reasons: first, because they knew that in Morley they had their best possible friend whom it would be impolitic to annoy; and second, because they feared that a disapproval of the reform proposals would give encouragement to the Extremist agitation in India. Old friends of the Congress in England, men like Hume and Wedderburn, also advised acceptance with gratitude. The Congress at its annual session in December 1908 considered the proposals contained in Morley's final dispatch of November last to be 'a large and liberal instalment of reforms' and expressed 'its most sincere and grateful thanks' to the Viceroy and the Secretary of State.[4] This atmosphere of gratitude and satisfaction, however, gave way to disappointment and grief when the rules and regulations framed under the Act were announced towards the end of 1909. The Congress condemned the separate electorates created for the Muslims as designed to aggravate communal differences. It considered the franchise to be illiberal and rooted in the distrust of the educated classes. It regretted that the non-official majorities in the provincial legislative councils had been rendered illusory by the system of nomination, that the Punjab and the United Provinces had been denied executive councils,

[1] Minto to Morley, June 17, 1909, Minto Papers, M.1009, No. 31. Also, 'But what will the next great change be, and when? Not in our time.' Minto to Morley, February 25, 1909, ibid., M.1009, No. 10.

[2] Lord Crewe spoke for most of his contemporaries when he remarked in the House of Lords on February 24, 1909: 'What will be the future of India fifty, sixty, or a hundred years hence need not, I think, trouble us. It is on the knees of the gods, and all we have got to do is to provide, as best as we can, for the conditions of the moment, having, of course, an eye to the future, but not troubling ourselves about what may happen in days when, to use Sheridan's words—"all of us are dead and most of us are forgotten".' 1 H.L. Deb. 5s., col. 215.

[3] Morley to Minto, July 27 and August 2, 1906, Minto Papers, M.1006, Nos. 6 and 8.

[4] *Report of the Twenty-Third Indian National Congress*, 1908, pp. 1–2.

and that the Central Provinces had not been given even a legislative council. But, while disapproving of these illiberal regulations and urging modifications, the Congress gratefully accepted the Act of 1909 as 'a fairly liberal measure'.[1] Strange though it might appear, Indian nationalists welcomed the reforms for the very reason which Morley and Minto had so emphatically and repeatedly disavowed. They interpreted them as an advance towards parliamentary self-government. Gokhale remarked that Indians had hitherto been engaged in agitating from outside, the reforms offered them an opportunity for responsible association with the administration. It was not still control over the administration, he said, or any large share in it, but the reforms had opened prospects of ultimate responsible administration. Undaunted by official disclaimers, he asserted confidently: 'From agitation to responsible association and from responsible association—a long and weary step—but the step will have to come to responsible administration.'[2]

The Morley-Minto reforms were a typical product of that nineteenth-century English liberalism which believed that statesmanship was mainly a question of determining how far popular demands should be conceded, but which seldom bothered to think out the fundamentals of policy, or relate it to a well-defined larger purpose. 'Lacking a clearly distinguishable and steadily developing British policy towards the growth of politics in India,' justly comments Professor C. H. Philips, 'Morley and Minto were driven to devising not so much a coherent plan as a series of expedients to meet the particular and admittedly difficult situation.'[3] 'Order *plus* Progress'[4] was an excellent maxim, but it could not be a substitute for a well-thought-out and farseeing policy. In a certain sense, Morley and Minto refused to face the basic question posed by Indian nationalism: 'What is the goal of British policy in India?' Perhaps, they thought that no new ideal was needed and that what had satisfied Burke, Macaulay and Mill would be sufficient unto their day and even beyond it. While ready to recognize the genuine wish of educated Indians for an increased share in the administration of their own country, Minto still believed that it was 'not so much political reform or political ambitions that, in the present stage of Indian history, I feel we ought to look to, but the means of giving most happiness and prosperity to the every-day lives of its

[1] *Report of the Twenty-Fourth Indian National Congress*, 1909, pp. 1-2.
[2] *Report of the Twenty-Third Indian National Congress*, 1908, p. 137.
[3] C. H. Philips, *India* (1949), p. 107.
[4] Morley to Minto, October 31, 1907, Minto Papers, M.1007, No. 61.

teeming multitudes'.[1] The Secretary of State and the Viceroy did not fail to recognize that modern Western ideas were at work in India, that a new spirit was abroad, and that differences of class and creed were gradually being obliterated by the new-born spirit of nationalism,[2] but they felt that India would have to take countless weary steps before she could acquire a true political personality. Without worrying themselves overmuch with that distant contingency, Morley and Minto applied themselves to 'the duty of the day' and 'the tasks of tomorrow'.[3] About the central purpose of British rule in India Morley at least had no doubt. It was 'to implant—slowly, prudently, judiciously—those ideas of justice, law, humanity, which are the foundation of our own civilization'.[4] The 'mighty *Raj*'. Morley knew, was 'intensely artificial and unnatural' and surely could not last; and his task, as he conceived it, was 'to make the next transition, whatever it may turn out to be, something of an improvement'.[5] He would have nothing to do with either of 'the two stupid ideas, that we have nothing to do but to keep the sword sharp, or on the other hand that we have nothing to do but to concede One Man One Vote'.[6] 'The only chance,' he wrote to Minto, 'be it a good chance or a bad chance, is to do our best to make English rulers friends with Indian leaders, and at the same time to do our best to train them in habits of political responsibility.'[7] The complex and inscrutable problem of India did not allow even a philosopher-statesman like Morley to look far ahead, but he did not fail to recognize the two main forces working for progress in India. More than a year after relinquishing charge of the India Office, Morley wrote that 'the prudently guarded expansion of popular government in India by the Councils Act, passed by Parliament in 1909' and 'the expansion of

---

[1] Minto to Morley, November 4, 1906, Minto Papers, M.1006, No. 27.

[2] 'There is one point which people do not understand at home, and which has only in quite recent years become recognizable, viz., the disappearance of religious and race antipathies in view of the possibility of a united nationality.' Minto to Morley, May 16, 1907, ibid., M.1007, No. 24.

[3] Morley, *Indian Speeches* (1909), p. 33.

[4] 'And what are we in India for? Surely to implant. . . .' Morley to Minto, October 7, 1908, Minto Papers, M.1008, No. 52.

[5] '. . . how intensely artificial and unnatural is our mighty *Raj*, and it sets one wondering whether it can possibly last. It surely cannot, and our only business is to do what we can to make. . . . ' Morley to Minto, August 15, 1907, ibid., M.1007, No. 48.

[6] Morley to Minto, October 31, 1907, ibid., M.1007, No. 61.

[7] 'One liberal experiment may fail. The tory experiment of grudging and half-and-half concession is sure to fail; sure to end in dangerous impotence. The only chance. . . .' Morley to Minto, April 2, 1909, ibid., M.1009, No. 22.

popular power, and the distribution of it as an organized force, in Parliament at home'—'these two changes ... are evidently destined in the fullness of time, perhaps no very long time, to prove themselves changes of the first order in their effects upon Indian policy in all its most extensive bearings'.[1] All these sage reflections, however, could not make amends for the lack of a definite vision and a clear-cut, forward-looking policy.

[1] Morley, 'British Democracy and Indian Government', *Nineteenth Century and After*, February 1911, p. 197.

II

WAR AND A NEW ANGLE OF VISION

A few radicals, belonging to the Liberal or the Labour Party in England, sympathized with the Congress ideal of self-government for India on the Dominion model, but the more influential and responsible Englishmen dismissed that ideal as inconceivable, impracticable, or dangerous. The vastness, diversity and backwardness of India, which made the introduction of self-governing institutions in that country so difficult; the lack of racial and sentimental ties between Indians and the British; the strong belief that constitutional principles could not be applied to a conquered dependency; and the fear that a self-governing India would at once 'cut the painter'—all militated against the idea of an Indian Dominion. We have already noted[1] how Morley, the Liberal Secretary of State, was as sceptical in this regard as Minto, the Conservative Viceroy. Lord Milner[2] remarked in 1908 that 'the idea of extending what is described as "Colonial Self-Government" to India, which seems to have a fascination for some untutored minds, is a hopeless absurdity'.[3] Curzon called it 'a fantastic and futile dream' and objected to it *'in toto'*, for it was 'incompatible with the continuance of British rule in India'.[4] Valentine Chirol[5] wrote: 'There can never be between Englishmen and Indians the same community of historical traditions, of racial affinity, of social institutions, of customs and beliefs that exists between people of our own stock throughout the British Empire. The absence of these sentimental bonds, which cannot be artificially forged,

[1] See above, p. 51.

[2] Alfred, Viscount Milner (1845–1925). Director-General of Accounts, Egypt 1889; Under-Secretary for Finance, Egypt 1890–2; High Commissioner for South Africa 1897–1905; created Viscount 1902; member of Lloyd George's War Cabinet 1916–18; Secretary of State for War 1918; Colonial Secretary 1918–21.

[3] Milner, 'The Two Empires', *Proceedings of the Royal Colonial Institute*, 1907–8, vol. xxxix, p. 333.

[4] *Proceedings of the Royal Colonial Institute*, 1908–9, vol. xl, p. 382. See also Curzon, 'The True Imperialism', *Nineteenth Century and After*, January 1908, p. 163.

[5] B. 1852; traveller, journalist and author; in charge of *The Times* foreign department 1896–1912; visited India seventeen times; member of the Royal Commission on Indian Public Services 1912–14; d. 1929.

makes it impossible that we should ever concede to India the rights of self-government which we have willingly conceded to the great English communities of our own race.... We must continue to govern India as the greatest of the dependencies of the British Crown....'[1] Reginald Craddock[2] expressed the opinion of the average British civil servant in India on the subject when, in a note on 'the origin and spread of Indian discontent' submitted to Morley, he wrote: 'Those who ... prattle about the Utopian dream of Colonial *Swaraj* are Extremists in a very thin disguise. The attempted distinction sought to be made between Colonial and Absolute *Swaraj* is all a sham. The party advocating the former must come over to the latter directly that there arose the slightest chance of the former being attained. Colonial *Swaraj* is a convenient device for rescuing disloyalty from the reach of the criminal law.'[3]

It was easy enough to point to the dangers and difficulties of granting self-government to India like the Dominions, but had these sceptics any alternative ideal? Could any responsible British statesman declare frankly, as Chirol had done, that Britain would never concede self-government to India and continue holding her as a dependency for ever? In 1899 Theodore Morison[4] had written that 'a statesman who ventured to advocate the ... policy that India should be kept in a state of perpetual vassalage ... would be hooted from public life'.[5] This was an overstatement, but there was an element of truth in it. No responsible English statesman could reject outright the Indian claim to self-government, or go uncontradicted if he dared to do so publicly. For instance, in 1909 Lord Courtney[6] had taken some of his fellow peers to task for attempting to lay down the maxim that Dominion self-government could never, under any circumstances, come to pass in India. 'We have had', Courtney had remarked, 'government for the people in India. It is impossible to carry that on without proceeding to govern-

[1] Chirol, *Indian Unrest* (1910), pp. 332–3.

[2] B. 1868; entered Indian Civil Service 1884; Chief Commissioner of the Central Provinces 1907–12; Home Member of Viceroy's council 1912–17; Lieutenant-Governor of Burma 1917–22: MP 1931–7; d. 1937.

[3] See copy of the note enclosed with Craddock's letter to James Dunlop Smith (Private Secretary to the Viceroy), January 24, 1910, Minto Papers, M.986, No. 37.

[4] B. 1863; joined the staff of the Mohammedan Anglo-Oriental College, Aligarh 1889; Principal of the College 1899–1905; member of Secretary of State's council 1906–16; d. 1936.

[5] Morison, *Imperial Rule in India* (1899), p. 1.

[6] Leonard Henry, first Baron Courtney of Penwith (1832–1918). Leader-writer to *The Times* 1865–81; Under-Secretary for the Home Office 1880; Secretary of the Treasury 1882–8; Deputy Speaker 1886–92; created Baron 1906.

ment through the people of India. By and by you will come more and more to government by the people.'[1] The noble Lords had felt the rebuke and dared not challenge. But the general concensus of opinion even amongst the reformers in England was that there was 'no necessity to trouble much about the ultimate goal'.[2] Thus it happened that, true to their empirical nature, the statesmen of the Morley-Minto era, despite all their uneasiness about the future of British rule in India, either did not feel the necessity of or evaded formulating a clear and definite forward-looking policy. But once the Congress had inscribed ideal of self-government for India within the Empire on its banner—however ambitious and impracticable it might seem—it was both a moral and a political challenge which the British Government would some day have to answer. An attitude of negation or evasion could not be maintained indefinitely.

Speaking on the second reading of the Indian Councils Bill in the House of Lords on February 23, 1909, Morley had remarked that the effect of his reforms had been, was being and would be to persuade those who hoped for 'autonomy or self-government of the colonial species or pattern' in India to give up their dream and be content with admission to co-operation with the British administration.[3] This was mere wishful thinking. Men do not give up their dreams so easily: and national dreams are, perhaps, the most tenacious. The eyes of most educated Indians were now fixed on the future and, despite the assertions of Morley and Minto to the contrary, they had welcomed the reforms of 1909 as an advance towards parliamentary self-government. Even those who stood for co-operation with the British administration did not consider it to be an end in itself. As was to be expected, Indian nationalists, instead of relinquishing their dream, began persuading the British Government to accept it as their own. In July 1911 Gokhale wrote that the political evolution to which Indian reformers looked forward was 'representative Government on a democratic basis'.[4] In his view 'the first requisite ... of improved relations on an enduring basis, between Englishmen and Indians', was 'an unequivocal declaration on England's part of her resolve to help forward the growth of representative institutions in India and a determination to stand by this policy, in spite of all temptations or difficulties'.[5] 'I think the time has come', Gokhale added, 'when a definite pronouncement on this subject should be made by the highest authority entitled to speak in the name of

[1] 1 H.L. Deb. 5s., col. 196.   [2] Ibid.   [3] Ibid., cols. 118–19.
[4] Gokhale, 'East and West in India', *Hindustan Review*, July 1911, p. 9.
[5] Ibid.

England, and the British Government in India should keep such pronouncement in view in all its actions.'[1] In October 1911 R. G. Pradhan[2] referred to the conflicting views expressed by British statesmen at different times about the goal of their rule in India and how they were 'a constant source of bewilderment and irritation to the Indian people'.[3] He demanded, therefore, of the British Parliament 'a solemn and authoritative declaration that within a fixed period, say of twenty or twenty-five years, self-government would be granted to India'.[4]

Nor did Indian nationalists stand alone in demanding a definition of British policy in India. Indian unrest had set reflective Englishmen thinking about the future and purpose of the *Raj*. The Bishop of Southampton,[5] for example, enquired in January 1908 whether the English administrators in India ever cared to think where their work in India was leading to. 'Is India', he asked, 'always to remain a subject country? Is that our intention? Is that our conception of our mission, or have we in our minds something better and nobler, something of more world-wide importance? Have we visions of an Indian nation as a far-off possibility, and are such visions the inspiration of our work? Do we feel that our duty to India and mankind can be only accomplished through the evolution of a united, free, intelligent, self-governing people, and that it cannot be accomplished through the indefinite continuance of foreign bureaucratic rule, however good and beneficent?'[6] The Bishop argued that Englishmen and Indians were working at cross purposes because they did not have the same aim. He pleaded for a meeting of minds on the subject of the future goal and a definite acceptance by the British people of the Indian ideal of self-government.[7]

The enlightened civil servant in India also felt the need for a definite, far-sighted policy. Lovat Fraser[8] noted in 1909: 'Many of our difficulties are due to the fact that we have never made up our minds as our purpose there.... Reflecting civil servants have said to me: "What are we here for? If I only knew that, I should know how to order my life and my duty." The civilian nowadays is perplexed and puzzled. He sees the conflict of rival ideas—the one that we are in India for the

---

[1] Gokhale, 'East and West in India', *Hindustan Review*, July 1911, p. 9.
[2] Journalist and pleader at Nasik; b. 1876; d. 1940.
[3] *Mahratta*, October 8, 1911.   [4] Ibid., October 15, 1911.
[5] Dr J. Macarthur. He had formerly been the Bishop of Bombay from 1898 to 1903.
[6] The Bishop of Southampton, 'The Unrest in India and Some of Its Causes', *The East and the West*, January 1908, p. 15.   [7] Ibid., pp. 1–20.
[8] B. 1871; editor of the *Times of India* for several years; on the editorial staff of *The Times* 1907–22; d. 1926.

good of the people, and the other that we are there for our own good.'¹ Lord Meston² disclosed later that the far-reaching and constantly-spreading spirit of nationalism in India made it impossible for the British officials in that country to carry on without a declared policy of what England meant to do in India and with India, and that it was largely in response to their appeals that the search for a policy was undertaken.³

The radicals in England demanded that the issue should be burked no longer. In July 1910 Josiah Wedgwood⁴ asked bluntly in the Commons: 'Do we actually want India some time to be free and self-governing or do we not?'⁵ If not, the British Government should, he argued, drop cant and say so. If, on the other hand, they did want her to be ultimately self-governing—'whether it be in twenty, fifty or a hundred years'—they should tell that frankly to the Indian people and lay their plans accordingly.⁶

In 1911–12 there was an episode which, though it brought forth renewed and more emphatic official disclaimers of the ideal of Dominion self-government for India, revealed that even the Government of India felt the need for looking ahead and at least one member of His Majesty's Government realized that a clear and authoritative enunciation of British policy in India was imperative. In a dispatch to the Secretary of State, dated August 25, 1911, the Government of India had pointed out that 'in the course of time, the just demands of Indians for a larger share in the Government of the country will have to be satisfied, and the question will be how this devolution of power can be conceded without impairing the supreme authority of the Governor-General in Council'.⁷ To the Government of India 'the only possible solution of the difficulty' appeared to be 'gradually to give the Provinces a larger measure of self-government, until at last India would consist of a

¹ 'Britain's Future in India', *The Times*, June 28, 1909; *The History of 'The Times'* (1952), vol. iv, pt. ii, p. 834.

² James Scorgie, first Baron Meston (1865–1943). Entered Indian Civil Service 1885; Lieutenant-Governor of the United Provinces 1912–18; Finance Member of Viceroy's council 1918–19; created Baron 1919.

³ 37 H.L. Deb. 5s., col. 1034. See also C. Ilbert and J. Meston, *The New Constitution of India* (1923), pp. 94–5.

⁴ Josiah Clement, first Baron Wedgwood (1872–1943). MP 1906–42; left Liberal for Labour Party 1919; Chancellor of the Duchy of Lancaster 1924; created Baron 1942.

⁵ 19 H.C. Deb. 5s., col. 2044. ⁶ Ibid., cols. 2044–5.

⁷ *Announcements by and on behalf of His Majesty the King-Emperor at the Coronation Durbar held at Delhi on December 12, 1911, with the Correspondence relating thereto*, Cd. 5979 (1911), p. 7. The dispatch was in connection with the proposed transfer of the capital of India from Calcutta to Delhi.

number of administrations, autonomous in all provincial affairs, with the Government of India above them all and possessing power to interfere in cases of misgovernment, but ordinarily restricting their functions to matters of Imperial concern'.[1] The dispatch was published, December 12, 1911, and was at once seized upon by Indian nationalists as indicating the aim and intention of the British Government in India. It became the subject of an animated discussion both in India and in England. During the debates in Parliament in February 1912 Curzon and Lansdowne accused the Liberal Government of contemplating the introduction of some sort of federal home rule in India.[2] The Secretary of State for India, Lord Crewe,[3] assured the House that nothing of the kind was intended, and that Lord Hardinge[4] had only casually spoken of 'the inevitable trend and tendency of things in India' towards further decentralization in all matters of a provincial nature.[5] A week later,— February 28th—however, Edwin Samuel Montagu,[6] the Under-Secretary of State for India, spoke at Cambridge in a totally different vein. He dwelt at length on the Liberal ideal of the Empire, based on freedom and free association. He remarked that Curzon as Viceroy was 'a mere administrator' who had no policy at all. He compared him to a chauffeur who spent his time polishing up the machinery, screwing ever nut and bolt of his car ready to make it go, but never driving it or knowing where to drive it to. Referring to the controversial passage in the Government of India dispatch, he remarked: 'That statement shows the goal, the aim towards which we propose to work—not immediately, not in a hurry, but gradually.... We cannot drift on for ever without stating a policy. A new generation, a new school of thought, fostered by our education and new European learning, has grown up, and it asks: "What are you going to do with us?" The Extremist politicians,

---

[1] Cd. 5979 (1911), p. 7.   [2] 11 H.L. Deb. 5s., cols. 164–5, 240.
[3] Robert Offley Ashburton Crewe-Milnes, second Baron Houghton and Marquis of Crewe (1858–1945). Viceroy of Ireland 1892–5; Lord President of the Council 1905–8 and 1915–16; Lord Privy Seal 1908–11; Colonial Secretary 1908–10; Secretary of State for India 1910–15; Ambassador at Paris 1922–8; Secretary of State for War 1931.
[4] Charles, Baron Hardinge of Penshurst (1858–1944). Entered Foreign Office 1880; Ambassador to Russia 1904–6; Permanent Under-Secretary of State 1906–10 and 1916–20; Viceroy of India 1910–16; Ambassador at Paris 1920–2.
[5] 11 H.L. Deb. 5s., cols. 243–4.
[6] B. 1879; MP 1906–22; Under-Secretary for India 1910–14; Financial Secretary to the Treasury 1914–16; Chancellor of the Duchy of Lancaster 1915; Minister of Munitions 1916; resigned December 1916; Secretary of State for India 1917–22; d. 1924.

who form the outside fringe of this school, have made up their minds as to what they want. One of their leaders, Mr Bipin Chandra Pal, has drawn up and published a full, frank, detailed, logical exposition of the exact form of *"swaraj"*, or, as may be roughly translated, "Colonial self-government", that they want. The Moderates look to us to say what lines our future policy is to take. We have never answered that, and we have put off answering them far too long. At last, and not too soon, a Viceroy has had the courage to state the trend of British policy in India and the lines on which we propose to advance.'[1]

Indian nationalists hailed with delight Montagu's interpretation of the passage in the dispatch. In England it only served to revive the controversy. On April 22, 1912, Bonar Law[2] in the Commons referred to Montagu's speech at Cambridge and pointed out the discrepancy between Crewe's interpretation and that of Montagu.[3] Montagu denied that there was any such discrepancy, but went on to add that when every moving section in India had got a policy, when there were preachers and teachers advocating their own ideals, it was not out of place to show to the people of India, as Hardinge had done in his dispatch, that there was a direction in which the British occupation was tending —'some definite aim and object'—and that they were in India 'not merely to administer, but to develop her on a plan'.[4]

Curzon raised the topic in the Lords on June 24, 1912 and referred to the gloss put upon the passage in the dispatch by Indian nationalists, which had received support from the Under-Secretary's remarks on two occasions.[5] Crewe, in his reply, not only repeated his earlier denial, but also referred to the political school in India who cherished the dream of Dominion self-government for their country and remarked: 'I say quite frankly that I see no future for India on those lines. I do not believe that the experiment . . . of attempting to confer a measure of real self-government, with practical freedom from Parliamentary control, upon a race which is not our own . . . is one which could be tried.'[6] Cromer[7] and Curzon received with great satisfaction this 'most emphatic and unmistakable repudiation'.[8] But still the anxiety was not

---

[1] *Speeches on Indian Questions by the Rt Hon Mr Montagu* (1917), pp. 258–9.

[2] Andrew Bonar Law (1858–1923), Tory statesman; Leader of the Opposition in the House of Commons 1911–15; Prime Minister 1922–3.

[3] 37 H.C. Deb. 5s., col. 789. [4] Ibid., col. 812.

[5] 12 H.L. Deb. 5s., cols. 143–6. [6] Ibid., cols. 155–6.

[7] Evelyn Baring, first Earl of Cromer (1841–1917). Financial Member of Viceroy's council in India 1880–3; British Agent and Consul-General in Egypt 1883–1907.

[8] 12 H.L. Deb. 5s., cols. 157, 160.

wholly removed. On July 29, 1912, Lord Inchape[1] raised the issue once again in the Lords and demanded a statement of the views of His Majesty's Government.[2] Crewe explained that there were three objects of British policy in India: 'to devolve upon local and provincial Governments as many of the functions of government as can safely be entrusted to them'; 'to employ as many Indians in the public services as can reasonably be employed'; and 'to combine the pursuit of the two first with the maintenance and permanence of British rule in India'.[3] The Government of India, Crewe asserted, did not and could not have a final goal in view. He once again referred to the dream of self-government like that of the Dominions cherished by some Indians and remarked: 'I repeat categorically what I said last time, that there is nothing whatever in the teachings of history so far as I know them, or in the present conditions of the world so far as I understand them, which makes the realization of such a dream even remotely possible.'[4] To Crewe the idea of an Indian Dominion was 'a world as remote as any Atlantis or Erewhon that ever was thought of by the ingenious brain of an imaginative writer'.[5] He advised Indians to set aside the vision of becoming prime minister of an Indian Dominion or commander-in-chief of an Indian army in future years and to settle down to closer co-operation with their Western governors.[6]

Only Courtney in the Lords deprecated the tendency 'to put the limit of impossibility on the development that may occur in India'.[7] He recalled the extraordinary changes going on in the Eastern world and the remark made to him by Sir Alfred Lyall[8] shortly before his death, 'It is not impossible that the twentieth century may see the complete withdrawal of Europe from Asia';[9] and observed: 'however comfortable it may be to ourselves to attempt to dismiss these speculations, we cannot get rid of them'.[10] Crewe agreed with Courtney that the future of India lay on 'the knees of the gods', but pointed out that his main purpose in making the statement was to repudiate the suggestion that the present Government were pursuing a policy in India which was intended to end in self-government or that he and his friends shared the

[1] James Lyle Mackay, first Earl of Inchape (1852–1932). Chairman and director of numerous banking and shipping concerns; member of Secretary of State's council 1897–1911; created Baron 1911; Viscount 1924; Earl 1929.
[2] 12 H.L. Deb. 5s., cols. 740–1.   [3] Ibid., col. 743.   [4] Ibid., cols. 744–5.
[5] Ibid., col. 745.   [6] Ibid., cols. 745–6.   [7] Ibid., col. 750.
[8] Famous Anglo-Indian administrator and author; b. 1835; entered Indian Civil Service 1856; Lieutenant-Governor of the North-West Provinces 1882–7; member of Secretary of State's council 1887–1902; d. 1911.
[9] 12 H.L. Deb. 5s., col. 750.   [10] Ibid.

dreams of Indian nationalists about Dominion self-government for that country.[1]

Crewe's invocation of what William Archer[2] called 'the dogma of perpetuity',[3] failed to silence the heretics in India or in England. On December 31, 1912, the Council of the All-India Muslim League adopted as one of its objectives 'the attainment of a system of self-government suitable to India'.[4] Returning from India after a short visit in 1912, Philip Kerr[5] wrote in the September *Round Table* that, whether the pace be fast or slow, the goal towards which events in India, propelled by British and Indians alike, were travelling was self-government like that of the Dominions.[6] Under a very suggestive title 'India: Old Ways and New', another contributor wrote in the December 1912 issue of the same quarterly that conditions in India were changing with a rapidity unknown to previous generations, which made it impossible for the English in that country to go on doing their work empirically, avoiding a philosophy or a creed. And he added: 'It is time we defined our ideas; that we knew clearly what it is that India wants, and how far and by what stages we are going to assist her to get it.'[7]

With all their habitual disinclination to speculate about the future, with all their distaste for the conscious and the explicit, the British could not for long avoid defining their policy in India. The need for such a definition was being felt by many. It was, in a fundamental sense, made inevitable by the challenge of Indian nationalism. The impact of the First World War only brought the issue to a head and allowed it to be treated from a new angle of vision.

In 1909 Lovat Fraser had predicted that the entanglement of Britain in difficulties elsewhere would be the signal for an uprising in India.[8] Returning from a visit to India immediately before the outbreak of the First World War, William Archer had noted that 'the moment England gets into serious trouble elsewhere, India, in her present

---

[1] 12 H.L. Deb. 5s., col. 751.   [2] Critic and journalist; b. 1856; d. 1924.
[3] William Archer, *India and the Future* (1917), p. 295.
[4] *Pioneer*, January 2, 1913.
[5] Philip Henry Kerr, eleventh Marquis of Lothian (1882–1940). Member of Milner's 'Kindergarten'; editor of the *Round Table* 1910–16; private secretary to Lloyd George 1916–21; succeeded to the title 1930; Under-Secretary of State for India 1931–2; Ambassador at Washington 1939–40.
[6] 'India and the Empire', *Round Table*, September 1912, pp. 623–5. See also J. R. M. Butler, *Lord Lothian* (1960), p. 175.
[7] *Round Table*, December 1912, p. 52.
[8] 'Britain's Future in India', *The Times*, June 28, 1909.

temper, would burst into a blaze of rebellion'.[1] Germany, too, had probably counted on some such eventuality. When, however, the war broke out in August 1914 India belied the prophets of evil and proved to be 'Germany's greatest disappointment'. Enthusiastically and unanimously the country stood on the side of Great Britain. There was a remarkable outburst of genuine and spontaneous loyalty amongst all sections of the Indian people. Politicians in India behaved admirably. They voiced 'their feelings of unswerving loyalty and enthusiastic devotion to their King-Emperor, and an assurance of their unflinching support to the British Government' and offered to share in the heavy financial burdens imposed by the war on the United Kingdom.[2] Even the erstwhile Extremists, men like Pal and Tilak, preached co-operation with the Government in the war effort.

Imperial strategy had so far been based on the assumption that in the event of a war India would have to be reinforced with additional troops from home. But no sooner did hostilities commence in 1914 than Hardinge, instead of asking for more troops, pledged India's last man and last gun to the British Government. An Indian expeditionary force was at once dispatched to the Western front where it arrived just in time to fill the gaps in the thin red line during the critical winter of 1914, which could not be filled from any other source until the Kitchener armies and the Dominion contingents had been adequately trained and equipped. In the following months the Government of India kept up a steady flow of Indian reinforcements to the Western front and denuded the country almost entirely of regular British troops and her large reserves of artillery, ammunition and transport. Large Indian forces were also employed in the campaigns in East Africa and in the Middle East. In all, India sent one million men to the battlefield. Over £146 millions were voted from the revenues of British India towards the cost of the war, and the princes and other wealthy Indians made generous gifts.[3]

The Congress meeting at Madras in December 1914 conveyed to the King-Emperor and the people of England 'its profound devotion to the Throne, its unswerving allegiance to the British connection, and

---

[1] William Archer, op. cit., p. 17.
[2] Resolution passed in the Imperial Legislative Council, September 8, 1914. *Proceedings of the Council of the Governor-General of India*, 1914–15, vol. liii, pp. 16–17.
[3] For India's contribution to the war see J. W. B. Merewether and F. E. Smith, *The Indian Corps in France* (1917); and the Government of India publication *India's Contribution to the Great War* (1923).

its firm resolve to stand by the Empire, at all hazards and at all costs'.[1] It noted 'with gratitude and satisfaction' the dispatch of Indian troops to the Western front and offered to the Viceroy 'its most heartfelt thanks for affording to the people of India an opportunity of showing that, as equal subjects of His Majesty, they are prepared to fight shoulder to shoulder with the people of other parts of the Empire in defence of right and justice, and the cause of the Empire'.[2]

The Montagu-Chelmsford Report considered the behaviour of Indian political leaders during the first two years of the war to be 'worthy of all praise' and wondered 'whether a bolder policy from the outset of the war, and a franker inviting of India's co-operation in all forms of war effort might not have done much to steady men's minds'.[3] The *Round Table* commented in December 1915: 'It is not easy to see what more they could have done, and it is certain that they might easily have done less.'[4]

The reasons for India's loyal and generous response to the war are not difficult to understand. The magnitude of Indian unrest had been much exaggerated and its character misunderstood in official circles and in the British press. At heart India was still loyal. The Morley-Minto reforms had been sufficiently liberal to ease the tension in India and arrest the growing estrangement between the rulers and the ruled. The revocation of the partition of Bengal in 1911 had healed a festering sore. Hardinge's policy of trust and conciliation had done much to restore the waning faith and confidence of educated Indians in the British Government. There was a widespread recognition in India of the justice and righteousness of the cause for which England was fighting. Many welcomed the opportunity offered to India of acting on a world-wide stage. Hardinge's decision to dispatch Indian troops to the European front was universally applauded in the country. V. S. Srinivasa Sastri[5] compared it to Cavour's decision to send Piedmontese armies to fight along with the English and the French in the Crimean War,[6] and not a few hoped that the fields of Flanders and France would give birth to a new India. Their loyalty was fortified by their patriotism.

[1] *Report of the Twenty-Ninth Indian National Congress*, 1914, p. 1.
[2] Ibid., p. 2.
[3] *Report on Indian Constitutional Reforms*, Cd. 9109 (1918), p. 20.
[4] *Round Table*, December 1915, p. 100.
[5] B. 1869; President of the Servants of India Society 1915–27; President of the National Liberal Federation of India 1922; Agent of the Government of India in South Africa 1927–9; Vice-Chancellor of Annamalai University 1935–40; d. 1946.
[6] Srinivasa Sastri, *Self-Government for India under the British Flag* (1916), p. 1.

By loyally co-operating with the Empire in its hour of peril, Indians hoped to advance their claims for sharing in its privileges.

India's splendid rally to the cause of the Empire both surprised and gratified the British people, who had been hearing so much and so often of Indian unrest in the preceding years. And the more they were surprised and gratified, the more vocal and fulsome were their admiration and gratitude. 'The Indian Empire', wrote *The Times*, 'has overwhelmed the British nation by the completeness and unanimity of its enthusiastic aid.'[1] Prime Minister Asquith[2] remarked that in all the moving exhibition of national and imperial patriotism which the war had evoked there was none which had more touched the feelings of the British people than the magnificent response which the princes and the peoples of India had made to their need.[3]

It was the revelation that India had proved to be not a cause of anxiety but a source of immense strength to the Empire in its time of trouble, which caused even the most conservative imperialist in Britain to view the problems of her internal development and place in the Empire from a changed angle. As Chirol wrote: 'If India was willing to fight shoulder to shoulder with the other nations of the Commonwealth for the British Empire, then she was qualifying for closer partnership. Closer partnership could never, however, become a living reality unless India was capable of developing qualities essential to self-government on the same lines as all the other members of the British Commonwealth. Here at last was a meeting-ground for British Imperialists who believe in the Empire as one of the greatest instruments of human progress and are alive to the enormous value of India to the Empire; and for Indian Nationalists who, whilst equally alive to the enormous value of the British connection for India, believe no less firmly in the evolution of an Indian nation capable of self-government.'[4] The Under-Secretary of State for India, Charles Roberts,[5] emphasized the same point in the Commons on November 26, 1914. It was premature, he said, to attempt to anticipate the consequences that might follow from 'this striking and historic event—the participation of India in force in the World War of the Empire'.[6] 'But it is clear', he added, 'that India claims to be not a mere dependent but a partner in

[1] *The Times*, September 10, 1914.
[2] Herbert Henry Asquith, first Earl of Oxford and Asquith (1852–1928). Home Secretary 1892–5; Chancellor of the Exchequer 1905–8; Prime Minister 1908–16; created Earl 1925.
[3] 66 H.C. Deb. 5s., col. 955.   [4] *The Times*, June 6, 1918.
[5] B. 1865; MP 1906–18 and 1922–3; Under-Secretary of State for India 1914–15; d. 1959.   [6] 68 H.C. Deb. 5s., col. 1357.

the Empire, and her partnership with us in spirit and on battlefields cannot but alter the angle from which we shall all henceforward look at the problems of the government of India.'[1] And he hoped that 'the common endeavours of these days' would enable India to realize that she was occupying, and was 'destined to occupy, a place in our free Empire worthy alike of her ancient civilization and thought, of the valour of her fighting races, and the patriotism of her sons'.[2]

Participation in the war gave India a new sense of self-esteem. She felt that she had been tried and not found wanting, that thereby her status had been raised, and that it should be recognized. The proclaimed ideals of the war opened a new vista of hope for her subject people. At the 1914 Congress Mrs Annie Besant[3] remarked that India was 'not content to be any longer a child in the nursery of the Empire.... She is showing the responsibility of the man in Europe. Give her the freedom of the man in India.'[4] And Mrs Besant demanded this freedom not as a reward but as a matter of right. The President of the 1914 session of the Congress, B. N. Basu, declared that what India wanted above all was that her government should be autonomous within the Empire. India desired, he said, neither subordination nor separation, but 'a joint partnership on equal terms'.[5] By a formal resolution the Congress appealed to the British Government 'to deepen and perpetuate' 'the profound and avowed loyalty' manifested by the Indian people and 'make it an enduring and valuable asset of the Empire' by removing all invidious restrictions between His Majesty's Indian and other subjects, 'by redeeming the pledges of Provincial autonomy contained in the Dispatch of August 25, 1911, and by taking such steps as may be necessary for the recognition of India as a component part of a federated Empire, in the full and free enjoyment of the rights belonging to that status'.[6]

India's immense contributions to the war, the high praise they earned from British statesmen, and the proclaimed ideals of the Allies—all raised expectation in India to the highest pitch. Far away from the scene of actual conflict, Indian politicians had ample time to watch the trend of events. With a vigilant eye and an alert ear they noted the doings and sayings of British and Allied statesmen. After a few months

---

[1] 68 H.C. Deb. 5s., col. 1357.   [2] Ibid., col. 1358.
[3] B. 1847; went to India 1895; President of the Theosophical Society 1907–33; founded the Central Hindu College at Benares 1898; President of the Indian National Congress 1917; d. 1933.
[4] *Report of the Twenty-Ninth Indian National Congress*, 1914, p. 86.
[5] Ibid., p. 36.   [6] Ibid., p. 4.

of the war they detected—rightly or wrongly—a certain caution and restraint in the references of British statesmen to India, in striking contrast to the exuberance of earlier days. They noted a tendency amongst Englishmen to take India's services for granted and even to rate them lower than those of the Dominions. India figured rarely in the schemes for the future and it was feared that her services would be forgotten. Hardinge's viceroyalty and the outbreak of the war had submerged old distrust and suspicions, but not eliminated them. And when in March 1915 the House of Lords rejected the proposal for the creation of an executive council for the United Provinces, which had been recommended by the legislative council and the Lieutenant-Governor of that province and was supported by the Government of India and the Secretary of State, on the well-worn pleas that it was the demand of a microscopic minority and that personal rule suited the East, members in the Imperial Legislative Council asked more in sorrow than in anger: 'Is this the first fruit of that change in the angle of vision which had been promised by a high authority?'; 'If this is the attitude of our ex-Viceroys and ex-Governors towards us during the war, what will it be after the war? They have been paying us high and extremely flattering compliments upon our loyalty and devotion to the British Crown, and yet in the same breath they tell that we are in such a backward and primitive condition that even an executive council would be too good for us.'[1] The incident was both revealing and instructive.

The discussions throughout the Empire of schemes of Imperial federation convinced many an Indian politician that important changes were imminent in the constitution of the Empire. Indian nationalists claimed that their country had proved her loyalty to the Empire and was willing to remain steadfast to the British connection in the same way as the Dominions, but like the latter she must be given 'Home Rule'. The suggestion made in certain quarters that an Imperial parliament or council, composed of representatives from the Dominions and the United Kingdom, should be responsible for the government of India and other dependencies caused profound misgivings in India. At once the press and platform rang with the cry: 'Shall the Dominions rule India?'; 'Was this to be the reward for all our loyalty and sacrifices?'; 'Will India be the Cinderella of the Empire?' Smarting under the treatment of Indians in the Dominions, Indian opinion reacted violently to any suggestion of allowing the Dominions to have a say

[1] *Proceedings of the Council of the Governor-General of India*, 1914–15, vol. liii, pp. 606, 609, 637.

in Indian affairs. Indian politicians felt that a policy of silence and trustfulness might end in the tightening of fetters and their having to serve more masters and worse masters. They, therefore, began to demand that before India joined any Imperial federation she must have self-government like the Dominions and elevated to equal status.

Like many of his countrymen, Lord Willingdon,[1] the Governor of Bombay, had been profoundly impressed with India's loyal and magnificent services in the war, and felt that she should be rewarded handsomely. Early in 1915 he asked Gokhale privately to submit to him a scheme of minimum reforms which would satisfy India after the war. On February 17, 1915, two days before his tragic death, Gokhale submitted his scheme[2] to Willingdon, in which he recommended, among other things, almost complete provincial autonomy, with a legislature of 75-100, of which four-fifths was to be elected, and an executive of 6-3 English and three Indians—not dependent on the vote of the majority, its relations with the legislature being roughly similar to those between the Imperial Government and the *Reichstag* in Germany; a Government of India, increasingly amenable to a non-official majority and freed from the leading strings of the Secretary of State, whose council was to be abolished and position steadily approximated to that of the Secretary of State for the Colonies. Willingdon wrote to leaders at home to make a reassuring move, but 'either got no answer or no encouragement'.[3] Pherozeshah Mehta soon followed Gokhale to the grave, and the Congress was robbed of the moderating influence of two of its most prominent leaders. Under the influence of the excitement of the times, the uncertainty as to the intentions of the Government, and the apprehensions regarding India's position in a probable federation of the Empire, the political cauldron in India began to boil. Mrs Besant acted as the peacemaker between the Moderates and the Extremists and began preparations for launching a 'Home Rule' movement. The followers of Gokhale and Mehta were anxious that nothing should be done which might embarrass the authorities in any way during the period of the war, but neither did they wish to allow India's case to go by default. The loyalty of the Moderates was as firm as their patriotism. They stood for a gradual and

[1] Freeman Freeman-Thomas, first Marquis of Willingdon (1866-1941). MP 1900-10; Governor of Bombay 1913-18 and of Madras 1919-24; Governor-General of Canada 1926-20; Viceroy of India 1931-6.

[2] Srinivasa Sastri, *Life of Gopal Krishna Gokhale* (1937), pp. 112-13; *The Times*, August 15, 1917.

[3] Willingdon to Lloyd George, January 22, 1916: cited in Lloyd George, *War Memoirs* (1934), vol. iv, p. 1739.

peaceful advance of India towards self-government, in co-operation with their British rulers. For themselves they believed 'with the fervour of a religious faith'[1] that India would some day achieve her self-government within the Empire and that British statesmen would prove true to their traditional genius and recognize India's aspirations as legitimate and worthy of encouragement. But how could they—without appearing ridiculous—avow their faith openly while the solemn disclaimers of Morley and Crewe were fresh in public memory? These disclaimers, the Moderates knew, had made large classes of people in India distrustful of British good intentions and hostile to British rule. Clearly there was need that these unfortunate disclaimers themselves should first be disclaimed. And this, the Moderates felt, could easily be done if the British Government made an authoritative and unequivocal declaration that it was their aim and intention to grant India self-government similar to that enjoyed by the Dominions in the fullness of time. There was yet another reason why the Moderates considered such a declaration of British policy in India necessary. They were wise and practical-minded enough to realize that the war had given rise to excessive hopes and demands in India which could not be fully satisfied by the reforms likely to be granted by the authorities at the end of the war. Dissatisfaction with post-war reforms might even lead to a recrudescence of serious unrest in the country. But if the Government could be persuaded to avow an intention of leading India to self-government, the differences between the rulers and the ruled would be narrowed down to questions of method and pace of advance. In such a situation it would not be difficult for moderate and reasonable men to throw the weight of their co-operation and influence on the side of the authorities, thus ensuring the peaceful but steady political progress of India.

The desire of the Moderates for a definite statement of British policy in India found earnest expression in the presidential address delivered by Sir Satyendra Prasanno Sinha[2] to the 1915 session of the Congress held at Bombay. Sinha remarked on the occasion that nothing but 'a rational and inspiring ideal' could 'still the throbbing pain in the soul

---

[1] The phrase quoted is S. P. Sinha's. See *Speeches and Writings of Lord Sinha* (1922), p. 86.

[2] B. 1864; Advocate-General of Bengal 1905–9; Law Member of Viceroy's council 1909–10; President of the Indian National Congress 1915; member of the council of Governor of Bengal 1917–19; created Baron 1919; Under-Secretary of State for India 1919–20; Governor of Bihar and Orissa 1920–1; member of the judicial committee of the Privy Council 1926–8; d. 1928.

of awakening India'.[1] After reiterating that self-government within the Empire was the goal of Indian nationalism, he went on to appeal to the British people 'to declare their ungrudging approval of the goal to which we aspire, to declare their inflexible resolution to equip India for her journey to that goal and furnish her escort on the long and weary road'.[2] Such a declaration by Britain, Sinha said, would be the most distinguished way of marking her appreciation of India's loyalty and services; it would touch the heart and appeal to the imagination of Indians far more than any specific political reforms. These latter, he argued, might fall short of the high expectations raised by the utterances of English statesmen as to the future place of India in the Empire and cause general disappointment, but an authoritative declaration of Britain's resolve to lead India to self-government would, without causing such disappointment, convince the Indian people that the pace of reforms would be reasonably accelerated and that henceforth it would be only a question of patient preparation. Sinha referred to the 'unhappy statements and even actions of responsible [British] statesmen'[3] in the recent past which had, he said, aroused a widespread suspicion in India that Britain did not contemplate giving India freedom even in the most distant future. He demanded, therefore, 'an authentic and definite proclamation with regard to which there will be no evasion, no misunderstanding possible',[4] 'a frank and full statement of the policy of the Government as regards the future of India, so that hope may come where despair holds sway and faith where doubt spreads its darkening shadow'.[5] And he warned that unless the British Government 'steadily, consistently and unflinchingly' adhered to the policy of preparing India for ultimate self-government within the Empire 'the moderate party amongst us will soon be depleted of all that is fine and noble in human character'.[6]

That was how Sinha—the most loyal and moderate and sensible of Indians—tried to pin down the British nation and Government, and tempt them into making a declaration of policy. Lord Chelmsford[7] revealed later that 'the ball was set rolling' by Sinha's remarkable address to the Congress in December 1915.[8] It apparently inspired him—the future Viceroy of India—and many others to think about the goal of

[1] *Report of the Thirtieth Indian National Congress*, 1915, p. 23.
[2] Ibid., p. 30. [3] Ibid., p. 23. [4] Ibid., p. 25. [5] Ibid., p. 30. [6] Ibid., p. 24.
[7] Frederick John Napier Thesiger, third Baron and first Viscount Chelmsford (1868–1933). Governor of Queensland 1905–9 and of New South Wales 1909–13; Viceroy of India 1916–21; First Lord of the Admiralty 1924.
[8] 69 H.L. Deb. 5s., cols. 266–7. See also C. H. Setalvad, *Recollections and Reflections* (1946), p. 284.

British policy in India and to realize the need for its announcement.

The ruling Viceroy, Lord Hardinge, was a wise and imaginative statesman, fully alive and sympathetic to the new developments in India. Convinced that peace and tranquillity in India and the future good relations between India and the British Empire would depend to a large extent upon what concessions were made to legitimate Indian aspirations, he had already in August 1915 drawn up a memorandum on the reforms which he thought should be introduced in India at the end of the war.[1] In October 1915 he had sent his memorandum to the Secretary of State, along with the overwhelmingly favourable comments on it of the heads of local governments and the members of his executive council. Hardinge openly avowed his friendliness to the Indian ideal of self-government. Speaking at the United Service Club at Simla on October 8, 1915, he remarked that it was 'not enough for... [England] now to consider only the material outlook of India', she must cherish the aspirations for liberty of which she had herself sown the seed in the country. He asked the English officials in India to prepare themselves for the 'far more glorious task' of the future, that of 'encouraging and guiding the political self-development of the people', and he himself looked forward 'with confidence to a time when... India may be regarded as a true friend of the Empire and not merely as a trusty dependent'.[2] Although in his valedictory address to the Imperial Legislative Council on March 24, 1916, Hardinge discouraged 'extravagant hopes... and unrealizable demands' with regard to post-war reforms in India, he did not fail to add: 'I do not for a moment wish to discountenance self-government as a national ideal. It is a perfectly legitimate aspiration and has the warm sympathy of all moderate men.'[3] Hardinge's remarks encouraged Indian politicians to think that it would not be very difficult to persuade the authorities to make a formal

[1] 'Memorandum by H.E. the Viceroy upon Questions Likely to Arise in India at the End of the War', Austen Chamberlain Papers, A.C. 22/91.

The main recommendations of Hardinge were: commissions for Indians in the army; the modification of the Arms Act; the abolition of the Indian excise duty on cotton goods; the modification of the regulations of the central and provincial legislative councils (elected majority in the provinces, increase of elected members at the centre, wider electorates); the relaxation of control exercised by the centre over the provinces, and by the Secretary of State over the Government of India; India's representation at the Imperial Conference; the abolition of indentured labour; state-aid for Indian industries; the appointment of Indians to the Privy Council; and the increased employment of Indians in the public services.

[2] *Times of India*, October 11, 1915.

[3] *Proceedings of the Council of the Governor-General of India*, 1915–16, vol. liv, p. 559.

and definite declaration that self-government for India was the ultimate goal of their policy.

Chelmsford came as Viceroy to India in April 1916 with his mind made up that a declaration of British policy was necessary.[1] At the very first meeting of his executive council he propounded two questions:

'(1) What is the goal of British Rule in India? [and] (2) What are the steps on the road to that goal?'[2] The deliberations of the council led to the conclusion that 'the endowment of British India as an integral part of the British Empire with self-government was the goal of British Rule' and that an advance towards this goal should be made along three roads, namely, the development of local self-government; the more responsible employment of Indians in the administration; and the expansion of the provincial legislative councils.[3] On November 24, 1916, the Government of India sent a dispatch to the Secretary of State, containing their final proposals for reform, along with the comments of the local governments on them.[4] The two main features of the Government of India dispatch related to the reform of the provincial legislative councils and the declaration of the goal of British rule in India. As regards the provincial legislative councils, the dispatch had recommended that their electorates should be widened, that the number of Indian representatives in them should be increased, and that they should have elected majorities.[5] In making these recommendations the Government of India had followed the lines laid down by the reforms of 1892 and 1909. They had proposed no immediate enlargement of the constitutional powers of the provincial legislative councils and had expressly told the Secretary of State that they had 'no wish to develop the councils as quasi-parliaments'.[6] As regards the declaration of the goal of British rule in India, the Government of India had proposed a long and verbose formula:

[1] See the remark made by Crewe in the Lords on December 12, 1919: 37 H. L. Deb. 5s., col. 986.
[2] *Proceedings of the Indian Legislative Council*, 1917–18, vol. lvi, p. 17.
[3] Ibid., pp. 17–18.
[4] Government of India Dispatch, Home Department, Political, No. 17, dated November 24, 1916, Austen Chamberlain Papers, A.C. 22/91.
[5] Ibid., pp. 19–24.
[6] Ibid., p. 20. The Government of India had rejected the method of advance—by way of dyarchy—suggested in the Duke memorandum (see below, p. 85). On this point see Chelmsford to Austen Chamberlain, May 30, 1917 (telegram), Private Telegrams, Austen Chamberlain Papers, A.C.45; and the remark made by Chelmsford in the House of Lords on November 24, 1927: 69 H.L. Deb. 5s., cols. 267–8.

'The goal to which we look forward is the endowment of British India as an integral part of the Empire, with self-government, but the rate of progress towards that goal must depend upon the improvement and wide diffusion of education, the softening of racial and religious differences, and the acquisition of political experience.

'The form of self-government to which she may eventually attain must be regulated by the special circumstances of India. They differ so widely from those of any other part of the Empire that we cannot altogether look for a model in those forms of self-government which already obtain in the great Dominions. In all parts of the Empire which now enjoy self-government, it has been the result, not of any sudden inspiration of theoretical statesmanship, but of a steady process of practical evolution, substantially facilitated by the possession of a more or less common inheritance of political traditions, social customs and religious beliefs.

'British India has been built up on different lines, and under different conditions, and must work out by the same steady process of evolution a definite constitution of her own. In what form this may eventually be cast it is neither possible nor profitable for us to attempt now to determine, but we contemplate her gradual progress towards a larger and larger measure of control by her own people, the steady and conscious development of which will ultimately result in a form of self-government, differing perhaps in many ways from that enjoyed by other parts of the Empire, but evolved on lines which have taken into account India's past history, and the special circumstances and traditions of her component peoples, and her political and administrative entities.

'Our most anxious desire is to see a real and immediate advance made towards this goal, and in the belief that the time has now come when the rate of progress may be accelerated on definite lines we propose:

(a) To develop urban and rural self-government in the direction of giving greater powers to the local boards and councils, and making these more predominantly non-official and elective in character, while at the same time extending the franchise in the wards or other constituencies by which the elected members are chosen.

(b) To increase the proportion of Indians in the higher branches of the public service, and thereby to enable Indians to take a more important part in the administration of the country.

(c) To pave the way for an ultimate enlargement of the constitutional powers of the provincial legislative councils—(i) through an increase in the elected element; and (ii) through a material expansion of the constituencies by which the elected members are chosen, so as to bring about a state of things under which they will become more truly representative of the interests of the people as a whole.'[1]

Unfortunately, the Government of India could not take the Indian public into their confidence. Indian politicians had expected some announcement of policy in Chelmsford's opening speech to the Imperial Legislative Council in September 1916, but they were disappointed. It was already rumoured that the Government of India were busy considering a scheme of future reforms, but when Indian members enquired in the Council whether it was so, and would the Government publish their proposals before final decision was reached, the Home Member replied that the Government were 'unable to make any statement in the matter'.[2] Anxious lest their case go by default, nineteen non-official members of the Imperial Legislative Council hurriedly put their heads together and produced a memorandum, containing what they called their 'humble suggestions' regarding post-war reforms in India, and submitted it to the Viceroy in September 1916.[3]

Aided by the unnecessary reticence of the Government of India, Indian nationalists closed their ranks. The Extremists re-entered the Congress and before the year 1916 was out the Muslim League had signed a concordat with its old antagonist. Meeting together at Lucknow in the last week of December 1916, the Congress and the League put forward a joint demand that 'the King-Emperor should be pleased to issue a proclamation that it is the aim and intention of British policy to confer self-government on India at an early date', that 'definite steps should be taken towards self-government by granting the reforms contained in the [Congress-League] scheme', and that 'in the reconstruction of the Empire India [should] be lifted from the position of a dependency to that of an equal partner in the Empire with the self-governing Dominions'.[4] The main reforms demanded by the Congress and the League were: provincial autonomy; four-fifths of the central and provincial legislative councils to be elected; not less than half the members of the central and provincial governments to be elected by their respective legislative councils; the executives to be bound to act in accordance with the resolutions passed by their legislative councils

[1] Government of India Dispatch, Home Department, Political, No. 17, dated November 24, 1916, p. 16, Austen Chamberlain Papers, A.C. 22/9.
[2] *Proceedings of the Indian Legislative Council*, 1916–17, vol. lv, pp. 45–6, 51.
[3] The memorandum is reproduced in Srinivasa Sastri, *Self-Government for India under the British Flag*, Appendix I, pp. i–vii. Its proposals were later incorporated in the Congress-League scheme.
[4] *Times of India*, December 30, 1916, January 1–2, 1917.

unless they were vetoed by the Governor-General or Governors, in that event, if the resolution were passed again after an interval of not less than one year, it should in any case be put into effect; the relations of the Secretary of State with the Government of India to be similar to those of the Colonial Secretary with the Dominion governments; and India to have an equal status with the Dominions in any body concerned with Imperial affairs.[1]

In the absence of any alternative proposals on behalf of the Government, the Congress-League scheme monopolized the political stage in India and opinion began to crystallize fast in its favour. The Home Rule Leagues of Besant and Tilak daily gained fresh converts. In February 1917 the Maharaja of Bikaner[2] publicly expressed the deep sympathy of the princes for 'the legitimate aspirations of our brother Indians'.[3] Never before had such a unanimity of opinion been witnessed in India on any political issue. Hindus and Muslims; Extremists and Moderates; politicians and princes—all seemed to be united in their desire for self-government for India. This unique phenomenon could not fail to impress the British Government. It was not long before liberal non-official Anglo-Indian opinion reinforced the Indian demand for a declaration of British policy. 'We have never met an intelligent man', wrote the *Times of India* on May 15, 1917, 'who doubted the goal of British policy in India; it is clearly and irrevocably, the attainment of full self-government within the Empire.' The paper could 'discern no possible ill, and many positive advantages', in a 'clear and emphatic announcement' of this goal. 'Unless the end is clearly in view,' it added, 'there can be no logical or definite purpose behind such constitutional changes as are made or contemplated.'[4]

An India Office committee, headed by Sir William Duke,[5] examined the Government of India dispatch of November 24, 1916, and submitted its report to the Secretary of State on March 16, 1917.[6] The committee did not think that the proposals of the Government of India with

[1] *Times of India*, December 30, 1916, January 1-2, 1917.
[2] Ganga Singh Bahadur, Maharaja of Bikaner (1880-1943). Succeeded 1887; assumed ruling powers 1898; Chancellor of the Chamber of Princes 1921-6.
[3] K. M. Panikkar, *His Highness the Maharaja of Bikaner: A Biography* (1937), p. 174. [4] *Times of India*, May 15, 1917; see also June 21 and August 2, 1917.
[5] B. 1863; entered Indian Civil Service 1882; Lieutenant-Governor of Bengal 1911; member of the council of Governor of Bengal 1912-14; member of Secretary of State's council 1914-20; Permanent Under-Secretary of State, India Office 1920-4; d. 1924.
[6] 'Report on Government of India Dispatch, Home Department, No. 17, Political, dated November 24, 1916', March 16, 1917, Austen Chamberlain Papers, A.C. 22/91.

regard to the provincial legislative councils constituted a coherent and well-thought-out plan of reform, or that they embodied sound and constitutional lines of political advance.¹ It pointed out that a mere increase in the number of elected Indian representatives in the councils would effect 'no progress in or towards self-government', but simply 'perpetuate and aggravate a vicious system which makes it the main function of the Legislative Councils to oppose and criticize the Government while remaining completely free from responsibility for the results of their action'.² The committee considered that 'it would be hazardous to increase their numbers while withholding responsibility' and suggested that 'training in functions ought to precede any considerable increase of numbers'.³ Nor did the committee give its support to the enunciation of an ultimate goal for Indian constitutional development, such as formulated by the Government of India. 'We doubt the wisdom', said its report, 'of dangling before the Indian politicians a formula of political progress, hedged with restrictions that nullify its meaning, and calculated to embarrass, by the vagueness of its promises, our successors in Indian government. We feel that the situation demands not the visionary prospect of a development beyond the realization of generations, but a frank and clear statement embodying practical progressive reforms capable of achievement within a definite future that can be foreseen.'⁴

The Secretary of State for India, Austen Chamberlain,⁵ agreed with the committee's criticism of the Government of India scheme and wrote to the Viceroy accordingly.⁶ As regards a declaration of British policy

¹ 'Report on Government of India Dispatch, Home Department, No. 17, Political, dated November 24, 1916', March 16, 1917, pp. 1-2, Austen Chamberlain Papers, A.C. 22/91. ² Ibid., p. 7.   ³ Ibid.   ⁴ Ibid., p. 8.

⁵ B. 1863; MP 1892–1937; Chancellor of the Exchequer 1903–5 and 1919–21; Secretary of State for India 1915–17; member of the War Cabinet 1918; Foreign Secretary 1924–9; First Lord of the Admiralty 1931; d. 1937.

⁶ 'After all, we want to train Indians in self-government. A mere increase in the number of their representatives does not really advance this object, unless we can at the same time fix these men with some definite powers and with real responsibility for their actions.' Austen Chamberlain to Chelmsford, May 2, 1917, 'Extracts from Mr Chamberlain's Private Letters to the Viceroy', Austen Chamberlain Papers, A.C. 22/91.

Again, on May 15, 1917, Austen Chamberlain wrote to Chelmsford: 'My difficulty in regard to this scheme is, first, that it makes no real progress towards Self-Government; and, secondly, that it will perpetuate and aggravate a vicious system which makes it the main function of the Legislative Councils to oppose and criticise the Government while remaining completely free from responsibility for the results of their action.... The vital difficulty of this scheme, as it seems to me, is that, while increasing the number of representatives, it does nothing to

in India, however, Austen Chamberlain had begun to realize its necessity,[1] though he considered the formula proposed by the Viceroy to be unnecessarily elaborate and formal. 'I do not dispute your goal,' he wrote to Chelmsford, 'though I dislike the elaboration and the formality of your definition. I should prefer to say in the least formal manner possible and in the shortest words, that our object is to develop free institutions with a view to ultimate Self-Government within the Empire, and I should not attempt to define, at a time so distant from any point at which we could expect this aspiration to be realized, the form which such self-government must take or the extent to which our aspiration can ultimately be realized.'[2] Austen Chamberlain was also anxious that any such statement of the goal of British policy in India should be 'accompanied by a very clear declaration that this is a distant goal' and that 'the rate of progress and the times and stages by which it is to be reached must be controlled and decided by His Majesty's Government'.[3]

A resourceful combination of intellectuals and politicians in England, known as the Round Table,[4] had for some time past been considering the problem of India from an angle from which it had not hitherto been

---

secure any increase in their sense of responsibility; it gives them no real training in affairs and will merely multiply the number of irresponsible critics who, dissatisfied with their own impotence and deprived of all sense of responsibility for the results of their actions, may become a grave embarrassment to Government. I can see no use in multiplying elected representatives until we are prepared to entrust them with some degree of responsibility in financial or administrative matters.' Ibid.

[1] 'I am coming round to your view that a statement of our object is necessary.' Austen Chamberlain to Chelmsford, May 2, 1917, 'Extracts from Mr Chamberlain's Private Letters to the Viceroy', Austen Chamberlain Papers, A.C. 22/91.

[2] Austen Chamberlain to Chelmsford, May 15, 1917, ibid.

[3] Chelmsford to Austen Chamberlain, May 2, 1917, ibid.

[4] Lord Riddell noted in his diary the remark made by Lloyd George in 1921: 'L.G. in talking of the Round Table Group . . . remarked: "It is a very powerful combination—in its way perhaps the most powerful in the country. Each member of the Group brings to its deliberations certain definite and important qualities, and behind the scenes they have much power and influence".' *Lord Riddell's Intimate Diary of the Peace Conference and After, 1918–23* (1933), pp. 329–30. The prominent members of the Round Table were: L. S. Amery, Robert Brand, Robert Cecil, Valentine Chirol, Reginald Coupland; G. L. Craik, Lionel Curtis, Geoffrey Dawson, John Dove, Patrick Duncan, Richard Feetham, Edward Grigg, Lionel Hichens, Philip Kerr, D. O. Malcolm, William Marris; James Meston, Lord Milner, F. S. Oliver, Lord Selborne, Arthur Steele-Maitland and A. E. Zimmern.

considered either by Indian nationalists or the Indian Government, namely, how far was India adapted, or could be adapted, for inclusion in a possible federation of the British Empire. The beginnings of the Round Table's interest in India can be traced back to 1906, when two prominent Indian civil servants—William Marris[1] and Sir James Meston—went on secondment to South Africa to help in reorganizing the local civil service and there came in close contact with members of Milner's 'Kindergarten', particularly Lionel Curtis[2] and Philip Kerr. In 1909 those members of the 'Kindergarten' who had returned to England organized the Round Table, with the primary object of bringing about an 'organic union' of the Empire by the establishment of a federal 'Imperial government' and deputed Curtis and Kerr to go to Canada as missionaries of the movement. Curtis and Kerr took Marris with them on their visit to Canada in September 1909. It was during this visit, Curtis tells us, while walking together one day through a forest on the Pacific slopes and discussing with Marris Indian anarchist troubles, that the latter told Curtis that 'self-government ... however far distant, was the only intelligible goal of British policy in India'.[3] Referring to this incident, Curtis wrote later: 'I have since looked back to this walk as one of the milestones in my own education. So far I had thought of self-government as a Western institution, which was and would always remain peculiar to the peoples of Europe.... It was from that moment that I first began to think of "the Government of each by each, and of all by all" not merely as a principle of western life, but rather of all human life, as the goal to which all human societies must tend. It was from that moment that I began to think of the British Commonwealth as the greatest instrument ever devised for enabling that principle to be realized, not merely for the children of Europe but for all races and kindreds and peoples and tongues. And it is for that reason that I have ceased to speak of the British Empire and called the book in which I published my views, *The Commonwealth of Nations*.'[4]

[1] B. 1874; entered Indian Civil Service 1896; lent to the Transvaal Government 1906–8; Joint-Secretary in the Home Department, Government of India 1917–18; Governor of Assam 1921–2 and of the United Provinces 1922–7; member of Secretary of State's council 1927–9; d. 1945.
[2] B. 1872; a leading exponent of federalism; Fellow of All Souls College, Oxford; one of the most influential 'backroom' figures of his day; d. 1955.
[3] Curtis, *Dyarchy* (1920), p. 41.
[4] Ibid., p. 42. This explanation for the choice of the term 'Commonwealth of Nations' by Curtis may be compared with the one he gave to Professor W. K. Hancock later. See Hancock, *Survey of British Commonwealth Affairs*, vol. i, *Problems of Nationality* (1937), p. 54.

During the early years of its inquiries, however, the Round Table thought of Imperial federation primarily in terms of readjusting the mutual relations of the self-governing parts of the Empire. It envisaged an 'Imperial Parliament', consisting exclusively of representatives from the United Kingdom and the white Dominions, and responsible for defence, foreign affairs and the government of large dependencies like India—responsibility for the last being considered inseparable from that for the first two. But in the summer of 1912 three prominent members of the Round Table—Philip Kerr, William Marris and James Meston—urged that India should be allowed a few seats in the projected 'Imperial Parliament'.[1] The arguments which they advanced in support of their proposal were as follows:

The problem of India is unique and demands special treatment. India cannot be dismissed under the label 'dependency', for she is the Empire. She is Britain's greatest economic and military asset. Her vast population of 300 millions—three-fourths of the total population of the British Empire—contains a fair number of men who are as educated, cultured and loyal as any in other parts of the Empire. India cannot be transferred like an inert mass into the new Imperial organization. She has a vocal public opinion which will have to be taken into account. Indians will demand—have in fact already demanded—representation at the 'Imperial Parliament' and it will be impossible to say 'no' to them. They will plead their military contribution to the Empire and the need for being placed in a position to be able to counteract what they consider to be the evil influence of ignorant and hostile colonials; they will invoke the solemn pledges of equal rights and privileges repeatedly given to them in the past. Their demand will be supported by liberal opinion at home. Indians will strenuously resist their subordination to a legislature containing colonials. On whatever ground it is done, Indians will interpret their exclusion from the 'Imperial Parliament' as being motivated by racial prejudice. It will cause extreme bitterness which will not only add to the difficulties of Indian administration, but also prompt Indians to seek their destiny outside the British Empire. The declared policy of the British Government is to associate more and more Indians with the administration and to increase their representation on the local legislative councils; the admission of two or three Indians to the 'Imperial Parliament' will be merely an extension of this wise and liberal policy.

[1] See Kerr, 'Memorandum on the Representation of India', no date, but probably written in June 1912; Marris, 'Memo. on India and the Empire', June 1912; and Meston, 'Memo. on India and the Empire', June 1912, Curtis Papers.

Kerr, Marris and Meston did not restrict themselves to pleading for India's representation at the 'Imperial Parliament'. They went on to argue that self-government was the only intelligible goal of British policy in India and to demand that Britain should explicitly recognize this goal and try to develop India on the lines of the self-governing Dominions.[1]

This attempt to get the Round Table to revise its original stand on India was resisted by a minority in the group, chief amongst whom were George Lillie Craik[2] and Dougal Orme Malcolm.[3] They argued that as India was not self-governing—and would not be so for generations to come—she could not be represented at the 'Imperial Parliament'. They even doubted whether it would be wise to have India in the *British* Empire when—if ever—she became self-governing. Their main objection, however, to the admission of Indians to the 'Imperial Parliament' was that it would make the federal scheme totally unacceptable to the Dominions.[4]

There were others, like Chirol, who supported India's representation at the 'Imperial Parliament', in view of her great importance to the Empire, but were frankly sceptical about her ever becoming self-governing like the Dominions.[5]

Curtis, 'the Prophet' of the group, favoured the presence of a few Indians in the 'Imperial Parliament' as assessors, in order to acquaint the real rulers of India with the Indian point of view. But he maintained that as long as India was not self-governing she could not be really 'represented' at the 'Imperial Parliament'. To invite Indians to share in the government of the Empire while they were not yet responsible for their own internal government would, he argued, be a violation of the fundamental principle of the federation; it would also be impolitic, for it would create a wrong impression in the minds of Indians that their country was ripe for self-government when in fact it was not—there being no genuine electorates even for a province or district.[6]

---

[1] Kerr, 'Memorandum on the Representation of India'; Marris, 'Memo. on India and the Empire'; and Meston, 'Memo. on India and the Empire', Curtis Papers.   [2] B. 1878; barrister; Managing Director of the Commonwealth Trust Ltd.; d. 1929.

[3] B. 1877; private secretary to Lord Selborne in South Africa 1905–10; President of the British South Africa Company 1937–55; d. 1955.

[4] See Craik, 'Note on the Principle of Indian Representation', July 1912; and Malcolm, 'Memorandum', July 1912, Curtis Papers.

[5] Chirol, 'Memo. on India', July 1912, ibid.

[6] Curtis, 'Note on Philip Kerr's Memorandum', no date, but probably written in June 1912, ibid.

But, while Curtis opposed the proposal of Kerr, Marris and Meston for India's immediate and special representation at the 'Imperial Parliament', he had already been converted to their view that self-government for India should be the goal of British policy. He had incorporated this new outlook in the doctrine of the 'commonwealth' which he formulated early in 1912. 'For a commonwealth', wrote Curtis, 'to govern communities not deemed as [sic] included in its citizenship is to violate its own essential principles.'[1] He argued that a 'commonwealth' governing a dependency without having as its main object the training of the inhabitants of that dependency up to the status of citizens in order to enable them to assume the full rights and duties of citizenship, was acting like a despot and proving itself false to the law of its being. He pleaded that 'Indians should be regarded as fellow-citizens of one super-commonwealth with ourselves, and that to prepare them first for the control of their sub-commonwealth and finally for an equal share in the control of the super-commonwealth should be our guiding principle'.[2]

Curtis's doctrine of the 'commonwealth' in itself—leaving aside its federalist overtones—represented almost a revolution in imperialist thinking. It rejected the current imperialist dogma that non-white communities were incapable of self-government and that they should remain satisfied with good British government. It affirmed that to prepare the subject communities of the Empire for self-government was the supreme duty of the Empire, the spiritual end for which it existed.

The discussions in 1912 did not apparently enable the Round Table to reach any definite conclusion as regards India's place in a possible federation of the Empire. Most members of the group, including Curtis, were still inclined to think that the mutual relations of Great Britain and the Dominions—the self-governing parts of the Empire—should be adjusted first, and that the problem of India, being less urgent and more difficult, could wait.

The war encouraged the Round Table to intensify its campaign for closer Imperial union. It also served to underline the immense economic military and political value of India to the Empire and convinced the group that India could not be left out of any scheme of Imperial reorganization. Almost all prominent British statesmen pointed out—in reply to Curtis's query—that an Imperial cabinet without a representative of India was inconceivable.[3]

[1] Curtis: cited in Craik, 'Note on the Principle of Indian Representation', p. 4, Curtis Papers.   [2] Curtis, 'Note on Philip Kerr's Memorandum', p. 1, ibid.
[3] Curtis, *Dyarchy*, p. 77.

When in 1915 a section of the Round Table, specially interested in India, was engaged in writing the chapters relating to India, intended to form part of the proposed second volume of *The Commonwealth of Nations*, it sought the co-operation of some members of the India Office. A study group was organized, which met regularly once a fortnight in London during the autumn of 1915. Those who attended the meetings of this study group included Curtis, Kerr, Reginald Coupland,[1] Sir William Duke, Sir Lionel Abrahams,[2] M. C. Seton,[3] C. H. Kisch[4] and J. E. Shuckburgh.[5] The group began by agreeing that the attitude taken by Indians in the war had proved that the country was riper than had been supposed for further constitutional reforms. Curtis, however, insisted that it was imperative to decide what was the goal of British policy in India before discussing any further steps in constitutional advance. The only conceivable goal, it was recognized, was self-government. A closer examination of the term 'self-government' revealed that it was ambiguous. 'The only meaning of self-government as a goal which bore the test of examination was responsible government for India within the Commonwealth on lines which could not stop short of those by which the Dominions had reached their present position.'[6] It was obvious that India could not advance by one step to full responsible government and that her progress towards it must be by stages. It was also realized that any further progress on the lines of the Morley-Minto reforms would lead to disaster, for a further increase of the non-official element in the legislative councils would give the latter the power of paralysing government at every turn, but not the power and responsibility of conducting government for themselves.

[1] B. 1884; Beit Lecturer in Colonial History, Oxford 1913-18; editor of the *Round Table* 1917-19 and 1939-41; Beit Professor of History of British Empire, Oxford 1920-48; d. 1952.

[2] B. 1869; entered India Office 1898; Assistant Under-Secretary 1911-17; d. 1918.

[3] B. 1872; entered India Office 1898; Secretary, Judicial and Public Department 1911-19; Assistant Under-Secretary 1919; Deputy Under-Secretary 1924-33; d. 1940.

[4] B. 1884; entered India Office 1908; Private Secretary to Permanent Under-Secretary 1911 and to Parliamentary Under-Secretary in addition 1915; Private Secretary to Secretary of State for India 1917-21; Secretary, Financial Department 1921-33; Assistant Under-Secretary 1933-43; Deputy Under-Secretary 1943-6; d. 1961.

[5] B. 1877; entered India Office 1900; Assistant Secretary, Political Department, 1912-17; Secretary 1917-21; transferred to Colonial Office 1921; Assistant Under-Secretary 1921-31; Deputy Under-Secretary 1931-42; d. 1953.

[6] Curtis, *Dyarchy*, p. xxii.

The essence of the problem was, therefore, to find a method of introducing true responsible government in a limited and manageable field of administration, which could be contracted or extended in accordance with the practical results attained, without imperilling the structure of government itself. The method by which this gradual and safe advance to responsible government could be made in India was suggested in a memorandum prepared for the group by Sir William Duke.[1] It was later nicknamed 'dyarchy' and became the basis of the Montagu-Chelmsford reforms. Chelmsford had shown interest in the inquiries of the group and at his request the final draft of the Duke memorandum was sent to him in May 1916.

In October 1916 Curtis reached India to study the situation on the spot and stayed there for about a year and a half. He discussed the problem of Indian reforms with Chelmsford, Willingdon, Meston, Marris, Chirol,[2] Malcolm Hailey[3] and others. As luck would have it, one of the very first letters which Curtis wrote to Kerr in November 1916, giving his impressions of the Indian situation, endorsed by Chirol, Marris and Meston, leaked out. It was given wide publicity in the Indian press and created quite a furore in the country. His association with high officials, and especially with Chirol who was disliked by Indian nationalists for his writings in *The Times*, made him look a highly sinister figure to the childishly suspicious imagination of political India. It was feared that he and his friends were busy hatching a plan of Imperial federation which would condemn India to be subordinated to the Dominions as well as to Britain. The Indian press heaped abuse upon him, the Congress session of 1916 was full of references to him, and in the Imperial Legislative Council members asked questions about his alleged designs. Curtis then came into the open and started his campaign of educating Indian public opinion regarding the future constitutional reforms, the meaning of responsible government and the plan of dyarchy, through his famous *Letters to the People of India*. Though Curtis contributed much towards the political training of India and exercised considerable influence over a certain section of moderate Indian opinion, he introduced a rather upsetting element into the already tense atmosphere of the country. It is also possible that the

[1] Originally issued under the title *Suggestions for Constitutional Progress in Indian Polity* (1916), it later became famous as the 'Duke Memorandum'.

[2] Chirol was on one of his frequent visits to India at the time.

[3] B. 1872; entered Indian Civil Service 1895; Chief Commissioner of Delhi 1912–18; member of Viceroy's council 1919–24; Governor of the Punjab 1924–8; Governor of the United Provinces 1928–30 and 1931–4; director of the African Research Survey 1935–8; created Baron 1936.

chances of acceptance of the Montagu-Chelmsford Report in India were prejudiced because many Indian politicians traced the shadow of Curtis across it.

As private secretary to the Prime Minister, Lloyd George, Philip Kerr exerted his influence in favour of India's representation at the Imperial War Conference, the announcement of August 1917, and the Montagu-Chelmsford reforms.[1] Curtis provided many of the arguments of the Montagu-Chelmsford Report. It was actually written by Marris. The *Round Table* lent the weight of its authority and support to the policy of the reforms. Curtis's great influence with men like Milner and Selborne[2] and his tireless campaign in favour of the speedy enactment of the reform proposals were no mean assets to Montagu in his battle to launch India on the path to responsible self-government within the Empire.

While Curtis was carrying on his political campaign in India and the question of a declaration of British policy was still hanging in the balance, a step was taken which was fraught with momentous consequences for the future of the British Empire. In April 1917 India was admitted to the membership of the Imperial Conference. But, though an event of far-reaching significance, it was not, as is commonly believed, an entirely novel or sudden development, for India had, in a way, been represented at the 'Imperial' Conference ever since 1902.

The first Colonial Conference held in 1887 was a motley gathering of 121 delegates, representing the United Kingdom, the self-governing Colonies, the Crown Colonies, and the Protectorates. India was not represented at this Conference, though the Secretary of State for India, Lord Cross, attended its formal opening session.[3] Apparently because the Conference did not include any representative of the Empire of India, it was officially designated 'Colonial' and not 'Imperial'.[4] The second Colonial Conference in 1897 was restricted to the representatives of the mother country and the self-governing Colonies. Before the meeting of the third Colonial Conference in 1902, which was to be like the second a 'Conference between the Secretary of State for the Colonies and the Premiers of Self-Governing Colonies', it was known

[1] See Butler, op. cit., pp. 82, 175–6.
[2] William Waldegrave Palmer, second Earl of Selborne (1859–1942). Under-Secretary of State for the Colonies 1895–1900; First Lord of the Admiralty 1900–5; High Commissioner for South Africa 1905–10; Chairman of the Joint Select Committee on the Government of India Bill 1919.
[3] *Proceedings of the Colonial Conference*, 1887, vol. i, C. 5091 (1887), p. 1.
[4] Ibid., p. 371.

that one of the principal items on its agenda was the question of a preferential tariff within the Empire. The Bengal Chamber of Commerce—an organization of British commercial interests in India—urged that, in view of the importance of the subject to be discussed, India should be represented at the forthcoming Conference.[1] The Government of India and the Secretary of State backed their demand.[2] The Colonial Secretary, Joseph Chamberlain,[3] agreed, for his ultimate aim was free trade within the Empire and he desired that any preliminary arrangement made at the next Conference should be as comprehensive as possible.[4] 'A representative of the India Office', T. W. Holderness,[5] accordingly, attended meetings of the Colonial Conference in 1902.[6] Thus began, like so many things British, in a rather casual and unobstrusive manner, the representation of India at the 'Imperial' Conference. Holderness was present at the Conference of 1902 not merely as an observer from a sister department of the state, but also as a watchdog of 'Indian interests'. Far more significant, however, was the mere fact of his presence. It created a precedent for India's representation at the 'Imperial' Conference whenever matters interesting and affecting her were under discussion.

[1] See copy letter from the Secretary, Bengal Chamber of Commerce to the Secretary, Government of India, Finance and Commerce Department, June 20, 1902: encl. Arthur Godley (Under-Secretary of State, India Office) to the Under-Secretary of State, Colonial Office, July 16, 1902, Colonial Office Records at the Public Record Office, London, (hereafter referred to as C.O.) 323/475, f. 403.

[2] See Arthur Godley to the Under-Secretary of State, Colonial Office, July 16, 1902, and encl. copy letter from the Under-Secretary, Government of India, Finance and Commerce Department, June 26, 1902, C.O. 323/475, ff. 401, 402.

[3] B. 1836; President of the Board of Trade 1880–5; President of the Local Government Board in the third Gladstone Cabinet 1886; resigned on the introduction of the Home Rule for Ireland Bill; Colonial Secretary 1895–1903; d. 1914.

[4] See Colonial Office minutes and copy letter from C. P. Lucas (Assistant Under-Secretary of State, Colonial Office) to the Under-Secretary of State for India, July 21, 1902, C.O. 323/475, ff. 400, 404.

[5] B. 1849; entered Indian Civil Service 1872; Secretary in the Revenue and Agricultural Department, Government of India 1898–1901; Secretary in the Revenue, Statistics, and Commerce Department, India Office 1901–12; Permanent Under-Secretary of State, India Office 1912–19; created Baron 1920; d. 1929.

[6] Agreement to admit a representative of the India Office was reached after the Conference had begun its sessions, on July 21, 1902. See C.O. 323/475, f. 404. Holderness attended the Conference on July 22, August 1, 5, 8, 11, 1902. See 'Conference between the Secretary of State for the Colonies and the Premiers of Self-Governing Colonies. Minutes of Proceedings and Papers laid before the Conference', Colonial Office, October 1902, Miscellaneous No. 144, Confidential, pp. 62, 126, 145, 167, 182, P.R.O.

The resolutions of the 1902 Conference in regard to preferential tariffs within the Empire were duly communicated to the Government of India, who expressed themselves resolutely opposed to the idea.[1] Their objections—contained in a strongly-worded but reasoned dispatch to the Secretary of State, which was published—provided additional ammunition to Chamberlain's opponents when he launched his tariff reform campaign in late 1903. India figured prominently in the tariff reform controversy. The free-traders accused Chamberlain of having forgotten the largest and most powerful unit of the Empire. They emphasized the value of India and of Indian trade—equal to that of all the self-governing Colonies put together—to Great Britain. They painted in lurid colour the grave economic and political consequences which might follow in India an abandonment of the free trade system by Britain. The demand arose from various quarters that India should be adequately represented at the 'Imperial' Conference.

An informal but influential group in Britain, who were busy examining the problem of Imperial reorganization at the time and for whom Sir Frederick Pollock[2] acted as spokesman, recommended that India should be represented at future Conferences by her Secretary of State.[3] The council of the British Empire League passed a resolution to the same effect in July 1905.[4] The *British Empire Review* went even further. It protested 'emphatically' against the suggestion that India could be 'sufficiently represented' by her Secretary of State alone. 'The day has gone by', it wrote, 'when the right of India to direct representation in an Imperial Council, both in her own interests and in those of the Empire, can be ignored, or the most august of the outlying possessions of the Crown continue to be treated on the level of a Crown Colony.'[5]

Alfred Lyttleton,[6] the successor of Joseph Chamberlain at the Colonial Office, was probably one of the undisclosed members of the Pollock group. At any rate the influence of their proposals is clearly shown in his dispatch of April 20, 1905 to the self-governing Colonies.[7]

[1] *Views of the Government of India on the Question of Preferential Tariffs*, October 22, 1903, Cd. 1931 (1904).

[2] Jurist; b. 1845; Corpus Professor of Jurisprudence, Oxford 1883–1903; d. 1937.

[3] *The Times*, October 17, 1904; also February 9, October 30, 1905 and March 14, 1907; and *Proceedings of the Royal Colonial Institute*, 1904–5, vol. xxxvi, pp. 288–304.   [4] *British Empire Review*, August 1905, pp. 21–2.

[5] Ibid., November 1904, p. 103.

[6] B. 1857; lawyer and statesman; Colonial Secretary 1903–5; d. 1913.

[7] *Correspondence Relating to the Future Organization of Colonial Conferences*, Cd. 2785 (1905).

Regarding the composition of the future Conference, which it proposed should better be called 'the Imperial Council', the Lyttelton dispatch said: 'The Secretary of State for the Colonies would represent His Majesty's Government. India, whenever her interests required it, would also be represented. The other members of the Council would be the Prime Ministers of the Colonies represented at the Conference of 1902.'[1]

The meeting of the fourth Colonial Conference, due in 1906, was delayed. In the mean time the Unionists went out of power and were replaced by the Liberals. The new Parliament contained quite a few members who vigorously championed the cause of India's representation at the forthcoming Conference.[2] One of them, Sir Henry Cotton, even suggested in 1906 that the British Government should not only invite a representative official of the Government of India to attend the Conference, 'but also a representative of the people themselves, chosen, if need be, by the Government from among the non-official members of the Legislative Councils'.[3] The Liberal Government favoured the representation of India at the Conference.[4] On May 29, 1906, the Prime Minister, Sir Henry Campbell-Bannerman,[5] announced in the Commons: 'The practice adopted at the previous Conferences provides for the presence of representatives of different Departments of the Government and under this arrangement the representation of India will be secured.'[6] Asquith reiterated the same assurance in Parliament on February 19, 1907. He also declared: 'The question of the representation of India at future Conferences will no doubt enter into the discussion of the future constitution of the Conference itself.'[7] The character and manner of India's proposed representation at the Colonial Conference of 1907 were explained by Morley, the Secretary of State for India, in a letter to Minto, the Viceroy: 'About the Colonial Conference which is to assemble by and by, we have promised—as you know—that India should be represented, but of course it cannot be represented in the same sense in which Canada or Australia is. The idea

---

[1] Cd. 2785, p. 3.
[2] E.g. Charles Dilke, J. D. Rees and Henry Cotton. See 157 H.C. Deb. 4s., cols. 940–1; 158 H.C. Deb. 4s., cols. 297, 1380; 169 H.C. Deb. 4s., cols. 721, 743.
[3] 158 H.C. Deb. 4s., col. 1380.
[4] 'We are of the opinion that India should be represented.' Campbell-Bannerman, May 21, 1906: 157 H.C. Deb. 4s., col. 941.
[5] B. 1836; M.P. 1868–1908; Chief Secretary for Ireland 1884–5; Secretary for War 1886 and 1892–5; Prime Minister 1905–8; d. 1908.
[6] 158 H.C. Deb. 4s., col. 297.
[7] 169 H.C. Deb. 4s., col. 721. See also C.O. 532/2.

is that the Secretary of State for India should be there, with a sort of assessor, perhaps two: I am thinking of Sir James Mackay and Mr Holderness.'[1]

The Colonial Conference of 1907 was attended by Morley,[2] Mackay[3] and Holderness.[4] The India Office presented a 'memorandum on preferential tariffs in their relation to India' to the Conference.[5] Mackay also put forward ably the Indian point of view on the subject of preferential trade at the meetings of the Conference.[6] The representatives of the Colonies, particularly those of Australia, jealous of their freedom and status, did not take kindly to India's presence at the Conference table.[7] Their objections appear to have been mainly on three grounds: first, that India was not self-governing;[8] secondly, that her representation would only mean an additional vote and influence for Great Britain in the deliberations of the Conference;[9] and thirdly, that the paramount consideration of the British Government for their Indian trade made them averse to the scheme of preferential tariffs on which the Colonies were very keen.[10]

At the 1907 Conference the self-governing Colonies decided to style themselves 'Dominions'. By another resolution it was agreed that future Conferences should be designated 'Imperial' and devoted to the discussion of questions of common interest 'as between His

---

[1] Morley to Minto, February 15, 1907, Minto Papers, M.1007, No. 9.

[2] Present only on the first and tenth days. *Minutes of Proceedings of the Colonial Conference*, 1907, Cd. 5323 (1907), pp. 3, 295.

[3] Mackay was the regular representative of the India Office at the Conference, present on all days, except one. Ibid. See also A. Godley to the Under-Secretary of State, Colonial Office, March 14, 1907, C.O. 532/2.

[4] Present on the ninth, tenth, eleventh and twelfth days. See Cd. 3523, pp. 296, 400; and *Published Proceedings and Précis of the Colonial Conference*, April 30 to May 14, 1907, Cd. 3406 (1907), pp. 6, 9, 15, 18.

[5] *Papers Laid before the Colonial Conference*, 1907, Cd. 3524 (1907), pp. 453–7.

[6] Cd. 3523, pp. 297–304.   [7] Ibid., pp. 294, 325.

[8] 'Mr Deakin [the Australian Premier] ... actually contended that India had no right to a place at the Conference table, because not self-governing. I dealt faithfully with him on the point. I laugh when I think of a man who blows the imperial trumpet louder than other people, and yet would banish India, which is the most stupendous part of the Empire—our best customer, among other trifles—into the imperial back-kitchen.' Morley to Minto, May 2, 1907, Minto Papers, M.1007, No. 26.

[9] When Asquith casually referred to Sir James Mackay as 'representing' India, Deakin interjected, 'He represents the British Government'. Cd. 3523, p. 294.

[10] The Australian Minister for Trade and Customs, Sir William Lyne, complained at the Conference: 'I do not like your absolutely ignoring the whole of the British Colonies excepting India.' Ibid., p. 325.

Majesty's Government and his Governments in the self-governing Dominions beyond the seas'.[1] The peers of the Empire thus separated themselves for its subject communities. The constitution of the Imperial Conference now became fixed. Self-government was the qualification for its membership and it could only be attended by ministers.[2]

The published report of the proceedings of the 1907 Conference does not reveal what was actually the decision of the Conference on the subject of India's representation at its future meetings. Ministerial replies to questions in Parliament, however, indicate that, though the Conference was henceforth to be confined to the autonomous governments of the Empire, the Secretary of State for India could be present when Indian interests required it.[3] 'India will be represented at the Imperial Conference by the Secretary of State in all matters in which her interests are or may be involved,' assured the Prime Minister on March 22, 1911.[4] India, accordingly, made a brief appearance at the Imperial Conference of 1911. The Secretary of State, Lord Crewe, along with Sir Herbert Risley,[5] an official of his department, was present on the eleventh day of its meeting and addressed the Conference on the need for treating sympathetically the question of Indian immigrants to the Dominions.[6]

India's services in the First World War strengthened her claim for full representation at the Imperial Conference. In July 1915 a non-official member of the Indian Legislative Council gave notice of a resolution which demanded that in future the Government of India should, like those of the Dominions, be directly represented at the Imperial Conference. The Viceroy, Lord Hardinge, and his executive council favoured the acceptance of the resolution and wrote to the Secretary of State, Austen Chamberlain, to that effect.[7] After consulting the Cabinet, Austen Chamberlain authorized the Viceroy to accept

---

[1] Cd. 3523, p. v.
[2] See the replies of the Prime Minister and the Colonial Secretary to questions in the Commons on March 27 and April 6, 1911, respectively. 23 H.C. Deb. 5s., cols. 899, 2420.
[3] 23 H.C. Deb. 5s., cols. 198, 397, 899, 2419–20.   [4] Ibid., col. 397.
[5] B. 1851; entered Indian Civil Service 1873; Secretary in the Home Department, Government of India 1902–9; member of Viceroy's council 1909–10; Secretary in the Judicial and Public Department, India Office 1910–11; d. 1911.
[6] *Minutes of Proceedings of the Imperial Conference*, 1911, Cd. 5745 (1911), pp. 394–9.
[7] Hardinge to Austen Chamberlain, July 29, 1915 (telegram), Private Telegrams, Austen Chamberlain Papers, A.C. 45.

the resolution, but asked him to make it clear that, while the British Government would give a sympathetic consideration to the demand, they could not bind themselves to its principles or details, and that the ultimate decision in the matter would rest with the Imperial Conference itself.[1]

On September 22, 1915, the resolution was formally moved in the Indian Legislative Council by Sir Muhammad Shafi,[2] who claimed that not merely on the ground of the magnitude of her interests affected should India in justice have a voice in Imperial deliberations, the part she had played in the war showed that she was actually worthy of exercising the privilege for which she asked.[3] The Viceroy spoke immediately after the mover and announced that his Government gladly accepted the resolution and, if the Council passed it, would readily take action upon it. He told the Council that he had been 'authorized by His Majesty's Government, while preserving their full liberty of judgement, and without committing them either as to principles, or details, to give an undertaking that an expression of opinion from this Imperial Legislative Council, in the sense of the Resolution that is now before us, will receive most careful consideration on their part, as expressing the legitimate interest of the Legislative Council in an Imperial question, although the ultimate decision of His Majesty's Government must necessarily depend largely on the attitude of other members of the Conference'.[4] Hardinge himself answered some of the possible objections that could be raised against India's membership of the Imperial Conference. Much had happened, he said, since the last Conference was held in 1911 which would leave a lasting mark upon the British Empire and to him it was inconceivable that Dominion statesmen would not have realized the great and important position that India occupied within the Empire. 'It is true', Hardinge went on, 'that India is not a self-governing Dominion but that seems hardly a reason why she should not be suitably represented at future Conferences. India's size, population, wealth, military resources, and, lastly, her patriotism demand it.'[5] Hardinge asserted that no Conference could afford to debate great Imperial issues in which India was vitally concerned, and at the same time to disregard her. How could questions of the defence of the Empire be discussed without India which was 'the

[1] Austen Chamberlain to Hardinge, August 11 and 26, 1915 (telegrams), Austen Chamberlain Papers, A.C. 45.
[2] B. 1869; barrister of the Lahore High Court; President of the Muslim League 1913 and 1927; member of Viceroy's council 1919-24; d. 1932.
[3] *Proceedings of the Council of the Governor-General of India*, 1915-16, vol. liv, pp. 37-41.   [4] Ibid., pp. 42-3.   [5] Ibid., p. 43.

greatest military asset of the Empire outside the United Kingdom'; or of commerce without 'England's best customer'? asked Hardinge.[1] He concluded by saying: 'To concede the direct representation of India at future Imperial Conferences does not strike me as a very revolutionary or far-reaching concession to make to Indian public opinion and to India's just claims, and I feel confident that if, and when, this question is placed in its true light before the Governments of the self-governing Dominions, they will regard it from that wider angle of vision from which we hope other Indian questions may be viewed in the near future, so that the people of India may be made to feel what they really are, in the words of Mr Asquith, "conscious members of a living partnership all over the world under the same flag".'[2]

The Council passed the resolution unanimously and the Government's attitude in meeting it more than half-way gladdened the hearts of Indian politicians. The proposal was well received in the United Kingdom and the Dominion press. The *Round Table* pleaded for India's representation at the Imperial Conference. It argued that constitutional niceties need not be pressed too far. The Imperial Conference was not a sovereign body. It had no executive authority or legislative power. It was a purely deliberative and consultative piece of machinery which could easily accommodate a representative of a great dependency like India. What India asked for, said the quarterly, might be an anomaly, but mere logic and pedantry should not decide a question which was essentially one of Imperial statesmanship. If India was disappointed in the matter, her people would feel it acutely, for with them it was far more a gain of status and recognition that was sought than any material advantage. The *Round Table* also suggested that any existing differences between India and the Dominions, such as those concerning Indian immigrants, stood a better chance of being solved by Indian and Dominion representatives talking over the matter face to face at the Imperial Conference, more so now because the trenches and the hospitals had afforded to each a wholly new understanding of the other's character.[3]

In a confidential memorandum submitted to the Secretary of State in October 1915, Hardinge not only reiterated the arguments he had advanced in favour of India's direct representation at the Imperial Conference in his speech to the Indian Legislative Council, but even added a few more. He referred, for instance, to the Conference in 1909

[1] Proceedings of the Council of the Governor-General of India, 1915–16, vol. liv, p. 43.   [2] Ibid.
[3] 'India and the Imperial Conference', *Round Table*, December 1915, pp. 86–119.

on 'the naval and military defence of the Empire' from which India was excluded, 'although it must have been known to all those present that the Empire, as it stands, could not go on without the Indian Army to help it in its defence in many quarters of the globe, and that the annual military expenditure of India was then several times the total military expenditure of all the self-governing Dominions'.[1] 'Although India had no voice in the proceedings of this Conference,' Hardinge added, 'proposals seriously affecting Indian interests, to which public opinion in India would have been strongly opposed, and to which I am convinced, no Government of India could possibly agree, were nevertheless made as a result of the meeting. I refer to the proposal for a larger naval contribution from India.'[2] Hardinge also referred to the statements already made in the press that the Dominions were to have a voice in the future peace negotiations and remarked that if an Imperial Conference was to be held for this purpose, India's direct representation at it would be 'specially desirable', 'in view of the great Indian interests involved in Persia, Arabia and Mesopotamia, and of the part played by India in the war'.[3] Hardinge urged that India was 'the keystone of the structure of the British Empire, and ought to be recognized and reckoned with as such'.[4] It would be no more incongruous, he said, to place India alongside the self-governing Dominions than it was to classify her with the Crown Colonies. He suggested that her position 'as that of a great, but not self-governing, dependency' would be sufficiently defined if she were represented at the next Imperial Conference by her Secretary of State and one or two official representatives from India as colleagues selected in consultation with the Viceroy.[5]

The Government of India under Chelmsford—Hardinge's successor to the viceroyalty—continued pleading earnestly with the Home Government for India's representation at the Imperial Conference. On June 16, 1916, they wrote to the Secretary of State that 'the interests of India in the Empire, no less than the interests of the Empire in India, fully justify her admission in some definite form to the deliberations of an imperial council'.[6] Again on November 24, 1916, the Government of India urged that India's claim for representation should not be prejudiced by the fact that she was not, and could not for a long time become, a fully self-governing nation. 'That very fact', they argued,

[1] 'Memorandum by H.E. the Viceroy upon Questions Likely to Arise in India at the End of the War', p. 25, Austen Chamberlain Papers, A.C. 22/91.
[2] Ibid.   [3] Ibid., p. 26.   [4] Ibid., p. 25.   [5] Ibid., p. 26.
[6] Cited in the Government of India dispatch, Home Department, Political, No. 17, dated November 24, 1916, p. 10, Austen Chamberlain Papers, A.C. 22/91.

'indeed constitutes the strongest possible reason why her interests and claims should receive the most impartial and punctilious attention at the hands of the conference. Her vast territory, her huge population, her undeveloped resources, her great potential wealth when once those resources are prudently developed, and last, but not least, her loyal support to the Empire during the present crisis, plead most eloquently on her behalf. It would ill become a great Empire, as it reckons up the sum total of its own assets, to dwell with pardonable pride on that territory, that population, those resources, and that loyal support of India, and then to turn a cold shoulder to her just petition.'[1]

The Government of India were preaching to the converted. The British Government had already decided in favour of admitting India to the Imperial Conference.[2] It was the self-governing Dominions which had really to be persuaded to accept India at the Conference. Austen Chamberlain had informed Hardinge privately in August 1915: 'I fear we must anticipate great difficulties with [the] self-governing Dominions.'[3] The India Office had to work hard to overcome these difficulties. It seized every available opportunity to plead India's case before the Dominions and to mollify their objections to India's full representation at the Imperial Conference. One such instance of special pleading on behalf of India deserves mention. Speaking before a conference of the Empire Parliamentary Association in London in the summer of 1916, Lord Islington,[4] the Under-Secretary of State for India, strongly urged India's inclusion into the inner circle of the Empire because of 'her size, her geographical position, volume of trade, intellectual and political development, and ... her proved loyalty to the Crown'.[5] He earnestly appealed to the delegates from the various parliaments of the Dominions present on the occasion to 'act as influential missionaries' to their respective parliaments 'to induce them to realize what India is, what its position is, what its value is, within

[1] Government of India dispatch, Home Department, Political, No. 17, dated November 24, 1916, p. 10, Austen Chamberlain Papers, A.C. 22/91.
[2] Sir George Barnes, the Commerce Member of the Viceroy's council, told the Bengal Chamber of Commerce on July 29, 1916, that 'India's participation in the councils of the Empire had been promised definitely [This seems to be an exaggeration.] by the Secretary of State for India and the Prime Minister'. *The Times*, July 31, 1916.
[3] Austen Chamberlain to Hardinge, August 11, 1915 (telegram), Private Telegrams, Austen Chamberlain Papers, A.C. 45.
[4] John Poynder Dickson-Poynder, Baron Islington (1866–1936). Governor of New Zealand 1910–12; Chairman of the Royal Commission on Indian Public Services 1912–14; Under-Secretary of State for the Colonies 1914–15 and for India 1915–18. [5] 'India and the Empire', *Imperial Problems* (1916), p. 21.

the Empire—the part that it is playing and will continue increasingly to play in the future as a component part of the Empire'.[1] 'How inextricably interwoven are her interests with ours; and ours with hers,'[2] remarked Islington. There was not, he said, a single problem of Imperial interest in which India was not directly concerned. And he emphasized repeatedly that no Imperial organization could be lasting or effective, complete or adequate to its purpose, which did not include within it a representative of the Empire of India.

The Dominions were not to be converted so easily. It was not simply a case, as Islington had suggested, of their old ideas about India dying hard. The Dominions were extremely jealous of their self-governing status and could not easily allow it to be obscured or compromised by getting mixed up with the less developed parts of the Empire. They might even have suspected a sinister design on the part of Downing Street to bring them down to the level of India. Moreover, the Dominions were determined to remain white and they feared that India's elevation to the membership of the Imperial Conference would be the thin end of the coloured wedge.

Whatever the reasons—and here we can only guess—the Dominions did not welcome the idea of admitting India to the Imperial Conference when it was first mooted to them officially in (September?) 1916. The Prime Ministers of Australia and Canada—William Hughes and Robert Borden—expressed themselves definitely adverse. Those of New Zealand and South Africa—William Massey and General Botha—remained non-committal.[3] But the Secretary of State for India, Austen Chamberlain, was insistent on India's inclusion and he had behind him the support of the Government and the people of India. He argued that it would be 'little short of an outrage', in view of India's enormous sacrifices in the war and the hopes aroused in that country by the utterances of British statesmen themselves, to deny her a place in the Imperial Conference. The primary concern of the forthcoming Conference, he added, would be to concert measures in the further prosecution of the war and to this end consultation with the Government of India, who had been bearing such a large part of the burden, was absolutely essential.[4] The Prime Minister, Lloyd George,[5] supported Austen Chamberlain and the War Cabinet decided unani-

[1] *Imperial Problems* (1916), p. 27.   [2] Ibid.
[3] Sir Charles Petrie, *The Life and Letters of the Right Hon Sir Austen Chamberlain* (1940), vol. ii, p. 73.   [4] Ibid.
[5] B. 1863; MP 1890–1945; President of the Board of Trade 1905–8; Chancellor of the Exchequer 1908–15; Prime Minister 1916–22; created Earl 1945; d. 1945.

mously in favour of India's inclusion.[1] In order to overcome the difficulty created by the lack of understanding with the Dominions, it was agreed to give the Conference a different designation and summon it 'on a special basis, outside the official constitution'.[2]

On December 25, 1916, when Lloyd George summoned the Imperial War Conference, the Secretary of State for India was invited to represent India. Austen Chamberlain telegraphed to the Viceroy, Chelmsford, to select two gentlemen from India to assist him at the proposed gathering.[3] The Imperial War Conference and the Imperial War Cabinet commenced their sittings in London in March 1917. India was represented on both bodies by her Secretary of State, aided by three delegates from India, Sir James Meston, Sir S. P. Sinha and the Maharaja of Bikaner. The Indian delegates were warmly welcomed and they created a good impression both inside the Conference and outside. Austen Chamberlain immediately took advantage of this fact and with 'the active good will' of the Colonial Secretary, Walter Long,[4] pushed forward the claim of India for full representation at the regular Imperial Conference.[5] On April 4, 1917, the Conference decided to pass a resolution recommending a modification of the constitution of the regular Imperial Conference so as to permit of India's participation at its future meetings.[6] A formal resolution to this effect was duly passed on April 13.[7] On Sinha's suggestion, which was readily accepted, India also found a mention in the famous constitutional resolution moved by Sir Robert Borden on April 16, 1917, which claimed for the Dominions and India a 'right to an adequate voice in foreign policy and in foreign relations'. But while the Dominions were described in this resolution as 'autonomous nations of an Imperial Commonwealth', India could only be called 'an important portion of the same'.[8]

The Indian delegates not only participated in the proceedings of the

[1] Petrie, op. cit., vol. ii, pp. 73–4.

[2] Lloyd George, op. cit., vol. iv, pp. 1737–8. See also Petrie, op. cit., vol. ii, p. 74.

[3] *The Times*, December 27, 1916. It was later decided to invite a representative of the Indian states as well.

[4] Walter Hume, first Viscount Long of Wraxall (1854–1924). President of the Board of Agriculture 1895–1900; President of the Local Government Board 1900–5 and 1915–16; Colonial Secretary 1916–18; First Lord of the Admiralty 1919–21; created Viscount 1921.

[5] See Austen Chamberlain to Walter Long, April 3, 1917, and Walter Long to Austen Chamberlain, April 4, 1917, Austen Chamberlain Papers, A.C. 16/52.

[6] Imperial War Conference, 1917. *Extracts from Minutes of Proceedings and Papers Laid before the Conference*, Cd. 8566 (1917), pp. 15–16.

[7] Ibid., pp. 22–3.   [8] Ibid., pp. 49–50, 61.

Imperial War Conference, they 'attended ... every meeting of the Imperial War Cabinet, sat on its Committees, and saw every confidential paper, and heard every confidential statement that was made in the course of the sittings of that body'.[1] How real and far-reaching was the progress made in 1917 in respect of India's position in the Empire can be gleaned from a letter of the Secretary of State to the Viceroy, dated May 15, 1917, communicating to the latter the decisions of the Imperial War Cabinet as regards its future meetings. 'An Imperial Cabinet', Austen Chamberlain informed Chelmsford, 'is to meet once a year. This Cabinet will comprise those British Ministers specially concerned with Imperial questions, including the Secretaries of State for India and the Colonies. There will also be convoked the Prime Ministers of the self-governing Dominions and a representative of the Government of India who will come on the same footing as they do, and is the nearest approximation which India can produce under present circumstances to a Prime Minister. We have further secured that in all future Imperial Conferences India will be represented on a footing of perfect equality with the self-governing Dominions.'[2]

'The admission of India to the Conference,' says Professor Keith Hancock, 'which should normally have been the sequel to Indian self-government, was a recognition of the fact that self-government was India's destiny. It was, so to speak, a payment in advance which India had earned by her extraordinary services.'[3] The resolution passed by the Imperial War Conference on April 13, 1917, was, wrote Lloyd George later, 'important, not merely because it opened the door for the future appearance of India alongside the Dominions at Imperial Conferences, but because it marked the first Imperial recognition of the altered status of India. It was one of the preliminary stages of the reforms on Indian administration, which started that great country on the pathway towards full self-government within the British Commonwealth.'[4]

[1] See the remark made by Austen Chamberlain at a private meeting of the Empire Parliamentary Association, held in London on July 31, 1918, to which Sir Satyendra Sinha delivered an address on 'Indian Constitutional Reforms'. *Indian Constitutional Reforms* (1918), p. 3, Austen Chamberlain Papers, A.C. 22/91.
[2] Austen Chamberlain to Chelmsford, May 15, 1917, 'Extracts from Mr Chamberlain's Private Letters to the Viceroy', Austen Chamberlain Papers, A.C. 22/91.
[3] Hancock, op. cit., vol, i. p. 169.
[4] Lloyd George, op. cit., vol. iv, pp. 1763-4.

WAR AND A NEW ANGLE OF VISION

The Indian delegates to the Imperial War Conference of 1917—Bikaner, Meston and Sinha—ardently pleaded India's case for ultimate self-government within the Empire from various platforms in England and created a very favourable impression. Commenting on their speeches—particularly those of Bikaner—*The Times* wrote on May 2, 1917: 'The question is whether the time is not now upon us for something more than pious aspirations about the future of India. . . . The broad lines of British policy in India are perfectly clear. It looks steadily forward to a gradual increase of the self-governing function, and is only concerned to regulate that increase as good order within and security against aggression from without require. But this policy is too seldom expressed in terms, and we believe that the moment to declare it with authority is now, while the war is still in progress, and not as a reply to agitation when the war is over.'[1] In private Bikaner, Meston and Sinha pressed the need for an announcement of British policy upon the Secretary of State for India and apparently succeeded in converting him to their point of view.[2]

Willingdon had, as noted above,[3] since long favoured a bold and liberal gesture in India. He was in close touch with the leaders of moderate Indian opinion and sympathetic to their aspirations. Moreover, his province—Bombay—was particularly affected by the 'Home Rule' agitation of Besant and Tilak. In the autumn of 1916 he had strongly advised the Government of India and the Secretary of State to make an early declaration of their policy in order to strengthen the hands of the moderate nationalists, but was told that it would be useless to make a general declaration until the authorities were prepared to state specifically the reforms which they intended to carry out at the earliest.[4] In May 1917 Willingdon renewed his pressure upon the Viceroy and with better effect.[5] On May 18, 1917, the latter telegraphed to the Secretary of State requesting an immediate announcement of British policy in India. The Viceroy pointed out that the political situation in India had materially altered during the past few months as a result of the revolution in Russia, the publication of statements as to the right of the peoples to govern themselves, the reception accorded

[1] *The Times*, May 2, 1917.
[2] See the remark made by Bikaner to this effect on March 7, 1919, reproduced in *Speeches and Writings of Lord Sinha*, Appendix, pp. xix–xx.
[3] See above, p. 70.
[4] See Austen Chamberlain to Chelmsford, November 27, 1916, and Chelmsford to Chamberlain, December 1, 1916 (telegrams), Private Telegrams, Austen Chamberlain Papers, A.C. 45.
[5] See Chelmsford to Austen Chamberlain, May 18, 1917 (telegram), ibid.

to the representatives of India at the War Conference in England, and India's admission to the Imperial Conference. The absence of any definite announcement of policy was, he wrote, causing embarrassment to the local governments, alienating the moderates, and leaving the field free to the extremist propaganda. The Viceroy realized the difficulties of making a declaration of policy while not yet being in a position to state specifically what their proposals for reform were, but he considered the declaration necessary 'in order to arrest the further defection of moderate opinion'.[1]

On May 22, 1917, Austen Chamberlain invited the attention of the Cabinet to the very serious problems with which the Government of India were faced and asked for an early decision on the action to be taken. He circulated to his colleagues the reform proposals submitted by the Government of India in November 1916, along with his comments, and his suggestions for making known the policy of the British Government.[2] Lloyd George's small War Cabinet was, however, overburdened with work and could not find time early to deal with the Indian issue.[3] And when at last it did take up the question on June 29th, and again on July 5th, valuable time was wasted in a fruitless discussion over the meaning of the term 'self-government'. Lord Balfour,[4] in particular, objected to the use of the term 'self-government' in any declaration for the reason that in the mouths of Englishmen it had acquired a definite meaning, namely, a parliamentary form of government, and in his view it was unwise to graft parliamentary democracy on to India.[5] The result was that when Austen Chamberlain suddenly resigned on July 14, 1917, over the Mesopotamian affair,[6] the Cabinet,

[1] Telegram from the Viceroy to the Secretary of State, Home Department, May 18, 1917, 'Indian Political Reforms, Collection of Telegrams (unparaphrased) between Viceroy and Secretary of State', pp. 1–3, Austen Chamberlain Papers, A.C. 22/91.
[2] 'Memorandum by the Secretary of State for India on Indian Reforms', ibid.
[3] Austen Chamberlain, *Down the Years* (1935), p. 132.
[4] Arthur James, first Earl of Balfour (1848–1930). Chief Secretary for Ireland 1887–91; First Lord of the Treasury 1891–2 and 1895–1902; Prime Minister 1902–5; First Lord of the Admiralty 1915–16; Foreign Secretary 1916–19; Lord President of the Council 1919–22 and 1925–9; created Earl 1922.
[5] Lord Ronaldshay, *The Life of Lord Curzon* (1928), vol. iii, p. 164. Ronaldshay did not disclose the name of Balfour, but simply referred to him as 'one prominent member of the Cabinet'. It is significant that Curzon considered Balfour's note to be 'very stubborn and rather reactionary'. See Curzon to Austen Chamberlain, August 25, 1917, Austen Chamberlain Papers, A.C. 14/39.
[6] A Royal Commission which inquired into the mismanagement of the campaign in Mesopotamia accused the Government of India of administrative in-

even after having discussed the question twice, had failed to reach any decision on the form of the announcement or whether it should be made at all.

In India the political situation had meanwhile further deteriorated. The internment of Mrs Besant in June 1917 had led to a country-wide agitation. The publication of the Report of the Mesopotamian Commission at the end of June, containing severe strictures on the Government of India for their lack of judgement and administrative efficiency, had dealt another blow to their prestige. The debate in the Commons on the Report turned out to be a censure motion on the Government of India. Montagu, in a bitter and impassioned speech, described the Government of India as 'too wooden, too iron, too inelastic, too antediluvian'[1] and pleaded for a more responsible and democratic administration. He outlined his vision of future India as 'a series of self-governing Provinces and Principalities, federated by one central Government'[2] and remarked: 'But whatever be the object of your rule in India, the universal demand of those Indians whom I have met and corresponded with is that you should state it. . . . The history of this War shows that you can rely upon the loyalty of the Indian people to the British Empire—if you ever doubted it! If you want to use that loyalty you must take advantage of that love of country which is a religion in India, and you must give them that bigger opportunity of controlling their own destinies, not merely by councils which cannot act, but by control, by growing control, of the Executive itself.'[3]

Montagu's speech gladdened the hearts of Indian nationalists. He had ever since his days as the Under-Secretary of State for India (1910–14) been known for his deep sympathy with Indian national aspirations. And when on July 18, 1917—within a week of his performance in the Mesopotamian debate—Montagu was appointed as Chamberlain's successor at the India Office, the event was widely acclaimed in India and gave rise to excessive expectations. It horrified certain Conservative circles in England. Even the sober *Times* called it 'a blunder' and 'an unfortunate selection'.[4] Both this over-optimism and this dislike were to be unfortunate elements in the Indian situation in the years to come. Indian politicians now became more active than ever before. The Committee of the Indian National Congress and the

---

efficiency. There was no suggestion that blame attached to Austen Chamberlain, but as it was his department which was involved he felt it to be his duty to resign.

[1] 195 H.C. Deb. 5s., col. 2205.   [2] Ibid., col. 2209.
[3] Ibid, cols. 2209–10.   [4] *The Times*, July 18, 1917.

Council of the Muslim League met together at Bombay in the last week of July and reiterated their demand that the Imperial Government be pledged to the policy of making India a self-governing member of the Empire. They also urged the authorities to adopt the Congress-League scheme of post-war reforms, to publish the official proposals for discussion, and to reverse 'the policy of repression'. In order to secure these objectives they decided to send a deputation to England and even threatened to launch a campaign of passive resistance in India.[1]

Recognizing 'the gravity and urgency of the situation' in India, the Viceroy repeatedly impressed upon the Secretary of State the view that, whatever be the decision regarding the nature and extent of future reforms, 'it would be fatal to put off any longer an unmistakable declaration in India of our future policy'.[2] Montagu energetically took up the threads where Chamberlain had left them. On July 30, 1917, he circulated a memorandum to the Cabinet, drawing their attention to the rapidly deteriorating situation in India and to the increasing insistence of the Viceroy and the heads of provincial governments for an immediate announcement of policy.[3] But he could not get the Cabinet to find the time to discuss the question soon.[4] On August 7th he was still pleading with the Prime Minister: 'You can save India. You can set your foot, and force England to set its foot, firmly on a path of progress on democratic lines. . . .'[5]

Montagu was anxious that any declaration of British policy must include the word 'self-government', not only because it was so current in India discussion, but also because he feared that its avoidance might cause dissatisfaction in India and thus defeat the very purpose of making the declaration.[6] The formula which he had suggested to the Cabinet in his memorandum of July 30th was substantially the same as that

[1] *Times of India*, July 30, 1917.
[2] See 26 H.L. Deb. 5s., col. 768, and 31 H.L. Deb. 5s., col. 597.
[3] 'Indian Reforms', Memorandum, dated July 30, 1917, copy enclosed with Montagu's letter to Austen Chamberlain, August 7, 1917, Austen Chamberlain Papers, A.C. 15/48.
[4] See Montagu to Austen Chamberlain, August 7, 1817, ibid. On August 15th Montagu wrote to Austen Chamberlain: 'The number of times that I have sat trembling for a Cabinet summons, the number of times that I have hoped to see the Prime Minister, the number of messages that I have got from the Viceroy—all this would make a story which would bring tears to your eyes. . . .' Ibid.
[5] F. Owen, *Tempestuous Journey: Lloyd George, His Life and Times* (1955), p. 416.
[6] See Montagu to Austen Chamberlain, August 7, 1917, and encl. op. cit., p. 2, Austen Chamberlain Papers, A.C. 15/48.

WAR AND A NEW ANGLE OF VISION

proposed earlier by Austen Chamberlain. It read: 'His Majesty's Government and the Government of India have in view the gradual development of free institutions in India with a view to ultimate self-government within the Empire.'[1]

This, however, did not satisfy Lord Curzon, who like most members of the Cabinet disliked the phrase 'self-government'.[2] He devoted a good deal of time and thought to the phraseology of the proposed declaration. In order to make it 'rather safer and certainly nearer to my own point of view',[3] he redrafted it as follows on the eve of its publication: 'The policy of His Majesty's Government, with which the Government of India are in complete accord, is that of the increasing association of Indians in every branch of the administration, and the gradual development of self-governing institutions, with a view to the progressive realization of responsible government in India as an integral part of the British Empire.'[4]

It was this formula which the Cabinet sanctioned on August 14th and Montagu repeated in the Commons six days later—on August 20th—in reply to a question from Charles Roberts. Montagu also

---

[1] 'Indian Reforms', op. cit., p. 3, ibid.; and Ronaldshay, op. cit., vol. iii. p. 167.
[2] Montagu to Austen Chamberlain, August 7, 1917, Austen Chamberlain Papers, A.C. 15/48.
[3] Ronaldshay, op. cit., vol. iii, p. 168.
[4] Ibid., p. 167. It is not possible, in the present stage of our knowledge, to account for the choice of the phrase 'responsible government' in preference to 'self-government' by Curzon and the Cabinet. The following comments by Montagu on the point are interesting, but not very enlightening: 'For some reason which I am absolutely unable to understand, people prefer "responsible Government" to "Self-government". I do not know the difference. If there is a difference, "Self-government" might mean that India was to be placed under a Hindu or Parsee dictator, but "responsible Government", I should have thought, meant that that Hindu or Parsee dictator would be responsible to some form of Parliamentary institutions. So I think they [the Cabinet] have given more than your formula would have necessitated.' Montagu to Austen Chamberlain, August 15, 1917, Austen Chamberlain Papers, A.C. 15/48. On August 21, 1917 Montagu wrote to Chelmsford: 'It was a strange discussion. I had hoped that the word "self-government" would be used, because it appeared in every one of your communications and because I thought it was a pity to boggle at a word so current in Indian discussion. The Cabinet in its wisdom preferred "responsible Government" to "Self-Government". It requires a better educated man than myself to know the difference, but if it lies anywhere, "responsible Government", I should have thought, pledges one to more than "self-government".' Cited in Sir David Waley, 'Life of the Hon. Edwin Samuel Montagu' (Unpublished), p. 174. I am indebted to Lady Waley for her kind permission to make use of this quotation here.

declared that substantial steps in pursuance of this policy would be taken as soon as possible and that he would be proceeding to India shortly to discuss matters with the Government of India and receive representations from Indians. 'I would add', he went on, 'that progress in this policy can only be achieved by successive stages. The British Government and the Government of India on whom the responsibility lies for the welfare and advancement of the Indian peoples, must be the judges of the time and measure of each advance, and they must be guided by the co-operation received from those upon whom new opportunities of service will thus be conferred, and by the extent to which it is found that confidence can be reposed in their sense of responsibility.'[1]

Speaking in the House of Lords two months later, Curzon remarked that the announcement of August 20, 1917, did not contain 'any definite drawing up of a programme, any sketch of what exactly was to be done. It was nothing of that sort. It was a broad general declaration of principle, and the lines upon which . . . our administration of that country ought to proceed in the future.'[2] But what was the 'principle' and what were 'the lines' of advance which Curzon had in mind? What was really his intention in substituting the phrase 'responsible government' for 'self-government' in the proposed declaration? Was he thinking of 'responsibility' only in a moral and not in a constitutional sense? We can do no more than guess, for Curzon never opened his mind to the public on these points and his official biographer finds it 'tossing painfully in a sea of indecision' and 'extremely difficult to understand'.[3] Curzon was anxious to make the announcement as safe, indefinite and non-committal as possible. But by the introduction of that phrase 'responsible government' he definitely and irrevocably committed Great Britain at least on one point—the policy of introducing parliamentary self-government in India on the English model. No sooner was the announcement made than public opinion, both in India and England, tended to fasten on that well-known term and it was recognized on all hands that technically and historically it meant a government responsible to the elected representatives of the people. When, therefore, Curzon later took fright at the proposals of the Montagu-Chelmsford Report and denounced them as being designed 'to lay the foundations of a Parliamentary system in India' which would 'lead by stages of increasing speed to the ultimate disruption of the Empire', Montagu was justified in pointing out that the charge should more

[1] 97 H.C. Deb. 5s., cols. 1695–6. [2] 26 H.L. Deb. 5s., col. 787.
[3] Ronaldshay, op. cit., vol. iii, p. 166.

properly be laid at the door of the announcement itself.[1] Lord Selborne considered the announcement of August 20th to be 'unfortunately worded' for it bound the British Government to the establishment of parliamentary government in India on the English or the Dominion model.[2]

The announcement laid down clearly and definitely the ultimate aim of British rule in India. It recognized India to be potentially a Dominion. 'In this pronouncement', wrote Curtis, 'the goal prescribed for India is identified with that already attained by the self-governing Dominions.'[3] The long phrase 'the progressive realization of responsible government in India as an integral part of the British Empire' was, as Professor Coupland remarked, 'a terse and accurate description of the rise of the self-governing Colonies to Dominion Status'.[4] Lloyd George's testimony should be conclusive on this point, for he presided over the Government which sanctioned the terms of the declaration of 1917. He admitted in 1929 that it was decided in 1917 that 'there should be accorded to the people of India a considerable measure of self-government' and 'that gradually, if the experiment were successful . . . we would extend it until India ultimately enjoyed full partnership in the Empire on equal terms with our great Dominions'.[5]

Progress towards the goal was, however, to be gradual, by successive stages. The British Government and the Government of India were to be the judges of the time and measure of each advance, and they were to be guided by the co-operation received from Indians and the extent to which confidence could be reposed in their sense of responsibility. In this respect, the declaration was a conditional pledge, but a pledge none the less, binding, as Curzon put it, 'not only upon Government but upon Parliament and upon the country'.[6]

In spite of all the great care and caution bestowed upon the drafting of the declaration, it was inaccurate on two points. It spoke of 'India' while its policy was meant to apply only to 'British India'. It spoke of 'the British Government and the Government of India, on whom the responsibility lies for the welfare and advancement of the Indian peoples' and who 'must be the judges of the time and measure of each advance', while constitutionally speaking this responsibility and authority belonged only to Parliament. Both these inaccuracies were rectified when the Act was passed in 1919.

[1] Ronaldshay, op. cit., vol. iii, pp. 169–74. [2] 37 H.L. Deb. 5s., col. 1005.
[3] Curtis, *Dyarchy*, p. 362.
[4] R. Coupland, *The Indian Problem, 1833–1935* (1942), p. 54.
[5] 231 H.C. Deb. 5s., col. 1316. [6] 37 H.L. Deb. 5s., col. 1039.

The declaration of 1917 was not only 'the most momentous utterance ever made in India's chequered history',[1] it was also a landmark in British Imperial history, for it marked a definite repudiation of the concept of 'the two Empires'[2]—the concept that there could be, under the British flag, one form of constitutional evolution for the West and another for the East, or one for the white races and another for the non-white. On February 16, 1788, Burke had protested against what he called 'a plan of *geographical morality*, by which the duties of men in publick and private situations, are not to be governed by the relation to the great Governour of the Universe, or by their relation to mankind, but by climates, degrees of longitude, parallels not of life but of latitudes'.[3] The announcement of August 20, 1917, did away with the 'geographical morality' of British Imperial policy. Taken together with the admission of India to the Imperial Conference four months earlier, it signified the passing away of the Second British Empire and the beginning of what Zimmern called 'the Third British Empire',[4] the transformation, in principle, of the Empire into a Commonwealth of Nations.

[1] *Report on Indian Constitutional Reforms*, Cd. 9109 (1918), p. 5.
[2] The phrase is Lord Milner's. See *Proceedings of the Royal Colonial Institute*, 1907–8, vol. xxxix, pp. 329–37.
[3] *The Works of the Right Honourable Edmund Burke* (1826 ed.), vol. xiii, p. 154. Opening speech in the impeachment of Warren Hastings.
[4] A. E. Zimmern, *The Third British Empire* (1926).

III

THE INDIAN NATIONAL CONGRESS AND THE COMMONWEALTH

The announcement of August 20, 1917, was universally welcomed in India not merely because it contained an authoritative declaration of British policy which Indian nationalists had demanded, but more so because the man who made it was considered to be a champion of India's demand for self-government. 'We recognize in him [Montagu]', wrote the *Bengalee*, commenting on the announcement, 'the friend of India and of the aspirations for liberty and constitutional freedom, as equal subjects of the Crown, which are now throbbing in our hearts.'[1] The cold and cautious phraseology of the announcement, however, aroused some apprehension and was attributed to the influence of Tories like Curzon and Milner in the Cabinet. The claim that the British Government and the Government of India were to be the sole judges of the time and measure of each advance was resented. It was hoped and asserted, on the contrary, that the people of India should have an effective voice in the matter. The *Amrita Bazar Patrika* also demanded that 'a definite declaration of the nature of responsible government proposed to be granted and the time when it may be conferred should . . . be made without delay'.[2]

When Montagu reached India in November 1917 the Congress submitted to him and the Viceroy a memorandum containing its demands. The memorandum provides the best clue to an understanding of the mind of contemporary nationalist India. It expressed satisfaction and gratitude for the declaration of British policy in India, but hinted at the element of uncertainty as to the future steps and objected to the decision with regard to them being left exclusively to the Governments of Great Britain and India. It demanded an assurance that successive steps in the direction of self-government would be taken 'at regular intervals not far removed from one another' and that each instalment of reform would be a 'substantial one'.[3] 'Where is the guarantee, it is asked by Indians who have a painful experience of imperfectly redeemed pledges and half-fulfilled promises, that a great effort may

[1] *Bengalee*, August 22, 1917.   [2] *Amrita Bazar Patrika*, August 22, 1917.
[3] *Congress Memorandum* (1918), p. 14.

107

not again be necessary for them to induce a future Government to make the next forward move?'[1] The memorandum suggested that either a section should be inserted in the Government of India Act or a Royal proclamation issued making it definite and certain that a steadfast endeavour would be made to reach the appointed goal 'within a reasonable space of time' and that at stated intervals the progress made would be reviewed 'by a competent and impartial authority—say a joint committee of the two Houses of the British Parliament—and the next step taken, the whole journey being completed in about twenty-five years'.[2]

The memorandum demanded for India a position of equality with the Dominions. The position of a mere dependency, it said, was wounding to the self-respect of a proud and ancient people who were heirs to a great civilization. It pointed out that the events of the last two years had added an element of urgency which necessitated 'their insistence upon the elevation of their country to a status of equality with the Dominions in all inter-Imperial matters. It has become clear that the latter will in future have a potent voice in the settlement of Imperial problems. They are no longer to be in the position of daughter-States; they are referred to as sister-States; forming with Britain the five free nations of the Commonwealth. If, as some writers suggest, a Parliament and (or) a Council of the Empire should be established with representation therein of the United Kingdom and the Dominions, and if all affairs of the Empire are to be disposed of by them (it), the present House of Commons and the House of Lords concerning themselves exclusively with the affairs of Britain, it is obvious that there will result the governance of India by the Dominions in conjunction with Britain.'[3] The memorandum warned that Indians would offer a most resolute resistance to any such development, for, even if the attitude of the Dominions towards India were unexceptionable, Indians could never agree to the widening of the area of subjection. It asserted that if the fabric of the Empire was to be refashioned on some such lines, the indispensable condition from the Indian standpoint was that India should be represented at any projected Imperial Council or Parliament by elected members, the extent of India's representation being determined by the same criteria as might be applied to the Dominions. The memorandum demanded that even if no such far-reaching changes were to take place, India's representatives at the Imperial Conference should be chosen by the elected members of the central and provincial legislatures.[4]

[1] *Congress Memorandum* (1918), p. 14.
[2] Ibid., pp. 14–15.   [3] Ibid., p. 15.   [4] Ibid., pp. 15–16.

The memorandum affirmed that the claim of Indians for eventual self-government rested 'on more grounds than one. Above and beyond everything is the natural right of every people, inherent and inalienable, to be in their own country what other peoples are in their native lands. It is their birthright, and their very self-respect and the honour of their nation demand its unflinching assertion.'[1] This by itself, the memorandum added, should be an all-sufficient reason with the British people, whose whole history was an inspiration to others aspiring to be free, who had a passionate love for liberty and who were making such sacrifices in the cause of freedom and justice in the present war.

The memorandum avowed 'India's fidelity to England', but pointed out that, more than the gratitude for past and present benefits, it was the hope of achieving self-government with her help which was the secret of that attachment.[2]

Similar sentiments were voiced at the annual session of the Congress held at Calcutta towards the end of December 1917. The main demands made at this session were: a definition of the term 'responsible government'; the fixation of a time limit for the achievement of complete self-government; the enactment of the Congress-League scheme as the first step; an effective voice for the people of India in the determination of the future steps; and a status of equality for India with the Dominions.[3]

The Congress met in a special session at Bombay towards the end of August 1918 to consider the reform proposals contained in the Montagu-Chelmsford Report and pronounced them 'disappointing and unsatisfactory'.[4] It demanded the introduction of dyarchy in the central government; the transfer of all subjects, except law, police and justice, to the responsible government in the provinces; 'the declaration of the rights of the people of India as British citizens'; 'the same measure of fiscal autonomy [for India] which the self-governing Dominions of the Empire possess'; and a statutory guarantee that 'full responsible government should be established in the whole of British India within a period not exceeding fifteen years'.[5]

When the Congress met for its annual session in December 1918 at Delhi, the war had ended. It reiterated the demands made at the special session at Bombay and in one respect went even further. Yielding to the pressure of public opinion, the Congress urged that full responsible

---

[1] *Congress Memorandum* (1918), p. 17.   [2] Ibid.
[3] *Report of the Thirty-Second Indian National Congress*, 1917, *passim*.
[4] *Report of the Special Session of the Indian National Congress held at Bombay*, August 29–September 1, 1918, Appendix, p. ii.   [5] Ibid., pp. i–vi.

government be granted to the provinces at the very outset. The pronouncements of President Wilson and Lloyd George about self-determination had added another weapon to the armoury of Indian nationalists. The Congress demanded that the principle of self-determination should be applied to India also, and that, as the first step towards the practical application of that principle, Parliament should pass an Act 'which will establish at an early date complete Responsible Government in India' and 'when complete Responsible Government shall be thus established, the final authority in all internal affairs shall be the Supreme Legislative Assembly as voicing the will of the Indian Nation'.[1] The Congress further resolved 'that in the reconstruction of Imperial polity, whether in matters affecting the inner relations of the nations constituting it, in questions of foreign policy or in the League of Nations, India shall be accorded the same position as the self-governing Dominions'. The Congress also urged that 'in justice to India, it should be represented . . . to the same extent as the self-governing Dominions' by elected representatives at the Peace Conference.[2]

'The shadow of Amritsar . . . [had] lengthened over the fair face of India'[3] in 1919; the Muslims were uneasy about the probable fate of Turkey; but the Congress responded loyally and gallantly to the spirit of the Royal proclamation of December 23, 1919. Though it judged the Act of 1919 to be 'inadequate, unsatisfactory and disappointing', the Congress decided to work it 'so as to secure an early establishment of full Responsible Government'.[4]

Going through the proceedings of the Congress during the years 1917–19 today, one doubts whether the Congress deserved the abusive epithets 'extremist' and 'revolutionary' which its critics in India and

[1] *Report of the Thirty-Third Indian National Congress*, 1918, Appendix A, pp. vi–vii.

[2] Ibid., p. vii. The Congress also elected three of its members—B. G. Tilak, M. K. Gandhi and Hassan Imam—to represent it at the Peace Conference. Tilak, who was then in England, was later instructed by the Congress to go to Paris for this purpose, but he was not allowed to do so by the British Government and had to content himself with addressing a letter to Georges Clemenceau, the President of the Peace Conference. See S. L. Karandikar, *Lokamanya Bal Gangadhar Tilak* (1957), pp. 570–4.

[3] The Duke of Connaught, February 9, 1921: *Legislative Assembly Debates*, 1921, vol. i, pt. i, p. 17. On April 13, 1919, General Reginald Edward Harry Dyer opened fire without warning on a crowd in Amritsar which had inadequate means of dispersal, killing some four hundred and wounding more than a thousand.

[4] *Report of the Thirty-Fourth Indian National Congress*, 1919, Appendix A, p. 176.

England hurled at it. The presidents of these sessions[1] were loyal, moderate, respectable, and sensible persons. The Congress still gave pride of place to the loyalty resolution in its proceedings. Its tone was respectful of royalty, the British people and Parliament. It never expressed any desire to break away from the British Empire. In fact, some of the speeches in these sessions might compare favourably with those of the pre-war years in their gushing loyalty and warm attachment to the British throne. Not satisfied with passing a resolution 'loyally congratulating' His Majesty the King-Emperor on the successful termination of the war, the 1918 Congress decided to present 'an address of congratulation' to him and 'a petition to the High Court of Parliament in England enunciating our demand for Responsible Government as an integral part of the British Empire'.[2] The 1919 Congress tendered 'its respectful thanks to His Majesty the King-Emperor for His Gracious Proclamation', welcomed the announced visit of the Prince of Wales to India and assured him of 'a warm reception by the people of this country'.[3] However much the Congress might have differed with the Moderates in the manner of expressing its dissatisfaction over the reforms, the modifications it urged were hardly different from those suggested by the Moderates. If anything, the Congress voiced more correctly the feelings of the politically-alert Indians than the Moderates who concealed their dissatisfaction in a thick fog of make-believe oratory. Moderatism can err as grievously in politics as its opposite and it may well be argued whether the Indian Moderates, by plumping for the Montagu-Chelmsford reforms, did not mislead the British Government in the matter of Indian opinion with regard to those reforms. By their precipitate defection from the Congress in 1918, the Moderates certainly contributed something towards making that organization 'extremist' in later years. Till 1919, however, the Congress had not gone 'extremist' or 'revolutionary'. A change had undoubtedly been coming over the Congress. The events and ideas of the war had made their impact. 'The iron of Amritsar' had entered into its soul. It now tooks its stand on the natural and inalienable right of all men to be free and on the principle of self-determination. But it still urged the British Parliament to recognize and apply the

---

[1] Mrs Annie Besant: Calcutta, 1917; Hassan Imam: Bombay special session, 1918; M. M. Malaviya: Delhi, 1918; Motilal Nehru: Amritsar, 1919.
[2] *Report of the Thirty-Third Indian National Congress*, 1918, Appendix A, pp. i, ix.
[3] *Report of the Thirty-Fourth Indian National Congress*, 1919, Appendix A, p. 173.

principle of self-determination to India. Strange self-determination indeed! It demanded a declaration of the rights of the Indian people, but as 'British citizens', as 'Indian subjects of His Majesty'—to be made by 'the Imperial Parliament'. The 'full' and 'complete Responsible Government' which the Congress desired to be established in India at an early date did not yet go beyond 'all internal affairs'. Nor should it be forgotten that until the beginning of 1920 the Congress stood committed to strict constitutionalism and to the policy of working the reforms in a spirit of co-operation.

It was the events of the next few months—the Treaty of Sèvres with Turkey,[1] the Hunter Committee Report,[2] the approval of General Dyer's action by a strong element in the House of Commons and a majority of the House of Lords, and the immense public subscription raised for him—which acted as a catalyst. Before Gandhi[3] transformed the Congress in 1920, he was himself to undergo a profound transformation.

Gandhi began his political career in South Africa in the 1890s as a convinced and pronounced believer in the excellence of the British constitution and in the value of the British connection. The secret of his loyalty to the Empire was his belief that the British constitution recognized, in principle if not always in fact, the equality of all races, and that it was possible for Indians to grow to their full stature within and with the help of the Empire. In spite of his unhappy experiences in South Africa, Gandhi never wavered in this faith. He hoped that by loyal service and sacrifice his countrymen would qualify for equal partnership in the Empire. He himself served with distinction in the Boer War and the Zulu rebellion on the side of the English. In his book *Hind Swaraj*, published in 1909, Gandhi vigorously supported the ideals and methods of the Moderates in India and denounced those of

---

[1] The terms of the Treaty—published in May 1920—proposed to deprive Turkey of her control over Thrace, Smyrna, Syria, Palestine and Mesopotamia. They were denounced bitterly by the Indian Muslims as being unduly harsh, contrary to earlier assurances given by British statesmen, and an interference with the Khilafat. The Treaty was concluded in August 1920, but it was not ratified and was later superseded by the Treaty of Lausanne in 1923.

[2] *Report of the Committee appointed by the Government of India to investigate the Disturbances in the Punjab, etc.* [presided over by Lord Hunter, lately Solicitor-General for Scotland], Cmd. 681 (1920).

[3] Mohandas Karamchand Gandhi, b. 1869; called to the Bar 1889; went to South Africa 1893; returned to India 1915; leading figure of the Indian National Congress till his assassination in 1948.

THE INDIAN NATIONAL CONGRESS AND THE COMMONWEALTH

the Extremists. Though extremely critical of many aspects of Western civilization, Gandhi genuinely loved the English people and admired the outstanding qualities of their character. His beau ideal in politics was Gokhale and, though his methods later differed considerably from Gokhale's, he ever retained the stamp of his master's personality.[1]

Throughout the period of the First World War Gandhi laboured strenuously in the cause of the defence of the Empire. He preached 'absolutely unconditional and wholehearted co-operation with the Government on the part of educated India' in the war effort and emphasized what he considered to be the elementary truth that if the Empire perished, with it would perish their cherished political aspirations for their own country.[2] He disappointed Mrs Besant in 1915 when he refused to join her in launching a Home Rule movement in India. He told her in so many words that he did not share her distrust of the English people and would do nothing which might embarrass them during the war.[3] He would have liked his countrymen to 'withdraw all the Congress resolutions, and not whisper "Home Rule" or "Responsible Government" during the pendency of the war'.[4] The Secretary of State, Montagu, while in India in 1917, noted in his *Diary* after an interview with Gandhi: '[Gandhi] does not understand details of schemes; all he wants is that we should get India on our side. He wants the millions of India to leap to the assistance of the British throne.'[5] Busy recruiting soldiers for the war, Gandhi wrote to the Viceroy, Chelmsford, in April 1918 that he loved the English nation and wished 'to evoke in every Indian the loyalty of Englishmen'.[6] To Mohammed Ali Jinnah,[7] who was then engaged, along with Besant and Tilak, in popularizing the gospel of Home Rule, he wrote on July 4, 1918: 'Seek ye first the recruiting office and everything will be added unto you.'[8]

In spite of the ill-timed Rowlatt Act[9] and the unfortunate Amritsar

[1] See Gandhi, 'A Confession of Faith', *Young India*, July 13, 1921.
[2] D. G. Tendulkar, *Mahatma* (1951), vol. i, p. 280.
[3] K. Dwarkadas, *Gandhiji through My Diary Leaves* (1950), pp. 10–11.
[4] Tendulkar, op. cit., vol. i, p. 278.
[5] Montagu, *An Indian Diary* (1930), p. 58.
[6] Tendulkar, op. cit., vol. i, p. 278.
[7] B. 1876; barrister of the Bombay High Court; President of the Muslim League 1916, 1920, and from 1934 till his death in 1948; Governor-General of Pakistan 1947–8.
[8] Tendulkar, op. cit., vol. i, p. 282.
[9] This Act authorized the Government of India in 1919 to retain the summary powers vested in them during the war. It was based upon the recommendations of a committee which inquired into seditious activities in India and was presided over by Sir Sidney Rowlatt of the King's Bench in England.

incident, Gandhi pleaded with his people to work the reforms of 1919 in a spirit of genuine co-operation and goodwill. 'The Reforms Act', he wrote, 'coupled with the Proclamation is an earnest of the intention of the British people to do justice to India.'[1] He advised his countrymen not to subject the reforms to carping criticism but to settle down quietly to work so as to make them a thorough success and thereby qualify for further advance. At the Amritsar session of the Congress held towards the end of December 1919, the latter-day apostle of non-co-operation would not even brook the idea of grudging acceptance or Irish obstructionism which Tilak and C. R. Das[2] contemplated practising in the councils. 'I shall challenge that position,' he remarked, 'and I shall go across from one end of India to the other and say we shall fail in our culture, we shall fall from our position . . . if we do not respond to the hand that has been extended to us.'[3] Gandhi also made the Congress pass a resolution condemning the excesses committed by the Indian mobs in the Punjab and Gujerat. The events of the next few months, however, turned the great loyalist and co-operator into a rebel and a non-co-operator.

The terms of the Treaty of Sèvres with Turkey, published in May 1920, were considered by most Indians to be a breach of the pledges given earlier by British statesmen. The Report of the Hunter Committee appeared to them as an attempt to whitewash the culprits in the Amritsar 'massacre'. The manner in which Dyer's action was acclaimed by the general body of Europeans in India and their friends in England filled Indians with pain and indignation. Gandhi became convinced that 'the present representatives of the Empire' had become 'dishonest and unscrupulous', that they had no real regard for the wishes of the Indian people and counted the honour of India as of little consequence.[4] To an enraged and aggrieved people he suggested the way of non-violent non-co-operation to enforce the national will and secure redress of the Khilafat and the Punjab wrongs. The non-co-operation movement was launched on August 1, 1920. A special session of the Congress held at Calcutta in September 1920 approved of and adopted Gandhi's programme and affirmed that 'the only effectual means to vindicate national honour and prevent repetition of similar wrongs in future is the establishment of *Swaraj*'.[5]

[1] 'The Royal Proclamation', *Young India*, December 31, 1919.
[2] B. 1870; barrister of the Calcutta High Court; President of the Indian National Congress 1921; formed with Motilal Nehru the Swaraj Party 1923; d. 1925.
[3] *Report of the Thirty-Fourth Indian National Congress*, 1919, p. 123.
[4] *Young India*, July 28, 1920.   [5] Tendulkar, op. cit., vol. ii, p. 12.

The special session of the Congress held at Calcutta in September 1920 also appointed a committee to revise the constitution of the Congress. The draft report of this committee recommended that the goal of the Congress should be the attainment of *Swaraj* by all legitimate and peaceful means. Commenting on the draft constitution Gandhi remarked that the altered creed represented 'the exact feeling of the country at the present moment' and was 'but an extension of the original'.[1] As long as no break with the British connection was attempted, it was, he claimed, strictly within even the existing creed. The extension lay, he pointed out, in the contemplated possibility of a break with the British connection. 'In my humble opinion,' Gandhi added, 'if India is to make unhampered progress, we must make it clear to the British people that, whilst we desire to retain the British connection, if we can rise to our full height with it, we are determined to dispense with it, and even to get rid of that connection, if that is necessary for full national development. I hold that it is not only derogatory to national dignity, but it actually impedes national progress superstitiously to believe that our progress towards our goal is impossible without [the] British connection. It is this superstition which makes some of the best of us to tolerate the Punjab wrong and the Khilafat insult. This blind adherence to that connection makes us feel helpless. The proposed alteration in the creed enables us to rid ourselves of our helpless condition.'[2]

The Congress debated the question at its Nagpur session in December 1920. Gandhi moved the main resolution in the Subjects Committee on December 27th. It read: 'The object of the Indian National Congress is the attainment of *Swaraj* by the people of India by all legitimate and peaceful means.'[3] Radical opposition within the Congress found vent in an amendment, moved by N. R. Alekar,[4] demanding that the object of the Congress should be 'the establishment of an Indian Republic... to be achieved by all just and effective means'.[5] The moderates, led by Malaviya and Jinnah, desired the Congress to be committed to *Swaraj* 'within the British Commonwealth'.[6] The Subjects Committee, however, favoured Gandhi's draft. An illuminating discussion took place the next day, December 28, 1920, in the open session of the Congress. Gandhi defined his position clearly. 'I do not, for one moment, suggest', he remarked, 'that we want to end the British connection at all costs, unconditionally. If the British connection is for the

[1] 'The Congress Constitution', *Young India*, November 3, 1920.   [2] Ibid.
[3] *Times of India*, December 29, 1920.   [4] Pleader of the Nagpur High Court.
[5] *Times of India*, December 29, 1920.   [6] Ibid.

advancement of India, we do not want to destroy it. But if it is inconsistent with our national self-respect, then it is our bounden duty to destroy it.'[1] He pointed out that the new creed was elastic enough to include both those who, like himself, believed that by retaining the British connection they could purify themselves and purify the British people, and those who had no such belief.

Lajpat Rai[2] pointed out that the change in the Congress creed was an announcement in the clearest possible terms of the change in mentality which had come over the country. The Congress could not exclude from its ranks those patriots who had conscientious objection to signing the existing creed or those who believed in complete independence outside the British Empire. He did not think that the majority of Congressmen or of thinking people in the country were prepared to say that they would at once go in for complete independence or that they would not remain in the British Commonwealth if it were possible for them to do so honourably. The change in the creed was, he remarked, 'a notice to the British public and the British Government that although we do not at the present aim, directly aim, to get out of this British Empire, or, what we may call the British Commonwealth, but if we remain in the British Commonwealth . . . we shall not remain at the dictation of anybody or by fear. We shall remain there by our own free choice and free will. . . .'[3] India, Lajpat Rai said, would decide when the time came whether she could remain a member of the British Commonwealth on terms of equality. He did not think that such a Commonwealth yet existed. 'As to the British Empire, I would rather be a slave than willingly consent to be a part of an empire which enslaves so many millions of human beings.'[4] He emphasized that the word *Swaraj* had been left unqualified deliberately for the purpose of enabling them to remain within the Commonwealth if they chose to do so when a real Commonwealth had been established, or to go out if they so desired.

Left-wing opposition to Gandhi's resolution had exhausted itself in the Subjects Committee, but the right-wingers did not fail to register their protest again in the open session. Jinnah opposed the change in the creed mainly on two grounds: first, that it was virtually a declaration of independence and as such inopportune; and secondly, that the

[1] *Report of the Thirty-Fifth Indian National Congress*, 1920, p. 47.
[2] B. 1865; author, lawyer and social reformer; President of the Indian National Congress (special session at Calcutta) 1920; d. 1928.
[3] *Report of the Thirty-Fifth Indian National Congress*, 1920, p. 50.
[4] Ibid., p. 52.

means chosen for its achievement were inadequate. He argued that the resolution was nothing but 'a declaration of complete independence'[1] and it was a 'camouflage'[2] to leave the word *Swaraj* undefined. The majority in the nation may have the will to declare for independence, but they had not yet the means to carry it out. 'You will never get your independence without bloodshed', Jinnah warned, and added, 'you are exposing your hand to your enemies.'[3] He assured his audience that his 'only reason' in opposing the proposition was that it was 'not the right step to take at this moment'.[4] Jinnah also objected to the limitation in methods by which *Swaraj* was to be achieved. 'Non-co-operation by legitimate and peaceful methods', he said, 'may be an excellent weapon for the purpose of bringing pressure upon the Government. But let me tell you once more that the weapon will not succeed in destroying the British Empire. I therefore object to the methods; because if you want complete independence let us not be limited to methods.'[5]

Josiah Wedgwood, who, along with two other members of the Labour Party, Benjamin Charles Spoor[6] and Holford Knight,[7] attended the Nagpur session of the Congress, deplored the change of creed on the ground that it might make the union between the Congress and the Labour Party more difficult, if not impossible.[8]

From moderate Madras came two amendments seeking to define *Swaraj* as 'full responsible government' similar to that enjoyed by the self-governing Dominions of the British Empire.[9] The mover of one of these amendments, S. Satyamurti,[10] referred to the remark of Sir Robert Borden (?) that 'If Canada tomorrow declares her independence, not one British gun should be fired against her'.[11] Satyamurti pointed out that India could attain the same status as the Dominions within the Empire and the right of secession if she so desired. The movers of both the amendments emphasized that care should be taken not to alienate friends in Britain.

The Congress, however, decided to follow Gandhi. When his

---

[1] *Report of the Thirty-Fifth Indian National Congress*, 1920, p. 54.
[2] Ibid. p. 55.   [3] Ibid., p. 54.   [4] Ibid.   [5] Ibid., p. 56.
[6] B. 1878; MP 1918–28; member of the National Executive of the Labour Party 1919; Parliamentary Secretary to the Treasury and Chief Whip of the Labour Party 1924; d. 1928.   [7] B. 1877; barrister; MP 1929–35; d. 1936.
[8] *Report of the Thirty-Fifth Indian National Congress*, 1920, p. 60.
[9] Ibid., pp. 61–7.   [10] Journalist and lawyer at Madras; b. 1887; d. 1943.
[11] *Report of the Thirty-Fifth Indian National Congress*, 1920, p. 63. The speaker probably meant Bonar Law. For the latter's remark in 1920 to a similar effect see 127 H.C. Deb. 5s., col. 1125.

resolution was put to the vote only two, out of the 14,000 delegates, voted against it.[1]

The debate at Nagpur revealed clearly the trend of thought within the Congress about membership of the British Commonwealth. Freedom within the Empire if possible, but without if necessary had now come to be the objective of the Congress. It was not yet a repudiation of the British connection, or, as Jinnah thought, a declaration of complete independence. It was considered derogatory to national self-respect to make a fetish of the British connection and to insist that India must evolve within the Empire irrespective of the attitude of the British Government. The change in the creed was deemed necessary to give expression to the general wish of the rank and file which was either hostile or indifferent to the British connection, to distinguish the Congress objective from that of the Liberals, to enable those who, like Shaukat Ali,[2] had 'suspended' their allegiance to the British Crown to continue staying within the organization, and to assert India's right of self-determination. The word 'Empire' was disliked. It had become a term of abuse, meaning enslavement and exploitation. No speaker, however, declared himself against the idea of a true Commonwealth of nations; but it was felt that the British Empire was not yet such a Commonwealth. All were agreed that India could not accept any inferior status within the Commonwealth and that she must have the right to opt out of it if she so chose. Even those who wanted India to strive for self-government within the British Empire took it for granted that Dominion Status implied the right of secession. Believers in the British connection could combine idealism with expediency in varying degree. It was easier, in their view, to attain self-government within the Empire; and freedom in association with Britain was preferable to freedom without any association with Britain.

The Nagpur Congress was the largest so far held. The *petit bourgeois* mass flooded the session. The leaders would have gladly moved at a slower pace, but the crowd had taken the reins in its hands and drove the former.[3] At Nagpur in December 1920 the Congress broke definitely and decisively with the Moderates. But it was not yet a complete victory for the young radicals. As one of them commented later: 'Regarding both the goal and the means, the decision of the Nagpur Congress represented the golden mean between the views of the Right-Wingers like Pandit Malaviya and Mr Jinnah and the youth-

[1] *Report of the Thirty-Fifth Indian National Congress*, 1920, p. 85.
[2] B. 1873; Secretary of the Central Khilafat Committee; d. 1937.
[3] See Gandhi, 'The Congress', *Young India*, January 5, 1921.

ful Left-Wingers who swamped the Congress for the first time in 1920. The latter desired the goal of the Congress to be complete independence to be attained by all possible means. It was Mr Gandhi, however, who by virtue of his tremendous influence and popularity was able to keep the Left-Wingers at bay.'[1]

During the days of the anti-partition agitation in Bengal, Aurobindo Ghose and B. C. Pal had raised the slogan of absolute autonomy and unqualified *Swaraj* for India. Its effect had been electrifying but shortlived. After 1909 the cry of complete independence had almost died down in India. Aurobindo Ghose had retired from politics and Pal had become a convert to the idea of Imperial federation. The 'Home Rulers' did not contemplate a severance of the British connection. Montagu, while in India, noted in his *Diary* in November 1917 that 'revolutionary or not, loathing or not as they may do the Indian Civil Service, none of these Indians show any signs of wanting to be removed from connection with the British throne'.[2] Even that stormy petrel Tilak did not advocate *Swaraj* outside the British Empire. The manifesto of his Congress Democratic Party, which Tilak issued in April 1920, read: 'This party believes in the integration or federation of India in the British Commonwealth for the advancement of the cause of humanity and the brotherhood of mankind, but demands autonomy for India and equal status as a sister state with every partner in the British Commonwealth, including Great Britain.'[3] Gandhi's non-co-operation movement was certainly not conceived in a spirit hostile to to the British connection. In the later half of the year 1920, however, the demand for complete independence outside the British Empire began to gain strength in India. It was encouraged in part by the events which gave birth to the Khilafat and non-co-operation movements. It was inspired by the similar demand being made in Ireland and Egypt at the time. But it was an Englishman, Charles Freer Andrews,[4] who did most to popularize the cry in India.

In September 1920 Andrews publicly declared that he saw 'no possible recovery of self-respect [by Indians] except by claiming an independence from British domination not less than that of Egypt'.[5]

---

[1] S. C. Bose, *The Indian Struggle, 1920-34* (1935), p. 58.
[2] Montagu, op. cit., p. 58.
[3] Cited in S. L. Karandikar, *Lokamanya Bal Gangadhar Tilak* (1957), p. 635.
[4] B. 1870; joined Cambridge Brotherhood in Delhi; author, journalist and social reformer; d. 1940.
[5] B. Chaturvedi and M. Sykes, *Charles Freer Andrews* (1949), p. 155.

During the next few months he deluged India with speeches, articles and pamphlets preaching the immediate need of independence for India outside the British Empire.[1] He condemned the idea of self-government for India within the Empire as the product of a 'subservient mind'.[2] Future historians, he wrote, would find it hard to believe that Indians could have sunk so low in character as to boast that they were 'British subjects' and 'British citizens' at the very time when they were being treated like helots and outcastes in the British Dominions. 'India was', Andrews emphasized, 'already, for all practical purposes, outside the British Empire.'[3] The Dominions had 'ignominiously hurled India, by their savage exclusion laws and white race policies, outside the Empire'.[4] He denounced as 'ludicrously absurd'[5] the notion that a vast sub-continent could remain permanently tied to an island in the North Sea. He pointed out that India was a mother country herself and not a daughter community like the Dominions. She had no vital, intimate, organic relation with Britain. Race, language, climate, religion, and culture—all differentiated India from Britain. She could not like Australia, Canada and New Zealand be assimilated to the British way of life. She could never in reality become 'an integral part of an Empire, which must always remain peculiarly and centrally British'.[6] Indians 'were foreigners and must always remain foreigners, in the midst of an Empire of kinsmen'.[7]

Andrews told Indians not to delude themselves with the hope that the British Empire would one day accord them an equal, honourable and self-respecting place within it. The people in the Dominions were more than ever determined to deny Indians equality and justice. And as to the English people, however much 'Home Rule within the British Empire' might be substituted for the present autocratic administration, he was 'quite certain, as an Englishman—knowing my countrymen, as no Indian could possibly understand them—that there would always be some residuum of subjection in India's position; some remaining mark of dependence'.[8]

India's connection with England was, Andrews remarked, a result of brute conquest. It might have done some good at some stage, but

[1] See his *How India Can Be Free* (1921); *Indian Independence: The Immediate Need* (1921); *The Indian Problem* (1921); *The Claim for Independence: Within or Without the British Empire* (1921); and also his introduction to S. E. Stokes, *The Failure of European Civilization as a World Culture* (1921).
[2] Andrews, *The Claim for Independence*, p. 39.
[3] Andrews, *How India Can Be Free*, p. 10.
[4] Ibid. [5] Andrews, *The Claim for Independence*, p. 24.
[6] Ibid., p. 25. [7] Ibid., p. 23. [8] Ibid., p. 35.

subjection for a long time to a foreign yoke was the most potent cause of national degeneration. British rule in India, he affirmed, had now become a dead hand, which must be removed entirely and immediately if India was to have a natural and unfettered growth. India's orientation towards Great Britain and her dependence on the latter vitiated her whole life and culture. She could never be herself again and regain her soul unless and until she was completely independent. Andrews also warned that by remaining within the Empire India would be running the risk of involvement in the wars of the Empire and assisting in the perpetuation of Western economic and financial vested interests.

Andrews believed that Indians did not need the sword in order to be free. If they only developed the will to be free and realized that it was shameful to assist the foreigner, the British Empire in India—he quoted Seeley in support of his thesis—would collapse in no time. He felt that the real revolution that was needed in India was in the minds of men. The slave mentality of the people themselves had to be changed. And this, he told Indians, could not be done unless they put before themselves the correct and ennobling ideal of independence outside the British Empire.

The case for India's independence outside the British Empire was never before or in after years presented with such convincing logic and telling eloquence as it was by Andrews in the years 1920-1. His preaching made a tremendous impression in India, not least on such alert young minds as that of Jawaharlal Nehru.[1] It failed, however, to convince Gandhi, who claimed to know Englishmen better. Gandhi wrote to his friend on November 23, 1920: 'In its present condition the English connection is hateful. But I am not as yet sure that it must be ended at any cost. ... The connection must end on the clearest possible proof that the English have hopelessly failed to realize the first principle of religion, namely brotherhood of men.'[2] At the Nagpur Congress in December 1920 he expressed his dissent publicly from the views of Andrews.[3] In July 1921 he wrote in *Young India* about Andrews, 'who,

---

[1] B. 1889; President of the Indian National Congress 1929, 1936, 1937, 1946 and 1951-4; Prime Minister of India from 1947 till his death in 1964.

Nehru later wrote in his *Autobiography* (1942 ed.), p. 66: ' ... it seemed to me not only to make an unanswerable case for independence but also to mirror the inmost recesses of our hearts. The deep urge that moved us and our half-formed desires seemed to take a clear shape in his simple and earnest language.... It was wonderful that C. F. Andrews, a foreigner and one belonging to the dominant race in India, should echo the cry of our inmost being.'

[2] Cited in Chaturvedi and Sykes, op. cit., p. 156.

[3] See *Report of the Thirty-Fifth Indian National Congress*, 1920, p. 47.

unlike me, considers that there is no room in the British Empire for a self-respecting and self-governing India, and who expects that some day I shall myself be driven to that position'.[1] 'I am', Gandhi added, 'differently constituted. I never give up hope as long as there is the least chance, and I have faith enough in the British people to feel that, whilst they will test our determination and strength to the uttermost, they will not carry it to the breaking point.'[2] As Gandhi sat listening to the fiery speech of Maulana Hasrat Mohani[3] at the Ahmedabad Congress in December 1921, pleading for the declaration of complete independence as the goal of India, he remarked to Andrews, who was seated on the dais beside him, 'This is your *shararat* [mischief], Charlie'.[4] Andrews wrote in 1922: 'A short time before Mahatma Gandhi's arrest, when I was with him in Ahmedabad, he blamed me very severely indeed for my lack of faith in the British connection and for my publicly putting forward a demand for complete independence. He said to me openly that I had done a great deal of mischief by such advocacy of independence. If I interpret him rightly his own position at that time was this. He had lost faith in the British Administration in India—it was a Satanic Government. But he had not lost faith in the British Constitution itself. He still believed that India could remain within the British Empire on the basis of racial equality, and that the principle of racial equality would come out triumphantly vindicated after the present struggle in India was over. Indeed, he held himself to be the champion of that theory, and the upholder of the British Constitution. . . . I said to him, "It would almost seem as if you had more faith in my own countrymen than I have myself". He said to me, "That may be true"—and I felt deeply his implied rebuke.'[5]

Gandhi was the strangest rebel the world had ever known—a man who loved the English, had invincible faith in English character, and claimed to uphold the British constitution while waging a non-violent war against it. The British Empire got the adversary it deserved. Though Gandhi's non-violent non-co-operation was a weapon which he thought could be used against any antagonist anywhere, when he wielded it against the British he knew that it was irresistible. 'An Englishman', he told Andrews, 'never respects you till you stand up to

---

[1] 'Indian Republic', *Young India*, July 13, 1921.   [2] Ibid.
[3] Saiyid Fazl-ul-Hasan Hasrat Mohani, b. 1878; journalist, poet and politician; President of the All-India Muslim League 1921; d. 1951.
[4] Chaturvedi and Sykes, op. cit., p. 179.
[5] *Indian Review*, June 1922, p. 366; Introduction to *Speeches and Writings of M. K. Gandhi* (1922 ed.), pp. xv–xvi.

him. Then he begins to like you. He is afraid of nothing physical; but he is very mortally afraid of his own conscience if ever you appeal to it and show him to be in the wrong. He does not like to be rebuked for wrong-doing at first; but he will think over it, and it will get hold of him and hurt him till he does something to put it right.'[1]

At the Ahmedabad session of the Congress in December 1921 Maulana Hasrat Mohani moved a resolution suggesting that the object of the Congress should be the attainment of 'complete independence, free from all foreign control'.[2] He pointed out that the concept of Colonial self-government was not applicable to India as she was not a Colony. He asserted that Britain would never willingly concede self-government to India. He desired that they should place before themselves 'the highest ideal possible'.[3] His main contention, however, was that the Khilafat question could not be solved unless India achieved complete independence and thereby dealt a blow at the might of the British Empire. 'So far as India alone is concerned,' Mohani remarked, 'the Colonial form of self-government may suffice, but so far as the Khilafat is concerned, *Swaraj* can have only one meaning and that is complete independence. The Khilafat question is not possible of solution so long as British Imperialism is not broken. The British will not retrace their steps from Iraq, Arabia and the Jazirat-ul-Arab and the whole world will not be free from their domination so long as their Imperialism is not broken.... The Colonial form of self-government would not solve the Khilafat question but it would, on the other hand, go against the Khilafat for this reason that it will strengthen British Imperialism.'[4]

Those who supported Mohani's resolution argued that their goal should be clearly defined; that Colonial self-government was an impossibility both because Indians were not colonials and because the English would never voluntarily grant it to India; and that the only ideal consistent with their self-respect and position in the world was that of complete independence.[5]

Gandhi took Mohani and his supporters severely to task for 'raising a false issue' and 'throwing a bomb-shell in the midst of the Indian atmosphere'.[6] He condemned 'the levity' with which the proposition had been taken up, for it showed 'a lack of responsibility'.[7] He reminded them of their limitations, especially the lack of unity amongst the various communities in India, and warned them not to enter

[1] Andrews, *Mahatma Gandhi's Ideas* (1929), p. 249.
[2] *Report of the Thirty-Sixth Indian National Congress*, 1921, p. 50.
[3] Ibid., p. 53. [4] Ibid. [5] Ibid., pp. 55–6. [6] Ibid., p. 57. [7] Ibid.

waters whose depth they did not know. 'Are creeds such simple things like clothes which a man can change at will?' he asked and added, 'For creeds people die and for creeds people live from age to age.'[1] He described the existing creed of the Congress as 'an extensive creed'—'it takes in all, the weakest and the strongest'—and appealed to his audience to reject the 'limited creed of Maulana Hasrat Mohani which does not admit the weakest of your brethren'.[2] The Congress rejected Mohani's resolution by an overwhelming majority.

Writing in *Young India* on January 5, 1922, under the heading 'Independence', Gandhi returned to the theme again. The Maulana, he wrote, wanted to sever all connection with the British people even as partners and equals. It was theoretical to argue that the Khilafat question could not be solved without complete independence. If the British people remained hostile to the Islamic world, Gandhi affirmed, there would be nothing left for Indians but to insist on complete independence. 'But assuming', he argued, 'that Great Britain alters her attitude, as I know she will when India is strong, it will be religiously unlawful for us to insist on independence. For it will be vindictive and petulant. It would amount to a denial of God, for the refusal will then be based upon the assumption that the British people are not capable of response to the God in man. Such a position is untenable for both a believing Mussalman and a believing Hindu.'[3] 'India's greatest glory', Gandhi told his countrymen, 'will consist not in regarding Englishmen as her implacable enemies fit only to be turned out of India at the first available opportunity but in turning them into friends and partners in a new commonwealth of nations in the place of an Empire based upon exploitation of the weaker or undeveloped nations and races of the earth and therefore finally upon force.'[4]

Gandhi was the supreme and unquestioned leader of India during the period of the non-co-operation movement—1920–2. Not only was his word law unto his numerous followers, he also created a profound impression on the minds of those in India who did not always agree with him. It is worth while, therefore, to ascertain how he visualized *Swaraj* for India and the nature of her connection with the British Empire.

Gandhi repeatedly emphasized during these years that by *Swaraj* he meant 'the parliamentary government of India in the modern sense of the term'.[5] 'In so far as I can see,' he wrote in December 1920, '*Swaraj*

---
[1] *Report of the Thirty-Sixth Indian National Congress*, 1921, p. 57.
[2] Ibid., pp. 57–8.   [3] *Young India*, January 5, 1922.   [4] Ibid.
[5] Ibid., December 29, 1920.

will be a parliament chosen by the people with fullest power over the finance, the police, the military, the navy, the courts, and the educational institutions. . . . Under that *Swaraj*, the nation will have the power to impose a heavy protective tariff on such foreign goods as are capable of being manufactured in India, as also the power to refuse to send a single soldier outside India for the purpose of enslaving the surrounding or remote nationalities.'[1] Gandhi, however, denied that he had any 'clear-cut scheme', or that any one man could produce such a scheme, for, as he put it, it was not one man's *Swaraj* that was wanted. All that he was doing, he said, was to lay down some 'broad outlines'. The actual scheme of *Swaraj* was to be 'framed by the authorized representatives of the nation'—freely elected through universal adult franchise.[2]

Gandhi was well acquainted with South African politics and his writings bristle with references to the examples and precedents from the history of that country. And then, Irish history was a perennial source of inspiration to Indian nationalists, a running lesson in tactics and strategy. The conclusion of the treaty between Great Britain and Ireland on December 6, 1921, encouraged great hopes in India and led to the demand for the calling of a round table conference to settle the Indian question. The examples of South Africa and Ireland strengthened Gandhi's belief that India could attain *Swaraj* within the British Empire. On January 5, 1922, he wrote: 'Let us see clearly what *Swaraj* together with the British connection means. It means undoubtedly India's ability to declare her independence, if she wishes. *Swaraj* therefore will not be a free gift of the British Parliament. It will be a declaration of India's full self-expression. That it will be expressed through an act of Parliament is true. But it will be merely a courteous ratification of the declared wish of the people of India even as it was in the case of the Union of South Africa. Not an unnecessary adverb in the Union scheme could be altered by the House of Commons. The ratification in our case will be a treaty to which Britain will be a party. Such *Swaraj* may not come this year, may not come within our generation. But I have contemplated nothing less.'[3]

Gandhi repeatedly pointed out during the years 1920–2 that by *Swaraj* he meant 'full responsible government on Dominion lines' or 'full Dominion Status' for India with freedom to secede from the

---

[1] *Young India*, December 8, 1920.
[2] Ibid., February 16, 1921, January 19, 1922, February 23, 1922.
[3] Ibid., January 5, 1922. See also *Young India*, December 15, 1921, and January 19, 1922.

Empire.[1] As early as September 22, 1920, he had remarked: 'If it is to be partnership, it must be partnership at will.'[2] On October 6, 1920, he wrote: 'We must have absolute equality in theory and in practice, and ability to do away with the British connection if we so wish.'[3] Again on June 29, 1921, he said: 'In a free Commonwealth, every partner has as much right to retire if the rest go wrong, as it is his duty to remain so long as the rest are faithful to certain common principles.'[4] From this position, that India must have full Dominion Status and the right to secede from the Empire if she so chose, Gandhi and the Congress did not depart in later years.

The non-co-operation movement distintegrated almost immediately after Gandhi abruptly sounded the call to retreat in February 1922 and after his own arrest in the following March. From the height of their exaltation, optimism and self-confidence, Congressmen swung to the depths of exhaustion, despair and agonizing self-introspection. It was realized, almost with a tinge of regret, that in the heat of their righteous indignation Congressmen and Khilafatists had committed a grave blunder in boycotting the councils. If they had sought election in 1920, they would have obtained commanding majorities and they could have used that power either to dominate the political machine or to bring it to a standstill. There were also many within the Congress who had never fully believed in the Gandhian programme, but their scepticism had given way before the miracle-maker and they had found the current too strong for them. But now that the holy man was in the Yerveda prison, his following dispirited and disheartened, and his promised '*Swaraj* in one year' as distant as ever, many realized the truth of Tilak's remark, 'Politics is a game of worldly people and not of *sadhus* [saints]'.[5] And the wordly people felt the need of a more realistic campaign and decided to enter the legislatures.

The Swarajists represented the right wing of the Congress. They were constitutionalists at heart. They admitted that the non-co-operation movement had played a significant part in rousing the masses from their slumber and in creating a surge towards freedom, but they did not disguise from themselves the fact that it had failed to force the hands of the authorities. They pointed out that the country was in no mood for a further bout of non-co-operation and that instead of wasting

[1] *Young India*, April 6, 1921, January 19 and February 23, 1922.
[2] Ibid., September 22, 1920.   [3] Ibid., October 6, 1920.
[4] Ibid., June 29, 1921.
[5] Cited in T. V Parvate, *Bal Gangadhar Tilak* (1958), p. 524.

their time in sulkiness it was advisable to utilize the councils for putting pressure on the authorities for a further constitutional advance. The battle for *Swaraj* was to continue, they said, only its form and weapons were to change in order to suit the circumstances of the country. To the followers of the Mahatma it was treason against their absent leader, the old Moderate heresy rearing its ugly head within the Congress. They defeated the proposal made by C. R. Das and Motilal Nehru[1] to enter the councils at the Gaya Congress held towards the end of December 1922. Undaunted by this rebuff, the constitutionalists announced the formation of the Congress-Khilafat Swaraj Party on January 1, 1923. The manifesto of the new organization declared that 'While the goal of the party is the attainment of *Swaraj*, the immediate objective of the party is the speedy attainment of full Dominion Status'.[2] What this latter objective signified was explained in the programme of the party published in February 1923. It meant, said the programme, 'the securing of the right to frame a constitution adopting such machinery and system as are most suited to the conditions of the country and the genius of the people'.[3] The same point was emphasized in the election manifesto of the party published on October 14, 1923.[4] A compromise was effected at the special session of the Congress held at Delhi in mid-September 1923 and the Swarajists were allowed to contest the elections to be held towards the end of the year. The Swarajists virtually routed the Liberals and gained impressive victories in the elections for both the provincial and central legislatures. They struck a working alliance with the Independents and came to the councils determined to force the hands of the Government to revise the Act of 1919.

On February 3, 1924, a conference consisting of the Swarajists and the Independents held at Delhi passed a resolution, moved by Jinnah, asking the Government 'to take steps immediately for the establishment of full responsible Government'.[5] By another resolution the conference proposed the appointment of a committee or a round table conference, consisting of the representatives of the various communities and interests in India, to consider and recommend measures for the establishment of full responsible government in India.[6] On February 5, 1924 a Labour Government came into office in England. This encouraged hopes of a liberal response to the demand which Indian

---

[1] B. 1861; advocate of the Allahabad High Court; President of the Indian National Congress 1919 and 1928; d. 1931.
[2] *The Indian Annual Register*, 1923, vol. ii, p. 143.
[3] Ibid., p. 221.   [4] Ibid., pp. 218–19.
[5] *The Indian Quarterly Register*, 1924, vol. i, p. 70.   [6] Ibid., p. 71.

nationalists had already decided to make in the Assembly. On February 8, 1924, Motilal Nehru introduced a motion in the Indian Legislative Assembly containing the so-called 'National Demand'. It urged the Governor-General in Council 'to take steps to have the Government of India Act revised with a view to establish full responsible Government in India and for the said purpose:

(*a*) to summon at an early date a representative Round Table Conference to recommend with due regard to the protection of the rights and interests of important minorities the scheme of a constitution for India; and
(*b*) after dissolving the Central Legislature, to place the said scheme for approval before a newly elected Indian Legislature for its approval and submit the same to the British Parliament to be embodied in a Statute.'[1]

Motilal Nehru made it clear that what he and his friends inside the Assembly were demanding was 'a complete overhauling of the Government of India Act'.[2] They were not asking, he said, 'for complete responsible government to be handed over to us tied up in a bundle', but that the British Government should recognize the right of Indians to self-determination and convene 'a round table conference, or committee, or whatever other name you may give it' to examine the entire problem of the future government of India.[3] 'We have come to ask you', he remarked, 'to meet us so that we may put our heads together—to hear us and to let us hear you and then come to some definite conclusion.'[4] He wanted the proposed conference to be really representative—consisting of the representatives of the Government and of the various interests in the country. Such a conference, Motilal Nehru insisted, would afford 'an opportunity . . . to the Government to right itself with the people, and to the people to right themselves with the Government';[5] it would 'restore old relations and . . . obliterate the sad memory of past events'.[6] He denied that his party had entered the Assembly only for obstructive purposes. 'We have come here', he said, 'to do something which we have not been doing so far . . . we have come here to offer our co-operation, non-co-operators as we are, if you will care to co-operate with us. That is why we are here. If you agree to have it, we are your men; if you do not, we shall, like men, stand upon our rights and continue to be non-co-operators.'[7]

[1] *Legislative Assembly Debates*, 1924, vol. iv, pt. i, p. 367.
[2] Ibid., p. 368.   [3] Ibid., p. 369.   [4] Ibid., p. 371.
[5] Ibid., p. 545.   [6] Ibid., p. 546.   [7] Ibid., p. 370.

For three days speaker after speaker on the non-official side in the Assembly emphasized the unanimity with which all sections of politically-minded India combined to demand immediate and substantial political advance. If the revision of the Act of 1919 was to take place either by a commission or a conference in co-operation with all the elements in the political life of India, this was perhaps the finest opportunity. All political parties in India were agreed that the Act of 1919 had exhausted its possibilities, that it was no use continuing whipping the dead horse of dyarchy, and that delay, instead of solving any problem or removing any one of the alleged numerous obstacles in the path of self-government, would only serve to estrange the two peoples. They demanded that immediate steps should be taken for a comprehensive settlement of the Indian problem, and that the Indian constitution should be placed on a permanent footing with provision for automatic advance towards full responsible government. The British Government and the Government of India, however, did not think that the time had yet arrived for such steps to be taken.[1] Their response, appointing a committee to inquire into the working of the Act of 1919, deeply disappointed even the moderate-minded Indians.

The Swarajists realized the weak position of the Labour Government—in office but not in power, and that, too, for the first time—and did not expect it to concede their demand wholesale, but they certainly did expect a more liberal response than they received from the party in England which had ever since the end of the war so enthusiastically supported India's claim for self-determination and self-government. Strangely enough, their hopes were revived when a strong Conservative Government came into power in England early in 1925. Some Swarajist leaders, especially C. R. Das, felt that it would be in a better position to end the political deadlock in India. They even expected the new Secretary of State, Lord Birkenhead,[2] to repeat his performance in the settlement of the Irish question in 1921. In March 1925 Das came out with what was widely considered in India to be a generous offer of co-operation to the Government. He severely condemned methods of violence and expressed with almost poetic fervour his belief in the Commonwealth ideal. He discounted the possibility of a resumption of civil disobedience and offered to co-operate with the Government if

[1] The attitude of the British Government and the Government of India is examined in Chapter VI.
[2] Frederick Edwin Smith, first Earl of Birkenhead (1872–1930). MP 1906–18; Attorney-General 1915–19; Lord Chancellor 1919–22; Secretary of State for India 1924–8; d. 1930.

the latter showed a change of heart and assured that *Swaraj* would come automatically in the future.[1] The Swarajists made some other small gestures of peace to indicate that they were eager for reconciliation and co-operation.[2] Even Gandhi blessed their efforts. On Das's untimely death in June 1925 he appealed to the Government to respond to Das's sincere offer in a generous manner. 'Cannot this glorious death', he wrote, 'be utilized to heal wounds and forget distrust', and added, 'May the fire, that burnt yesterday the perishable part of Deshbandhu Das, also burn the perishable distrust, suspicion and fear.'[3] Gandhi even transferred all power to Motilal Nehru and merged the Congress into the Swaraj Party in order to support the latter's bid for settlement with the Government.

Lord Birkenhead's first statement in Parliament as Secretary of State for India on July 7, 1925.[4] disappointed the Swarajists. He expressed his personal dislike of dyarchy but wanted Indians to work it. He asserted that the preamble to the Act of 1919 contained the 'permanent and static' policy of the British Government.[5] He ridiculed the idea that India was an entity or a nation and declared that he was 'not able in any foreseeable future to discern a moment when we may safely, either to ourselves or India, abandon our trust'.[6] But Birkenhead did hold out the prospect of an early appointment of the Statutory Commission if Indian leaders showed 'a sincere and genuine desire to co-operate with us in making the best of the existing constitution'.[7] In September 1925 Motilal Nehru put forward a motion in the Legislative Assembly reiterating the Swarajist demand of 1924.[8] But in two essential respects it was a further climb-down. The Swarajists expressed their willingness to accept a commission provided it was representative of the important elements in Indian political life. And secondly, in order to make it doubly clear that what they demanded was not immediate full responsible government, Motilal Nehru's motion specifically laid down that defence, political relations[9] and foreign affairs were to remain reserved subjects for a fixed term of

[1] See P. C. Ray, *Life and Times of C. R. Das* (1927), pp. 247–56.
[2] Motilal Nehru agreed to serve on the committee for considering ways and means of recruiting Indian officers for the army, and Vithalbhai Patel contested and won the election for the presidentship of the Legislative Assembly.
[3] Tendulkar, op. cit., vol. ii, p. 255.
[4] 61 H.L. Deb. 5s., cols. 1069–92.
[5] Ibid., col. 1076.   [6] Ibid., col. 1091.   [7] Ibid., col. 1085.
[8] *Legislative Assembly Debates*, 1925, vol. vi, pt. ii, pp. 854–5.
[9] By 'political relations' in India was meant the relations of the Government of India with the Indian princely states.

years.[1] No political party in India demanded less than this and the Swarajist motion was supported by almost all the elected members of the Assembly. The Government of India, however, could not see their way to accept the motion. Yet another chance of making politics in India run on constitutional lines was missed in 1925. The deadlock continued.

The situation as Lord Irwin[2] found it when he succeeded Lord Reading[3] as Viceroy in 1926 was described by him in a letter to his friend Geoffrey Dawson:[4] 'I am always racking my brain as to how to get out of this futile and vicious circle by which we say, no advance without co-operation, and they say no co-operation without advance. I cannot help feeling that it is a question much more psychological than political. One of the extreme Swaraj people said to me the other day that if only they could trust us it wouldn't matter to them whether they waited five or fifty years. How then to make them believe that we mean what we say?'[5] Irwin had put his finger on the root of the Indian problem. But it was too late. The Swarajists had already withdrawn from the councils in despair.

The Swarajists were eager to remain in the councils. They did not want to return to the fold of their critics in the Congress as repentant sinners. The *non possumus* attitude of the authorities drove them into ploughing the barren fields of non-co-operation and obstruction—the very thing which neither they nor the Government desired. Throughout the constitutional debates of 1924–5 no feelings inimical to the British connection were expressed in the Assembly. The tone of the Swarajists, though defiant, was one of earnest appeal to the authorities to help them evolve within the Empire in a constitutional manner. It was a Motilal Nehru, painfully conscious of his defeat and humiliation, who walked out of the Assembly on March 8, 1926 saying: 'Sir, the co-

[1] Motilal Nehru even said: 'Make us masters in our own home, but whatever else is outside the home and pertains more to your Imperial interests, you are welcome to keep.' *Legislative Assembly Debates*, 1925, vol. vi, pt. ii, p. 863.

[2] Edward Frederick Lindley Wood, first Baron Irwin, and third Viscount and first Earl of Halifax (1881–1959). Under-Secretary for Colonies 1921–2; President of the Board of Education 1922–4 and 1932–5; Viceroy of India 1926–31; Secretary of State for War 1935; Lord Privy Seal 1935–7; Foreign Secretary 1938–1940; Ambassador at Washington 1941–6.

[3] Rufus Daniel Isaacs, first Marquis of Reading (1860–1935). Lord Chief Justice 1913–21; Ambassador at Washington 1918–19; Viceroy of India 1921–6; Foreign Secretary 1931.

[4] B. 1874; editor of *The Times* 1912–19 and 1923–41; d. 1944.

[5] Irwin to Dawson, May 18, 1926: cited in *The History of 'The Times'*, vol. iv, pt. ii, p. 863.

operation we offered has been contemptuously rejected and it is time for us to think of other ways to achieve our object.'[1] He meant, he said, 'no menace or threat', but was going out 'in all humility with the confession of our failure to achieve our object in this House on our lips ... to devise those sanctions which alone can compel any Government to grant the demands of the people'.[2]

At almost every session of the Congress, ever since 1920, some young enthusiasts moved a resolution demanding that the Congress should declare its goal to be complete independence outside the British Empire. The usual arguments, with which we have become familiar, were used in favour of it. But every time the Congress rejected the resolution with an overwhelming majority. There were many reasons why the Congress refused to accept the proposed change. First and foremost was the influence of Gandhi, who incessantly emphasized that *Swaraj* within the Empire was preferable to that outside the Empire, and that it would be a greater triumph for the Congress to win freedom without severing the British connection. Secondly, the Congress was still dominated by the older group of nationalists, who, in spite of all their alleged radicalism, were cautious and conservative politicians. Though anxious for a speedy attainment of self-government, they stood for ordered and peaceful progress. The British connection was something of a fetish with them. They even feared that a declaration of complete independence would give encouragement to violent and revolutionary activities in the country. The third important reason was, that the country was not, in their view, ready for such a change. Communal antagonism was becoming increasingly bitter. The country was badly divided and demoralized. Even the Congress was a house divided against itself. The Swarajists and the pure Gandhi-ites were engaged in an acrimonious controversy over tactics. In 1923 a committee appointed by the Congress to examine what changes should be made in the Congress constitution had reported that while most Congressmen individually favoured the ideal of complete independence, they were opposed to any change in the existing creed of the organization as it would narrow the Congress platform and introduce another element of controversy within its ranks.[3]

As long as Gandhi was in prison the opponents of change took shelter behind the authority of his name and views to foil the attempts of the 'Young Turks' within the Congress. Gandhi's first message to

[1] *Legislative Assembly Debates*, 1926, vol. vii, pt. iii, p. 2139.
[2] Ibid., p. 2143.   [3] *The Indian Annual Register*, 1923, Supplement, p. 114.

his countrymen on his release early in February 1924 was that they should regard Englishmen as their friends and not enemies, that their fight was against the system and not against the men administering it, and that in so far as they had failed to understand this distinction they had harmed their own cause.[1] In his presidential address to the Belgaum Congress in December 1924 he clearly defined his attitude. 'In my opinion,' Gandhi remarked, 'if the British Government mean what they say and honestly help us to equality, it would be a greater triumph than a complete severance of the British connection. I would therefore strive for *Swaraj* within the Empire but would not hesitate to sever all connection, if severance became a necessity through Britain's own fault. I would thus throw the burden of separation on the British people. The better mind of the world desires today not absolutely independent States warring one against another but a federation of friendly interdependent States. The consummation of that event may be far off. I want to make no grand claim for our country. But I see nothing grand or impossible about our expressing our readiness for universal interdependence rather than independence. It should rest with Britain to say that she will have no real alliance with India. I desire the ability to be totally independent without asserting the independence. Any scheme that I would frame, while Britain declares her goal about India to be complete equality within the Empire, would be that of alliance and not of independence without alliance. I would urge every Congressman not to be insistent on independence in each and every case, not because there is anything impossible about it, but because it is wholly unnecessary till it has become perfectly manifest that Britain really means subjugation in spite of her declaration to the contrary.'[2]

During the years 1924–6 the Swarajists were knocking at the gates of the authorities for Dominion Status with reservations. They had struck a working alliance with other parties in order to put pressure on the Government to make a forward move. Even the impatient idealists within the Congress realized that it would be inexpedient to force a change in the Congress creed at this time, for it might mean wrecking the impressive unity which the Swarajists had been able to secure. Though some of the irresponsible and irrepressible sort amongst them continued formally to move resolutions at consecutive Congress sessions, it was nothing more than a gesture of protest and impatience. By the middle of 1926 it was evident that the Swarajists had failed. The Government had refused to be coerced. Even Dominion Status

[1] Tendulkar, op. cit., vol. ii, p. 166.
[2] *Report of the Thirty-Ninth Indian National Congress*, 1924, pp. 25–6.

remained a dim, distant and doubtful prospect. The alliance of the Swarajists with other groups in the Assembly had broken down. Amongst the Swarajists themselves certain sections led by M. M. Malaviya, M. R. Jayakar[1] and N. C. Kelkar[2] had swung round to what they called 'responsive co-operation' with the Government. Communal tension showed no signs of abatement. In the elections held towards the end of 1926 the Swarajists suffered a set-back. The three years of the Swarajist experiment had been an unmitigated failure. A dangerous feeling of impatience gripped the younger and more radical elements within the Congress. If only the ideal were high enough, they thought, if only the fire of struggle burnt bright and fierce, all evil within the country would be consumed and all obstacles overcome. Socialistic and communistic ideas were gaining currency in India. Racial bitterness was increasing. The young were spoiling for a fight. The Congress, they felt, was degenerating into a debating society, only a shade different from the Liberals. The Swarajist heresy, they were convinced, had brought the Congress down to '*Babu* politics'; it must be eradicated.

At the Congress session held at Gauhati in December 1926 the radicals made a rather determined effort to get the Congress committed to complete independence and severance of the British connection. But once again Gandhi foiled their attempt. He asked the advocates of independence to tell him why they wanted the severance of the British connection. 'Have you got repugnance against the white skin?'[3] he enquired. When one of the separatists replied that the British would never grant India equality of status, Gandhi pointed out that that was totally different from rejecting British association on any terms. He accused the advocates of independence of lack of faith in human nature and in themselves. He told them that instead of thinking that the British would never undergo a change of heart it would be more honest to admit that there was no change of heart in the British because Indians were weak and undeserving. The Balfour Committee Report[4]

---

[1] B. 1873; barrister of the Bombay High Court; member of the Bombay Legislative Council 1923–5; member of the Indian Legislative Assembly 1926–30; Judge of the Federal Court of India 1937–9; member of the judicial committee of the Privy Council 1939–41; Vice-Chancellor of Poona University 1948–56; d. 1959.
[2] B. 1872; a close associate of Tilak, and editor of the *Kesari* and the *Mahratta*; d. 1947.   [3] *Times of India*, December 30, 1926.
[4] Report of the Inter-Imperial Relations Committee set up by the Imperial Conference of 1926 under the chairmanship of the first Earl of Balfour, which defined the status of the Dominions. See below, p. 235.

and General Hertzog's[1] satisfaction with the results of the Imperial Conference of 1926 had added strength to Gandhi's elbow. He told the separatists that between Britain and the Dominions there was a partnership at will on terms of equality. 'Take the instance', he remarked, 'of South Africa. There is that haughty nation, the Dutch Boers. Even they do not bring in such a resolution. General Hertzog has returned from London completely converted, knowing that if he wants to declare independence today, he can get it. I shall not be satisfied with any constitution that we may get from the British Parliament unless it leaves that power with us also, so that if we choose to declare our independence we could do so.'[2] In an article in *Young India* on January 13, 1927, Gandhi again chastised the advocates of independence and demolished their arguments more effectively.[3]

While Gandhi was busy trying to keep his unruly followers in check, the British Government unwittingly offered the latter a real boon in the form of the Simon Commission[4] of 1927. Amidst the atmosphere of universal indignation aroused in India by the appointment of an all-white Commission, the radical idealists, led by Jawaharlal Nehru, found it easy to make the Congress at its Madras session in December 1927 pass a resolution declaring 'the goal of the Indian people to be Complete National Independence'.[5] It was their reply, they said, to 'the arrogant and insulting challenge' thrown down by Lord Birkenhead. The creed of the Congress, as defined by the constitution of 1920, remained unchanged, but the separatists had now unfurled their banner.

Gandhi[6] was very angry. He denounced the resolution as 'ill-conceived'.[7] 'Do men conceive their goals in order to oblige people and to resent their action?'[8] he asked. 'My ambition', he wrote, 'is much higher than independence. Through the deliverance of India, I seek to deliver the so-called weaker races of the earth from the crushing heels of Western exploitation in which England is the greatest partner. If

[1] James Barry Munnik Hertzog (1866–1942), Prime Minister of South Africa 1924–39. [2] *Times of India*, December 30, 1926.
[3] 'Independence', *Young India*, January 13, 1927.
[4] The Statutory Commission, appointed in accordance with the provisions of the Government of India Act, 1919, to review the working of constitutional reforms in India, with Sir John Simon, MP, as its Chairman.
[5] *The Indian Quarterly Register*, 1927, vol. ii, p. 380.
[6] Gandhi had not taken any part in shaping Congress policy at the Madras session. He was absent from the meeting of the Working Committee which accepted Jawaharlal Nehru's resolution. Motilal Nehru was away in England.
[7] Tendulkar, op. cit., vol. ii, p. 402.
[8] 'Independence v. Swaraj', *Young India*, January 12, 1928.

India converts, as it can convert, Englishmen, it can become the predominant partner in a world commonwealth of which England can have the privilege of becoming a partner if she chooses. . . . This is big talk I know. For a fallen India to aspire to move the world and protect weaker races is seemingly an impertinence. But in explaining my strong opposition to this cry for independence, I can no longer hide the light under a bushel. Mine is an ambition worth living for and worth dying for. In no case do I want to reconcile myself to a state lower than the best for fear of consequences. It is, therefore, not out of expediency that I oppose independence as my goal.'[1]

Ever since 1906 Congressmen had been debating whether India should strive for *Swaraj* within or without the British Empire. *Swaraj* remained as distant as ever, but (or because of it?) the academic controversy over the ideal became increasingly sharper. For nationalism the banner is as important as the forward march. The 1927 Congress, in passing the resolution on independence, had done what Gandhi had so far successfully resisted—it had fixed an abstract label on the national struggle and turned that label into a test for patriots. Its unfortunate results were soon evident in India. Into that land of discord it introduced yet another element of fierce and passionate controversy. Throughout the succeeding two years India was torn by what came to be known as the Dominion Status-*versus*-Independence controversy. It pursued the deliberations of the All-Parties Conference and even threatened to split the Congress. We cannot afford to follow the controversy in the various camps and in all its details and shall content ourselves with noting its essential features.

The 1927 session of the Congress at Madras, which declared 'the goal of the Indian people to be Complete National Independence', also decided to co-operate with other political parties in India in order to frame a *Swaraj* constitution for the country. An All-Parties Conference was organized for this purpose. This Conference appointed a committee, presided over by Motilal Nehru, to draft a constitution for India. The report of this committee—commonly known as the Nehru Report—recommended a constitution for India on the lines of the self-governing Dominions, drawing heavily on the Irish model. Only on the basis of the ideal of Dominion Status, said the Report, was 'the maximum degree of agreement obtainable amongst the parties in India'.[2] It, however, emphasized that Dominion Status was viewed 'not

[1] *Young India*, January 12, 1928.
[2] *All-Parties Conference: Report of Committee* (1928), p. 25.

as a remote stage of our evolution but as the next immediate step'.[1] The advocates of independence opposed the ideal of Dominion Status at every stage of the deliberations of the All-Parties Conference. They even organized Independence Leagues to propagate their creed. The Nehru Report, while it accepted the ideal of Dominion Status as being 'the greatest common factor of agreement among the well recognized political parties in India',[2] had allowed any individual or party which believed in independence to work for it. Motilal Nehru and the older leaders of the Congress were anxious that the Congress should approve of the Report *in toto* if it was to carry any force behind it. In their view Dominion Status had 'come to mean something indistinguishable from independence except for the link with the Crown'.[3] Secondly, because 'the maximum degree of agreement was only obtainable on this basis',[4] Dominion Status was, in their view, preferable to a theoretically higher ideal of independence. Thirdly, in order that the precarious alliance with other political groups in the country, especially the Liberals, might not be disrupted, and also in order that the Report might receive a sympathetic consideration from the authorities, it was considered prudent and safe not to aim too high.

The viewpoint of the 'Independence-wallahs' was best presented by Jawaharlal Nehru during the year 1928 from various platforms.[5] He condemned Dominion Status as a timid and uninspiring ideal. It could not be the rallying cry of a militant and revolutionary nationalism. Instead of encouraging the spirit of struggle, suffering and sacrifice, it damped that spirit where it existed and prompted men to seek the easy, sheltered paths of compromise and submission. The advocates of Dominion Status believed and encouraged others to believe that their objective could be won by sweet reasonableness and logic. This was a great delusion. The national demand would have to be backed by force, by sanctions devised through mass organization and mass action. The votaries of Dominion Status retarded the cause of national freedom, instead of advancing it, for they encouraged the false belief that such sanctions were not necessary.

In attacking the ideal of Dominion Status, Jawaharlal Nehru in fact attacked the reformist psychology of the Liberals and of moderate Congressmen. He accused them of having no vision of a new India.

[1] *All-Parties Conference: Report of Committee* (1928), p. 1.
[2] Ibid.   [3] Ibid.   [4] Ibid., p. 25.
[5] For the speeches of Jawaharlal Nehru in 1928 on the issue see R. Dwivedi, *The Life and Speeches of Pandit Jawaharlal Nehru* (1929), pp. 67–181; *The Indian Quarterly Register*, 1928, vol. i, pp. 401–5, 416–20; *The Indian Quarterly Register*, 1928, vol. ii, pp. 22, 33–5, 437–8, 453, 458–64.

Those who thought in terms of Dominion Status, he said, wanted only an Indianization of the administration—the substitution of the brown in place of the white rulers, while retaining intact the existing political, social and economic order. Independence stood, he claimed, for a new state and a new society—democratic and socialistic. Indians could not, he argued, do away with landlords, princes and capitalists while maintaining the British connection. He also feared that Dominion Status, though it might give India a larger measure of political liberty, would keep her economically tied with a thousand strings to British capitalism.

Jawaharlal Nehru considered the very idea of a vast and ancient country like India remaining a Dominion of England to be ridiculous and humiliating. He did not believe in reforming imperialism by entering into a partnership with it. The British Commonwealth, in spite of its high-sounding name, he pointed out, did not stand for true international co-operation. It was an exclusive system whose membership would deprive India of the freedom to develop contacts with the world at large, especially with the other countries of Asia. He did not stand for a narrow, isolated nationalism, but he felt that a true commonwealth of nations could not grow out of the British Empire.

British foreign policy, especially as witnessed in Britain's dealings with countries in the Middle East and with China, came in for severe criticism at the hands of Indian nationalists. Jawaharlal Nehru denounced Britain as the greatest enemy of national freedom, of disarmament and peace throughout the world. One of his great objections to Dominion Status was that it would mean the involvement of India in the reactionary foreign policy of Great Britain. As early as 1927-8 he had begun feeling that 'imperialism' was preparing for a war. He believed that a firm and unequivocal declaration on the part of India that she would not allow her manpower and resources to be exploited for waging 'an imperialist war' might have a restraining influence on British policy. He attacked the Nehru Report for postulating a joint foreign policy for India and Great Britain.

Jawaharlal Nehru considered Great Britain to be 'the arch-priest of imperialism'[1] and India the pivot of her imperial policy. In order to retain her hold on India, Britain had subjugated the other parts of Africa and Asia. Indian soldiers had been used to do 'the dirty work of British imperialism'.[2] The independence of India would be a deathblow to British imperialism and the signal for the liberation of other oppressed nationalities.

[1] Dwivedi, op. cit., p. 146.   [2] Ibid., p. 101.

The idea that the Congress, having declared complete independence as its objective at Madras in 1927, should, as a matter of expediency, accept the ideal of Dominion Status was highly distasteful to Jawaharlal Nehru. He told his elders at the Calcutta Congress in December 1928 that if they were 'prepared to pull down the flag of independence' they must give him and men of his thinking 'the liberty to hold on to that flag'.[1] 'This is a vital issue', he said, 'and we feel with regard to it that there can be no compromise. It is a matter with us of the deepest conviction, it is a matter with us of what we think is the honour of the country....'[2] And he warned that the issue might lead to a fratricidal struggle similar to that which tore Ireland after the conclusion of the treaty of 1921.

Jawaharlal Nehru, however, always took care to emphasize that their struggle was not directed against England or the English people. 'Our quarrel is not with the people of England but with the imperialism of England,'[3] he said. 'The day England sheds her imperialism', he affirmed, 'we shall gladly co-operate with her.'[4] India could have no truck with British imperialism. Nor could she have 'a real measure of freedom within the limits of the British Empire'.[5] 'Before a new bridge is built', he insisted, 'on the basis of friendship and co-operation, the present chains which tie us to England must be severed. Only then can real co-operation take place.'[6]

The Dominion Status-*versus*-Independence controversy in 1928-9 was but a symptom of the deeper schism within the Congress. It was conflict between palsied age and fiery youth, between an upper-middle-class leadership and a lower-middle-class following within the organization. A wave of leftist ideas was rolling forward in India. Youth Leagues, Volunteer Corps, and Independence Leagues were being organized all over the country. The Soviet Union, China, Turkey and Egypt attracted the attention of younger men. More and more young Congressmen began to drift away from pure Gandhi-ism and call themselves socialists and communists. Even secret revolutionary and terrorist societies grew up. The communists exploited the industrial unrest in the country. The Congress old guard became more than ever anxious for a settlement with the Government. The Viceroy, Lord Irwin, had by the force of his character and the sincerity and nobility of his utterances held out hope. It was encouraged by the remark of

---

[1] *The Indian Quarterly Register*, 1928, vol. ii, p. 34.
[2] Ibid.   [3] Dwivedi, op. cit., p. 137.   [4] Ibid., p. 146.
[5] Ibid., p. 104.   [6] Ibid., p. 95.

Ramsay MacDonald[1] at the British Commonwealth Labour Conference on July 2, 1928: 'I hope that, within a period of few months rather than years, there will be a new Dominion added to the Commonwealth of our Nations, a Dominion that will find self-respect as an equal within this Commonwealth. I refer to India.'[2] Gandhi was not very happy with the young radicals within the Congress. In preference to Jawaharlal Nehru and Vallabhbhai Patel,[3] he put 'the crown of thorns'—the presidentship of the Congress—on the head of Motilal Nehru, considering him to be an influence for conciliation—'an eminently worthy ambassador of a nation that is in need of and in the mood to take an honourable compromise'.[4] 'Let the impatient youth of the country wait a while,'[5] he remarked. When 'the impatient youth' threatened to reject the Dominion Status ideal of the Nehru Report at the Calcutta Congress in December 1928, Gandhi used all his personal influence and persuasive skill in favour of that ideal. The radicals demanded that the Congress should launch a campaign of civil disobedience at once. Gandhi requested them to wait at least for two years. With great difficulty a compromise was arrived at which postponed the launching of a mass civil disobedience campaign by twelve months, during which the British Government was required to accept the Nehru Report as a constitution for India. Gandhi did his best to take the sting out of the ultimatum. He appealed to the authorities not to treat the resolution as a threat, but as an address. 'If there is the slightest trace of a change of heart of the Government they will understand it as the yearning of a nation which is trying to throw off thraldom,'[6] he remarked. 'If the Viceroy', he added, 'is a worthy representative of his King and his nation, he will take note of this resolution even though it does not contain the clause which I should have liked to be inserted.'[7] Gandhi cancelled his proposed visit to Europe in 1929 and waited in faith and hope.

The Viceroy did not disappoint Gandhi. As 'a worthy representative

---

[1] B. 1866; MP 1906; visited India twice, in 1909 and 1912; Prime Minister 1924, 1929–31 and 1931–5; d. 1937.

[2] *The Indian Quarterly Register*, 1928, vol. ii, p. 293.

[3] B. 1875; called to the Bar 1913; practised at Ahmedabad; President of the Indian National Congress 1931; Deputy Prime Minister of India from 1947 till his death in 1950.

[4] 'Crown of Thorns', *Young India*, July 26, 1928.   [5] Ibid.

[6] *The Indian Quarterly Register*, 1928, vol. ii, p. 42.

[7] Ibid., p. 43. Gandhi wanted a clause to be introduced into the resolution to the effect that a copy of the resolution, along with the Nehru Report, should be sent to the Viceroy.

of his King and his nation', he rightly understood his 'double duty', to see that the King's Government was carried on and to serve as an intermediary between India and Great Britain.[1] The story of his visit to England in mid-1929 and the famous announcement which he made on his return on October 31, 1929, has been told by Irwin himself and many others[2] and need not be repeated here. After stating that His Majesty's Government would meet representatives of British India and the Indian states for securing the greatest possible measure of agreement for the final proposals to be submitted to Parliament, Irwin declared that he had been 'authorized on behalf of His Majesty's Government to state clearly that in their judgement it is implicit in the declaration of 1917 that the natural issue of India's constitutional progress, as there contemplated, is the attainment of Dominion Status'.[3]

Irwin's declaration revived trust and hope. Though the younger Congressmen were suspicious of this 'ingeniously worded announcement, which could mean much or very little',[4] Gandhi and his senior lieutenants welcomed it. To friends in England, who wrote to Gandhi to reciprocate the gesture of the Labour Government, he replied that he was 'dying for co-operation'. 'My non-co-operation', he wrote, 'is a token of my earnest longing for real heart co-operation in place of co-operation falsely so called. . . . I can wait for the Dominion Status constitution, if I can get the real Dominion Status in action, if today there is a real change of heart, a real desire on the part of the British people to see India a free and self-respecting nation and on the part of the officials in India a true spirit of service.'[5] The Congress, in association with the Liberals, issued a manifesto offering to co-operate in drafting a Dominion constitution if certain acts were done and certain points clarified. The signatories to the manifesto interpreted Irwin's announcement to convey that the proposed Round Table Conference was 'to meet not to discuss when Dominion Status is to be established, but to frame a scheme of Dominion constitution for India'.[6] Though the President-elect of the forthcoming Congress session, Jawaharlal Nehru, allowed himself 'to be talked into signing'[7] the manifesto, a

---

[1] See Irwin's address to the members of the Legislative Assembly on January 28, 1929: *Legislative Assembly Debates*, 1929, vol. i, p. 8.

[2] Halifax, *Fulness of Days* (1957); J. Coatman, *Years of Destiny* (1932); A Campbell-Johnson, *Viscount Halifax* (1941); S. Gopal, *The Viceroyalty of Lord Irwin* (1957).   [3] *The Times*, November 1, 1929.

[4] J. Nehru, *An Autobiography* (1942 ed.), p. 195.

[5] Tendulkar, op. cit., vol. ii, p. 502.

[6] *The Times*, November 4, 1929.

[7] J. Nehru, *An Autobiography*, p. 197.

section of the extremists, led by Subhas Chandra Bose,[1] refused to support it. But still it was a remarkable achievement that the Congress and the Government should have come so near to each other.

Irwin's statement raised a storm of protest in England. The prolonged and severe post-mortem conducted by Parliament brought back the old suspicions in India. Congress leaders sought an assurance from the Viceroy that the sole function of the proposed conference would be to frame a Dominion constitution for India. Irwin, more cautious than ever because of the fierce attacks being made on him in England, could not give any such assurance. Congress leaders, thereupon, withdrew their support of Irwin's declaration.

The Congress assembled at Lahore towards the end of December 1929 and, according to schedule, declared the Nehru Report to have lapsed and unfurled the flag of independence. At the stroke of midnight on December 31st it passed a resolution, with barely a score of persons, out of many thousands, dissenting, which defined the word '*Swaraj*' in the Congress constitution to mean 'Complete Independence'.[2] It considered that nothing was to be gained 'in the existing circumstances' by the Congress being represented at the proposed Round Table Conference, and decided to prepare for launching a civil disobedience campaign.[3]

Did the Congress at Lahore in voting for complete independence also vote for the severance of all connection with the British Commonwealth? Professor Coupland thought it did.[4] The facts, however, would not support his conclusion. The resolution passed by the Lahore Congress in 1929 simply declared that 'the word "*Swaraj*" in Article I of the Congress Constitution shall mean Complete Independence'.[5] It said nothing about the British connection. Nor did it define what complete independence meant. In fact, an attempt made to do so was foiled by Gandhi. Subhas Chandra Bose moved an amendment to the resolution, proposing, among other things, the addition of a rider to complete independence—'implying thereby complete severance of the British connection'.[6] Bose's amendment was vigorously opposed

---

[1] B. 1897; President of the Indian National Congress 1938 and 1939; escaped to Germany 1942; formed the Indian National Army 1943; died in an air crash 1945.
[2] *The Indian Quarterly Register*, 1929, vol. ii, p. 300.   [3] Ibid.
[4] 'Thus the Congress had accepted Pandit Jawaharlal Nehru's view that India must sever all connexion with the British Commonwealth.' R. Coupland, *The Indian Problem*, p. 100.
[5] *The Indian Quarterly Register*, 1929, vol. ii, p. 300.   [6] Ibid, p. 302.

by Gandhi, and the Congress—agreeing with Gandhi—rejected it with an overwhelming majority. The clever Mahatma had once again confounded the radicals. The latter were to have nothing but their pound of flesh. Gandhi satisfied their clamour for complete independence but did not allow them to get the Congress committed to secession from the British Commonwealth.

There were three main groups within the Congress at the Lahore session.[1] On the right stood a powerful section of the old guard, led by M. M. Malaviya, Sarojini Naidu,[2] N. C. Kelkar and M. A. Ansari,[3] which pleaded for caution and delay. It suggested that there should be no change in the party's creed until another all-party conference considered the matter again. Its position was extremely weak in the open session of the Congress, but it showed surprising strength in the Subjects Committee.[4] On the extreme left stood the radicals, led by Subhas Chandra Bose, who wanted a total break under any conditions. They pressed for a more radical programme of action, including the establishment of a parallel government in India. In the centre was Gandhi, supported by the elder Nehru and the other faithfuls, determined to fulfil the pledge taken at Calcutta in 1928, but equally determined that the struggle should be disciplined and peaceful, and that the door of honourable compromise should not be closed. It was Gandhi who secured an overwhelming victory at the Lahore session of the Congress. And inasmuch as Gandhi triumphed, we are safe to conclude that the Congress only voted for independence and not for secession at Lahore in 1929.

This conclusion is further confirmed by the future behaviour of Gandhi and the Congress. Soon after the Lahore Congress Gandhi wrote: '... the independence resolution need frighten nobody. I had repeatedly declared that for me, as for all other Congressmen, Dominion Status could mean only virtual independence; that is partnership at will for mutual benefit and to be dissolved at the instance of either partner.'[5] In a letter to Irwin on March 4, 1930, Gandhi assured him to the same

[1] For the proceedings of the Lahore session see ibid., pp. 286–311, and the *Times of India*, December 27–31, 1929.
[2] B. 1879; poetess and politician; President of the Indian National Congress 1925; Governor of the United Provinces 1947–9; d. 1949.
[3] B. 1880; medical practitioner at Delhi; President of the All-India Muslim League 1920, of the Indian National Congress 1927, and of the All-Parties Conference 1928; d. 1936.
[4] Malaviya's amendment secured 77 votes against 114 in the Subjects Committee.
[5] *Speeches and Writings of Mahatma Gandhi* (1933 ed.), p. 734.

effect.[1] The Viceroy wrote to the King on March 13, 1931, that he was sure that Gandhi wanted to find the way to peace and that it was 'definitely untrue to suggest, as I see it suggested from time to time, that he [Gandhi] is out to break the unity of Your Majesty's Empire'.[2] Irwin communicated to the King what Gandhi had told him, that in his view 'the highest form' of complete independence for India was the one that could be attained 'in association with Great Britain'.[3]

A resolution passed by the next session of the Congress held at Karachi in March 1931 contemplated the maintenance of the British connection, with 'the right to either party to end the partnership at will'.[4] It was this resolution which Gandhi carried with him as the 'mandate' of the Congress when he went to attend the second session of the Round Table Conference later in 1931. At the Conference he clearly stated that what the Congress desired was not secession from the British Commonwealth, but only freedom to secede. 'If we are intent upon complete independence,' Gandhi remarked, 'it is not from any sense of arrogance; it is not because we want to parade before the universe that we have now severed all connection with the British people. Nothing of the kind. On the contrary, you will find in this mandate itself that the Congress contemplates a partnership—the Congress contemplates a connection with the British people—but that connection to be such as can exist between two absolute equals.'[5] 'Time

---

[1] 'But the resolution of Independence should cause no alarm if the word "Dominion Status", mentioned in your announcement, has been used in its accepted sense. For has it not been admitted by responsible British statesmen that Dominion Status is virtual Independence?' Ibid., p. 739.

[2] H. Nicolson, *King George the Fifth* (1952), p. 508.

[3] Gandhi told Irwin: 'I want to see India established in her own self-respect and in the respect of the world. I therefore want to see India able to discuss with Great Britain on terms of equality, and Great Britain willing to discuss with India on such terms. I know perfectly well that we want British help in many things for a long time yet—defence, administration and so on—and I am prepared to have safeguards, or as I prefer to call them, adjustments, provided these are really in the interests of India and you will allow us to discuss them with you on equal terms. If we can reach agreement on those lines, I shall be satisfied that I have got *Purna Swaraj* or *complete independence*, and India will have got it in what to me is the highest form in which it can be attained, namely, in association with Great Britain. But if Great Britain will not help me in this way, and if this achievement in partnership cannot be brought about, then I must pursue my end of *Purna Swaraj* or *complete independence* in isolation from Great Britain, and this I definitely regard as the second best.' Ibid. [4] *Times of India*, March 30, 1931.

[5] Indian Round Table Conference, Second Session, September 7–December 1, 1931. *Proceedings of the Federal Structure Committee and Minorities Committee* (1932), p. 17.

was', he added, 'when I prided myself on being, and being called, a British subject. I have ceased for many years to call myself a British subject; I would far rather be called a rebel than a subject. But I have aspired—I still aspire—to be a citizen, not in the Empire, but in a Commonwealth; in a partnership if possible—if God wills it an indissoluble partnership—but not a partnership superimposed upon one nation by another. Hence you find here that the Congress claims that either party should have the right to sever the connection, to dissolve the partnership.'[1] As for the words 'Dominion Status' or 'complete independence', he did not care. 'Call it by any name you like,' he remarked, 'a rose will smell as sweet by another name, but it must be the rose of liberty that I want and not the artificial product.'[2]

By 1928-9 Motilal Nehru and Gandhi had realized that they had had their innings. Conscious of the hiatus between themselves and the younger generation and convinced that the battle of the future would have to be fought by younger men, they decided that it would be better if the latter began to take responsibilities in the presence of their elders.[3] It was an extremely wise decision. The transference of power to new hands was made in 1929 and the recipient was carefully chosen. The crown of the Congress was placed on the head of Jawaharlal Nehru. He was known to be rash, impetuous and extremist, but Gandhi judged correctly that responsibility would mellow and sober him, and take the edge of his extreme leftism. At the Lahore session in 1929 Jawaharlal Nehru occupied a position somewhere between the majority group led by Gandhi and Motilal Nehru and the more irrespressible and irresponsible radicals led by Subhas Chandra Bose who were anxious for a complete break with Britain. He declared himself 'a socialist and a republican'[4] and remarked: 'Independence for us means complete freedom from British domination and British imperialism. Having attained our freedom, I have no doubt that India will welcome all attempts at world co-operation and federation, and will even agree to give up part of her own independence to a larger group of which she is an equal member.'[5] He reiterated his opposition to Dominion Status, but left the door open to friendship with Britain: 'India could never be

[1] *Proceedings of the Federal Structure Committee and Minorities Committee* (1932), p. 17.
[2] Indian Round Table Conference, Second Session, September 7–December 1, 1931. *Proceedings*, Cmd. 3997 (1932), p. 393.
[3] See J. Nehru, *A Bunch of Old Letters* (1958), pp. 58, 61–2; and Tendulkar, op. cit., vol. ii, pp. 488–90.
[4] J. Nehru, *India and the World* (1936), p. 27.   [5] Ibid., p. 23.

an equal member of the Commonwealth unless imperialism and all it implies is discarded.'[1] Jawaharlal Nehru was the most internationally-minded of Congressmen. Not only was he free from narrow nationalism, he had no bitterness against the British people as such.[2] As he wrote a little later: 'All my predilections (apart from the political plane) are in favour of England and the English people, and if I have become what is called an uncompromising opponent of British rule in India, it is almost in spite of myself.'[3]

The second leader whom Gandhi chose to preside over the Congress session at Karachi in March 1931 was Vallabhbhai Patel. Cool, calculating and conservative, Patel was almost the exact opposite of Jawaharlal Nehru. He lacked the latter's idealism and international outlook. But he was gifted with a strong sense of realism which made him recognize the many practical advantages which India could derive from her continued association with the Commonwealth. In his presidential address to the Karachi Congress, Patel made it clear that complete independence did not mean, 'was not intended to mean, a churlish refusal to associate with Britain', and that it did 'not exclude the possibility of equal partnership for mutual benefit, and dissolvable at the will of either party'.[4] He referred to 'a strong body of opinion [in India] to the effect that before a partnership [with Britain] could possibly be conceived there must be a period of complete dissociation' and remarked, 'I do not belong to that school.'[5]

This choice of good leaders was yet another service that Gandhi rendered to India and the Commonwealth. Lieutenant-Commander Kenworthy[6] had remarked in the House of Commons on February 14, 1922: 'Gandhi has been abused by everyone, including, of course, the Secretary of State for India. . . . I think the time may come when we shall rather congratulate ourselves on having a man of Gandhi's eminence with the ideas which he apparently possesses. It may be fortunate that the agitation in India is led by a Gandhi and not by a De

---

[1] *India and the World* (1936), p. 24.
[2] 'Anger and resentment have often filled my mind at various happenings, and yet as I sit here [in prison], and look deep into my mind and heart, I do not find any anger against England or the English people.' J. Nehru, *An Autobiography*, p. 418.
[3] Ibid, p. 419.
[4] *Congress Presidential Addresses*, second series (1935), p. 907.
[5] Ibid.
[6] Joseph Montague Kenworthy, tenth Baron Strabolgi (1886–1953). Served in the Royal Navy 1902–19; MP 1919–31; left Liberal for Labour Party 1926; succeeded to the title 1934.

Valera.'[1] The truth of Kenworthy's prophetic remark was vindicated twenty-five years later in his own lifetime.

[1] 150 H.C. Deb. 5s. cols. 936–7. Éamon De Valéra, b. 1882; Commandant in the National Uprising 1916; President of the Irish Republic 1919–22; rejected the Anglo-Irish Treaty 1922; President of the Executive Council of the Irish Free State 1932–7; Taoiseach (Head of the Government) 1937–48, 1951–4 and 1957–9; President of Ireland since 1959.

IV

THE NATIONAL LIBERAL FEDERATION OF INDIA AND THE COMMONWEALTH

'Rally the Moderates' had been the watchword of Morley and Minto. So was it of Montagu and Chelmsford. It was not so much the clamour of the radicals as the friendly pressure of the moderate and sober elements in India which had persuaded the authorities to make the declaration of August 20, 1917. The Montagu-Chelmsford reform proposals were also framed in close consultation with the leading Moderates within the Congress. Some of the latter, such as S. P. Sinha, B. N. Basu and S. Nair, were already in the inner councils of the Government. Others, like Srinivasa Sastri, T. B. Sapru,[1] C. Y. Chintamani[2] and C. H. Setalvad,[3] were taken by Montagu into his confidence and told of the proposed scheme of reforms.[4] They were evidently not pleased with the scheme, for they felt that it did not go far enough and would not satisfy the country. But they were all profoundly impressed with Montagu's personality, his honesty, earnestness and sincerity of purpose. They found him extremely sympathetic and determined to do his very best for India. And, above all, they were made to recognize the immense difficulties under which the Secretary of State was labouring—a coalition government in England, the danger of encountering opposition from Curzon and Milner in the Cabinet, the known antipathy of the Government of India to any weakening of central authority, and the already pronounced hostility of the civil services and Anglo-India circles, both in England and India, to any

[1] B. 1875; advocate of the Allahabad High Court; Law Member of Viceroy's council 1920–3; President of the National Liberal Federation of India 1923 and 1927; d. 1949.
[2] B. 1880; editor of the *Leader* (Allahabad); member of the United Provinces Legislative Council 1916–23 and 1927–36; Minister in the U.P. Government 1921–3; President of the National Liberal Federation of India 1920 and 1931; d. 1941.
[3] B. 1866; advocate of the Bombay High Court; Minister in the Bombay Government 1921–3; President of the National Liberal Federation of India 1928 and 1937; d. 1947.
[4] See Montagu, op. cit., pp. 163, 236, 274.

sweeping reforms. The Moderates were, in effect, told to be realistic and not to look at the shortcomings of the first instalment, but to ask 'whether it led assuredly to self-government'.[1] Reasonable and loyal as the Moderates were, they decided to make the most of whatever was attainable under the circumstances and, in any case, not to let the Secretary of State down, for, if they were only half-converted to his scheme, they had become full converts to Montagu himself.[2]

Montagu was conscious of the fact that his scheme fell 'far short of the circumstances of the country',[3] that it stood 'no chance of public acceptance'[4] and would be 'none too popular with the extremists'.[5] He was, therefore, anxious to secure in advance the support of the Moderates, the more so in order to convince the Cabinet and Parliament that the scheme would be worked by at least some party in India. This did not prove to be very difficult, for the Moderates were themselves willing to be wooed. They were already feeling uneasy within the Congress, where the Extremists were busy displacing 'these old-stagers', as they called them, from their positions of influence within the organization, or making the pace too hot for those who had managed to survive their iconoclastic fervour. The Moderates realized that in order to save themselves and the reforms—for the Extremists were a threat to both—it was necessary to break away from the Extremists and accept the reforms gracefully. While Montagu was still in India, he had assured himself that the Moderates would support the reforms, secede from the Congress—were, in fact, already doing so—form a party of their own, run their own newspapers, send a deputation to England to support him, and would be, in their turn, supported by the Government of India.[6]

On February 19, 1918, Srinivasa Satsri's weekly paper, the *Servant of India*, made its first appearance. It enunciated its policy in the words borrowed from the late M. G. Ranade: 'Liberalism and moderation will be our watchwords. The spirit of Liberalism implies a freedom from race and creed prejudices and a steady devotion to all that seeks to do justice between man and man, giving to the rulers the loyalty that is due to the law they are bound to administer, but securing at the same time to the people the equality which is their right under the law. Moderation implies the conditions of never vainly aspiring after the

---

[1] Montagu, op. cit., p. 119.
[2] See C. P. Ramaswami Aiyer, 'Montagu: A Personal Tribute', *Indian Review*, January 1925, pp. 73–6.
[3] Montagu, op. cit., p. 236.   [4] Ibid., p. 248.   [5] Ibid., p. 55.
[6] Ibid., pp. 71, 104, 133–4, 217, 236, 363.

impossible or after too remote ideals, but striving each day to take the next step in the order of natural growth by doing the work that lies nearest to our hands in a spirit of compromise and fairness.'[1] Here was the creed of the Indian Moderates put in a nutshell. Even before the Montagu-Chelmsford Report was published, the Moderates had begun canvassing support for it.[2] Attempts were already being made to organize a separate party of the Moderates. For instance, as early as November 10, 1917, Prithwis Chandra Ray[3] had written a letter to Moderate Congressmen throughout India, saying: 'In co-operation with some very influential friends, I am making a serious effort to find out if there is, in any quarter, any particular desire to establish a moderate organization, and, if so, on what lines it should be founded. It is proposed to hold an informal conference of leading moderate politicians of all India sometime during the next Christmas holiday to discuss the advisability of such an organization and to take such steps as may be necessary in consequence of its decision.'[4] Ray had emphasized that the time had come for establishing such an organization in view of 'the fact that the moderate party had been swept off the field of politics by a new broom' and the Congress and all its machinery had 'practically been captured by the extremist party'.[5] In June 1918 a National Liberal League was actually organized in Bengal, with S. N. Banerjea as its President. Its declared objective was 'the attainment of responsible government [for India] as an integral part of the British Empire by methodical and ordered progress'.[6] The contention of the Moderates later, that they were scared by the manner in which the Extremists reacted to the Montagu-Chelmsford Report into abstaining from the Congress and into forming an organization of their own, is hardly borne out by the facts. Their minds were, in truth, already made up.

When the Report was published on July 8, 1918, the Moderates, though they urged improvements, welcomed the reform proposals contained therein as a real and substantial step towards self-government and a sympathetic and honest attempt to give effect to the declara-

---

[1] Cited in *Indian Review*, February 1918, p. 155.
[2] See C. R. Das, *India for Indians* (1921), pp. 125-6.
[3] B. 1870; editor of the *Indian World* 1905-14 and of the *Bengalee* 1921-4; 'founder' of the National Liberal League, Bengal 1918.
[4] Cited in Stanley A. Wolpert, *Tilak and Gokhale: Revolution and Reform in the Making of Modern India* (1962), p. 286.
[5] Ibid.
[6] *Englishman*, June 13, 1918.

tion of August 20, 1917.¹ They boycotted the special session of the Congress called to consider the Report and decided to summon a conference of their own. While the Congress subjected the Montagu-Chelmsford scheme of reforms to severe criticism and pronounced it 'disappointing and unsatisfactory', a resolution moved by S. N. Banerjea, welcoming it as 'a genuine effort and a definite advance',² was passed in the Imperial Legislative Council on September 7, 1918, by an overwhelming majority of 46 to 2. The first All-India Moderates' Conference, which met at Bombay on November 1 and 3, 1918, expressed its 'cordial welcome', 'hearty support' and 'grateful appreciation' of the reform proposals 'as constituting a distinct advance on present conditions' and 'a real and substantial step towards the progressive realization of responsible government'.³ It, however, suggested certain 'necessary modifications and improvements therein'.⁴ They were: the introduction of the principle of responsibility in the Government of India; half the members of the proposed Council of State to be elective; the power of certification by the Governor-General to be limited to matters concerning defence, foreign affairs, relations with the Indian states, peace and order; half the members of the Viceroy's executive council to be Indians; and the grant of fiscal autonomy to India.⁵

S. N. Banerjea, as President of the Conference, defined the Moderate creed as 'co-operate when we can; criticize when we must'.⁶ He spoke of 'the change, the profound change in the spirit and policy of the Government'⁷ and remarked that the period of propagandism was over and that of reconstruction had begun. While he appealed to the people to rally to the support of the scheme, he warned the authorities of the grave consequences of any undue delay in the enactment of the reforms or any attempt to whittle them down. 'We have endeavoured', he said, 'to do our duty. The Government must fulfil its part.'⁸ The Moderates sent a strong delegation to England which, while urging modifications, vigorously supported the scheme before the Joint Select Committee in 1919 and had the satisfaction of getting it improved in certain respects.

The Government of India had written to the Secretary of State on March 5, 1919, that the Moderates represented 'the ablest and most

---

[1] For Indian reactions to the Montagu-Chelmsford Report see S. Satyamurti (ed.), *The Montagu-Chelmsford Reform Proposals* (1918).
[2] *Proceedings of the Indian Legislative Council*, 1918–19, vol. lvii, p. 93.
[3] *Times of India*, November 4, 1918.
[4] Ibid.   [5] Ibid.   [6] Ibid., November 2, 1918.   [7] Ibid.   [8] Ibid.

respected Indian opinion'.[1] 'Ablest' it certainly was, but it is doubtful if it was the 'most respected'. The Moderates were men of political wisdom and experience. They stood for circumspection, balance, sense and ordered progress. But they were no longer the type from which Indian public opinion was busy choosing its popular idols. *The Times* had suggested that meeting in a conference was not enough, the Moderates must 'bestir themselves' and, if they wished for political power, 'they must struggle against their opponents'.[2] Energy, activity and fighting quality were not, however, the strong points of the Moderates. At best they could sail in fair weather with the wind provided by a generous and liberal government. But the post-war weather in India was by no means fair and the Government of India's primary task of governing had not in any way been lightened by doing what they considered to be the maximum possible in the direction of reforms. Scarcity, high prices, a devastating influenza epidemic, Muslim uneasiness about Turkey and the Khilafat, and the slow process of lawmaking at Westminster were hardly conducive to the growth of moderation in India. The passage of the ill-timed Rowlatt Act, despite protests by the Moderates, exposed their position and shook their prestige. While official opinion lamented that the Moderates lacked backbone and had failed the very first 'test', the Moderates felt that the ground underneath their feet was being cut by the unwisdom of the Government. And then, in April 1919 came the Amritsar incident which put the reforms and the Moderates into the dark shade from which they never emerged.

When the second Moderates' Conference met at Calcutta on December 30, 1919, the Reform Act had been passed and the King-Emperor's proclamation had created a very favourable impression. S. N. Banerjea, and Mrs Besant enthusiastically declared that 'India was at last free'.[3] The Conference showed a genuine appreciation of the new spirit and an earnest desire to co-operate with the Government. Sir B. C. Mitter[4] condemned the 'extravagant' demands of the Extremists and their

---

[1] *Letter from the Government of India to the Secretary of State for India, dated March 5, 1919, and enclosures, on the questions raised in the Report on Indian Constitutional Reforms*, Cmd. 123 (1919), p. 1.

[2] *The Times*, August 19, 1918.

[3] *Round Table*, March 1920, p. 397. Mrs Besant had now become a supporter of the reform scheme, though she had earlier denounced it as 'unworthy to be offered by England or to be accepted by India'.

[4] B. 1872; barrister of the Calcutta High Court; Standing Counsel to the Government of India 1910–17; member of the Bengal Legislative Council 1910–1916 and of the Council of State 1921; d. 1930.

attitude of 'distrust of the great English people'.[1] 'England throughout her long and glorious history has always been', he argued 'the champion of freedom and the protector of oppressed nationalities.'[2] He recalled how England had helped Greece and Italy to win their independence and how she had recently given self-government to the defeated Boers and gone to war for the freedom of Belgium. 'To be a component part', he affirmed, 'of the Empire of which England is the centre seems to me to be the guarantee of our progressive advance to the full measure of that imperial citizenship of which civil freedom is the watchword. If we secure such freedom in association with the British Empire it will rest on a rock of adamant impervious to the ravages of times and vicissitudes of fortune.'[3] Sir P. S. Sivaswamy Aiyer,[4] the President of the Conference, remarked that they had met 'to celebrate with heartfelt rejoicing the auspicious event which has started India on the path of self-government and is destined within a measurable period of time to lead her to the goal of full responsible government'.[5] He referred to the 'short course of apprenticeship of a decade or two' as 'not unnecessary' in the art of responsible government.[6] Though he regretted that their suggestion for the introduction of dyarchy in the Government of India had not been accepted, he hailed the Act as 'a generous measure' and expressed the hope that full provincial autonomy would be achieved 'at the end of the first decade' and the goal of full responsible government in the country 'within twenty years'.[7] He concluded by saying: 'I trust that from this day India will be described as a "Dominion" and not a Dependency of the Empire and I look forward to the day when India will walk proud and erect among the nations of the earth conscious of a partnership on equal terms in the greatest Empire which the world has seen and a right of British citizenship which will connote equal privileges for all members in all lands over which the British flag waves, proud of the glorious contribution she can make to the strength of the Empire, to the thought and culture of the world and to the moral forces that will tend to make this world a better and happier one for all.'[8]

[1] *Report of the Proceedings of the Second Session of the All-India Conference of the Moderate Party*, 1919, p. 4.
[2] Ibid., p. 10.   [3] Ibid.
[4] B. 1864; Advocate-General of Madras 1908–12; member of Governor's council 1912–17; President of the National Liberal Federation of India 1919 and 1926; d. 1946.
[5] *Report of the Proceedings of the Second Session of the All-India Conference of the Moderate Party*, 1919, p. 14.
[6] Ibid., p. 20.   [7] Ibid., p. 35.   [8] Ibid.

The Liberals, as the Moderates officially styled themselves in 1920,[1] claimed—and rightly so—that they stood for the policy of the wise founders of the Congress, whose watchword was constitutional progress in close co-operation with the British Government. They asserted that they represented the spirit of the old Congress whose name had been usurped by others. The Liberals belonged to the prosperous and the well-to-do classes and were opposed to radical social and political changes. They were busy and elderly men—mostly eminent lawyers, businessmen and landlords—whose politics was of the drawing-room or council-chamber variety—respectable, quiet, compromising and moderate. They were out of touch with the thoughts and emotions of youth. The Liberal Party contained in its ranks many active politicians who were able men with long records of public service. Its influence in the country was, however, small and its following insubstantial. It represented, as Jawaharlal Nehru put it, 'bourgeoisdom *in excelsis* with all its pedestrian solidity'.[2] The Liberals were not, in fact, made for the rough and tumble of a nationalist struggle. Their politics was more like arguing a case or participating in a grand debate. They never had a satisfactory party organization and though small in number had their own caves and groups.

They earned no little odium for holding offices and co-operating with the Government at a time when self-sacrifice and non-co-operation were the favourite slogans. They were accused of having merged themselves with the bureaucracy. The authorities also in their wisdom spared no Liberal of any consequence of some title or honour. This proved to be disastrous for them. They came to be called 'Liberal Knights' contemptuously and condemned for having sold themselves 'just for a riband' and 'a handful of silver'.

The Liberals always remained convinced adherents to constitutional means. Mass agitation, non-co-operation, civil disobedience and aggressive policies were hateful to them. They condemned them as not only undesirable in themselves, but also as tending to alienate the British people. They hoped to achieve their objectives by a display of 'wisdom, experience, moderation, power of persuasion, quiet influence and real efficiency'.[3] They attempted to steer their course between the

---

[1] At its second annual conference at Calcutta, December 30, 1919–January 1, 1920, the Moderate Party adopted the name by which it was thereafter known—the National Liberal Federation of India. See *Report of the Proceedings of the Second Session of the All-India Conference of the Moderate Party*, 1919, p. 115.

[2] J. Nehru, *An Autobiography*, p. 411.

[3] Srinivasa Sastri: cited in ibid., p. 421.

two extremes of the Government and the Congress. They blamed the Government for their unwise policies of repression and of slow and suspicious reform which gave birth to extremism in India and kept it alive. On the other hand, they denounced the Congress for its 'disloyal' and 'semi-revolutionary' policies which ruined the chances of success of the Montagu experiment. Doling out their superior wisdom, the Liberals made themselves distasteful to both the nationalists in the Congress and the authorities. Their 'practical idealism', on which they prided themselves, was not practical enough to the Government, nor any idealism to the nationalists. The authorities accused them of flirting with the agitators and of not being courageous enough to court unpopularity by sincerely supporting the Government. To ardent nationalist imagination they appeared to be timid, reactionary men, who neither dreamt nor acted, who talked the strange, discredited language of yesterday and behaved like courtiers. The Liberals, Chintamani wrote, 'found themselves in the unenviable position of the proverbial earthen pot between two brass vessels'.[1]

The attitude of the Liberals towards British rule was discerning and discriminating. They did not underrate the manifold advantages which India had derived, and continued to derive, from British rule—the inestimable benefits of peace and security; law and order; English education and works of public utility; the political unification of the sub-continent and the growth of a spirit of nationality. 'Would there have been an India but for the almost providential intervention of the British?' 'And, what held India together today and saved her from disintegrating and relapsing into Chinese chaos but the "steel frame" of the British *Raj*?' 'Who guarded India's long sea coast and her, historically the most vulnerable, north-western frontier securely but the strong arm of the British Empire?' the Liberals enquired of the impatient idealists who talked of destroying the *Raj* and driving out the British. As anxious as any other nationalist to see their country attain self-government at the earliest date, the Liberals recognized that, considering as a whole, British rule was a favourable circumstance in the present evolution of India and any precipitate withdrawal of it would be disastrous. They did not talk of destruction before reconstruction could begin. They believed in building upon the existing foundations gradually. The nationalist accused them of admiring the architecture and the edifice of the British *Raj* and thinking solely in terms of replacing its owners. Nor did the Liberals think, as so many Indian nationa-

[1] C. Y. Chintamani and M. R. Masani, *India's Constitution at Work* (1940), p. 7.

lists were inclined to do, that British rule was the cause of all the ills of which their country was suffering and that all would be well once the 'satanic' *Raj* was gone. Their pursuit of ideals was tempered by a perception of practical limitations. Their nationalist ardour did not blind them to the fact that their nation was still in the making and that the British connection, far from being the dead hand, was a guarantee of its peaceful and orderly evolution.

The Liberals were steeped in English liberal tradition and were great admirers of English institutions and the English way of life. They were men who had drunk deep of English history, literature, law and politics. Most of the Liberal leaders were highly anglicized. They paid frequent visits to England and had close personal contacts with British officials in India and public men in England. They did not share in the general reaction against Western ideals and institutions to which Gandhi gave a vigorous encouragement in India. 'If there is one thing', said Sivaswamy Aiyer in 1924, 'which I value more than anything else as an important factor for the regeneration of this country, it is the British connection. I value the co-operation of the English people. I value their collaboration with us in the political, in the economic sphere. . . . I value not merely these things, but I value also the English institutions, political, judicial and administrative. I value English culture.'[1]

The Liberals took pride in calling themselves British citizens and fellow-subjects of the Empire. They claimed self-government in their own country and equality of treatment for Indians throughout the Empire on the basis of their common allegiance to the same Crown. The idea of belonging to the biggest, the mightiest and the freest Empire that the world had ever seen appealed to their imagination, and they demanded an equal share in its glories, privileges and obligations. Nor were they unconscious of the unique position that India occupied within the Empire and the special relation in which their country stood with regard to the Crown. 'Do not forget', Sapru told the Imperial Conference in 1923 feelingly, 'that my country, India, is the one country which makes the British Empire truly Imperial. I take pride in that.'[2] Loyalty to the person and the throne of the sovereign was a real and living sentiment with them. There was something of Oriental deference

---

[1] *Legislative Assembly Debates*, 1924, vol. iv, pt. i, p. 726.

[2] Imperial Conference, 1923. *Appendices to the Summary of Proceedings*, Cmd. 1988 (1923), p. 73.

and attachment in this feeling. It was also inspired by a great admiration for constitutional monarchy in England and a vivid perception of the part played by the Crown as a bond of the Empire, to the equal membership of which they aspired. And, above all, the Crown was associated in their imagination—as in that of so many Indians of the older generation—with the historic proclamations of 1858, 1908, 1911 and 1919.

The Liberals had a faith and an enthusiasm for the British Commonwealth almost akin to those of liberal and enlightened imperialists. They had no sympathy with the imperial idea as a symbol of power and domination. They disliked imperialists like Rhodes and Kipling who gloried in 'painting the map red', though they often themselves talked with pride of India's membership of the vastest and the mightiest Empire in history. They were frankly critical of imperialists whose credo was the race and who considered the racial bond as fundamental to the unity of the Empire. 'I am one of those men', said Sapru, 'who say that the British Empire can never be described as an exclusively white Empire.'[1] The talk of the civilizing mission of the Empire and of 'the White Man's burden' left them cold. The theory of trusteeship smacked to them of cant and often evoked caustic comments. With all their admiration for the British people and their ideals and achievements, the Liberals could not persuade themselves to believe that the British were the disinterested guardians of subject peoples. Though they readily acknowledged the many advantages derived by Indians from British rule, they did not fail to enumerate the equally enormous advantages—material, military, moral and political—which Great Britain herself derived from her control of India. These latter, they felt, vitiated the outlook of Englishmen towards the problem of Indian self-government and made them hesitate in applying fully to India the principles and ideals which they professed. Englishmen, they believed, were deeply interested in maintaining the *status quo* and retaining their hold on India, for they feared the consequences of the political emancipation of India as regards their vested interests. And they quoted the statements of English statesmen themselves to prove that their fears were not imaginary. They ridiculed, therefore, the attitude of paternal benevolence exhibited by a certain type of British imperialist and likened his mentality to that of Sir Joseph Bowley—a character in Dickens—the self-styled friend and father of the poor.[2]

[1] *Appendices to the Summary of Proceedings*, Cmd. 1988 (1923), p. 86.
[2] See Sivaswamy Aiyer, *Indian Constitutional Problems* (1928), pp. 354-5.

What appealed to the Liberals most in the imperial idea was its emphasis on the ideals of justice, equality, freedom and brotherhood—almost the very ideals which they attributed to the genius and traditions of the British people. Sir Stanley Reed[1] recalls how in 1922 Srinivasa Sastri 'electrified a sun-dried audience at Simla with his confession of faith—the British Commonwealth is the greatest instrument for human freedom the world has ever seen'.[2] Sastri remarked on the occasion[3] that the true nature and the great benevolent influence of the British Commonwealth were not always best understood by Englishmen themselves and, perhaps, it was necessary not to be an Englishman to do so. As a member of the Servants of India Society, he said, he had never wavered in the faith which the basic article of that organization enunciated that 'the connection of India with England is somehow on high intended to fulfil some high purposes for the benefit of the world'.[4] 'I take it', he added, 'that this great political organization [the British Commonwealth] stands unique amongst the political institutions of the world for one thing above all others . . . and that is the reconciliation of the East and the West, the bringing together in happy harmony the people of varied races and varied complexions, the blending together under one law, under one sovereign, under the Imperial Parliament, peoples of adverse nationalities, various cultures, hitherto felt in many other political organizations to be irreconcilable and never to be brought under one flag.'[5] Sastri expressed his belief that wisely guided the British Commonwealth could provide a happy solution of all those conflicts of races, religions and cultures which menaced the peace of the world.

It was this ideal of a multi-racial Commonwealth, a lesser League of Nations, which appealed to the Indian Liberals. 'Think for a moment', Sapru asked the Commonwealth statesmen in 1923, 'what India means to you? . . . If we are incorporated within the Commonwealth, think what we shall mean to the peace of the world, with our ideals of self-government, bridging as we do the East and the West, shouldering burdens which are yours as well as ours for the service of humanity.'[6]

[1] B. 1872; editor of the *Times of India* 1907–23; MP 1938–50.
[2] Reed, *The India I Knew* (1957), p. 164.
[3] Banquet at the Viceregal Lodge, Simla, May 12, 1922, on the eve of Sastri's departure to Australia, New Zealand and Canada as a representative of the Government of India to discuss with the Dominion governments the question of the status of Indian nationals in those Dominions.
[4] *Speeches and Writings of the Rt Hon V. S. Srinivasa Sastri* (1924), p. 250.
[5] Ibid., pp. 250–1.
[6] Cmd. 1988, p. 87.

The Liberals were ardent admirers of British culture and institutions, especially of British parliamentary democracy, and the British Commonwealth was to them a community of the freest, the most civilized and the most successfully evolved nations in the world. It is true that when they talked of their association with the British Commonwealth, what they had in mind was primarily India's relations with Britain, for their contacts with the Dominions were few and far from being pleasant. But they were conscious of the fact that the British Commonwealth was a microcosm of the world and its survival and development might well prove to be the precursor of 'the Parliament of Man, the Federation of the World'.

The disabilities imposed on Indian nationals domiciled in other parts of the Empire, however, sorely tried the faith of the Indian Liberals in the Commonwealth ideals of equality and liberty. At the annual session of the National Liberal Federation in December 1920, Govindaraghava Iyer[1] warned that 'if ever India became lost to Britain and the British Empire, it will not be so much on account of questions of internal administration, important and intricate as they are and may become, but on this question of the treatment of Indians in the Colonies'.[2] While the Liberals accepted the first part of the resolution of the Imperial Conference of 1921,[3] 'that each community of the British Commonwealth should enjoy complete control of the composition of its own population by means of restriction from any of the other communities', they drew attention to the second part of the same resolution which said that there was 'an incongruity between the position of India as an equal member of the British Empire and the existence of disabilities upon British Indians lawfully domiciled in some other parts of the Empire', and demanded the removal of those disabilities. During his tour of the Dominions in 1922, Sastri repeatedly emphasized that there was a necessary condition to India loyally remaining within the Empire and it was that her nationals who happened to be domiciled in the Dominions before the advent of the fact of exclusion should be fairly and justly treated. A narration of the indignities, privations and hardships to which Indians were subjected

[1] B. 1867; vakil of the Madras High Court; President of the National Liberal Federation of India 1921; d. 1935.
[2] *Report of the Proceedings of the Third Session of the National Liberal Federation of India*, 1920, p. 9.
[3] Conference of Prime Ministers and Representatives of the United Kingdom, the Dominions, and India held in June, July and August, 1921. *Summary of Proceedings and Documents*, Cmd. 1474 (1921), p. 8.

in many parts of the Empire, he told his audiences, would suggest that they were living in a barbarous empire and not the British Empire. Indians wanted to stay within the Empire, but if they could not be proud of their position in it, they might reluctantly be compelled to seek their destiny elsewhere, rather than continue in an Empire whereas a matter of deliberate policy disabilities of a humiliating character were imposed upon them.[1] 'Any inequality of Indian nationals', Sapru told the Imperial Conference in 1923, 'enters like iron into our souls ... it cuts to the quick our national pride and our new consciousness. It permeates and sours our whole outlook in regard to Imperial relationship.'[2] It was a question of 'Izzat' with Indians, he said, and 'When "Izzat" (which means honour) is at stake, we prefer death to anything else'.[3] He claimed that he was fighting for a great principle whose denial was a threat to the unity of the Empire. 'As a subject of King George ... I fight', he asserted, 'for a place in his household and I will not be content with a place in his stables.'[4] He reminded General Smuts, the South African Premier, of the assurances he had given when the principle of reciprocity was accepted in 1917, that once rid of the fear of being swamped by unlimited Indian immigration, the Indians who were domiciled in South Africa would be 'treated as human beings with feelings like our own and in a proper manner'.[5] He also took him to task for arguing that equal political rights did not follow from Imperial citizenship and common allegiance to the same Crown. While prepared to debate the constitutional and legal position before any competent authority, Sapru contented himself with pointing out: 'That allegiance with us is a real living thing. Shake that allegiance, and you shake the foundations of the entire fabric, with consequences which it is difficult to overestimate.'[6]

Despite their soreness on the question of the treatment of Indians in the Dominions, especially in South Africa, the Liberals were prepared to make allowances for the inability of the British Government to interfere in the internal affairs of the self-governing Dominions in order to secure redress for Indian settlers. They, however, treated British policy in Kenya as a test of the sincerity of British professions. This policy which culminated in the famous Kenya White Paper of July 1923 came as a rude shock to them, for it retained, under threat of rebellion from the white settlers, the racial bar in the Kenya highlands and imposed franchise discrimination and immigration restrictions on

---

[1] See *Speeches and Writings of the Rt Hon V. S. Srinivasa Sastri*, pp. 256–304.
[2] Cmd. 1988, p. 74.   [3] Ibid., p. 73.   [4] Ibid., p. 72.
[5] Ibid., p. 78.   [6] Ibid., p. 73.

Indians. Kenya was a Crown Colony and if the resolution of the Imperial Conference of 1921 did not bind South Africa it certainly bound the British Government. The restrictions were, therefore, galling not only in themselves, but because of the source from which they came and their general moral effect. To the Indian Liberals it was a great 'betrayal', an admission of 'moral bankruptcy' by British statesmen. Indians, said the enraged Liberals, were not equal members of the British Commonwealth, but 'helots in a Boer Empire'.[1] 'Kenya lost, everything lost,'[2] exclaimed Sastri. How could Indians plead for equal treatment in the Dominions when the British Government itself had condemned them to injustice and inequality in a Crown Colony? Speaking in the Council of State in March 1923, Sastri had warned: 'There will be very few friends left in India to plead for the cause of the British Empire. You will wipe out the friends of Britain by any such settlement.'[3] After the publication of the White Paper he remarked, more in grief than in anger, that he was 'a changed man' and that his faith in the British Empire and its mission had received a severe setback.[4]

In spite of all the make-believe in which the Liberals had indulged in regard to the Act of 1919, the fact remained that they were themselves dissatisfied with it and knew that it fell far short of the expectations of the country in general. One of them had even blurted out before the Joint Select Committee that if no simultaneous advance was made at the centre there would be an agitation in India which might 'stagger imagination'.[5] The Liberals had agreed to work the reforms more in a mood of wise resignation because of their faith in Montagu and the belief that the Act offered opportunities for further advance which it would be unwise to throw away in a fit of sulkiness. While the Congress looked the gift-horse of the Montagu-Chelmsford reforms rather closely in the mouth, the Liberals looked forward to riding the horse itself.

Left to themselves, there is little doubt, the Liberals would have sincerely and whole-heartedly worked the reforms for some time and demanded the grant of the next instalment only as a reward for proved merit. But, with the country in the full swing of the non-co-operation

---

[1] Hancock, op. cit., vol. i, p. 226.
[2] *Speeches and Writings of the Rt Hon V. S. Srinivasa Sastri*, p. 517.
[3] Ibid., p. 463. [4] Ibid., pp. 509, 526.
[5] N. M. Samarth: *Report of the Joint Select Committee on the Government of India Bill*, H.C. 203 (1919), vol. ii, p. 159.

movement, the Liberals could hardly afford to concentrate on their lessons with an easy conscience. The result was that hardly had the Act been put into operation than the Liberals themselves began pressing for its revision. In September 1921 a Liberal member[1] moved a resolution in the Legislative Assembly suggesting that steps should be taken to ensure the grant of full responsible government in the provinces and the transfer of all subjects, except defence, foreign and political relations, to responsible ministers at the centre in 1924, and the attainment of 'full Dominion Self-Government' in 1930.[2] The resolution was more in the nature of a feeler. It was inspired not only by the anxiety about the worsening political situation in the country and the need to placate public feelings, but also by the knowledge that responsible official circles realized that the transitional stage would have to be shortened.[3] The Home Member, Sir William Vincent,[4] confirmed this impression further when he observed during the debate on the resolution: '... nor do I personally believe that the present transitional scheme of this Government can last as long as is expected. I think we in the Government of India appreciate that as much as any one....'[5]

The Government spokesmen, Sir William Vincent and Sir Malcolm Hailey, while sympathizing with the natural desire of the members for a further advance, pointed out that insufficient time had elapsed to justify a change, the experience of the Assembly had not been tested, the electorates were not yet trained and the possibilities of expansion within the Act were not yet exhausted. As regards the demand for ensuring full responsible government in India by 1930, they observed that it was difficult to foresee that India would develop a spirit of citizenship and nationality and the power to defend herself in the near future, and unless these two fundamental conditions were fulfilled the country could not attain Dominion self-government. They added that the present moment was hardly opportune to approach Parliament for a further political advance and warned the Assembly not to encourage the elements opposed to Indian aspirations in England by any hasty and ill-considered demand.[6] At their suggestion, it was decided that the

---

[1] Rai J. N. Majumdar Bahadur.
[2] *Legislative Assembly Debates*, 1921, vol. ii, p. 956.
[3] See below, p. 210.
[4] B. 1866; entered Indian Civil Service 1887; member of Viceroy's council 1917–23; member of Secretary of State's council 1923–31; d. 1941.
[5] *Legislative Assembly Debates*, 1921, vol. ii, p. 1248.
[6] Ibid., pp. 1247–54, 1274–9.

Assembly should pass a resolution recommending to the Governor-General in Council that he should convey to the Secretary of State the view of the Assembly that the progress made by India on the path of responsible government warranted a re-examination and revision of the constitution at an earlier date than 1929. A resolution to this effect was passed unanimously by the Assembly on September 29, 1921, and was accepted by the Government.[1]

If the debate on the resolution did nothing else, it at least confirmed and encouraged the belief that a revision of the constitution would take place before 1929. The Liberal Federation at its annual session in December 1921 urged that 'in view of the experience obtained by the working of the Reforms Act, the rapid growth of national consciousness and the strong and growing demand among all sections of people for a fuller control over their destinies', full autonomy should be introduced in the provincial governments and all subjects, except defence, foreign and political relations and ecclesiastical affairs, should be transferred to popular control in the central government at the beginning of 1924.[2] The mover of the resolution, Sivaswamy Aiyer, dwelt at length upon the defects of the existing constitution and the gravity of the political situation in the country. He pointed out that the reforms had fallen far short of their expectations and that the mistake of the authorities in not accepting the modifications and improvements suggested by them was the main cause of the present agitation. The Liberals were demanding nothing new, he said, but 'simply reiterating the demand that was originally made'.[3]

Montagu's resignation in March 1922 struck the Indian Liberals like a thunderbolt, for they had placed almost all their hopes in him. With him as the Secretary of State, they were confident that the reforms would be worked in a liberal spirit, the period of transition would be shortened and India would attain Dominion Status at the earliest date.[4] His departure made them feel like waifs and they feared that the forces which had contrived to bring about his downfall would attempt a policy of reaction or at least of stagnation in Indian affairs. Subsequent events served only to confirm their worst fears. The new Secretary of

---

[1] *Legislative Assembly Debates*, 1921, vol. ii, pp. 1282–6.
[2] *Report of the Proceedings of the Fourth Session of the National Liberal Federation of India*, 1921, p. ii.
[3] Ibid., p. 50.
[4] See Srinivasa Sastri, 'Edwin Samuel Montagu', *Indian Review*, May 1925, pp. 372–5.

State, Lord Peel,[1] in his reply to the resolution of the Assembly of September 1921 revealed a *non possumus* attitude. The British Government turned down a scheme prepared by the Government of India for the complete Indianization of the army within 35 years. The War Office opposed a slight reduction in the British army in India which the Government of India had recommended as a matter of urgent economy and which even the Commander-in-Chief in India had considered absolutely safe. The Government of India, faced with an acute financial stringency, attempted to balance the budget by increasing the salt tax. The Assembly, annoyed at the behaviour of the War Office, refused to pass the grant and the Viceroy, Lord Reading, had to resort to certification. *The Times* had reminded the Assembly of the possibility of 'reverse steps' contemplated in the Act of 1919 and threatened it with serious consequences—'an examination of the whole problem from a new angle'—if it attempted to interfere with the budget.[2] In August 1922 came Lloyd George's famous 'steel-frame' speech.[3] This was followed by the refusal of the Viceroy and the Secretary of State to agree to the recommendation of Lord Willingdon, the Governor of Madras, that in view of the success of the reforms in his province, it should be granted full responsible government; and the appointment of the Lee Commission[4] in 1923, in spite of universal Indian opposition. The Liberals were convinced that a new breeze had begun to blow at Whitehall[5] and Simla. Soon after Montagu's resignation, most of the Liberals walked out of the provincial ministries, inveighing against the unworkability of the dyarchic system and the changed attitude of

[1] William Robert Wellesley, first Earl and second Viscount Peel (1867–1937). MP 1900–12; Under-Secretary for War 1919–21; Chancellor of the Duchy of Lancaster 1921–2; Secretary of State for India 1922–4; created Earl 1929.

[2] *The Times*, March 23, 1922.

[3] Speaking in the Commons on August 2, 1922, Lloyd George described the British civil service in India as the 'steel frame' of the *Raj* and remarked that he could see no period when Indians could dispense with its guidance and assistance. See 157 H.C. Deb. 5s., col. 1513.

[4] Royal Commission on the Superior Civil Services in India, with Viscount Lee of Fareham as its Chairman.

[5] That this conviction was not wholly baseless is proved by the following entry in the diary of the Commander-in-Chief, Lord Rawlinson (1864–1925): 'The fact is that the Home Government, having introduced the Reform schemes, are now afraid they are going too fast. They are trying to put on the brake, and the machine is inclined to run away from them. But we must either trust the Indian or not trust him. The schemes have got to be carried out honestly in their entirety, with a view to eventual Dominion self-government, or else we must return to the old method of ruling India by the sword. There is no half-way house.' See Sir Frederick Maurice, *The Life of General Lord Rawlinson* (1928), p. 307.

the officials. The Liberal honeymoon with the Government was over. Most non-official witnesses before the Muddiman Committee[1] in 1924 testified that the date of Montagu's resignation was the dividing line between the success and the failure of dyarchy.

Taking a leaf out of the history of the Dominions, especially South Africa, and encouraged by the recent example of Ireland, Mrs Besant launched a movement for a National Convention towards the end of 1922 in order to frame a constitution for India and negotiate on its basis with the British Government.[2] Prominent Liberals associated themselves with this project, if for no other purpose than to rally all the constitutionalists in the country and exert pressure on the authorities by formulating their demands in a precise form. Their efforts were, however, mainly directed towards demanding an early appointment of the Statutory Commission contemplated in the Act of 1919.

The Liberal Federation at its annual session in December 1922 'earnestly' urged 'the necessity of accelerating the pace for the attainment of complete self-government and towards that end the taking of steps for the immediate introduction of: (1) full responsible government in the provinces and (2) responsibility in the central Government in all departments, except the military, political and foreign'.[3] Sastri, as President of the session, warned the British Government that to be 'pedantic' about the ten-year limit for the appointment of the Statutory Commission would be not only 'inexpedient', but also 'a political blunder'.[4] By the middle of 1923 most of the provincial Liberal organizations had changed their creeds so as to include formally the demands for Dominion Status and responsible self-government as early as possible.[5] These demands were also contained in the Liberal

[1] A Committee appointed by the Government of India in 1924, with Sir Alexander Muddiman, the Home Member, as its Chairman to inquire into the working of the Government of India Act of 1919.
[2] Mrs Besant carried on her campaign for quite some time. The National Convention met several times during the years 1923–5. It drafted a Commonwealth of India Bill, which was introduced in the House of Commons by the Labour leader, George Lansbury, and received its first reading in December 1925. Though Mrs Besant's campaign proved abortive, it was, in a sense, the precursor of the All-Parties Conference of 1928 and the latter-day demand of the Congress for a Constituent Assembly. For the history of the National Convention see Besant, *Indian Problems* (1939), pp. 136–55; *India: Bond or Free?* (1939), pp. 225–46; *The India That Shall Be* (1939), pp. 26–88.
[3] *Report of the Proceedings of the Fifth Session of the National Liberal Federation of India*, 1922, p. i.   [4] Ibid., p. 29.
[5] *The Indian Annual Register*, 1923, vol. ii, pp. 115–20.

manifestoes on the forthcoming elections issued in August 1923.[1] At its annual session in December 1923, the National Liberal Federation modified its creed and declared its object to be 'the attainment by constitutional means of *Swaraj* (responsible self-government) and Dominion Status for India at the earliest possible date'.[2] It reiterated its earlier demands for political advance and an early appointment of the Statutory Commission. These demands the Liberals continued to press upon the authorities, both inside the legislature and outside, in subsequent years.

The Liberal leaders were fairly well acquainted with Imperial history and closely watched developments in intra-Commonwealth relations. Their familiarity with the literature on the subject of the development of responsible government in the Dominions may indeed seem remarkable today. They represented India at the Imperial Conferences and had close personal contacts with Imperial statesmen. They thus had opportunities of learning and becoming convinced that Dominion Status could give India everything politically that any proud and self-respecting nation could care to achieve. They knew that Dominion Status was not a static but a dynamic concept, and that ever since the Imperial Conference of 1917 it had been widened and enlarged to mean virtual independence both in the internal and international spheres. What had seemed to satisfy the recalcitrant nationalism of the Boers and the Irish should, they believed, certainly satisfy Indian nationalists, who were still struggling not for the forms but the substance of political power. Any doubts that they might have had in the matter were laid to rest after the publication of the Balfour Committee Report in 1926. At the 1926 session of the National Liberal Federation Chintamani remarked that the Balfour Report had 'conceded to the Dominions such a status of equality with the mother country that even a statesman like General Hertzog, who previously stood for separation from the British Empire, went back to South Africa and has been delivering speeches to tell his fellow-Boers that they need no longer be dissatisfied with their position within the Empire'.[3] The Balfour Report became a weapon in the hands of the Liberals in their fight against those Indian nationalists who demanded complete independence.

[1] *The Indian Annual Register*, 1923, vol. ii, pp. 109–12.
[2] *Report of the Proceedings of the Sixth Session of the National Liberal Federation of India*, 1923, p. 5.
[3] *Report of the Proceedings of the Ninth Session of the National Liberal Federation of India*, 1926, p. 93.

Dominion Status was, they urged on the authority of that Report, virtual independence. They accused the advocates of complete independence of alienating friends and strengthening the hands of reactionaries in England, of causing a division amongst their own ranks in India, and thus doing nothing but harm to the cause of India's political progress. The Liberals did not subscribe to the theory that Dominion Status could be used as a stepping-stone to complete independence. They believed that Dominion Status was desirable in itself. 'We Liberals believe', said C. P. Ramaswami Aiyer,[1] 'that there is nothing to lose but a great deal to gain by being within the British Commonwealth of Nations.'[2] 'Dominion Status', remarked Chimanlal Setalvad in 1928, 'meets all national aspirations and carries with it the protection, safety and all other advantages of partnership in the most powerful Empire in the world.'[3] The Liberals claimed that even as an ideal Dominion Status was higher than that of complete independence, for, while the former meant India's association on free and equal terms with the freest and most progressive nations of the world, the latter stood for a narrow isolationism.

Nor did the Liberals demand full Dominion Status at once. 'We want a Constitution', said Sapru in 1929, 'which shall give us Dominion Status automatically without any more investigation or examination by Parliamentary Committees or Commissions.'[4] The National Liberal Federation at its annual session in December 1929 demanded by a formal resolution the immediate enactment of 'a Constitution based on Dominion Status, with such safeguards and reservations as may be necessary for the period of transition'.[5] A statement issued by the Federation at this very session emphasized repeatedly that what the Liberals aimed at was 'Dominion Status for India, not as a distant goal or ideal, but capable of achievement within the shortest possible limit of time' and that they were prepared to accept all 'such safeguards and reservations including the protection of the interests and rights of minorities as may be necessary in the present conditions of India for the period of transition'.[6] This was also the demand of moderate Congressmen.

[1] B. 1879; vakil of the Madras High Court; member of Viceroy's council 1931 and 1942; Dewan of Travancore 1936–47.
[2] *Report of the Proceedings of the Eleventh Session of the National Liberal Federation of India*, 1928, p. 35.   [3] Ibid., p. 14.
[4] *Report of the Proceedings of the Twelfth Session of the National Liberal Federation of India*, 1929, p. 55.
[5] Ibid., Appendix A, p. i.
[6] Ibid., Appendix B., pp. iii–iv.

Lord Irwin was therefore correct when he wrote in November 1929 that there was 'a fundamental distinction between the general political thought of Great Britain and India' in the discussion of the term Dominion Status.[1] To the Englishman, he said, the phrase Dominion Status meant 'a constitutional state enjoyed within the Empire by a political entity over which His Majesty's Government retain no right of supervisory interference'.[2] To the Indian it meant 'something different', for very few responsible Indians ignored the fact that complete Dominion Status in this sense was not possible for at least some time to come.[3] 'Whatever he may feel it necessary to say in public,' wrote Irwin, 'the Indian is not so much concerned with *the achieved constitutional state*, in the British sense, as he is with what he would consider *the indefeasible assurance of such an achievement*. In all the constitutional discussions of the last two years, the underlying element in much of Indian political thought seems to have been the desire that, by free conference between Great Britain and India, a constitution should be fashioned which may contain within itself the seed of full Dominion Status, growing naturally to its full development in accordance with the particular circumstances of India, without the necessity —the implications of which the Indian mind resents—of further periodic inquiries by way of Commission.'[4]

The Liberals were the most formidable critics of British military policy in India and considered it to be 'the test of tests for the *bona fides* of the British Government'.[5] They demanded for the Government of India the same autonomy in military affairs which the Dominion governments enjoyed. They registered a vigorous protest against the underlying assumptions of the Esher Committee Report[6] that the army in India could not be considered 'otherwise than as part of the total armed forces of the Empire',[7] and against its recommendations intended to enable the War Office and the Imperial General Staff 'to exercise a considerable influence on the military policy of the Government of India'.[8] They feared that the acceptance of its recommendations would

[1] See Irwin's 'Note on "Dominion Status" as understood in Great Britain and India', November 1929: reproduced in A. Campbell-Johnson, *Viscount Halifax* (1941), p. 231.
[2] Ibid.   [3] Ibid.   [4] Ibid., p. 232.
[5] Srinivasa Sastri: *Report of the Proceedings of the Fifth Session of the National Liberal Federation of India*, 1922, p. 22.
[6] *Report of the Committee appointed by the Secretary of State for India to inquire into the administration and organization of the Army in India* [Chairman: Viscount Esher], Cmd. 943 (1920).   [7] Ibid., p. 3.   [8] Ibid., p. 4.

mean an increase in the already excessive military expenditure in India and result in 'making the War Office in England close its tentacles over the Army and the Military Department in India'[1] and condemn their country to remain a dependency for ever. At the annual session of the party in December 1920,[2] in the press and in the Legislative Assembly in 1921,[3] Liberal spokesmen insisted that the army in India should remain entirely under the control, real as well as nominal, of the Government of India and any co-ordination between the military policies and organizations of different parts of the Empire should be secured, as in the case of the Dominions, by discussion and agreement at conferences at which India was adequately represented.

The Liberals were convinced that quite a substantial part of the British army in India was maintained at India's expense for Imperial purposes. They demanded that it should be either withdrawn or paid for by the Imperial Government. They insisted that the numerical strength of the army in India should be determined in accordance with India's needs and be commensurate with her financial capacity. The primary purpose of the army in India, they asserted, must be, as it was alleged to be, the defence of India against external aggression and the maintenance of internal peace and security. They expressed their willingness to shoulder their part of Imperial obligations, but demanded that these obligations should be no more onerous than those resting on the self-governing Dominions, and should be subject to the same conditions as were applicable to those Dominions.

The Esher Report had assumed that Western Europe would no longer be an armed camp and that the centre of gravity had shifted to the Near and the Middle East, and it had looked forward, with unblushing frankness, to underprop British policy in those regions by the army in India.[4] This provided an easy target for Liberal attack. They accused the British Government of attempting hegemony over the Middle East with the Indian army as its sword and buckler. They protested against the large-scale employment of Indian troops in the Middle East as derogatory to India's position, self-respect and fair name. They demanded that Indian troops should not be used for

[1] Sivaswamy Aiyer: *Legislative Assembly Debates*, 1921, vol. i, pt. i, p. 186.
[2] See *Report of the Proceedings of the Third Session of the National Liberal Federation of India*, 1920, pp. 43–69.
[3] See *Legislative Assembly Debates*, 1921, vol. i, pt. i, pp. 182–97, 660–4; pt. ii, pp. 1447–51, 1683–1762.
[4] Cmd. 943, p. 3.

purposes of offence and 'imperial aggrandizement'.[1] We do not mean, they affirmed, to shirk our Imperial obligations and shall be found in our places when actual danger threatens the Empire, but 'we should be satisfied that those dangers have not been of your seeking, and that it is forced upon us by other Powers, without any provocation. If the United Kingdom wants to play high games of international politics, to dictate the fates of Powers in Europe, to parcel out kingdoms everywhere in the world, or to create or solve problems in the Near or Middle East, to play the role of saviours of oppressed nationalities or creeds, or to peg out new spheres of influence or to spread the benefits of Western civilization, then we shall not encourage you by any promise of support with our manpower.'[2] This was being said in 1921 by the loyal Liberals in the full knowledge of the fact that the Indian Legislative Assembly had no control whatsoever over military policy or expenditure!

Repeated reminders by British statesmen that India could not hope to achieve responsible government unless and until she was fully capable of self-defence annoyed the Liberals. They asserted that the idea that self-defence was an inseparable attribute of Dominion autonomy was a theory of recent growth and had not been rigorously enforced in the past in the case of the self-governing Dominions, where Imperial troops had continued to stay even after they had achieved responsible government. India, unlike the Dominions, had, ever since the beginning of the British connection, borne every rupee of the military expenditure incurred in maintaining internal order, external security, or in carrying on wars against the Indian states. Britain had never borne any part of the financial burden of India's defence—this fact, along with the numerous advantages, military, material, moral and political, which the Imperial Government had derived from the possession of India, should, they pleaded, dictate to the British Government a different and more favourable treatment of the Indian problem. Even if there were objections to the continuance of British troops in India after the grant of full responsible government—though they denied their full validity inasmuch as the British troops were paid for by Indian revenue and were not exactly Imperial troops—there should be none, the Liberals argued, to the continuance of British officers in the Indian

---

[1] See *Legislative Assembly Debates*, 1921, vol. i, pt. ii, pp. 1687, 1782. The number of Indian troops employed in Egypt, Mesopotamia and Persia, February 22, 1921, was 97,000. Ibid., p. 1712.

[2] Sivaswamy Aiyer, February 17, 1921: *Legislative Assembly Debates*, 1921, vol. i, pt. i, p. 197.

army till such time as Indian officers could be trained to replace them, for certainly it was no fault of theirs that India was not in a position to take up the responsibility of her self-defence immediately. After having denied Indians opportunities for military training and admission to the higher ranks in the army as a matter of deliberate policy, in spite of the repeated demands of Indians for at least half a century in the past, it was not fair, they said, to lay down as an axiom that India must first be capable of self-defence, with an Indian army—manned and officered wholly by Indians—before she could claim self-government. This appeared to them to be adding insult to injury.

The Liberals quoted authorities, especially the reports of the Peel Commission (1858–9) and the Eden Commission (1879), to prove that British military policy in India, as regards recruitment, the ratio of British to native troops, the exclusion of Indians from the artillery and higher ranks in the army, and general organization, had been based upon a deep-seated distrust of the people and princes of India and that its one dominating motive had been to provide against the risk of a general uprising in the country. They regretted that the same motive still continued to colour the attitude of the British Government towards the question of the Indianization of the army. They could not but give way to despair and treat as mere excuses for delay the arguments, such as those advanced by the Commander-in-Chief in 1925, that it was no simple matter to create a national army in India because India was not a nation, that India would not be able to dispense with the services of the British officers 'for many many years to come', and that he would 'resist strenuously' any attempt to hasten the process of Indianization of the army, for it would undermine its efficiency.[1]

The Liberals did not ask that Britain should continue to defend India indefinitely, but only that arrangements should be made for training Indians—officers and men—to enable them to undertake the burden of India's defence within a reasonable period of time. No words were more often quoted in the frequent debates on this question than those of Montagu, uttered in the House of Commons on December 5, 1919: 'Do not deny to India self-government because she cannot take her proper share in her own self-defence, and then deny to her people the opportunity of learning to defend themselves.'[2]

The Liberals appear to have taken to heart the advice given in 1921 by the Home Member, William Vincent,[3] and incessantly demanded

[1] *Legislative Assembly Debates*, 1925, vol. v, pt. ii, p. 1952.
[2] 122 H.C. Deb. 5s., col. 836.
[3] 'If I had been a non-official member of this Assembly, the one consideration

that arrangements be made for a rapid Indianization of the army. They condemned as 'wholly inadequate' the eight-units' scheme of Indianization[1] adopted by the authorities in 1922. If progress was to be made at this pace, they argued, it would take two hundred years before the entire Indian army would be officered by Indians.

The Liberals knew that the British Government were determined not to hand over the control of the Indian army to a responsible government in India—at least not in the near future. To prove, therefore, that they were reasonable, loyal and patient, the Liberals demanded the introduction of responsibility only in the civil administration and were content to leave the army, along with foreign affairs and relations with the Indian states, as a reserved subject in the hands of the Viceroy. Dissatisfied, however, with the attitude of the Government in the matter of army expenditure, the Liberal Federation suggested in 1924 that a fixed amount be allotted towards the same, any additional expenditure requiring the assent of the Legislative Assembly.[2] In 1926 the Skeen Committee[3] recommended fifty per cent Indianization of the army by 1952, but the vaccilations and delays of the Government of India, first in publishing the report of the Committee and later in accepting its unanimous recommendation, made even the Liberals despair. The Liberal Federation at its annual session in December 1926 demanded that the British Government should make an explicit declaration of their military policy in India and frame a scheme of complete Indianization 'within a reasonably short period'.[4] Rather reluctantly, the Liberals were driven to insist that the Government should fix a time-table for the Indianization of the army and make an Indian member of the Viceroy's executive council responsible for carrying it out.

---

that I would have constantly pressed upon the Government would have been the development of an Indian Army officered by Indians, because on that really rests very largely the future political progress of this country.' *Legislative Assembly Debates*, 1921, vol. ii, p. 1251.

[1] According to this scheme, eight units of the Indian army, out of a total of one hundred and thirty-two, were selected for Indianization. All Indian officers holding the King's commission were to be posted to these units, which were expected to be completely Indianized by about 1946.

[2] *Report of the Proceedings of the Seventh Session of the National Liberal Federation of India*, 1924, p. 40.

[3] The Indian Sandhurst Committee, headed by Lieutenant-General Sir Andrew Skeen, Chief of the General Staff in India.

[4] *Report of the Proceedings of the Ninth Session of the National Liberal Federation of India*, 1926, p. ii.

The Liberal position in regard to the problem of defence as it stood in 1928–9 may be summarized as follows: India should have the freedom to organize and administer her military forces like the Dominions. The utilization of the army in India for purposes extraneous to her defence must be conditional upon the assent of the Indian legislature. In order to carry out a military policy framed with due regard to the national interests of India, the portfolio of defence, which should continue to be treated as a reserved subject for some time, should be entrusted to a non-official Indian member of the Viceroy's executive council.

The Liberals were no doctrinaires. They never adopted a heroic pose by taking a stand on the rock of abstract principle. The doctrines of national sovereignty and self-determination appealed to them as nationalists, but as practical politicians they never allowed them to get the better of their judgement. Constitutionalists by temperament and mostly lawyers by profession or training, they frankly recognized the ultimate sovereignty of the British Parliament. Anxious to achieve their objectives with the consent and co-operation of the British people, they were always careful not to alienate their sympathies or hurt their *amour propre*. They had no illusions about the manner in which Parliament fulfilled its responsibilities towards India through the Secretary of State. Parliamentary sovereignty was in practice, they often bitterly complained, the sovereignty of half a dozen men in England and half a dozen men in India. Nor is it difficult to find in their writings and speeches frequent respectful references to freedom being the birthright of all men and the right of every people to determine the constitution best suited to them. But, as realists, the Liberals never directly or openly challenged the ultimate sovereign authority of Parliament in Indian affairs. Their position was best stated by Sapru when he observed: 'Constitutionally, Parliament is sovereign, and until India has got complete Responsible Government, it is correct in that sense to say that the responsibility for its welfare and advancement lies upon Parliament. But this constitutional position is by no means incompatible with the undoubted right of all subjects of the King to say when and how and on what lines further advance should be secured.'[1]

The Liberals, therefore, did not see any incongruity in supporting the project of a National Convention or the demand for a round table conference. Their preference for a Royal Commission instead of a round table conference, as demanded by the Swarajists, was mainly

[1] Sapru, *The Indian Constitution* (1926), pp. 8–9.

due to a recognition of the 'need not to neglect British opinion'.[1] A Royal Commission, they argued, was 'a thing understood in England', would mean 'no violent departure in agency' and would be 'best able to sift evidence and adjucate conflicting interests'.[2] As Sivaswamy Aiyer remarked, pleading for the immediate appointment of a Royal Commission instead of a round table conference, in the Legislative Assembly in 1924, the principle of self-determination was 'a sacred principle' and every nation had a right to determine for itself the form of government best suited to it, but prudence demanded that the machinery suggested should be 'acceptable to them [the British Government], not offensive to their *amour propre*'.[3] 'You must provide a dignified passage to a graceful concession,'[4] he added.

The Liberals maintained that, though the final authority lay with Parliament, Indians must have an effective voice in framing the future constitution for their country. The Liberal Federation at its Calcutta session in December 1925 reiterated its demand for an immediate appointment of the Statutory Commission and urged that 'Indian public opinion should be adequately represented thereon'.[5]

The Liberals had expected that as they were careful not to challenge British rights or wound British susceptibilities, the British Government would be equally considerate in respecting Indian rights and sentiments. In mid-1927, when speculation about the forthcoming Commission was rife and it was being rumoured—even suggested in certain Anglo-Indian circles—that an exclusively British and Parliamentary Commission might be appointed, prominent Liberals had warned the British Government that any such Commission would make no appeal to any section nor carry Indian confidence and support. They had asserted emphatically that Indians must sit on the Commission on equal terms and no provision for co-opted members or assessors would satisfy them.[6] 'It is the permanent interests of India that are at stake', Sapru had remarked in June 1927, 'and Indians must have a natural and moral right to take part in the shaping of their constitution for the future.'[7]

The appointment of an exclusively British Commission in Novem-

[1] Sapru, presidential address to the Indian National Convention at Delhi, February 22, 1924: *The Indian Quarterly Register*, 1924, vol. i, p. 74.
[2] Srinivasa Sastri: ibid., p. 77.
[3] *Legislative Assembly Debates*, 1924, vol. iv, pt. i, p. 728.   [4] Ibid.
[5] *Report of the Proceedings of the Eighth Session of the National Liberal Federation of India*, 1925, p. 3.
[6] See *Indian Review*, July 1927, p. 481; August 1927, pp. 529–34.
[7] *Englishman*, June 27, 1927.

ber 1927, despite their warnings and protests, was considered by the Liberals to be a deliberate affront to their honour and self-respect as Indians. They felt betrayed and humiliated and decided to boycott the Simon Commission. They demanded a mixed Commission on which Englishmen and Indians sat on equal terms, and no concessions made subsequently to liberalize the procedure of the Commission sufficed to make them alter their decision. Their attitude towards the Commission—repeatedly affirmed during the subsequent period—may be described thus: We accept that constitutionally the final and ultimate authority is Parliament, but this does not mean that the machinery for investigation and making recommendations to Parliament must be exclusively British or Parliamentary. The Act of 1919 did not preclude a mixed Commission. The appointment of an exclusively British agency for exploring the avenues of progress not only condemns Indians to the position of inferiority as petitioners and thus wounds their self-respect, it flagrantly denies the right of the Indian people to participate on equal terms in framing the future constitution for their country. The choice of the personnel of the Commission was destructive of the spirit of mutual confidence which alone could beget co-operation. Neither our self-respect nor our duty to our country allows us to go near the Commission. As Parliament has boycotted us, we too shall have nothing to do with its Commission at any stage, to any extent, or in any form.

The Liberals had always taken the announcement of 1917 to mean the promise of Dominion Status for India. In February 1924, however, Sir Malcolm Hailey, the then Home Member of the Viceroy's council, had attempted to draw a subtle distinction between responsible government and Dominion Status and suggested that the British Government had promised India the former and not the latter.[1] The Liberals had denounced Hailey's 'hair-splitting' and kept on insisting that the British Government stood committed to grant India Dominion Status. 'I venture to submit with confidence', said Sapru, 'that if British statesmen come to study their own declarations during the last seven or eight years and the declarations of the highest personages in the British Empire, they will find that so far as Parliament is concerned, so far as British statesmanship is concerned, it stands committed to Dominion Status for India.'[2] Sapru was right. But he and the other

[1] *Legislative Assembly Debates*, 1924, vol. iv, pt. i, p. 358.
[2] *Report of the Proceedings of the Eleventh Session of the National Liberal Federation of India*, 1928, p. 28.

Liberal leaders were old enough to remember instances in the past when attempts had been made by responsible British statesmen to explain away solemn promises and proclamations in a similar manner. They did not need to ransack the past, for there was a recent instance ready at hand. The manner in which the Act of 1919 had been interpreted in order to appoint a purely Parliamentary Commission in 1927 was enough to arouse Liberal suspicions and underline the need for seeking an authoritative reaffirmation of the goal to which the British Government stood committed by their earlier pronouncements. That the issue should be clarified became urgent because of other recent developments also. The Nehru Report had postulated Dominion Status as the immediate goal of India. The younger and more radical elements in the country had declared war on that ideal and the whole country was divided into 'Independence-wallahs' and 'Dominion-Status-wallahs'. The majority was still in favour of the latter. If the country was to be rallied round the idea of Dominion Status, if the trend towards complete independence was to be checked, there was need that the British Government reaffirmed unequivocally that they were pledged to grant India Dominion Status and took early steps towards that end.

The boycott of the Simon Commission had given no joy to the Liberals. Men whose watchword had been co-operation with the Government felt uneasy at being compelled to non-co-operate. The Liberals did not waste their time and effort in organizing black-flag demonstrations and shouting 'Simon, Go back'. They decided to meet the challenge twice thrown down before by Lord Birkenhead to frame a constitution for India, carrying behind it a fair measure of general agreement among the peoples of India. The Nehru Report was the outcome of their initiative and a triumph of Liberal ideals and principles.

Once again a situation similar to that in 1916 had been created. The moderates had been thrown into the arms of the extremists. The Government of India lacked the support and confidence of any reputable element in Indian political life. The 'Simon blunder' had proved to be very costly. But, though the Liberals had been forced to co-operate with the Congress, they soon began to chafe at this marriage of convenience. The extremists had exploited the situation. The Madras Congress in 1927 had declared for independence. And it was with extreme difficulty that Gandhi and Motilal Nehru had been able to secure even a conditional support for the Dominion Status objective of the Nehru Report at the 1928 session of the Congress.

The Viceroy, Lord Irwin, had begun to realize that the Simon

Report stood no chance of public acceptance in India and would only prolong the political deadlock.¹ 'By some means or other contact had to be regained and confidence in British purpose restored.'² He was fully aware of the Liberal dilemma and decided 'to get the more reasonable non-co-operators back into the discussion of the next stage of the Reforms'.³ The Liberals were urging upon the Viceroy, both in public and in private, the necessity of an immediate declaration by the Government that Dominion Status was the goal to which they stood committed by the announcement of August 1917, in order to remove the confusion and uncertainty created by Hailey's remark in 1924, and the summoning of a conference comprising representatives of all sections and interests in India for a comprehensive review of the entire Indian problem in collaboration with the British Government. These steps were necessary, they said, in order to ease the existing tension, to restore confidence in the sincerity and good intentions of the Government, to rally all those political parties and sections that did not profess extreme doctrines, to weaken the movement for independence, and, if possible, to prevent the Congress from acting on the ultimatum given at the Calcutta session in 1928. The coming of the Labour Government to power in England in June 1929 encouraged the Liberals to redouble their efforts. They openly assured that their co-operation was forthcoming in any 'honourable' way out of the present impasse.

The result of these energetic counsels was that the Viceroy, already convinced of the need 'to get at Indian opinion',⁴ went home in the summer of 1929, where he held discussions with the Labour Government and the leaders of other parties and on his return to India issued the historic declaration of October 31, 1929, containing a reaffirmation of the goal of Dominion Status for India as 'implicit in the declaration of 1917' and the proposal for summoning a Round Table Conference.⁵

The Liberals welcomed the announcement as clearing the mists and proposing a satisfactory change in procedure. They also persuaded the moderate leaders of the Congress to join them in doing so. The unfortunate debates in Parliament that followed Irwin's declaration robbed the latter of much of its grace and healing power. The Liberals regretted them, but were wise enough to recognize that they were inspired, in the main, by party spite at Westminster. Though the

---

¹ Campbell-Johnson, op. cit., p. 218.
² Halifax, *Fulness of Days* (1957), p. 117.
³ Dawson's memorandum on India, dated March 25, 1929: cited in Evelyn Wrench, *Geoffrey Dawson and Our Times* (1955), p. 272.
⁴ Ibid., p. 273.   ⁵ *The Times*, November 1, 1929.

Congress later stood aloof from the Round Table Conference, because the Viceroy could not give the assurance it asked for, namely, that the proposed Conference would meet to frame a Dominion Status constitution for India, the Liberals boldly stuck to their guns. They were anxious not to let the Viceroy and the Secretary of State down, especially at a time when they had dared so much for the sake of India and thereby invited 'Die-hard' wrath on their heads. They condemned the demand made by Gandhi and the Congress for a previous assurance as unreasonable for no government could give it. They were not slow to apprehend the great possibilities of the Round Table Conference, in particular, the renewed opportunity offered to bring pressure to bear on the authorities in the direction of accelerating the development process of British India in association with the Indian states.

At the plenary session of the Round Table Conference, which began on November 12, 1930, Liberal spokesmen declared their fervent and unfaltering conviction in the Commonwealth ideal. They emphasized the gravity of the situation in India, especially as regards the future of Indo-British relations. They characterized the movement for complete independence as 'a cry of despair, distrust and suspicion'.[1] They appealed to British justice, generosity and statesmanship for an early grant of Dominion Status to India, with such safeguards and reservations as might be considered necessary during the period of transition. 'Take your courage in your hands'; Sapru told the British statesmen, 'provide as many safeguards as you can, so long as those safeguards do not destroy the vital principle, and then go ahead with courage and faith. Courage and faith, together with the common sense of the people of India, will come to your rescue. Their whole future is at stake. But do not say "You shall march so many paces". The time has long since passed by when India could be told to hold its soul in patience and to march to that far-off ideal through the ages. I very respectfully beg of you to change your outlook on the whole situation.'[2] There was a note or urgency, earnestness and expectancy in the speeches of the Liberals at the Conference, verging almost on the pathetic.

[1] M. R. Jayakar: Indian Round Table Conference, First Session, November 12, 1930–January 19, 1931. *Proceedings*, Cmd. 3778 (1931), p. 41.
[2] Ibid., p. 32.

V

THE ALL-INDIA MUSLIM LEAGUE AND THE COMMONWEALTH

The Congress in its early years did not lack the support of a fair number of enlightened and liberal Muslims from all parts of India, but its efforts to secure the sympathy and co-operation of the educated Muslim community in general were foiled by some ultra-loyal Muslim leaders, chief amongst whom was Sir Syed Ahmed Khan.[1] Syed Ahmed Khan appealed frankly to the fears, prejudices and self-interest of his co-religionists in order to keep them away from the Congress. He impressed upon them the fact that they were economically and educationally backward and needed the patronage of the British Government if they were to hold their own against their more advanced countrymen. He described the Congress as 'Bengali' and 'seditious' and warned the Muslims not to 'give rise to suspicions of disloyalty'[2] by associating with it. He assured them that the demands of the Congress were inimical to their interests, that competitive examinations and representative institutions would, if allowed, only increase the predominance of the Hindus in the services and the legislatures. 'The object of the promoters of the National Congress is', he said, 'that the Government of India should be English in name only, and that the internal rule of the country should be entirely in their own hands.'[3] India, argued Syed Ahmed Khan, was not fit for representative institutions as she was 'peopled with different nations'.[4] The Hindus were four times more numerous than the Muslims. 'Therefore we can prove by mathematics that there will be four votes for the Hindu to every one vote for the Mahomedan. And now how can the Mahomedan guard his interests? It would be like a game of dice, in which one man had four dice and the other only one.'[5] Syed Ahmed Khan characterized the proposals of the Congress as 'monstrous and

[1] B. 1817; entered service of the East India Company as a clerk 1837; retired as Sub-Judge 1876; founded Mohammedan Anglo-Oriental College at Aligarh 1877; member of the Imperial Legislative Council 1878–83; knighted 1888; d. 1898.
[2] *Sir Syed Ahmed on the Present State of Indian Politics* (1888), p. 21.
[3] Ibid., p. 27.   [4] Ibid., p. 10.   [5] Ibid., p. 12.

unreasonable',[1] 'unrealizable and impossible'.[2] 'Can you tell me of any case in the world's history in which any foreign nation after conquering another and establishing its empire over it has given representative government to the conquered people?' he asked, and added, 'Such a thing has never taken place.'[3] He advised the Muslims in India 'to unite with that nation with whom we can unite. No Mahomedan can say that the English are not "people of the Book". No Mahomedan can deny this: that God has said that no people of other religions can be friends of Mahomedans except the Christians. He who has read the *Koran* and believes it, he can know that our nation cannot expect friendship and affection from any other people. . . . If we join the political movement of the Bengalis our nation will reap loss, for we do not want to become subjects of the Hindus instead of the subjects of the "people of the Book". . . . Whatever hope we have of progress is from them. The Bengalis can in no way assist our progress. And when the *Koran* itself directs us to be friends with them, then there is no reason why we should not act as God has said. Besides this, God has made them rulers over us. Our Prophet has said that if God place over you a black negro slave as ruler you must obey him. . . . We should be content with the will of God.'[4] And for a good many years the bulk of the educated Muslim community in India remained 'content with the will of God' and that of Sir Syed Ahmed Khan.

The Muslims in India were a far less heterogeneous community than the Hindus, but they did not have an all-India political organization of their own until 1906. The idea of having such an organization was often mooted, but it did not materialize. This was chiefly due to the lack of a strong and numerous middle class among them and to the personal rivalries among their leaders. Syed Ahmed Khan also, though he organized various associations for promoting Muslim interests and counteracting the influence of the Congress, remained until his death in 1898 opposed to political agitation on the lines of the Congress. It was the growing strength of the Congress, the attention paid to it by the Government after the coming into power of a Liberal Ministry in England in December 1905, and the knowledge that a further instalment of reforms was under consideration which spurred the Muslim leaders to action and organize the All-India Muslim League in December 1906.

The two main objectives of the League were 'to promote among the Mussalmans of India feelings of loyalty to the British Government' and

---

[1] *Sir Syed Ahmed on the Present State of Indian Politics* (1888), p. 18.
[2] Ibid., p. 15.   [3] Ibid., p. 39.   [4] Ibid., pp. 49–52.

'to protect and advance . . . [their] political rights and interests'.[1] Following the lines laid down by Syed Ahmed Khan in the eighties of the last century, the League looked with an eye of disfavour not merely on the Congress methods of agitation, but also on the Congress ideal of self-government for India on the Colonial model. Nawab Viqar-ul-Mulk,[2] one of the prominent leaders of the League, advised the youth of his community early in 1907 to eschew 'the agitational politics of the Congress', to regard themselves 'as soldiers of a British regiment' and 'to help in the continuance of the British rule', 'for if the British rule disappears from India, Hindus will lord it over it'.[3] The President of the League session of 1908, Syed Ali Imam,[4] accused the Congress of seeking 'not reform but revolution'[5] and denounced its objective of *Swaraj* as 'an almost impossible ideal'.[6] 'Throughout the troubled years 1907–10', said the Montagu-Chelmsford Report, 'the Muhammadans, with a few unimportant exceptions, held severely aloof from the revolutionary movement, and retained their traditional attitude of sturdy loyalty, secure in the feeling—which the partition of Bengal and the concession of communal representation in the reforms of 1909 had strengthened—that their interests were safe in the hands of the Government.'[7] But, it added, 'Since 1911 their attitude has been growing far less quiescent',[8] and went on to enumerate the causes which contributed to this change.

Though the year 1911 is generally recognized as marking a turning-point in the Muslim attitude towards the British Government, it is not difficult to detect signs of the coming change earlier. Indian Muslims, like their co-religionists elsewhere, had been affected by the Pan-Islam movement which began towards the end of the nineteenth century.[9] Through its emphasis on the solidarity of Islam and opposition to Western encroachments on Muslim states, Pan-Islamism came to

[1] *Pioneer*, January 2, 1907.

[2] Mushtaq Husain, Nawab Viqar-ul-Mulk (1841–1917). In Nizam's service at Hyderabad 1875–92; one of the founders of the All-India Muslim League; Honorary Secretary of the Aligarh College 1907–12.

[3] Cited in Ram Gopal, *Indian Muslims: A Political History* (1959), pp. 101–2.

[4] B. 1869; called to the Bar 1890; member of Viceroy's council 1910–15; Judge of the Patna High Court 1917; President of the Nizam's Executive Council 1919–22; d. 1932.

[5] *Speech of Mr Syed Ali Imam, Bar-at-Law, President of the All-India Muslim League, Amritsar Session,* 1908, p. 21.

[6] Ibid., p. 23.   [7] Cd. 9109, p. 22.   [8] Ibid.

[9] See H. Kohn, *A History of Nationalism in the East* (1929), pp. 48–9; V. Chirol, 'Pan-Islamism', *Proceedings of the Central Asian Society*, November 14, 1906, pp. 1–17.

acquire an anti-Christian and anti-imperialist character. The demonstrative enthusiasm of the Indian Muslims for the Sultan of Turkey and their severe condemnation of Britain for her pro-Greek attitude in the Greco-Turkish war in 1897 had given the authorities in India cause for anxiety.[1] Old Syed Ahmed Khan was alarmed at this trend for he perceived in it a threat to his Grand Design of 'an Anglo-Muslim alliance'.[2] He tried to counteract it, but without any apparent success. In May 1906 Minto wrote to Morley: 'There is, as you no doubt know, a pan-Islamic movement working in India in no friendly sense towards our rule, and, even in present circumstances, it will probably make itself felt.'[3] Developments in other Muslim states also found their echo in Muslim India. The nationalist movement in Egypt, the grant of a parliamentary constitution in Persia in 1907, and the Young Turk revolt in Turkey in 1908 exercised their influence upon young Muslim minds in India. With the growth of Western education amongst the Muslims, the sympathies of the younger generation naturally turned towards the Congress and the nationalist movement. The Secretary of the Aligarh College, Nawab Mohsin-ul-Mulk,[4] complained to the Principal of the institution, William A. J. Archbold,[5] in August 1906 that 'young educated Mohammedans seem to have a sympathy for the Congress'.[6] In a note submitted to Morley in 1906, Theodore Morison, an ex-Principal of the Aligarh College and an eminent authority on the Indian Muslims, wrote: ' . . . a generation of young Mohammedans is springing up, not only in Aligarh, but in all the big towns of Northern

[1] See, for example, A. P. Macdonnel, the Lieutenant-Governor of the North-West Provinces, to Elgin, the Viceroy, July 16 and August 22, 1897, Elgin Papers, MSS. Eur. F.84/71, Nos. 36 and 53; and a memorandum on the Pan-Islamic movement enclosed with the dispatch of the Government of India to the Secretary of State, Foreign Department, No. 110 of 1899, Political and Secret Letters and Enclosures from India, vol. 114, India Office Library.

[2] A. H. Albiruni, *Makers of Pakistan and Modern Muslim India* (1950), pp. 57-8; Sharif-al-Mujahid, 'Pan-Islamism', *A History of the Freedom Movement* (1961), vol. iii, pt. i, p. 105.

[3] Minto to Morley, May 9, 1906, Minto Papers, M.1005, No. 40.

[4] Mehdi Ali Khan, Nawab Mohsin-ul-Mulk (1837-1907). Joined service of the East India Company as a clerk and rose to be a Deputy-Collector in 1867; in Nizam's service at Hyderabad 1874-94; Honorary Secretary of the Aligarh College 1899-1907.

[5] B. 1865; Principal of the Aligarh College 1905-8 and later of the Government College, Dacca and the Muir Central College, Allahabad; played an important role in organizing the historic Muslim Deputation which waited on the Viceroy, Minto, October 1, 1906; d. 1929.

[6] Mohsin-ul-Mulk to Archbold, August 4, 1906: enl. Minto to Morley, August 8, 1906, Minto Papers, M. 1006, No. 9.

India which has learned English, and whose thoughts run easily in the Congress mould. For some time this young Mohammedan party has been restless, and it has only been kept to heel by the personal ascendancy of the leaders and the young Moslem's respect for his elders and betters. . . . Congress ideas are in the air, and you can't keep them out of any people's eyes and ears when once they have begun to read English. Ideas can only be combated by ideas, and you won't keep the young generation away from the Congress unless you have another programme and another set of ideas to set up against theirs. . . . I don't think the Mussalmans will long stand out against the blandishments of the Congress. . . .'[1] It was a sign of the times that the Aga Khan[2] was, towards the end of 1905, in favour of Muslims joining the Congress,[3] that the young Mohammad Ali Jinnah acted as the private secretary to Dadabhai Naoroji and attended the Congress session at Calcutta in 1906, and that a Muslim barrister, Abdul Rasul,[4] took a prominent part in the anti-partition agitation in Bengal. Syed Ahmed Khan must have turned in his grave when a product of his College—that seminary of loyalism—Hasrat Mohani became a follower of Extremists like Aurobindo Ghose and Bal Gangadhar Tilak, and who was in 1908 convicted of sedition. It was during this period that the young Mohammad Iqbal[5] wrote his famous patriotic poems, singing the glories of the motherland, lamenting for her fallen state, and inviting men of different creeds in his country to worship in a 'New Temple'. Similarity of education, commented the Aga Khan a little later, had contributed towards the creation of a similar outlook amongst the educated Hindus and Muslims, and 'influenced the increasing approximation of political views and sentiments amongst educated men of different communities' in India.[6] It was partly in order to check this drift of young, liberal Muslims towards the Congress and to provide an alternative outlet

---

[1] Note by Mr Theodore Morison: encl. Morley to Minto, June 22, 1906, Minto Papers, M. 1005, No. 69.

[2] Aga Sultan Mahomed Shah, third Aga Khan (1875–1958). Head of the Ismaili Muslims; Permanent President of the All-India Muslim League 1906–13; led the Indian Delegation to the League of Nations Assembly in 1932, 1934, 1935, 1936 and was the first Indian to be elected its President in 1937.

[3] The Aga Khan disclosed this fact in 1927. See *Times of India*, December 30, 1927.

[4] B. 1872; barrister of the Calcutta High Court; d. 1917.

[5] B. 1876; poet and philosopher; President of the All-India Muslim League 1930; d. 1938.

[6] The Aga Khan, 'The Indian Moslem Outlook', *Edinburgh Review*, January 1914, p. 9.

for their public spirit that the older, conservative leaders of the community had hastened to organize the Muslim League in 1906.[1]

It was, however, not English education, but English foreign policy, which shook the foundations of Muslim loyalty to the British Government in India. One of the main considerations which had made the Indian Muslims loyal to the British *Raj* was that the latter was friendly towards the Muslim states, especially Turkey. The continued deterioration in the relations between England and Turkey ever since the last decade of the nineteenth century had given the Indian Muslims cause for anxiety. The Muslims in India had always been suspicious of what they considered to be the anti-Turkish bias of the Liberal Party in England. They were seriously disturbed when that party came into power in England at the end of 1905. In 1906 a controversy developed in India over what should be the attitude of the Muslims in case a war broke out between England and Turkey. There was one school which maintained that the Muslim's primary allegiance and loyalty were to the Sultan of Turkey as the Khalifa of Islam. Mian Fazl-i-Husain,[2] for example, asserted that in the event of a war between England and Turkey 95 per cent of the followers of the Prophet in India would repudiate their allegiance to the British Crown.[3] Nawab Mohsin-ul-Mulk, on whom had fallen the mantle of Syed Ahmed Khan, challenged the view that the Khalifa was in any way the ruler of the Muslims. The Muslims in India, he wrote, were full of sympathy and reverence for the Sultan and wished with one heart for the stability of the Turkish Empire, but they were the subjects of the King-Emperor and owed

---

[1] The address presented by the Muslim Deputation to Minto on October 1, 1906 said that 'recent events have stirred up feelings, especially among the younger generation of Mahomedans, which might in certain circumstances and under certain contingencies easily pass beyond the control of temperate counsel and sober guidance'. *Pioneer*, October 3, 1906. The scheme for a 'Moslem All-India Confederacy' which Nawab Salimullah of Dacca circulated to Muslim leaders towards the end of 1906 and which formed the basis of the All-India Muslim League laid down the following objectives: '(a) To controvert the growing influence of the so-called Indian National Congress, which has a tendency to misinterpret and subvert the British rule in India or which may lead to that deplorable situation, and (b) To enable our young men of education, who for want of such an Association have joined the Congress camp, to find scope, on account of their fitness and ability, for public life.' *Bengalee*, December 14, 1906.

[2] B. 1877; barrister of the Lahore High Court; member of the Punjab Government with short interruptions 1921–30; member of Viceroy's council 1930–5; d. 1936.

[3] *Paisa Akhbar*, June 11, 1906: cited in Joseph Chailley, *Administrative Problems of British India* (1910), p. 76.

allegiance to him alone. The Nawab earnestly prayed that friendly relations between Great Britain and the Porte might be firmly established, but added that 'if God forbid, there be a war between our Government and any Mahomedan power, we should, as loyal subjects be on the side of our own Government, but as Mahomedans, we should also be sad about it'.[1] The Nawab had very correctly expressed the attitude of the vast majority of Muslims in India over the issue.

The course of British foreign policy continued to aggravate the anxieties of the Indian Muslims. They frankly disliked the Anglo-Russian Convention of 1907, for it disturbed their traditional belief that Russia was the enemy and Turkey the friend of the British Government. In 1911, when Italy went to war with Turkey over Tripoli and Great Britain remained neutral the Muslims in India felt aggrieved. They desired that in deference to the religious susceptibilities of her seventy million Muslim subjects in India Great Britain should have supported Turkey.

Events in India also added to the dissatisfaction of the Muslims. The revocation of the partition of Bengal in November 1911 came as a rude shock to them. Eastern Bengal was a predominantly Muslim province and its re-amalgamation with Bengal was naturally resented by the Muslims. Nawab Viqar-ul-Mulk wrote that the action of the Government in reversing the partition had proved conclusively that no reliance could be placed in their plighted word. He also referred to the feelings of disappointment and disillusionment caused among the Muslims by the Government's decision and their drift towards the Congress. 'By this decision', he wrote, 'Government displayed improper indifference to the Muslims, and the result is that some educated Muslims have begun to say that it is not in Muslim interest to keep aloof from the Hindus. They suggest that we should say "Goodbye" to the Muslim League and join the Indian National Congress—and this is what the Congress has been after for many years.'[2] The Nawab, however, considered this to be a counsel of despair. 'It is true', he remarked 'that many a time disappointments point the way to suicide ... but suicide is never advisable.'[3] He insisted that the Muslims should not join the Congress, for, as he pointed out: 'The *Swaraj* of the Congress is fatal to the Mussalmans. The disappearance of the British Government from or even any decrease of its influence in India would be a calamity for us.'[4]

[1] 'Khalifa and Khilafat', *Englishman*, June 26, 1906.
[2] Albiruni, op. cit., pp. 111–12.   [3] Ibid., p. 112.'
[4] Lal Bahadur, *The Muslim League* (1954), p. 87.

Early in 1912 Russia, now the friend of England, perpetrated massacres in Persia. The event shocked the Muslims in India. The cry of 'Islam in danger' was raised. It was exploited by certain radical Muslims for anti-British purposes. Shibli Nomani[1] had observed: 'For the last thirty years, efforts have been made to uplift the Muslims in the name of nationhood, but the failure of these efforts is only too obvious. The followers of the Prophet do not respond to the call of nationhood. Appeal to them in the name of religion and you will see what a splendid response you get.'[2] This is exactly what Zafar Ali Khan[3] through his paper, the *Zamindar*, and Abul Kalam Azad[4] through his *Al-Hilal* attempted to do. Pan-Islamism and nationalism became allies. Azad strongly advocated a change in the objectives of the Muslim League so as to bring it into line with the nationalist movement in India, for, according to him, there was no conflict between Islam and sympathy with Islamic countries on the one hand, and Indian nationalism on the other. Azad's preaching to the Muslims to give up subservient politics fell upon ready ears. The Balkan War in 1912 had caused widespread anxiety amongst the Muslims in India. Following upon the conquest of Morocco by France, the seizure of Bosnia-Herzegovina by Austria, the declaration of independence by Bulgaria, and the Italian brigandage in Tripoli, the Balkan War confirmed them in their belief that there was a sinister conspiracy amongst the Western countries to dismember and swallow Turkey. The sentiment of cohesion, always strong amongst the Muslims, blazed into a rapid flame. The Balkan War came to be regarded as 'a struggle between the Cross and the Crescent',[5] 'the ultimatum of Europe's temporal aggression'.[6] Poets and writers, religious and political leaders vied with one another in arousing sympathy for the cause of Turkey and Islam. Funds were raised to support Turkey and prayers offered in mosques for her success. A medical mission, led by Dr M. A. Ansari, was dispatched to her aid in December 1912. In the summer of 1913 a new organization, the *Anjuman-i-Khuddam-i-Kaaba*, was founded, whose members took an oath to sacrifice life and property in defence of the holy shrine against non-Muslim aggression. Its Secretary, Shaukat Ali, also planned to send

[1] B. 1857; Assistant Professor of Arabic at the Aligarh College 1882–98, author; a prominent leader of the Nadwat-ul-Ulema; d. 1914.
[2] Albiruni, op. cit., pp. 126–7.
[3] Prominent Khilafat leader of the Punjab.
[4] B. 1889; President of the Indian National Congress 1923 and 1939–46; Minister for Education in the Government of India from 1947 till his death in 1958. [5] Cd. 9109, p. 22.
[6] Mohamed Ali, *My Life: A Fragment* (1942), p. 57.

volunteers to fight for Turkey.¹ How profoundly the Muslims of India were disturbed by the Balkan War and the reverses of Turkey may be gleaned from a curious fact in the life of Mohamed Ali.² When the news reached India in the autumn of 1912 that the Bulgars were only 25 miles from the city of Constantinople, Mohamed Ali in his helpless rage and sorrow attempted to commit suicide.³

It was in these circumstances that the advanced section of the Muslims found it easy to push the Muslim League nearer to the Congress. Even the conservative Muslims favoured a *rapprochement* with the Hindus in order to put stronger pressure on the British Government to modify its anti-Turkish policy. Meeting at Lucknow on December 31, 1912, under the presidency of the Aga Khan, the Council of the League passed a resolution which recommended that the aims of the League should be:

'(1) To promote and maintain among Indians feelings of loyalty towards the British Crown;

'(2) To protect and advance the political and other rights and interests of the Indian Mussalmans;

'(3) To promote friendship and union between the Mussalmans and other communities of India; and

'(4) Without detriment to the foregoing objects, the attainment of a system of self-government suitable to India by bringing about through constitutional means a steady reform of the existing system of administration by promoting national unity and fostering public spirit among the people of India; and by co-operating with other communities for the said purposes.'⁴

The League at its annual session held on March 22–3, 1913, at Lucknow, under the chairmanship of Muhammad Shafi, ratified the change in the creed of the organization as recommended by its Council.⁵ Due to the influence of the advanced section and the efforts of certain peacemakers like Jinnah⁶ and Mrs Sarojini Naidu, the League also passed a resolution expressing 'its firm belief that the future development and

---

¹ Lal Bahadur, op. cit., p. 89.
² B. 1878; Chief Educational Officer, Baroda 1904–10; editor of the *Comrade* 1911–14; a prominent Khilafat leader; President of the Indian National Congress 1923; d. 1931.
³ Mohamed Ali, op. cit., pp. 49–50.
⁴ *Pioneer*, January 2, 1913.   ⁵ Ibid., March 24, 1913.
⁶ Jinnah was not yet a member of the Muslim League. He attended the League session in March 1913 as a guest.

progress of the people of India depend exclusively on the harmonious working and co-operation of the various communities' and its hope 'that the leaders on both sides will periodically meet together to restore the amicable relations prevailing between them in the past and find a *modus operandi* for joint and concerted action in the questions of the public good'.[1] But it was not yet quite the victory of the advanced party. A proposal, that the League should adopt the Congress goal of Colonial self-government, made by a Congress Muslim, Mazhar-ul-Haq,[2] found little favour. The League leaders were in no mood to accept the principle of numerical representation which parliamentary democracy of the Colonial type would lead to. Shafi remarked: 'The adoption of the alternative proposal put forward by some of our friends that the League should set up Colonial form of government in India as its ultimate goal is, in my opinion, inadmissible as well as politically unsound. The political conditions, internal and external, prevailing in the British Colonies have no analogy whatsoever with those obtaining in India. . . .'[3] It was, however, clear that the League had drawn closer to the Congress. The Secretary of the League, Saiyid Wazir Hasan,[4] remarked that 'the ideal of self-government which the All-India Muslim League had placed on its programme was an important step towards the formation of that great nationality for the building of which all Indians were aspiring'.[5] He pointed out that the spread of Western education had widened the political outlook of the Muslims and made them realize 'that the progress of their common motherland must depend on a hearty co-operation among all her sons'.[6] He expressed the hope that 'when once the two communities shared the same temper as regards Western education, and the educational disparity between them was removed, national unity would be assured'.[7] Nawab Syed Mahomed,[8] the President of the annual session of the Congress held at Karachi in December 1913, hailed the resolutions of the League as 'a happy sign of the advancing times'.[9] Referring to the criticism of the Congress ideal of Colonial self-government made

[1] *Pioneer*, March 26, 1913.
[2] B. 1866; called to the Bar 1891; practised at Calcutta and Bankipur; President of the All-India Muslim League 1915; d. 1921.
[3] *Pioneer*, March 24, 1913.
[4] B. 1874; advocate of the Allahabad High Court; Secretary of the All-India Muslim League 1912–19; Judicial Commissioner of Oudh 1920; Chief Judge 1930–4; President of the All-India Muslim League 1936; d. 1947.
[5] *India*, October 17, 1913, p. 190.   [6] Ibid., p. 189.   [7] Ibid.
[8] B. 1869; businessman and politician of Madras; d. 1919.
[9] *Report of the Twenty-Eighth Indian National Congress*, 1913, p. 37.

by Shafi, he remarked that the term Colonial self-government was in no way restrictive. It was, he said, definite only in one respect, that it affirmed and proclaimed 'the acceptance of the unalterable and necessary conditions of British supremacy'.[1] 'In my opinion,' he concluded, 'both the ideals are identical and I do not find any substantial difference in them, but only a difference in language . . . [for] it goes without saying that no Colonial form of Self-Government can do good to India which is not modified by and adjusted to the conditions of this country.'[2] By a formal resolution the 1913 Congress expressed 'its warm appreciation of the adoption by the All-India Muslim League of the ideal of Self-Government for India within the British Empire' and endorsed the plea of the League for harmonious co-operation between the two communities.[3]

The outbreak of the First World War further radicalized Muslim opinion in India. When Turkey entered the war against England in November 1914 Indian Muslims were placed in a very awkward situation. The Government of their King-Emperor was fighting against that of their Khalifa. They regretted the choice of the Turk and loyally supported the British Government, but in their hearts they remained uneasy about the fate of Turkey and sympathized with her. The public assurances given by His Majesty's Government, that the question of the Khilafat was one which must be decided by Muslims without interference from non-Muslim powers, served to steady Muslim opinion in India to a large extent. Only a few Pan-Islamists, like the Ali brothers (Mohamed Ali and Shaukat Ali), Azad and Zafar Ali Khan, openly avowed pro-Turkish sentiments. They were interned and their newspapers were supressed.

Muslim uneasiness about Turkey and the impact of the new ideas generated by the war gave an opportunity to the pro-Congress elements within the League to push the Congress-League *rapprochement* initiated in 1912–13 a step further. The 1915 session of the League was held at Bombay simultaneously with that of the Congress. It was presided over by a prominent Congressite, Mazhar-ul-Haq. 'We must have independence and open our eyes in fresh air,' demanded the President of the League, and added, 'Unless and until India has got a national government and is governed for the good of the Indian people, I do not see how she can be contented.'[4] The young, ardent Leaguers showed themselves more enthusiastic than the older Congress

---

[1] *Report of the Twenty-Eighth Indian National Congress*, 1913, p. 37.
[2] Ibid.   [3] Ibid., p. 10.   [4] *Times of India*, December 31, 1915.

leaders for Mrs Besant's plans to start a 'Home Rule' movement.[1] The League passed a resolution, moved by Jinnah, to set up a committee in order to draft a scheme of post-war reforms in consultation with the Congress.[2] The famous Congress-League scheme of 1916 was the result of the joint deliberations inaugurated at this session. The League had been emancipated from its old policy and began to flow with the current of nationalist agitation in India.

Presiding over the 1916 session of the League at Lucknow, Jinnah pointed out how the League had outgrown its original communal outlook and stood abreast of the Congress, 'ready to participate in any patriotic efforts for the advance of the country as a whole'.[3] He hailed 'the Hindu-Muslim *rapprochement*' as 'the first great sign of the birth of united India'.[4] As regards self-government for India, Jinnah remarked: 'It should be made clear by the Government in an authoritative manner that self-government is not a mere distant goal that may be attained at some future indefinite time, but that self-government for India is the definite aim and object of the Government to be given to the people within a reasonable time.'[5] Jinnah referred to the possibility of the reconstruction of the Empire and the formation of an Imperial Parliament or Council and warned the Government that India would never suffer to be ruled by the Dominions. He demanded that 'India's right should be recognized and her voice in that Imperial Parliament must be fully and properly secured and represented by her own sons'.[6] The news of the revolt of the Sherif of Mecca against the Sultan of Turkey in June 1916 had profoundly disturbed the Muslims, and it was generally believed that his rebellion had been instigated by the British. Jinnah warned the British Government not to interfere with the future of the Khilafat. He claimed that the feelings and sentiments of the Muslims in India, relating to their most cherished traditions, should receive consideration in the general policy of the Empire. 'The loyalty of the Mussalmans of India to the Government', he added, 'is no small asset.'[7]

The League and the Congress continued to speak and act in unison during the subsequent five or six years. They combined to put pressure on the authorities for a declaration of policy and welcomed it when it was made. They presented a joint address to the Secretary of State and the Viceroy in November 1917 demanding, among other things, the immediate adoption of the Congress-League scheme, the fixation of a

[1] See M. S. Kamath, *The Home Rule Leagues* (1918), p. 27.
[2] *Times of India*, December 31, 1915.
[3] M. H. Saiyid, *Mohammad Ali Jinnah: A Political Study* (1945), pp. 875–6.
[4] Ibid., p. 874.   [5] Ibid., p. 880.   [6] Ibid., p. 882.   [7] Ibid., p. 885.

time limit for the grant of complete self-government to India, and a place of equality for India with the Dominions in any reorganization of the Empire. These demands were reiterated at the annual session of the League held at Calcutta in December 1917.[1] Presiding over this session, the Raja of Mahmudabad[2] remarked: 'The interests of the country are paramount. We need not tarry to argue whether we are Muslims first or Indians. The fact is that we are both, and to us the question of precedence has no meaning.'[3] Jinnah, speaking at the same session, dismissed the fears of Hindu domination in a self-governing India as imaginary, 'a bogey, which is put before you by your enemies, to frighten you, to scare you, away from co-operation and unity which are essential for the establishment of Self-Government'.[4] 'This country', he added, 'has not to be governed by the Hindus, and let me submit, that it has not to be governed by the Mussalmans either and certainly not by the English. It is to be governed by the people and the sons of the country. I standing here, I believe I am voicing the feeling of whole India, demand the immediate transfer of a substantial power of the Government of the country.'[5]

When the Montagu-Chelmsford Report was published early in July 1918, prominent leaders of the League voiced their dissatisfaction with its proposals on grounds exactly similar to those of their counterparts in the Congress. The condemnation of the principle of communal representation contained in the Report gave them an added cause for anxiety. At an extraordinary session of the League held at Bombay on August 31 and September 1, 1918, to consider the Report, Sir Fazulbhoy Currimbhoy[6] observed that the reform scheme showed a gratuitous want of confidence and distrust of representative assemblies and individual Indians.[7] The Raja of Mahmudabad traced 'the sinister shadow of Mr Lionel Curtis' athwart the reform scheme.[8] In resolutions echoing the language and spirit of the Congress, the League pronounced the reform proposals to be disappointing and unsatisfactory and urged substantial modifications therein. The main demands of the League were: the transfer of all subjects, except law and order, in the provinces; the introduction of responsibility at the centre; the grant

[1] *Times of India*, January 1, 1918.
[2] Mohamed Ali Mohammad Khan, Raja of Mahmudabad (1877–1931). Home Member of the United Provinces Government 1921–6; President of the All-India Muslim League 1917, 1918 and 1928.   [3] *The Times*, January 8, 1918.
[4] *Indian Review*, January 1918, p. 54.   [5] Ibid.
[6] B. 1872; a Bombay businessman; member of the Bombay Legislative Council 1910–12 and of the Imperial Legislative Council 1913–16.
[7] *Times of India*, September 2, 1918.   [8] Ibid.

of fiscal autonomy to India; the retention of separate electorates; and the declaration of fundamental rights.[1] At its annual session in December 1918 the League, like the Congress, went further. It insisted that complete responsible government be granted to the provinces at once, and the principle of self-determination be applied to India.[2] The League delegates, Jinnah and Yakub Hasan,[3] reiterated these demands before the Joint Select Committee in August 1919.[4] The League, like the Congress, pronounced the act of 1919 'inadequate and unsatisfactory', but decided to work it in order to achieve self-government as early as possible.[5]

All through the war Muslim India had remained apprehensive about the probable fate of Turkey. Many believed that Turkey had been duped by Germany to throw in her lot with the latter, and they were not without hope that their loyal co-operation with the British Government would at least secure a not-too-severe punishment for Turkey. The assurances given by responsible British statesmen about the holy places and the future of the Turkish Empire had encouraged them in that hope. When at the end of the war rumours about the secret wartime agreements and the proposed harsh terms to Turkey got abroad, the Muslims in India felt that they had been deceived. Indian troops, of which the Muslims formed a fair proportion, had taken a prominent part in the campaigns against Turkey. There was a feeling of guilt and shame in numerous Muslim hearts when they reflected on how their men and money had gone to bring about the downfall of the Khalifa's empire. Representations began to be made to the British Government to treat Turkey leniently in deference to the services and sentiments of the loyal Muslims of India.

The Khilafat movement began in a perfectly loyal manner. At the annual session of the League in December 1918 it was urged that the British Government, possessing the largest Muslim empire, should sympathize with the feelings of the Indian Muslims regarding Turkey and the sacred places of Islam. In a long and interesting resolution the League said that, 'Having regard to the fact that the Indian Mussalmans take a deep interest in the fate of their co-religionists outside India and that the collapse of the Muslim powers of the world is bound to have an adverse influence on the political importance of the Mussalmans in the country and the annihilation of the military powers of

[1] *Times of India*, September 2, 1918.   [2] Ibid., January 2, 1919.
[3] B. 1875; member of the Madras Legislative Council 1916–20; d. 1940.
[4] H.C. 203, vol. ii, pp. 208–30.   [5] *Times of India*, January 3, 1920.

Islam in the world cannot but have a far-reaching effect on the minds of even the loyal Mussalmans of India, the All-India Muslim League considers it to be its duty to place before the Government of India and His Majesty's Government the true sentiments of the Muslim community and requests that the British representatives at the Peace Conference will use their influence and see that in the territorial and political redistribution to be made the fullest consideration should be paid to the requirements of the Islamic law with regard to the full and independent control by the Sultan of Turkey, Khalifa of the Prophet, over the Holy Places and over the Jazirat-ul-Arab as delineated in the Muslim books.

'The League further hopes that in determining the political relations of the Empire for the future His Majesty's Ministers shall pay the fullest consideration to the universal and deep sentiment of the Mussalmans of India that resolute attempts should be made to effect a complete reconciliation and lasting concord between the Empire and Muslim states based on terms of equity and justice, in the interests alike of the British Empire and the Muslim world.'[1]

In 1919 a Khilafat Conference was organized to rally the Muslim community in India in favour of these demands and exert pressure on the Government. Some of the radical and more bigoted elements amongst the Muslims began to talk of *jihad* (holy war) and *hijrat* (migration) in case the British Government did not abandon their antiTurkish policy. Others sought the advice of Gandhi, the rising star in the Indian political sky. The still loyal and moderate Mahatma advised the Muslims not to lose their faith in the British Government and to carry on their agitation in a loyal and temperate manner. 'But what shall we do', asked the Muslims, 'in case the British Government do not concede our demands?' 'Then', replied the Mahatma, 'remain non-violent, but cease to co-operate with the Government.' Thus was the idea of non-violent non-co-operation mooted tentatively for the first time at the Khilafat Conference at Delhi on November 23, 1919.[2] The harsh terms of the Treaty of Sèvres with Turkey published in May 1920 caused widespread gloom and indignation amongst the Muslims in India. Lloyd George had not redeemed even his 'pledge' of January 5, 1918.[3] On June 22, 1920, a letter signed by prominent Mus-

[1] *Indian Review*, January 1919, p. 13; *Times of India*, January 2, 1919.
[2] See *Young India*, December 3, 1919, and Gandhi, *An Autobiography* (1949 ed.), pp. 401–2.
[3] 'Nor are we fighting to deprive Turkey of its capital, or of the rich and renowned lands of Asia Minor and Thrace, which are predominantly Turkish in race.' *The Times*, January 7, 1918.

lim leaders of India was sent to the Viceroy.[1] It condemned the peace terms proposed to Turkey as a violation of the religious sentiments of the Muslims and contrary to the assurances given by British statesmen in the past. It pointed out that the British Empire, being 'the greatest Mahomedan power', could not treat Turkey, representing Khilafat, as a defeated enemy. It appealed to the Viceroy to secure a revision of the peace terms, or, in case he failed to get this done, to make common cause with the Indian Muslims, with whose just demands he apparently sympathized. 'We venture respectfully to suggest', said the signatories to the letter, 'that had India been a Dominion enjoying full self-government, her responsible Ministers would have, as a matter of course, resigned as a protest against such a serious breach of pledges and flouting of religious opinions as are involved in the peace terms.'[2] If the Government of India did neither of these two things by August 1, 1920, they intimated taking recourse to progressive non-violent non-co-operation. They denied that their decision implied any disloyalty or lack of respect towards the authorities. 'We claim', they observed, 'to be as loyal subjects of the Crown as any in India. But we consider our loyalty to an earthly sovereign to be subservient to our loyalty to Islam.'[3]

The Muslims of India had posed questions which vitally affected the continuance of the British *Raj* in India and the conduct of Imperial foreign policy. They asserted that they could not give their loyalty to a government which was inimical to Islam or Islamic countries. They also asserted—in so many words—that the British Empire was as much Muslim as British, and that its foreign policy could not be dictated merely by the governing classes of British birth and Christian faith. They claimed that the interests and sentiments of the 70 million Muslims of India were as much entitled to be heard as those of any other part of the Empire. A manifesto issued by the Khilafat Conference in 1920 remarked: 'The policy of the British Government has been definitely stated to be that of making India an equal partner. Recent events have awakened India to a sense of her dignity. In these circumstances, the British Empire, as one consisting of free nationalities, can only hold together if the just and fair demands of each component part of the Empire, in regard to matters which are of concern to a large section of its people, are adequately satisfied. It is therefore urged that the British ministers are bound not merely to press the Muslim, or rather the Indian, claim before the Supreme Council, but

[1] For the text of the letter see *Times of India*, June 25, 1920.
[2] Ibid. [3] Ibid.

to make it their own.'[1] There was material enough in these demands to give cause for reflection to those in England whose hearts were set upon a common foreign policy for a federated Empire.

The Muslim demand for a revision of the treaty with Turkey—powerfully backed by the Government of India and the India Office[2]—continued to be a complicating factor in Imperial politics for quite some time. Lloyd George and Curzon resented dictation by and on behalf of the Indian Muslims. They even got rid of Montagu, who was over-conscientious and zealous in supporting the Muslim demand. But the Muslim sentiments regarding Turkey, however unreasonable, could not be neglected with impunity. In September 1922, when the British Government threatened to go to war with Turkey over the Chanak incident, they were warned by the Viceroy that in any such contingency India would be 'ungovernable'.[3] The Government of India, voicing the demands of their Muslims, also influenced considerably the making of the final settlement with Turkey at Lausanne in July 1923.[4]

The Khilafat agitation gave an extremely dangerous turn to Muslim politics in India. August 1, 1920, the Khilafat Conference launched the non-co-operation campaign. At a special session of the Muslim League held at Calcutta, September 7th, Jinnah, as President, made a bitter attack on the authorities. He referred to the Rowlatt Act, the Punjab atrocities and the spoliation of the Ottoman Empire and the Khilafat and asserted that Indians could not rely either on the Government of India or His Majesty's Government to govern the country with justice and humanity or to represent India's voice in matters international. 'One thing there is which is indisputable,' he said, 'and that is that this Government must go and give place to a complete responsible Government.'[5] 'One degrading measure upon another,' he went on, 'disappointment upon disappointment, and injury upon injury, can lead a people to only one end. It led Russia to Bolshevism. It has led Ireland to Sinn Féinism. May it lead India to freedom.'[6] Though he did not

---

[1] *Foreign Affairs*, July 1920, Special Supplement.
[2] See Ronaldshay, op. cit., vol. iii, pp. 285 ff.; W. S. Churchill, *The World Crisis: The Aftermath* (1929), p. 392; H. Nicolson, *Curzon: The Last Phase* (1934), pp. 99 ff., 267 ff.
[3] Earl Winterton, *Orders of the Day* (1953), p. 116; *Fifty Tumultous Years* (1955), p. 55.
[4] See Second Marquess of Reading, *Rufus Isaacs, First Marquess of Reading* (1945), vol. ii, p. 232.   [5] *Englishman*, September 8, 1920.   [6] Ibid.

wholly approve of Gandhi's programme, Jinnah agreed that there was 'no other course left open to the people except to inaugurate the policy of non-co-operation'.[1] The League, however, voted for Gandhi's programme. The united appeal of Pan-Islamism and nationalism was irresistible.

At its annual session in December 1920 the League changed its creed to fall in line with that of the Congress. The objects of the League were declared to be: '(a) The attainment of *Swaraj* by the people of India by all peaceful and legitimate means; (b) to protect and advance the political, religious and other rights and interests of the Indian Mussalmans; (c) to promote friendship and union between the Mussalmans and the other communities of India; (d) to maintain and strengthen the brotherly relations between the Mahomedans of India and those of other countries.'[2] The Khilafat Conference held at Karachi in July 1921 declared it unlawful for any Muslim to serve in the army in India. It reassured the Sultan of Turkey of the allegiance of the Muslims in India to him and threatened the British Government that if the latter fought the Angora government 'directly or indirectly, openly or secretly', the Muslims in India would 'start civil disobedience and establish their complete independence at the next session of the Indian National Congress to be held at Ahmedabad and hoist the flag of the Indian Republic'.[3] The rise of Mustafa Kemal in Turkey and the Egyptian struggle for independence thrilled the hearts of Indian Muslims. When the League assembled at Ahmedabad towards the end of December 1921, its President, Maulana Hasrat Mohani, put forward a long and impassioned plea for the declaration of an Indian Republic on January 1, 1922, and the establishment of a parallel government.[4] Mohani demanded a definition of the word *Swaraj* and the form it would take in consonance with the desire of the Muslims. He himself advocated 'an Indian Republic on the lines of the United States of America'.[5] He characterized the British Empire as 'the worst enemy of the Muslim countries'[6] and hoped that every decline in its prestige and power would redound to the advantage of the Muslim world. Mohani also desired that no restriction should be imposed regarding the means by which complete independence was to be achieved. His lieutenant, Azad Sobhani,[7] moved a resolution in the Subjects Committee of the League, demanding that the object of the League should be 'the attain-

[1] *Englishman*, September 8, 1920.   [2] *Times of India*, January 3, 1921.
[3] *The Indian Annual Register*, 1922, vol. i, pp. 238–9.
[4] Ibid., Appendices, pp. 68–77.   [5] Ibid., p. 70.   [6] Ibid., p. 71.
[7] Prominent Khilafat and Communist leader of Kanpur.

ment of independence and the destruction of British Imperialism'.[1] The sane, experienced leaders of the League, however, applied a brake to the indiscreet enthusiasm of young fire-brand Pan-Islamists. They defeated Sobhani's resolution in the Subjects Committee and did not allow it to be moved in the open session of the League.[2]

The Khilafat and the non-co-operation movements, though they both failed disastrously to achieve their avowed objectives, combined to wreck the Montagu experiment. After the exciting events of 1920-2 no party in India was in a mood to work the dull reforms of 1919. Muslim opinion was no less persistent and strong than Congress or Liberal 'that immediate steps should be taken to establish *Swaraj*, i.e. full responsible government, by a complete overhauling of the Government of India Act, 1919'.[3] The leaders of the League declared themselves to be as ardent Swarajists as any other in India in the 'twenties. But the problem of *Swaraj* was far more complex for the Muslims than for the Hindus. Their fear of Hindu domination was deep-seated and they were determined to safeguard their individuality and interests as a community. In fact, as the prospect of *Swaraj* drew nearer, the Muslims began to devote their attention more anxiously to a clear definition and proper security of their position in a future self-governing India.

In 1921—the peak year of Hindu-Muslim political concord in India—the League President, Mohani, was constrained to remark that, in spite of the existing Hindu-Muslim unity, serious misunderstanding and suspicion persisted between the two communities. The Hindus, he said, had a lurking suspicion that given an opportunity of Muslim invasion of India the Muslims would help the invaders; the Muslims, on the other hand, feared that on the achievement of self-government the Hindus would acquire greater political power and use their numerical superiority to crush the Muslims. Mohani pointed out that in a merely reformed, as contrasted with an independent government, the Muslims would be under a double subjection—first, to the British Government, and, second, to the Hindu majority. If the English were eliminated, the Muslims would have only the Hindu majority to fear. This latter too could be negatived, Mohani added, if an Indian republic were established on a federal basis similar to that of the United States

[1] *The Indian Annual Register*, 1922, vol. i, Appendices, p. 78.
[2] *Times of India*, January 2, 1922.
[3] Resolution passed at the 1924 session of the League: *The Indian Quarterly Register*, 1924, vol. i, p. 663.

of America, 'for, while the Mussalmans as a whole are in a minority in India yet nature has provided a compensation; the Mussalmans are not in a minority in all the provinces. In some provinces such as Kashmere, the Punjab, Sind, Bengal and Assam, the Mussalmans are more numerous than the Hindus. In the United States of India the Hindu majority in Madras, Bombay and the United Provinces will not be allowed to overstep the limits of moderation against the Mussalmans.'[1] This interesting solution of the Hindu-Muslim problem continued to be advocated by Mohani in later years, and it profoundly influenced Muslim thinking.[2]

The League at its Lahore session in May 1924 dealt more realistically with the problem of safeguarding Muslim interests in any future constitutional advance. It laid down the 'basic and fundamental principles'[3] of any scheme of *Swaraj*. These were: the reorganization of India on a federal basis with full and complete provincial autonomy, the functions of the central government being confined to the minimum matters of common interest; no territorial redistribution to affect the Muslim

---

[1] *The Indian Annual Register*, 1922, vol. i, Appendices, pp. 71–2.

[2] It is tempting to connect this theory of hostages with the latter-day demand for Pakistan. Its implications were foreseen by a Punjabi Hindu, Lajpat Rai, who wrote in 1924: 'Maulana Hasrat Mohani has recently said that the Muslims will never agree to India's having Dominion Status under the British. What they aim at are separate Muslim States in India united with Hindu States under a National Federal Government. He is also in favour of smaller States containing compact Hindu and Muslim populations. . . . But it should be clearly understood that this is not united India. It means a clear partition of India into a Muslim India and a non-Muslim India.' Saiyid, op. cit., pp. 329–30. The Nehru Report noted in 1928: 'The Muslims being in a minority in India as a whole fear that the majority may harass them, and to meet this difficulty they have made a novel suggestion— that they should at least dominate in some parts of India.' *All-Parties Conference: Report of Committee*, pp. 28–9. At the first Round Table Conference Mohamed Ali echoed Mohani's sentiments and emphasized the fact that if there were provinces in which the Hindus were in a majority there were also provinces in which the Muslims were in a majority. 'That gives us our safeguard, for we demand hostages as we have willingly given hostages to Hindus in the other provinces where they form huge majorities.' Cmd. 3778, pp. 103–4. While the Round Table Conference was in session in London, Iqbal was unfolding his ideas to the League session at Allahabad in December 1930: 'I would like to see the Punjab, North-West Frontier Province, Sind and Baluchistan amalgamated into a single state. Self-government, within the British Empire or without the British Empire, the formation of a consolidated North-West Indian Muslim State appears to me to be the final destiny of the Muslims at least of North-West India.' Shamloo, *Speeches and Statements of Iqbal* (1948), p. 12. Mohani was a close friend of Iqbal, who is commonly believed to be the originator of the idea of Pakistan.

[3] *The Indian Quarterly Register*, 1924, vol. i, p. 662.

majority of population in the Punjab, Bengal and the North-West Frontier Province; separate electorates for all elective bodies; full religious liberty; and no measure to be passed in any elective body if opposed by the three-fourths of its Muslim members.[1]

Throughout the 'twenties the Muslims in India remained predominantly preoccupied with the problem of how best to safeguard their interests in any future political set-up in the country. This made them cease taking any marked interest in the question whether or not India was to remain in the British Commonwealth. It became for them very much a subsidiary question. Jealousy of the Hindus was stronger than antipathy to the British. It was elementary political prudence on their part not to be carried away by revolutionary zeal and annoy the British Government by talking of going out of the Empire, for they knew full well that if they fell foul of the Government they would be thrown to the mercy of the majority community to be treated as best or worst as the latter chose. Nor was the League as yet a mass organization.[2] Its leadership was in the hands of territorial magnates and upper-middle-class men—loyal and liberal by temperament, and conservative and compromising in politics.

The League ceased to appeal to the right of self-determination for India. It did not take its stand on the birthright of Indians to be free, nor challenge the right of Parliament to frame a constitution for India. As between a round table conference and the Statutory Commission its preference was for the latter, but it demanded that the Muslim community should be properly represented thereon. Though eager for a speedy constitutional advance, like the Swarajists and the Liberals, the League did not subscribe to the uncompromising and wrecking tactics of the Swarajists within the legislatures. In its methods and ideals it closely resembled the Liberal Party. But, though officially the League adopted this moderate line, there were within its ranks Muslims representing every conceivable shade of political thought in the country. It was, in fact, a microcosm of Muslim—nay, Indian—political life—an odd assortment of loyalists, liberals, nationalists and Pan-Islamists. The loyalists had their leaders in the Aga Khan and Muhammad Shafi, who considered co-operation with the British Government to be the greatest safeguard of Muslim interests. They accepted the goal of Dominion Status and trusted the British Government to gradually

[1] *The Indian Quarterly Register*, 1924, vol. i, p. 662.
[2] The total membership of the All-India Muslim League in 1927 was 1,330. See R. P. Dutt, *India Today* (1949 ed.), p. 434.

carry the country thereto. The liberals had their leaders in men like Jinnah, Ali Imam and Mahmudabad, whose attitude towards the British connection was similar to that of the Hindu liberals like Sapru, Sivaswamy Aiyer and Setalvad. The nationalist Muslims like the nationalists in the Congress, to which body they in fact belonged, could be divided into two groups. Those of the older generation— men like Ajmal Khan,[1] Azad and Ansari—were of the same view as the Hindu Congress leaders of their age-group, that Dominion Status was good enough if granted early. The young nationalist Muslims—men like Dr Sheikh Mohammad Alam,[2] Yusuf Meherally,[3] and Syed Abdulla Brelvi[4]—were like Jawaharlal Nehru and Subhas Chandra Bose in favour of complete independence. The Pan-Islamists—they still styled themselves Khilafatists—were a queer mixture. They had their leaders in the Ali brothers, Hasrat Mohani, Azad Sobhani and Shafi Daoodi.[5] They were ardent radicals and communalists at one and the same time. All of them were 'Independence-wallahs' and republicans. The Commonwealth ideal made no appeal to them, for their eyes were fixed upon Greater Islam. They condemned Dominion Status as Hindu *Raj*, propped up with British bayonets. Some of them were attracted towards socialism and even entertained vague visions of an alliance between Pan-Islamism and Bolshevism.[6]

The appointment of the Simon Commission in 1927 split the League into two. One section, led by Jinnah, was in favour of boycotting the Commission. The other, led by Shafi,[7] though it regretted the exclusion of Indians from the Commission, considered boycott to be inimical to the interests of the Muslim community and decided to co-operate with the Commission. The so-called Jinnah League met at Calcutta on December 30, 1927, and passed a resolution declaring emphatically that

[1] B. 1865; physician at Delhi; President of the All-India Muslim League 1919 and of the Indian National Congress 1921; d. 1927.

[2] B. 1892; barrister of the Lahore High Court; member of the Punjab Legislative Council.

[3] B. 1906; established Bombay Youth League 1928; founder member of the Congress Socialist Party; Mayor of Bombay 1942; d. 1950.

[4] B. 1892; editor of the *Bombay Chronicle* 1920–49; d. 1949.

[5] B. 1879; vakil of the Patna High Court; member of the Legislative Assembly 1924–35.

[6] Mohani, for example, was a communist. For poet Iqbal's socialistic sympathies see W. C. Smith, *Modern Islam in India* (1946), pp. 112–14. See also M. H. Kidwai, *Islam and Socialism* (1913) and *Pan-Islamism and Bolshevism* (1937).

[7] For Shafi's views see his *Some Important Indian Problems* (1930), pp. 221–50.

the Commission and its procedure as announced were unacceptable to the people of India and called upon the Muslims to 'have nothing to do with the Commission at any stage or in any form'.[1] Speaking on the resolution, Sir Ali Imam pointed out that the real issue was as to what was the relationship between India and England. Indians had been treated like serfs who would gratefully accept the crumbs falling from the table of British statesmen. During the war they were called partners and assured of a change in the angle of vision. 'I frankly tell you,' he remarked, 'I fully believed that there was a change in the angle of vision, but I have been disillusioned. We are now told we are not fit to sit at the same table. Are you going to go down? I, for one, an ex-sundried bureaucrat, refuse to take the insult lying down.'[2] Sir Ali explained that the resolution had been purposely worded in a manner to be acceptable to all schools of thought within the League, i.e. those who denied the right of Parliament to frame a constitution for India; those who stood for a round table conference; and those who, like himself, would have been satisfied with Indian members on the Commission. He added that the minimum that their self-respect and patriotism demanded was to assert their right to participate on equal terms in the framing of the constitution for their country.[3] Mohamed Ali asserted that no nation could concede to another the right to rule over it. 'I admit', he added, 'that I am unfit to wrest the rule back from English hands, but I do not concede any ethical basis to the British purpose in India. I challenge the preamble of the Act of 1919. My quarrel is not with the Jury. Even if it had consisted of Indians exclusively my objection would have remained.'[4] Jinnah remarked: 'We are denied equal partnership. We will resist the new doctrine to the best of our power. Jallianwalla Bagh[5] was a physical butchery, the Simon Commission is a butchery of our souls.'[6]

Even before the appointment of the Simon Commission in November 1927 the League and the Congress had, owing mainly to the efforts of Jinnah, started drawing closer to each other once again. In March 1927 Jinnah had put forward certain conditions on which the Muslims were prepared to give up separate electorates.[7] The Congress had

[1] *The Indian Quarterly Register*, 1927, vol. ii, p. 443.
[2] Ibid., p. 444.   [3] Ibid., pp. 444–5.   [4] Ibid., p. 446.
[5] The scene of General Dyer's action, April 13, 1919, at Amritsar.
[6] *The Indian Quarterly Register*, 1927, vol. ii, p. 451.
[7] This offer by Jinnah, which came to be known as the 'Delhi Proposals', demanded that Sind should be a separate province, that reforms should be introduced in the North-West Frontier Province and Baluchistan, that in the Punjab and Bengal representation should be in accordance with population, and that

welcomed his proposals, but they evoked a storm of indignant protest from Muslims in various parts of the country at what the latter considered to be an unauthorized and extremely undesirable attempt to surrender their Magna Carta. This had made even Jinnah hold back. But the universal resentment caused in India by the appointment of the exclusively British Simon Commission once again gave encouragement to these overtures for Hindu-Muslim unity. The Jinnah League cooperated with the All-Parties Convention in its early stages, but soon differences arose and the League delegates withdrew from the deliberations of the Convention.

When the Nehru Report was published towards the end of 1928, it was supported by a few liberal Muslims, like the Raja of Mahmudabad and Sir Ali Imam, and a few Congress Muslims, like Azad and Ansari. Jinnah and his followers, while they were critical of the Report on so many points, still worked for a *rapprochement* between the Congress and the Muslims. The prominent Khilafat leaders and the League under Shafi condemned it bitterly and organized a violent Muslim opposition to it. Their condemnation was based mainly on two grounds: they wanted separate electorates to be retained; and they insisted that the future constitution of India should be federal and not unitary, with a weak centre for minimum common interests and utmost autonomy for the provinces.

The Khilafat leaders attacked the Nehru Report for an additional reason. They were not prepared to accept the ideal of Dominion Status for India postulated in that Report. They accused the Nehru Report of having admitted in its preamble 'the bondage of servitude' and denounced the 'Dominion-Status-Wallahs' as 'cowards' and 'slaves'. The Khilafat Conference held at Calcutta towards the end of December 1928 passed a resolution declaring that complete independence, outside the British Empire, was the goal of the Indian Muslims.[1] 'The Quoran says', remarked Mohamed Ali at the Conference, 'that there is no Government but the Government of God. Therefore the Mussalmans of India, when they make complete independence their goal, say only what the Quoran asked them to do 1,310 years ago.'[2] Azad Sobhani observed that Dominion Status was another name for

---

in the central legislature Muslim representation should be no less than one-third. In case these conditions were accepted, the Muslims, it was said, would accept joint electorates with reservation of seats. See M. Noman, *Muslim India: Rise and Growth of the All-India Muslim League* (1942), pp. 244–5.

[1] *The Indian Quarterly Register*, 1928, vol. ii, p. 403.
[2] Ibid.

bondage and to live like a slave was not proper and consistent with Islam.[1]

Muslim opposition to the Nehru Report on communal lines found organized expression in the All-Parties Muslim Conference held at Delhi on December 31, 1928, and January 1, 1929, under the presidency of the Aga Khan. It was attended by representatives of almost all sections amongst the Muslims in India. The only notable absentees were Jinnah and his followers and the Congress Muslims. The Conference unanimously adopted a resolution, moved by Muhammad Shafi, which demanded a federal system of government for India, with complete autonomy and residuary powers vested in the constituent states; separate electorates for the Muslims; weightage for the Muslims in the provinces where they were in a minority; non-interference with the Muslim majority in the provinces where they constituted a majority of the population; one-third Muslim representation in the central legislature; due Muslim share in the cabinets and the services; and adequate safeguards for Muslim religion, culture and language. The final clause of the resolution read: 'This Conference emphatically declares that no constitution, by whomsoever proposed or devised, will be acceptable to Indian Mussalmans unless it conforms with the principles embodied in this resolution.'[2] The Conference wisely concentrated on formulating the joint demands of the Muslims in any future political set-up, for here agreement was easy. It did not concern itself with the question of Dominion Status *versus* independence, for here it was known that there were sections which stood committed differently. The All-Parties Muslim Conference provided the Indian Muslims with their 'code-book'.[3] In May 1929 Jinnah issued his famous 'Fourteen Points',[4] which laid down more precisely and clearly the basic Muslim demands. But Muslim politics in India remained in a hopelessly chaotic condition in the year 1929 and for quite some time thereafter. Shafi had his own All-India Muslim League. Jinnah continued to be the leader of another organization with the same nomenclature. The Delhi Conference group was another important element. The Ali brothers headed the Khilafat Conference. The Congress Muslims seceded from the Jinnah League in July 1929 and formed a separate organization of their own called the All-India Nationalist Muslim Party.

---

[1] *The Indian Quarterly Register*, 1928, vol. ii, p. 403.
[2] *Times of India*, January 2, 1929.
[3] The Aga Khan, *Memoirs* (1954), p. 210.   [4] Noman, op. cit., pp. 284–7.

What was the attitude of the Muslim League in the 'twenties towards the British connection and the Commonwealth ideal? The question is extremely difficult to answer. The League did not care to define its attitude in any formal or positive manner during this period. Perhaps it was not possible for it to do so. The League was, in the 'twenties, as we have already noted, an extremely heterogeneous organization. It contained within its ranks men of every conceivable shade of political thought in the country—communists and socialists, Congressmen and Liberals, rank communalists and high-minded patriots, yes-men and bitter enemies of the British Government in India. It was not easy to formulate a definite attitude which could be acceptable to all these diverse elements. Nor would any such formulation have redounded to the advantage of the League. Had the League committed itself to the ideal of complete independence outside the British Empire, it would have alienated the British Government and dangerously weakened its bargaining position. Had it, on the other hand, committed itself to the ideal of Dominion Status within the British Empire, it would have estranged some of its radical and most energetic elements and driven them to the Hindu camp.

During the exciting days of the Khilafat agitation when many Muslims had, to use Shaukat Ali's phrase, 'suspended' their allegiance to the British Crown, the League had in 1920 declared its objective to be 'the attainment of *Swaraj* by the people of India by all peaceful and legitimate means'. To the question whether *Swaraj* was to be attained within or without the British Empire, the usual answer was: 'Within, if possible, without, if necessary.' In 1921 an attempt made to get the League committed to complete independence outside the Empire was foiled by the League leadership. Kemal Pasha rendered a great service to the Muslims in India and also to the British Empire by abolishing the Sultanate in 1922 and the Khilafat in 1924. He thereby dealt a *coup de grâce* to the Khilafat agitation in India and spared the Muslims of any tormenting conflict of loyalties in the future. When the League gradually returned to normal politics towards the end of 1923 it was in a chastened and sober mood. It satisfied itself, like the Swarajists and the Liberals, with demanding 'full responsible government' as early as possible. Muslim attention during the subsequent years was entirely preoccupied with safeguarding their interests in any future constitutional advance. The League did not allow the vexed question of Dominion Status *versus* independence to intrude into its deliberations. Individuals declared their views as they chose, but the League did not concern itself with that unreal issue. It would, however, be safe to remark that, but for a few extremists—either of the Khilafat or the Congress variety—most of the prominent leaders of the League took the British connection for granted. They recognized in the latter a guarantee not only of Muslim interests but of India's safe and ordered progress towards self-government. To them, as to the Liberals and moderate Congressmen, *Swaraj* meant full responsible government and Dominion Status for India. The Raja of Mahmudabad spoke for most of his sober and responsible colleagues in the League when he registered an emphatic protest against 'the doctrine of independence in the sense of severance of British connection' in 1928. 'India's place in the British Commonwealth', remarked the Raja, 'is a place of undeniable security. Her association with the British Commonwealth is a valuable asset and in my judgement it will be folly to destroy this precious commodity with our own hands. It is my conviction that there is plenty of room for the growth, development and expression of Indian nationalism within the ambit of India's connection with England.'[1]

The loyal and moderate leaders of the League were alarmed at the rapid growth of the idea of complete independence in India in 1928–9. They joined hands with moderate Congressmen and the Liberals in putting pressure on the authorities to make a reassuring move in order to counteract this dangerous doctrine. Jinnah, for example, addressed a lengthy private letter to Prime Minister Ramsay MacDonald on June 19, 1929,[2] in which he warned the latter that the existing deadlock in India, if allowed to continue, would 'prove disastrous both to the interests of India and Great Britain'.[3] Indians, wrote Jinnah, boycotted the Simon Commission because its appointment and procedure relegated them to the position of suppliants and assessors. 'So far as India is concerned, we have done with it and when its report, whatever it may be, is published in due course, every effort will be made in India to damn it.'[4] Jinnah told the Prime Minister that there was no chance of persuading Indians to co-operate in the future stages of constitution-making unless the British Government made a wholly fresh move. 'India has lost her faith', Jinnah pointed out, 'in the word of Great Britain. The first and foremost thing that I would ask you to consider is how best to restore that faith and revive the confidence of India in the *bona fides* of Great Britain.'[5] Amongst the reasons for this loss of faith in British pledges and intentions, he emphasized

---
[1] *Times of India*, December 27, 1928.
[2] The letter is reproduced in full in M. H. Saiyid, op. cit., pp. 450–9.
[3] Ibid., pp. 450–1.   [4] Ibid., p. 451.   [5] Ibid., p. 453.

particularly the effect of Sir Malcolm Hailey's remarks in the Legislative Assembly in February 1924, virtually repudiating the idea that Great Britain was committed to grant India full self-governing Dominion Status. 'There is', Jinnah added, 'a section in India that has already declared in favour of complete independence, and I may tell you without exaggeration that the movement for independence is gaining ground, as it is supported by the Indian National Congress.... I would most earnestly urge upon you at this moment to persuade His Majesty's Government without delay to make a declaration that Great Britain is unequivocally pledged to the policy of granting to India full responsible Government with Dominion Status. The effect of such a declaration will be very far-reaching and go a great way to create a different atmosphere in the country and will be a severe antidote to the movement for independence.'[1] As regards the practical steps to be taken in order to secure the co-operation of Indian politicians in the future stages of constitution-making, Jinnah suggested that the British Government should, after they had received the proposals of the Simon Commission, but before they formulated their own, 'invite representatives of India, who would be in a position to deliver the goods (because completely unanimous opinion in India is not possible at present), to sit in conference with them with a view to reaching a solution which might carry, to use the words of the Viceroy, "the willing assent of political India" '.[2]

It was such well-meaning counsels which persuaded Lord Irwin and the Labour Government to make the famous announcement of October 31, 1929.

The announcement was welcomed by almost all sections of the Muslim community in India. At the plenary session of the Round Table Conference, which began in London on November 12, 1930, all the Muslim delegates demanded an early grant of Dominion Status, with safeguards for the transitional period, to India. 'I have been,' said Muhammad Shafi at the Conference, 'in the last 40 years of my public life in India, the strongest supporter of the British connection in India—so much so that on occasions I have been called a reactionary by my own countrymen. It is I who say that the situation in India is grave, very grave.'[3] He demanded on behalf of the Mussalmans of India a status for his country of equal partnership in the British Commonwealth. He assured the British Government that a happy and contented India would be a source of immense strength to the British

---

[1] M. H. Saiyid, op. cit., p. 456.   [2] Ibid., pp. 457–8.   [3] Cmd. 3778, p. 54.

Commonwealth.¹ Even the fiery Mohamed Ali demanded but 'the substance of freedom'.² Though he was 'a republican', he appealed to the King-Emperor to do justice to the people of India.³ 'British domination is doomed over India,' he said, but asked: 'Is our friendship doomed also?'⁴ 'We have a soft corner in our hearts for Great Britain. Let us retain it, I beseech you,'⁵ he added. Mohamed Ali warned that if they went back to India without the birth of a new Dominion, they would go back to a lost Dominion. 'I would', he remarked almost prophetically, 'even prefer to die in a foreign country so long as it is a free country, and if you do not give us freedom in India you will have to give me a grave here.'⁶

¹ Cmd. 3778, pp. 54–6.   ² Ibid., p. 98.   ³ Ibid., p. 97.
⁴ Ibid., p. 102.   ⁵ Ibid., p. 103.
⁶ Ibid., pp. 98–9. Mohamed Ali never returned to India. He died shortly afterwards (January 3, 1931) while still in England. He was buried in Mecca.

VI

INDIA, BRITAIN AND THE COMMONWEALTH, 1917-29

The Government of India Act of 1919 afforded evidence not only of Britain's desire to foster representative and responsible parliamentary institutions in India, but also of her intention to transfer power by stages to Indian hands. It was in the nature of a 'control experiment'. A beginning in responsible government was made in the provinces. Provincial government was divided into two compartments. Some subjects, finance and law and order in particular, were reserved to the control of the Governor and his official executive. Other subjects, such as education, agriculture, public health, local government, were transferred to the control of Indian Ministers responsible to the elected legislature. Responsible government was to be progressively realized by the transfer of further subjects to Ministers as and when it seemed justified in the light of experience. At the end of ten years a Commission was to examine the working of the system and to advise as to whether the time had come for complete responsible government in any province, or whether some subjects now reserved should be transferred, or if matters had gone badly, the reverse. The devolution of powers from the centre to the provinces was extended and legalized. The provincial legislatures were enlarged. In all of them the majority of the members were to be elected. The franchise was considerably widened. At the centre no comparable advance was made, but measures were taken to further Indian unity and to pave the way for the introduction of responsible government by the creation of a central legislature consisting of an Assembly and of a Council of State, the majority of whose members were elected. If they could not determine policy they could debate it.

There were two main conditions for the success of the difficult and delicate machinery created by the Act of 1919. The first—it was emphasized by the Government of India[1]—was 'a sufficiently long truce in the struggle for power'. The second—it was emphasized by Ramsay MacDonald[2]—was to persuade India that 'a really substantial

[1] Cmd. 123, p. 47. [2] 109 H.C. Deb. 5s., col. 1162.

beginning' was being made and an organization created which would by its own momentum lead progressively to complete self-government for India. Unfortunately, neither of these two conditions was satisfied in the event.

Even under the most favourable circumstances, dyarchy would have been 'a high test of human nature'[1] on all sides. In point of fact, the ironical imp who turns the wheel of fortune in human affairs could hardly have devised a setting less favourable to the inauguration of the reforms of 1919. The reflex action of the war, a devastating influenza epidemic, scarcity, high prices, stifled trade, the painful events of 1919, the uneasiness of the Muslims about the future of Turkey, and finally the non-co-operation movement—all combined to ruin the chances of their success.

Whereas most British officials and politicians believed that the concession of 1919 had been made by Parliament 'in the extreme of its generosity',[2] most Indians thought that it had not given them even 'four annas of genuine *Swaraj*'.[3] What Montagu had feared came to pass; his scheme proved to be 'much too small for the situation'[4] in India.

There was no more unfortunate remark in the Montagu-Chelmsford Report than that which told Indians '*Hanoz Dihli dur ast*'[5] ['Delhi is yet afar off'], for their eyes were now set on the citadel of power. The demand of Indian politicians for the fixing of a time limit arose—and it was so explained[6]—from a disbelief in the intentions of the British Government to transfer power to them. No such time limit could obviously be fixed; and it is no easy matter to remove distrust and suspicion. But unless Indians had some definite vision of the goal which they were going to reach in some foreseeable future, it is difficult to see how that goodwill and co-operation between the rulers and the ruled could be secured which was so necessary for the success of the Montagu-Chelmsford reforms. The tragedy of later years—so full of agonizing conflict—was due in the main to the failure of Indian politicians to realize the profound significance of the changes wrought in 1919 and that these changes had put into their hands the ultimate lever of power if only they knew how to use it; and the failure of most

---

[1] Ilbert and Meston; op. cit., p. 138
[2] Viscount Midleton: 37 H.L. Deb. 5s., col. 1029.
[3] C. R. Das: cited in Zetland, '*Essayez*' (1956), p. 135.
[4] Montagu, op. cit., p. 236.   [5] Cd. 9109, p. 232.
[6] See, for example, the remark made by Madhava Rao before the Joint Select Committee in 1919: H.C. 203, vol. ii, p. 124.

British statesmen, on the other hand, to recognize that the Act of 1919 marked the beginning of the end of British rule in India, to visualize the full implications of this process, and be prepared for all its consequences.

Montagu had originally envisaged full responsible government in the provinces after six years of the inauguration of his reforms.[1] Yielding to more conservative and cautious advice, he postponed this consummation till the next statutory inquiry.[2] The Montagu-Chelmsford Report, however, recommended a further transfer of subjects to the responsible branch of administration in the provinces at the end of five years.[3] The Government of India had second thoughts and opposed this recommendation.[4] The Joint Select Committee endorsed the view of the Government of India.[5] But hopes were still held out of an earlier revision of the Act of 1919. During the committee stage of the Government of India Bill in the House of Commons in December 1919 Labour members demanded that the proposed Statutory Commission should be appointed after six years instead of ten.[6] They also declared that if a Labour Government came into power it would expedite the appointment of the Commission.[7] Montagu and H. A. L. Fisher,[8] on behalf of the Government, assured that there was nothing in the Bill to prevent a revision of the constitution taking place before the expiry of the ten-year period.[9] The working of the Act of 1919 itself revealed that it could not last till 1929. In May 1921, Sir Alexander Frederick Whyte,[10] the President of the Indian Legislative Assembly, remarked: 'The political problem presented by the conjunction of an irremovable executive and a large constitutionally irresponsible majority would be ripe for treatment long before ten years are over.'[11] Montagu observed in August 1921: 'There is no use disguising the fact that transitional periods are a very awkward thing, full of anomalies and full of difficulties. . . . we cannot help recognizing these difficulties, finding in them every reason for accentuating the hope for an early termination of the

---

[1] Montagu, op. cit., pp. 186–7.   [2] Ibid.
[3] Cd. 9109, p. 211.   [4] Cmd. 123, pp. 46–7.
[5] H.C. 203, vol. i, p. 12.   [6] 122 H.C. Deb. 5s., cols. 497, 778.
[7] Ibid., col. 784.

[8] B. 1862; historian and statesman; member of the Royal Commission on the Public Services in India 1912–14; MP 1916–26; President of the Board of Education 1916–22; Warden of New College, Oxford 1925–40; d. 1940.

[9] 122 H.C. Deb. 5s., cols. 498, 782.

[10] B. 1883; MP 1910–18; First President of the Indian Legislative Assembly 1921–5; Political Adviser to the National Government of China 1929–32.

[11] *Times of India*, May 12, 1921.

transitional stage and the acquisition by India of full Dominion Status.'[1] Such remarks encouraged Indians to press for an early revision of the Act of 1919. During the course of a debate in the Indian Legislative Assembly in September 1921 members of the Government of India confirmed the impression that the Statutory Commission would be appointed earlier than 1929.[2] Whether or not Reading really meant it, the fact remains that his peace overtures in December 1921, during the visit of the Prince of Wales, gave his Indian confidants the impression that he was prepared to grant full responsible government to the provinces almost immediately and convene a round table conference of Indian leaders if the non-co-operation movement was withdrawn. Early in 1922 it became known in India that Lord Willingdon, the Governor of Madras, was pressing Reading and the Secretary of State that, in view of the success of reforms in his province and in order to excite the healthy rivalry of other provinces, Madras should at once be granted full responsible government. In the light of these facts it is easy to understand the optimism entertained by most Indian politicians regarding an early revision of the Act of 1919. That what Willingdon was eager to grant in 1922 was not actually conceded till 1937 may well represent the measure of Indian disappointment.

The non-co-operation movement, though it failed in its ostensible purpose, made 'the surge towards self-government . . . a strong and overmastering creed' in India.[3] Reading noted in April 1922 that, though there was a distinct movement on foot to bring the Congress back into constitutionalism, there would 'still be active agitation for a vast extension of reforms upon more satisfactory lines'.[4] He could, however, do little, even if he wanted, to satisfy this 'active agitation'. The refusal by a substantial part of political India to work the reforms, its apparent determination to take the fortress of power by storm, the boycott of the Prince's visit, the mounting tide of racial bitterness, the torrent of abuse and accusation hurled at the authorities—all these had stiffened public opinion in England against any further concession in India. The Englishman's sense of fair play felt outraged. Old doubts—which had never been laid at rest—about the capacity of Indians to work self-governing institutions were revived. All the fault was laid at Montagu's door. A feeling grew in official circles in England that they were 'going too fast' and an attempt was made 'to put on the brake'.[5]

It is possible that if the moderate leaders had shown greater vigour

---

[1] *Statesman*, August 16, 1921. [2] See above, p. 162.
[3] See *Round Table*, June 1922, p. 634. [4] Reading, op. cit., vol. ii, p. 249.
[5] Maurice, op. cit., p. 307.

and influence with the public in India, they might have been able to secure some extension of reforms in 1924. Their rout at the elections held towards the end of 1923 only strengthened the authorities in their determination to hold fast to the fort and await the forthcoming Swarajist assault. The Swarajists entered the legislatures in 1924 in a triumphant mood, with the declared intention of mending or ending them. They wanted to co-operate with the Government, but on their own terms. While eager for compromise, they often spoke and acted in a manner ill-calculated to achieve their objective. To have opened the door at the first push of the Swarajists would have been highly impolitic from the point of view of the Government. It would have driven the moderates and neutrals to the Swarajist camp and given a dangerous encouragement to the forces which demanded immediate *Swaraj* in India. The Government calculated correctly that the alliance of the Swarajists with the other groups in the Assembly was fragile. But they failed to understand the predicament of the Swarajists. The actions of the latter were being jealously watched by their critics outside in the Congress. The Swarajists could only meet the Government half-way. The Government miscalculated when they hoped that the Swarajists would at last settle down to the humdrum task of constitutional opposition in the Assembly.

Analysing the situation in India early in 1924, the *Round Table* correspondent emphasized how all political parties in the country were unanimous in their desire to secure a modification of the present constitution. He also drew attention to the universal and deep-rooted distrust of politically-minded India in the earnestness of the British Government to carry the country towards responsible government in the near future, and remarked: 'If the exigencies of British politics bring into office in Whitehall a Government which is prepared to consider an inquiry into the Indian constitution, with a view to possible revision within the next two years, it seems very probable that the Swarajists may gradually be weaned from their present idea of acting outside the limits of the existing polity. On the other hand, if no action is taken within the near future of a character which shows that Great Britain is prepared to consider immediate political advance the position of the Liberals will be still further weakened, and it is the writer's opinion that the difficulty of securing the adhesion of the majority of the politically-minded classes in India to any subsequent change will be correspondingly increased.'[1] This was a remarkably correct appraisal of the political situation in India. But, though the exigencies of

[1] *Round Table*, March 1924, pp. 359–60.

British politics brought into office in Whitehall a Labour Government, they did not allow the latter to act on the lines suggested by the correspondent of the *Round Table*. The attitude of the Labour Government of 1924 towards Indian aspirations was full of sympathy and understanding. They were, however, placed in an extremely awkward position just then—in office but not in power—to fulfil their pledges of earlier years. To have given an indication of yielding to the demands of the Swarajists would have at once exposed them to the charge of embarking upon a policy of 'abdication' in India by the opposition in Parliament, and ruined their chances of success in the forthcoming elections. In office for the first time, their behaviour was being closely scrutinized by their opponents in England. They, therefore, naturally tended to be timid and over-cautious. Lord Olivier,[1] the Secretary of State for India in the Labour Government, nevertheless suggested to Reading privately, with the consent of his colleagues, the appointment of 'a representative Delegation of British politicians of standing—six or seven—to meet a Delegation of similar calibre appointed by the Central Legislature of India to confer ... and see whether they could not come to an agreement'.[2] Reading 'did not think it opportune',[3] and the proposal was dropped. Pressed by the Opposition in Parliament, the Labour Government had to give an assurance that they did not intend to accelerate the appointment of the Statutory Commission or to go beyond the official inquiry into the working of the Act of 1919 proposed by the Government of India. This caused great disappointment to Indian nationalists who had reckoned on something more satisfactory and dramatic.

The Government of India interpreted the demand put forward by the Swarajists in the Assembly in February 1924 as one for the grant of immediate 'full self-governing Dominion Status'.[4] Their spokesmen—Malcolm Hailey, the Home Member, and Basil Blackett,[5] the Finance Member—pointed out that such a demand meant a repudiation of the essential condition of the declaration of 1917, which envisaged progress by stages. They drew attention to the numerous obvious difficulties

---

[1] Sydney Haldane, first Baron Olivier (1859–1943). Entered Colonial Office 1882; Governor of Jamaica 1907–13; Secretary of State for India 1924; created Baron 1924.

[2] 69 H.L. Deb. 5s., cols. 248–9.   [3] Ibid., col. 249.

[4] *Legislative Assembly Debates*, 1924, vol. iv, pt. i, p. 357.

[5] B. 1882; Entered the Treasury 1904; Secretary to the Royal Commission on Indian Finance and Currency 1913–14; Finance Member of Viceroy's council 1922–7; d. 1935.

in the way of India's rapid advance towards the goal of self-government—the problem of the Indian states, of the minorities, of developing an Indian army capable of defending the country unaided; the lack of confidence between the various communities in the country; and the danger of political advance out-running social conditions. Hailey was led during the course of his remarks on the occasion to draw a distinction between responsible government and Dominion Status. The declaration of 1917 and the preamble to the Act of 1919 had, he said, promised India the former and not the latter. Full Dominion self-government, he argued, was 'of somewhat wider extent' than responsible government, for it meant that not only would the executive be responsible to the legislature, but the legislature would in itself have the full powers which were typical of the modern Dominion, whereas responsible government was not necessarily incompatible with a legislature with limited or restricted powers.[1] 'It may be', he added, 'that full Dominion self-government is the logical outcome of responsible government, nay, it may be the inevitable and historical development of responsible government, but it is a further and a final step.'[2] Hailey opposed the idea of a round table conference primarily on two grounds: first, that it conflicted with Parliament's right of inquiry and decision, and, secondly, that it was not likely to be useful. He pointed out that interests in the country were not yet organized in such a manner as to make the proposed round table conference an authoritative convention, carrying a definite mandate from organized opinion. 'It will inevitably involve this—', he added, 'that at the last stage the Government will be brought in to decide between those conflicting interests, and incur once more all the odium and insinuations involved in the attempt to settle the claims of contesting interests. There may be unity against Government, but that unity breaks down when any attempt is made to proceed to constructive decisions.'[3]

The attitude of the Government of India was, however, apparently neither *non possumus* nor hostile. 'We are all Swarajists today,'[4] said Blackett. 'Our aim is the same and our purpose as high as that of any of those who wish the best for India,'[5] said Hailey. Let us not argue this case, he urged, 'as though we were contestants battling in a court of law for the possession of the future of India'.[6] Both Hailey and Blackett emphasized that their differences with the Swarajists were confined only to the method and pace of advance. It was not a problem,

---
[1] *Legislative Assembly Debates*, 1924, vol. iv, pt. i, p. 358.
[2] Ibid.   [3] Ibid., p. 765.   [4] Ibid., p. 539.   [5] Ibid., p. 366.   [6] Ibid.

they pointed out, of mere words or good feelings, but of administration, for there was a multitude to be moved. If the steady and safe course appealed to those in the Government, it was because they were practical men and experience had taught them to 'mistrust the morasses and dangers of the shorter ways in the valleys below'.[1] Blackett told the impatient nationalists, who continually pressed the driver of the car to go faster, not to forget 'that the driver also is human and that he is doing his best and that he cannot be expected to go on doing his best if all the time he is upbraided for his slowness and suspected, and indeed roundly accused to his face, of malingering. That is not the way in which to get the best out of any man.'[2] Whatever its shortcomings, he added, Englishmen were proud of their record in India, of the manner in which they had discharged their trust. Constant ridicule and vilification of their work in India touched them in a sentimental spot. It was not easy, Blackett said, for Englishmen to give expression to their deeper emotions, but the phrase 'the brightest jewel in the British Crown', uttered during the debate, did arouse deep emotions in their hearts. 'India', he went on, 'has become something more than part of the British Empire to countless Englishmen and Englishwomen. It has become an inspiration and an aspiration. . . . From her experiences in India England has learned to see a vision of a world order in which the conflicting problems and antagonisms of colour and race and creed could be resolved without armed struggle under a reign of law freely accepted by all. India has become the symbol and the test of that vision: and because of that England has realized that it is not enough to govern a country for the good of the people of that country even with the consent of the governed, and she has set before herself and India the goal of full responsible self-government for the Indian peoples as a full and free partner in the British Commonwealth of Nations. The desire to reach that goal has become for many people in England almost a passion—something more than a mere desire; it has become the absolute test of the position of the British Empire in the world.'[3]

Blackett and Hailey gave expression not only to the point of view of the Government of India, but that of enlightened Englishmen in general—a point of view as reasonable, convincing and appealing as any that a responsible Indian nationalist could put forward. But still the gulf between the two remained unbridged. Why? Motilal Nehru suggested the answer when he said of Hailey: 'My only trouble with

---

[1] *Legislative Assembly Debates*, 1924, vol. iv, pt. i, pp. 366, 539–40.
[2] Ibid., p. 540.   [3] Ibid., pp. 540–1.

him is that I cannot get him to feel as I feel.'[1] Blackett provided the answer when he remarked: 'That is the difficulty, the difficulty of mutual understanding, which is at the root of many of our troubles.'[2] For removing this great psychological difficulty an inquisition into the working of dyarchy—such as was undertaken by the Government of India—was hardly the appropriate step.

The Reforms Inquiry Committee, headed by Sir Alexander Muddiman, spent eighteen months over its thankless job. Before, however, it could submit its report the Labour Government had gone out of office and their place was taken by the Conservatives in England.[3] The new Secretary of State for India, Lord Birkenhead, had no sympathy with the Indian demand for a rapid political advance. He had 'a profound distrust of the Montagu-Chelmsford policy, and a belief that India would not be capable of supporting Dominion Status for centuries'.[4] He wrote to Reading on December 4, 1924: 'I think you know that alone in the Cabinet I distrusted, and indeed to some extent opposed, the Montagu-Chelmsford Report. To me it is frankly inconceivable that India will ever be fit for Dominion self-government. My present view is that we ought rigidly to adhere to the date proposed in the Act for a re-examination of the situation, and that it is not likely, unless matters greatly change in the interval, that such a re-examination will suggest the slightest extension. In the meantime, little as I have liked dyarchy, obviously it must be given its chance....'[5] The nationalist agitation for *Swaraj* in India 'inclined him rather to contract than to expand any further promises of constitutional reform'.[6] Even as late as September 1928 he wrote to Irwin: '... the Montagu Constitution was a mistake, ill-conceived and potentially extremely mischievous. I should, therefore, if I was dealing with the situation as a Mussolini might, correct the gravest and more obvious defects; give them nothing more; and resolutely face the chatter and abuse, for you get just as much chatter and abuse whatever you do.'[7] For dealing with the delicate situation in India just then, one wonders if Birkenhead, with his

---

[1] *Legislative Assembly Debates*, 1924, vol. iv, pt. i, p. 371.
[2] Ibid., p. 542.
[3] The change in government was, it is suggested, reflected not only in the recommendations of the majority report of the Committee, but also in the decision to take fresh evidence. See F. M. De Mello, *The Indian National Congress* (1934), p. 93.
[4] Second Earl of Birkenhead, *Frederick Edwin, Earl of Birkenhead: The Last Phase* (1935), p. 245.
[5] Ibid.   [6] Ibid., p. 246.
[7] Ibid., p. 261.

hectoring tone, his lack of real interest[1] in and sympathy for India, was in any way the right Secretary of State.

Birkenhead's first important pronouncement on India as Secretary of State in July 1925 was, however, studiously moderate. He demanded from Indian leaders positive evidence of the spirit of co-operation, for as long as Britain was confronted with 'a blank wall of negation', she could not be expected to make an advance.[2] As for expediting the statutory inquiry, he remarked that 'wise men are not the slaves of dates', but added in warning: 'The door of acceleration is not open to menace: still less will it be stormed by violence.'[3]

The Swarajists did give some proof of their desire to co-operate and accept responsibility, but it was considered inadequate. In September 1925 when they reiterated their demand for the convocation of a representative conference or commission, the Government of India—knowing the mind of the Secretary of State—advised them to lay aside their demand for immediate *Swaraj* for the moment, settle down to work the Act of 1919 and respond more fully to the Secretary of State's appeal for co-operation.[4] The demand for greater proof of co-operation stung Jinnah into a bitter diatribe. 'Will you bring', he asked the Government, 'a section of the politically-minded people, who happen to be the largest political party, will you bring them down on their knees? Will you bring Pandit Motilal Nehru to bow down to the throne at Viceregal Lodge, and say, "Sir, I am humble, I crawl before you, and will you now be graciously pleased to give a Royal Commission?" Is that what you want? What has Pandit Motilal Nehru been doing in this Assembly? Has he not been co-operating with you? ... I want to know what more you want, and may I know what evidence, what proof, documentary or oral, do you want me to produce or adduce that the responsible leaders are willing to co-operate with you? Have you no eyes, have you no ears, have you no brains?'[5]

Birkenhead had decided to appoint the Statutory Commission at the latest by the middle of 1927 'as a matter of elementary prudence' and 'safety', to prevent the choice falling to a Labour Government.[6] He wanted Reading to utilize such an acceleration as 'a useful bargain

---

[1] Birkenhead's lack of interest in Indian affairs is testified by: E. Cadogan, *The India We Saw* (1933), p. 4; L. S. Amery, *My Political Life* (1953), vol. ii, p. 298; and the Indian members of his council. For the last see *Hindustan Review*, December 1929, pp. 423–9.

[2] 61 H.L. Deb. 5s., col. 1077.   [3] Ibid.

[4] *Legislative Assembly Debates*, 1925, vol. vi, pt. ii, pp. 848–54, 890–6.

[5] Ibid., pp. 940–1.

[6] Birkenhead, op. cit., pp. 250–1.

counter or for further disintegrating the Swarajist Party'.[1] But when in December 1925 Reading suggested an immediate announcement of the appointment of the Commission, Birkenhead disregarded his advice and lost another opportunity of ending the deadlock in India.[2] The tendency to mark time and the anxiety to further disintegrate the Swarajist Party benefited no one. When Irwin arrived in India in April 1926, the country was already a land of despair. The Commission was appointed in 1927 when no one in India wanted it.

It was the considered judgement of the authors of the Montagu-Chelmsford Report that ever since 1858 the interest shown by Parliament in Indian affairs had not been either 'well-sustained or well-informed', and that it had 'ceased to assert control at the very moment when it had acquired it'.[3] And they reached the conclusion that 'Parliament's omission to institute regular means of reviewing the Indian administration' had been 'as much responsible as any single cause for our failure in the face of growing nationalist feeling in India, to think out and to work out a policy of continuous advance'.[4] They sought to remedy this defect by transferring the salaries of the Secretary of State for India and his Office to the Home Estimates, the institution of a Select Committee of Parliament on Indian affairs, and the revival of the old system of periodical inquiry into the Indian administration. In making these recommendations the authors of the Report virtually acceded to the long-standing demands of the Indian nationalists themselves. The periodic Commission which the Report suggested was intended to be 'some outside authority charged with the duty of re-surveying the political situation in India and of readjusting the machinery to the new requirements'.[5] It was to be an 'authoritative' Commission which should 'derive its authority from Parliament itself'.[6] The Report also indicated in general terms what the mandate of this proposed Commission should be.[7] Section 41 of the Government of India Act, 1919, accordingly provided for the appointment of a Statutory Commission 'at the expiration of ten years after the passing

[1] Birkenhead, op. cit., p. 251.   [2] Reading, op. cit., vol. ii, p. 342.
[3] Cd. 9109, p. 29.   [4] Ibid., p. 30.
[5] Ibid., p. 212. It was later claimed by some who had enjoyed the confidence of the authors of the Report that the genesis of the idea of a Statutory Commission lay in the anxiety—expressed by Indians and recognized by Montagu and Chelmsford—to obviate the risk of prolonging an admittedly transitory constitution and ensure progressive political advance in India. See Reed, op. cit., p. 186; *Times of India* (editorial), January 2, 1928; and Chintamani: *Report of the Proceedings of the Tenth Session of the National Liberal Federation of India*, 1927, p. 63.   [6] Cd. 9109, p. 212.   [7] Ibid.

of this Act' 'for the purpose of inquiring into the working of the system of government, the growth of education, and the development of representative institutions, in British India', and to 'report as to whether and to what extent it is desirable to establish the principle of responsible government, or to extend, modify, or restrict the degree of responsible government then existing therein'.[1] It was, however, not made clear by the Montagu-Chelmsford Report, or the Act itself, or during the debates in Parliament on the Government of India Bill in 1919, whether this proposed Commission was to be composed exclusively of members of Parliament. Had such a clarification been made when the Act of 1919 was being passed, the Imperial Government would have at least been spared the charges of bad faith brought against them by even the most moderate-minded Indians when the Simon Commission was appointed in 1927.[2]

All political parties in India in the 'twenties recognized the legislative supremacy of the Imperial Parliament. Even the Congress, which took its stand on the principle of self-determination, bowed to the sovereign and ultimate authority of Parliament. What it challenged was the assertion contained in the Preamble to the Act of 1919 that 'the time and manner of each advance can be determined only by Parliament'.[3] 'Now, that is a proposition', said Motilal Nehru, 'which we cannot accept, and as long as you insist upon that, so long we shall insist upon the contrary.'[4] Nor did Congressmen stand alone in ridiculing the doctrine of trusteeship and challenging the absolute and exclusive right claimed for Parliament to decide the fate of India. Liberals, Independents and Muslim Leaguers—all alike claimed that Indians should have an equal voice in framing the future constitution for their country, however much they might have differed from Congressmen in the manner of asserting that claim. Dominion precedents were frequently quoted by Indian nationalists in support of their demand to frame their own constitution and submit the same to Parliament for ratification. The recent example of Ireland and the remarks made by Imperial statesmen justifying the procedure followed in her case only

---

[1] Government of India Act, 1919, 9 & 10. Geo. 5 [ch. 101], p. 29.

[2] Dawson's comment is significant: 'The British Government are greatly to blame for the manner in which the Simon Commission was launched. Everyone had been allowed to anticipate a "mixed" Commission.' Cited in Wrench, op. cit., p. 272. It should also be borne in mind that never during the last sixty years had a Royal Commission been appointed to inquire into Indian affairs which did not include Indians as full members.

[3] 9 & 10. Geo. 5, p. 1.

[4] *Legislative Assembly Debates*, 1924, vol. iv, pt. iii, p. 1954.

strengthened the claim of Indian nationalists. The latter noted and remembered what Lloyd George had remarked during the debate on the Anglo-Irish Treaty on December 14, 1921: 'Here we are going to follow the example which has been set in the framing of every constitution throughout the Empire. The constitution is drafted and decided by the Dominion, the Imperial Parliament taking such steps as may be necessary to legalize these decisions.'[1] Did Sir John Simon[2] ever, during his unhappy experiences in India as Chairman of the Statutory Commission, recollect the speech he had delivered in Parliament on November 27, 1922, especially the following passage in it: 'I believe it would be true to say that Constitutions which promote prosperity and loyalty, and which have been found to be lasting Constitutions for subordinate States in our Empire, have, almost without exception, either actually or virtually, been formed by those who were to live under them themselves.'[3]

It is true that the attacks made by Indian nationalists on the Preamble to the Act of 1919 wounded British *amour propre* and prompted them to assert more emphatically its principles. This in its turn brought forth counter-assertions of the principle of self-determination. 'The Preamble contains the permanent and static policy of the British Government; Parliament will never divest itself of its trust; it will never agree to merely register your decrees,' said Government spokesmen. 'You are denying us our birthright; you are refusing to treat us as you treated your Dominions; you are exhibiting your physical might,' replied Indian nationalists. And so the debate continued throughout the 'twenties. It was a futile and dangerous game. The Indian problem could not be solved by a fiat of Parliament or 'the simple and soulful exercise of self-determination'. Statesmanship demanded accommodation and reconciliation of apparently divergent principles. As long as Indian nationalists made even a pretence of recognizing Parliament as the final and ultimate authority in Indian affairs, such a reconciliation was not difficult. With all its experience of dealing with Dominion nationalisms, and more especially that of the recent settle-

[1] 149 H.C. Deb. 5s., col. 42.
[2] B. 1873; Solicitor-General 1910; Attorney-General 1913; Home Secretary 1915–16; Chairman of the Indian Statutory Commission 1927–30; Foreign Secretary 1931–5; Home Secretary 1935–7; Chancellor of the Exchequer 1937–40; created Viscount; Lord Chancellor 1940–5; d. 1954.
[3] 159 H.C. Deb. 5s., col. 344. Simon was speaking in the debate on the Constitution of the Irish Free State and supporting the point made by Bonar Law, that 'as a matter of fact, the Constitutions of Canada, Australia and of South Africa were all drafted in those Dominions' (159 H.C. Deb. 5s., col. 329).

ment of the Irish question,[1] Parliament would not have found it very difficult to accommodate the far less intransigent claims of Indian nationalism. After all, what Indians demanded was, to quote Simon's description in 1922, 'by no means a novel or a revolutionary procedure'.[2] But for once the statesmen at the helm showed a lamentable lack of ingenuity and imagination. Both Irwin and Birkenhead were fully cognizant of the fact that most Indian parties and politicians disagreed with the claim of Parliament to dispose of the destiny of India as it chose,[3] but relying upon the weaknesses of Indian nationalism they made no serious attempt to accommodate the Indian point of view.

What India needed in 1927 was not a judicial inquest into the 1919 reforms, such as was entrusted to the Simon Commission. The working of dyarchy had proved nothing and settled nothing. It had been a foggy episode in which all parties had been groping. Its results had been so diverse and confused as to make it impossible to base any confident conclusions upon it and extract from its records any sure guidance for the future. Howsoever intelligent the 'jury' they could not find a solution to the Indian puzzle.[4] Even as 'rapporteurs' they were hardly likely to tell much that had not already been heard. The great need of the hour in India was to restore confidence in the good intentions of the Imperial Government. This could only be done by a sympathetic understanding of the Indian problem and by determining the political advance of the country in co-operation with its leaders. The most perfect and impartial findings of an excellent Commission could be of little use if they were not acceptable to the main body of Indian nationalists. The difficulties in the way of composing a mixed Commission were obvious and many, but certainly there were other ways of approaching the problem, and the considerations which prompted the Government of India and the Secretary of State not to search for these alternative methods do not reflect much credit on either.[5] There was not one concession that was made later—either by

---

[1] In the Irish settlement Parliament had made room for the national and self-derived statehood which Ireland claimed.   [2] 159 H.C. Deb. 5s., col. 343.

[3] See *Speeches by Lord Irwin* (1930), vol. i, p. 206; and Birkenhead, op. cit., p. 252.

[4] Simon admitted as much: 'I sometimes feel as though I had been asked to spend two years over a gigantic crossword puzzle, with the tip whispered into my private ear that the puzzle had *no* solution.' Simon to Dawson, January 12, 1929: *The History of 'The Times'*, vol. iv, pt. ii, p. 869.

[5] One of the most prominent considerations which weighed with Birkenhead in excluding Indians from the Commission was the fear that an 'alliance might be created between the Indian and the British Labour representatives'; Irwin was

way of liberalizing the procedure of the Commission or of supplementing its labours—which could not have been made earlier with more grace and better results. The appointment of an exclusively British Statutory Commission in 1927 very nearly caused the disruption of another Empire on the rock of juridical sovereignty. All tribute to Irwin who retrieved the situation in time. Yet another example of what Toynbee calls 'the British habit of "being only just in time" '![1]

Few in Parliament had disagreed with Crewe when in 1912 he authoritatively and emphatically repudiated the idea of Dominion self-government for India; fewer still disagreed with Montagu when he made the momentous announcement five years later recognizing that idea as the goal of British policy in India. This was a fact of some significance. The *volte-face* was accepted by many British politicians in a mood of wise resignation. As the Duke of Wellington had held 'rotten potatoes' responsible for Sir Robert Peel's right-about-turn over the Corn Laws in 1846, so did men like Curzon and Crewe blame the war for the 'changed angle of vision' in the matter of India in 1917. Some comforted themselves with the thought that the announcement of August 20, 1917, had spoken of responsible government in India merely as an ultimate goal which would not be attained for generations to come—not at least in their own lifetimes; others persuaded themselves to believe that Britain had always been pursuing the same policy in India and that the announcement had done nothing but stated it definitely and explicitly in so many words. Both these erroneous impressions precluded even responsible British statesmen from attempting to take into account the full implications of the declaration of 1917 or the significance of the forces released by the reforms of 1919. Nothing was changed in India, many of them believed, only a few more Indians had been admitted to the *arcana imperii*; a careful and cautious experiment was being made which would be extended or withdrawn as circumstances warranted. Britain's responsibility in India, said *The Times*, was 'no transient task'.[2] In vain did men like

---

'advised' that 'the Muslims certainly would not boycott, and if the Muslims did not boycott, the Hindus would hardly dare to do, so sharp was communal tension, and so keen would be the anxiety lest the decision might go against those who did not appear before the Commission to make their case'. See Halifax, op. cit., pp. 115–16.

[1] A. J. Toynbee, *The Conduct of British Empire Foreign Relations since the Peace Settlement* (1928), p. 29.   [2] *The Times*, August 21, 1917.

Professor Arthur Berriedale Keith[1] warn British statesmen not to labour under 'the impression that the development of responsible government in India will be a leisurely process, conducted at the rate of speed which seems good to them'.[2] In vain did Montagu tell Parliament that there was 'no use for pronouncements which take geological epochs to fulfil'.[3] But it is doubtful if even those who uttered these warnings or sympathized with Indian aspirations anticipated the headlong rush of Indian nationalism in the post-war era or had any clear and definite ideas about the further steps to be taken.

In 1926 Frederick Whyte was constrained to remark that neither the Government of India nor His Majesty's Government had ever so far attempted to look beyond the administrative and political problems of the day to grapple with the fundamentals of the Indian problem or to see it as a whole.[4] 'Rarely, if ever,' he wrote, 'has the Government of India or His Majesty's Government envisaged its Indian responsibilities as a constitutional problem requiring a foundation of principle as well as an edifice of carefully designed administrative architecture. The dispatches of the Secretary of State and the Governor-General in Council which deal with constitutional questions in India, including the Report on Constitutional Reforms by the late Mr Edwin Montagu and Lord Chelmsford, almost invariably approach the problem from the point of view of a particular—almost momentary situation in India itself.'[5] One could feel that Whyte might have excluded the Montagu-Chelmsford Report from the list of empirical, short-sighted and piecemeal attempts, for that Report certainly did not lack either principle or vision. A closer examination of the Report would, however, reveal that Whyte's verdict was not wholly unjust. The authors of that Report did try to look ahead, but the vastness and complexity of the problem they were called upon to deal with, the circumstances in which they conducted their inquiry, and their own personal limitations—arising almost from the ingrained habit of Englishmen to treat the issues of the day after tomorrow as unreal—prevented them from looking too far ahead. They laid down the policy; they made a beginning; and they awaited further incubation before the problem could be more satisfactorily treated. They did not conceive it to be their purpose to make arrangements for gradually winding up the British *Raj*. How

---

[1] B. 1879; Sanskrit scholar and constitutional lawyer; served in the Colonial Office 1901–14; Regius Professor of Sanskrit and Comparative Philology, Edinburgh 1914–44; d. 1944.
[2] *The Times*, October 8, 1920.   [3] 116 H.C. Deb. 5s., col. 2298.
[4] Whyte, *India, A Federation?* (1925), pp. 31–2, 315–16.   [5] Ibid., p. 31.

and when would responsible government be introduced at the centre? What of the problem of Indian defence or that of the Indian princely states? The Montagu-Chelmsford Report did not treat these as real issues. Vague general suggestions were made; they were repeated before the Joint Select Committee in 1919 and during the debates in Parliament; men like Curtis and Montagu were not lacking in good intentions or bright ideas; but there was no plan of campaign. 'The reforms of 1919', commented the Simon Report in 1930, 'did not make provision for a steady evolution towards an ultimate objective.'[1]

The result was that in 1922 Lloyd George still spoke of the British element in the Indian Civil Service as 'the steel frame' of the *Raj* and remarked that he could see no time when India could dispense with its guidance and assistance.[2] In 1925 Birkenhead admitted that the implications of provincial autonomy had 'never yet been closely analysed'.[3] No attempt was made to grapple with the problem of the princely states till 1930. Plans for the Indianization of the army remained halting, leisurely and unconvincing. Defence was often called 'the very article by which the republic stands or falls'.[4] India's incapacity in the matter was repeatedly emphasized as constituting an almost insuperable block on her rapid constitutional advance, but the British Government, in the 'twenties, do not appear to have reconciled themselves to the idea of handing over the control of the Indian army to a government responsible to an Indian legislature in any foreseeable future.[5] As late as 1930 the Simon Commission proposed that the subject of Indian defence should be reserved indefinitely as an Imperial responsibility and transferred to the Imperial Government.[6] Early in the 'twenties

---

[1] *Report of the Indian Statutory Commission*, vol. ii, Cmd. 3569 (1930), p. 7.
[2] 157 H.C. Deb. 5s., col. 1513.   [3] 61 H.L. Deb. 5s., col. 1087.
[4] Hailey: *Legislative Assembly Debates*, 1924, vol. iv, pt. i, p. 363.
[5] C. S. Ranga Iyer says in his book *How to Lose India?* (1935), p. 83, that Lord Winterton, for long Under-Secretary of State for India, once told him 'that he could not think of a day when the Indian Government consisting of Indians and responsible to India would be endowed with the same powers which ... the Dominions have in regard to the Army. He could only think of giving India autonomy in Civil affairs such as Rhodesia enjoyed.'
[6] The Report of the Commission described the North-West frontier as 'an international frontier of the first importance from the military point of view for the whole Empire' and remarked: 'India and Britain are so related that Indian defence cannot, now or in any future which is within sight, be regarded as a matter of purely Indian concern.' It recommended that the control and direction of the Indian army 'must rest in the hands of agents of the Imperial Government' and 'should not be regarded as a function of an Indian Government in relation with an Indian legislature'. See Cmd. 3569, pp. 173-4.

Indian political opinion became unanimous in demanding that the Act of 1919 should be completely overhauled and a constitution should be framed which would lead India automatically to complete responsible government in some reasonable time. For any such more or less final settlement of the Indian problem the British Government were ill-prepared. Their reply to Indian clamour and impatience was mainly by way of suggesting difficulties and emphasizing the evils of forcing the pace. 'Those who believe', remarked Hailey,[1] quoting the prophet Isaiah, 'do not go in haste.' But the root of the difficulty in India lay in the fact that Indians had ceased to believe in the British. 'I am rather surprised', Reading wrote to Olivier in 1924, 'at the practical unanimity among Indians of all shades and descriptions, with one or two rare exceptions of no importance. Their attitude is of such doubt of our intentions as to amount almost to mistrust.'[2]

It was tragic and ironical that Indian public opinion morally broke with Britain at almost the very moment when she committed herself publicly and definitely to the policy of self-government for India. But should not part of the explanation for this unfortunate happening be sought in the failure of British statesmen to show Indians clearly the steps by which they proposed to reach a definite goal? Did not the lack of a settled policy and a definite programme on the part of the British Government contribute something towards increasing the exasperation and intransigence of political India?

Nor did Indian impatience fail, in its turn, to react on the British. The latter, with their experience of the slow evolutionary growth of self-governing institutions in their own country and in the Dominions, could not but think that the development of a real parliamentary system in India—with her manifold divisions and immemorial traditions of autocracy—must be a gradual and very lengthy operation. Balfour expressed this point of view in the Lords on February 26, 1924.[3] He argued that it was a profound delusion to think that the British were acting as a drag upon the growth of free institutions in India. Freedom could not be created by a stroke of the pen. There was never a country where the difficulties of constitutional government were greater than they were in India. Institutions could not be imported as one imported a new locomotive from one civilization to another. 'Free institutions', he continued, 'on the British model or on the Dominion model are among the most difficult institutions in the world to manage properly.

[1] *Legislative Assembly Debates*, 1924, vol. iv, pt. i, p. 365.
[2] Reading, op. cit., vol. ii, p. 292.
[3] 56 H.L. Deb. 5 s., cols. 416–23.

Free government is very difficult government. The easy government is the government of an absolute autocracy. The notion appears to be that, if you leave India alone, India will at one stride—taking an example from Great Britain, from the great British Dominions, from the United States of America, from other great free and self-governing communities—join their ranks as a natural equal. That is entirely to ignore the teaching of history.'[1] But the Indian nationalists of the 'twenties were no longer inclined to listen to such lectures, however well-meant, from British statesmen. They were impatient to get rid of the British yoke. They looked upon British rule not as a school of freedom, but as a tyranny to be overthrown. Nor did all Britons reason as philosophically as Balfour did. Those who had served in India shook their heads at the strange new happenings in that country. Such things were unknown when they were at 'Dustypore' twenty-five years ago. Surely it must be the fault of Montagu who set out to disturb the placid, pathetic contentment of the Indian masses and injected a dose of democracy into that autocratic country. Sir William Joynson-Hicks[2] was determined to hold by the sword a country which had, he said, been conquered by the sword as an outlet for the goods of Great Britain.[3] Birkenhead was convinced that 'the surrender of India would be an act not only of great folly but of degenerate poltroonery', for it would mean the sinking of Great Britain 'into political and commercial insignificance'.[4] 'I am not able', he affirmed in 1925 as Secretary of State for India, 'in any foreseeable future to discern a moment when we may safely, either to ourselves or India, abandon our trust. There is, my Lords, no "Lost Dominion"; there will be no "Lost Dominion" until the moment—if ever it comes—when the whole British Empire, with all that it means for civilization, is splintered in doom.'[5] Preoccupied with pressing problems nearer home, most British politicians were slow to apprehend how rapid a transformation was passing over

[1] 56 H.L. Deb. 5 s., col. 417.

[2] B. 1865; MP 1908–29; Home Secretary 1924–9; created Viscount Brentford 1929; d. 1932.

[3] 'We did not conquer India for the benefit of Indians. I know it is said in missionary meetings that we conquered India to raise the level of Indians. That is cant. We conquered India as an outlet for the goods of Great Britain. We conquered it by the sword and by the sword we should hold it. I am not such a hypocrite as to say we hold India for the Indians. We hold it as the finest outlet for British goods in general, and for Lancashire goods in particular.' Joynson-Hicks: cited in Graham Pole, *India in Transition* (1932), p. 15.

[4] Cited in Sivaswamy Aiyer, op. cit., pp. 349–50.

[5] 61 H.L. Deb. 5 s., cols. 1091–2.

the Indian outlook. And thoughtless remarks such as those made by Joynson-Hicks and Birkenhead confirmed the worst suspicions of Indians about the real intentions of their rulers. Thus it happened that bred of impatience, on one side, and lack of appreciation, on the other, distrust grew, aggravating as the years passed the difficulty of bringing to bear on the Indian problem from either side the dispassionate judgement which its complexity demanded.

In 1917 the phrase 'Dominion Status' had not yet come into use. The historic announcement of August 20th of that year had only spoken of the goal of British policy as 'the gradual development of self-governing institutions with a view to the progressive realization of responsible government in India as an integral part of the British Empire'.[1] This was, however, universally interpreted as identifying the goal prescribed for India with that already attained by the self-governing Dominions.[2] The Montagu-Chelmsford Report underlined this interpretation when it visualized 'a completely representative and responsible Government of India on an equal footing with the other self-governing units of the British Commonwealth'.[3] Men like Curzon,[4] Milner[5] and Chirol[6] had now obviously reconciled themselves to the idea of a 'brown Dominion' within the Empire. Even those who, like Lord Sydenham,[7] disagreed with the measure and manner of political advance in India did not quarrel with the ultimate goal envisaged for her.[8] The only discordant voice in this chorus of approval was that of Lord Lansdowne, who dismissed the idea of India eventually finding 'her place alongside the self-governing British Dominions' as 'a dream',[9] and for this he was duly reprimanded by *The Times* next day.[10] During the debates in Parliament on the Montagu-Chelmsford reforms, speaker after speaker—irrespective of party affiliation—expressed the hope that India would in the fullness of time become a self-governing member of the Empire like the Dominions. The ideal

[1] 97 H.C. Deb. 5 s., col. 1695.
[2] See, for example, Curtis, op. cit., p. 362, and Ernest Barker, *The Future Government of India and the Civil Service* (1919), p. 5.
[3] Cd. 9109, p. 277. See also pp. 120 and 149.
[4] 37 H.L. Deb. 5 s., col. 1049.
[5] 41 H.L. Deb. 5 s., col. 312.
[6] *The Times*, November 6, 1917, June 6 and 27, 1918.
[7] George Sydenham Clarke, Baron Sydenham of Combe (1848–1933). Governor of Victoria 1901–3; Governor of Bombay 1907–13; created Baron 1913.
[8] 31 H.L. Deb. 5 s., col. 548. [9] Ibid., col. 787.
[10] *The Times*, October 25, 1917.

was variously expressed as 'self-government within the Empire',[1] 'equality with the other great portions of His Majesty's Dominions',[2] 'a sister nation in the British Empire',[3] 'one of the self-governing Dominions of the British Empire'[4] and even as 'dominion status'.[5]

In the debate on Irwin's announcement in 1929 Lord Reading remarked that the term 'Dominion Status' had 'never been used hitherto in any formal document'.[6] This was not true. The term occurs in the Crewe Committee Report of 1919 as an indication of the goal which India was to attain in course of time.[7] It occurs repeatedly in the Esher Committee Report of 1919–20.[8] In fact, the Esher Committee had been instructed by the Secretary of State for India to avoid framing their proposals in a manner likely to prove inconsistent with 'the gradual approach of India towards a Dominion status'.[9]

The instrument of Instructions issued to the Governors-General after the passing of the Act of 1919 read: 'For above all it is Our will and pleasure that the plans laid by Our Parliament for the progressive realization of responsible government in British India as an integral part of Our Empire may come to fruition, to the end that British India may attain its due place among our Dominions.'[10] The message of the King-Emperor read out by the Duke of Connaught before the Indian Legislature in February 1921 said: 'For years, it may be for generations, patriotic and loyal Indians have dreamed of *Swaraj* for their motherland. Today you have beginnings of *Swaraj* within my Empire, and widest scope and ample opportunity for progress to the liberty which my other Dominions enjoy.'[11]

Montagu, when Secretary of State, had often expressed his hope that India would attain full Dominion Status as early as possible.[12] Reading, who was critical of Irwin's Dominion Status declaration of 1929, had himself held out the same attractive ideal for India in his speeches as Viceroy,[13] even employing the phrase 'Dominion Status'.[14] Even

[1] 109 H.C. Deb. 5 s., col. 1158.   [2] Ibid., col. 1208.
[3] 116 H.C. Deb. 5 s., col. 622.   [4] Ibid., col. 2342.
[5] 109 H.C. Deb. 5 s., col. 1225.   [6] 75 H.L. Deb. 5 s., col. 377.
[7] See *Report of the Committee appointed by the Secretary of State for India to inquire into the Home Administration of Indian Affairs* (Chairman: Lord Crewe), Cmd. 207 (1919), pp. 11, 40.
[8] Cmd. 943, pp. 4, 7, 8, 32, 103.   [9] Ibid., p. 4.   [10] Halifax, op. cit., p. 121.
[11] *Legislative Assembly Debates*, 1921, vol. i, pt. i, p. 14.
[12] See above, pp. 210–11.
[13] *Speeches by the Earl of Reading* (1926), vol. ii, pp. 71, 125–6, 213, 283.
[14] Ibid., p. 423. Nor would it appear that Reading, in 1921, thought Dominion Status to be a very remote ideal. He wrote to Montagu on August 18, 1921: 'I am in entire agreement with you. I think it useless to make pronouncement of our

Winston Churchill,[1] than whom there was no greater critic of Irwin's declaration, had in 1921 'looked forward confidently to the days when the Indian Government and people would have assumed fully and completely their Dominion status'.[2] In fact, there was not one important British statesman who had not, at one time or another during the years 1917–29, indicated either literally or figuratively that Dominion Status was the glorious destiny in store for India. *The Times*, on November 5, 1929, quoted only ten such pronouncements made by responsible statesmen of all parties in England.[3] One could easily quote a hundred. Lord Passfield[4] was justified when he challenged the Lords in 1929: 'Is there any noble Lord who will get up and say that the goal of India in the fullness of time has not been declared to be Dominion *status*—declared over and over again?'[5]

The only objection that could be taken to Irwin's declaration of 1929—apart from its timing—was that the content and meaning of Dominion Status had widened and become more definite in recent years and that this enlarged and definitive Dominion Status could no longer be held out as the ultimate goal for India. But having repeatedly promised India Dominion Status, it was impossible to raise such an objection. The development and definition of Dominion Status could not be turned into an argument for 'lowering the sights' in the case of India. 'Can there be any doubt whatever, in any quarter of the House,' enquired Baldwin,[6] 'that the position of an India, with full responsible

---

policy to give India in the near future full Dominion Status and yet at the same time to hesitate to put her in the position to manage her affairs when they have been entrusted to her.' Reading, op. cit., vol. ii, pp. 209, 333–4.

[1] B. 1874; MP 1900; Under-Secretary for Colonies 1906–8; President of the Board of Trade 1908–10; Home Secretary 1910–11; First Lord of the Admiralty 1911–15; Minister of Munitions 1917; Secretary of State for War 1919–21; Colonial Secretary 1921–2; Chancellor of the Exchequer 1924–9; First Lord of the Admiralty 1939–40; Prime Minister 1940–5 and 1951–5.

[2] Speech made on June 15, 1921 at a dinner given by the Empire Development Parliamentary Committee to the Premiers of the Dominions and the representatives of India who were then in London for the Imperial Conference. Cited in *Report of the Joint Committee on Indian Constitutional Reform* (1932–3), vol. iic, Evidence, p. 1792.   [3] *The Times*, November 5, 1929.

[4] Sidney James Webb, Baron Passfield (1859–1947). Social reformer and historian; launched London School of Economics and Political Science 1895; created Baron 1929; Colonial Secretary 1929–31.

[5] 75 H.L. Deb. 5 s., col. 422.

[6] Stanley Baldwin, first Earl Baldwin of Bewdley (1867–1947). MP 1908–37; President of the Board of Trade 1921–2; Chancellor of the Exchequer 1922–3; Prime Minister 1923–4, 1924–9 and 1935–7; created Earl 1937.

Government in the Empire, when attained ... must be one of equality with the other States in the Empire?'[1] And he added: 'Nobody knows what Dominion status will be when India has responsible Government ... but surely no one dreams of a self-governing India with an inferior status.'[2] The honest and straightforward Irwin had no doubt that His Majesty's Government stood committed by solemn declarations to the policy of leading India on to Dominion Status.[3] He realized the need to remove the suspicion and misunderstanding created by Hailey's speech in the Indian Legislative Assembly in February 1924. Moreover, as he wrote later, 'whatever might be the exact definition of Dominion Status worked out by ingenious disciples of the law, it in no way touched my conviction that you could not, without losing India from the Commonwealth, hold out a future for her less honourable than that to which constitutional development had brought Canada or Australia'.[4]

When the war broke out in 1914, the Dominions enjoyed virtually complete self-government in all internal affairs. They amended, directly or indirectly, their constitutions. Their parliaments legislated within their borders without interference from London. They regulated their tariffs and immigration, and controlled their military and naval forces. A few theoretical limitations on their powers still existed, such as the legal supremacy of the Imperial Parliament, but these were of little consequence, for the Imperial Government scrupulously refrained from interfering in matters which concerned the Dominions alone. The Dominions had also succeeded by 1914 in acquiring almost complete control in practice over their own commercial treaties and were steadily increasing their influence in regard to political treaties in which they had a real and special interest. They also participated in several minor international conferences of a technical nature. But in more vital matters, such as the conduct of foreign policy, the diplomatic relations with other countries, the declaration of war and the making of peace, the participation in important international conferences, they took virtually no part. Here the mother country still exercised a trusteeship on their behalf.

The war enormously accelerated the historical movement towards greater Dominion autonomy and its broadening out so as to include control over foreign affairs as well. While the war demonstrated

[1] 231 H.C. Deb. 5 s., col. 1312.   [2] Ibid.
[3] 'I said nothing that had not been said, or directly implied, by speakers of every British party for several years past.' *Speeches by Lord Irwin* (1931), vol. ii, p. 356.
[4] Halifax, op. cit., p. 122.

strikingly the solidarity of the Empire, it also revealed the weakness of the machinery of Imperial co-operation. This made many recognize the necessity and cherish lively hopes of an Imperial federation. The federationists or centralists underestimated the force of Dominion nationalism and overrated that of the Imperial sentiment. They imagined that a promising start had been made towards their cherished goal of a closer union of the Empire in the shape of the Imperial War Cabinet and Conferences of 1917–18. But though the war had undoubtedly heightened the affection and reverence of the Dominions for the mother country, it had an even more marked effect in intensifying national consciousness within the Dominions. Moreover, the sudden but instructive initiation in the realities of high policy which the war had enabled them strengthened the conviction of at least some Dominion statesmen not to leave the issues of foreign policy in the hands of the British Government alone. The result was the famous resolution IX of the Imperial War Conference of 1917, which proposed the calling of a special Imperial Conference after the war to deal with 'the readjustment of the constitutional relations of the component parts of the Empire', and laid down that 'any such readjustment, while thoroughly preserving all existing powers of self-government and complete control of domestic affairs, should be based upon a full recognition of the Dominions as autonomous nations of an Imperial Commonwealth, and of India as an important portion of the same, should recognize the right of the Dominions and India to an adequate voice in foreign policy and in foreign relations, and should provide effective arrangements for continuous consultation in all important matters of common Imperial concern, and for such necessary concerted action, founded on consultation, as the several Governments may determine'.[1]

Both centralists and autonomists drew equal comfort from the ambiguous phraseology of the above resolution, but, as later events were to confirm, it in fact represented a triumph for the autonomists. It negatived the idea of formal federation; and it repudiated the continued subordination of the Dominions in external affairs.

At the end of the war the Dominions went a step further. They demanded—Canada taking the lead in the matter—and were granted separate representation at the Peace Conference. Though the façade of the diplomatic unity of the Empire was carefully maintained, the subsequent procedure in signing and ratifying the various Peace Treaties and the admission of the Dominions to the League of Nations were additional signs that a new movement towards decentralization had

[1] Cd. 8566, p. 5.

begun. The Dominions were now individual nations. They were the equals of Great Britain. They had achieved new weight and honour in the councils of the Empire and the world.

The years 1920-2 are called 'the period of co-operation'[1] and 'tentative centralization'[2] in Imperial affairs. An attempt was made during this period to keep alive the dying illumination of the war-years by the revival of a centralized executive in the guise of the 'Imperial Peace Cabinet' and the formulation of a common foreign policy for the Empire. For various reasons the proposal for a constitutional conference was allowed to lapse. But the victory of the centralists at the Imperial Conference of 1921 was short-lived, for very soon the tide of Dominion equality and autonomy swelled again, aided by the accidents of time and circumstance.

At the Imperial War Conference of 1917 General Smuts had complained that too many of the old ideas still clung to the new organism of the Empire, and that although in practice there was great freedom, yet in actual theory the status of the Dominions was of a subject character.[3] And he had expressed the hope that one of the most important tasks of the proposed constitutional conference to be held after the war would be to bring the theory of the Commonwealth into conformity with its practice. He reiterated his demand for a definition of Dominion Status at the Imperial Conference of 1921 and drew the attention of his colleagues to the fact that theoretical issues were practical politics in South Africa. In a private memorandum entitled 'The Constitution of the British Commonwealth', he emphasized the need to forestall the demands of nationalism in the Dominions and warned that 'unless Dominion Status was quickly solved in a way that would satisfy the aspirations of these young nations, separatist movements were to be expected in the Commonwealth'.[4] But the majority of the Conference remained passive, agreeing rather with W. M. Hughes, the Prime Minister of Australia, that the inequalities of strict law were 'figments, a few ancient forms' and that there was no need 'to set down in black and white the relations between Britain and the Dominions'.[5] It was accordingly decided that no advantage was to be gained by holding the constitutional conference envisaged in 1917.[6]

[1] A. G. Dewey, *The Dominions and Diplomacy* (1929), vol. ii, p. 62.
[2] R. MacGregor Dawson, *The Development of Dominion Status, 1900-36* (1937), p. 4.   [3] Cd. 8566, p. 47.
[4] Cited in C. M. van den Heever, *General J. B. M. Hertzog* (1946), p. 212.
[5] Conference of Prime Ministers and Representatives of the United Kingdom, the Dominions, and India, held in June, July and August, 1921. *Summary of Proceedings and Documents*, Cmd. 1474 (1921), p. 22.   [6] Ibid., p. 10.

Even when, towards the end of 1921, the Irish Free State was granted 'the same constitutional status in the Community of Nations known as the British Empire as the Dominion of Canada, the Commonwealth of Australia, the Dominion of New Zealand, and the Union of South Africa',[1] a definition of Dominion Status was studiously avoided. 'What does "Dominion status" mean?' asked Lloyd George speaking in the debate on the Anglo-Irish Treaty of 1921, but he refrained from answering it, preferring instead to speak of the dangers of definition. He recalled the anxiety of all the Dominion delegates at the Imperial Conference held earlier in the year to avoid 'any rigid definition'. 'That is not the way', he added, 'of the British constitution. We realize the danger of rigidity and of limiting our constitution by too many finalities.'[2] But a definition of Dominion Status could not long be avoided. 'Some definition', says Professor Mansergh, 'of the Commonwealth system there had to be. It was directly demanded ... by self-consciously nationalist Dominions, and in a fundamental sense it was made necessary by the inquiring, destructive temper of the age.'[3]

Before the time for 'Imperial stock-taking' came in 1926, several incidents, during the years 1922–5, had contributed towards an extension of the concept of Dominion Status. The first was the famous Chanak incident in September 1922, when the British Government asked the Dominions to stand by it in a threatened war with Turkey. The reactions of the Dominions to this call from the mother country were varied, but the attitude of Canada left the Imperial Government in no doubt that that Dominion was not prepared to underwrite automatically all the wars of Great Britain. This suggested, by implication, that although Great Britain might be involved in war, a Dominion might not take part in actual hostilities, thereby drawing the distinction between, what came to be called, a state of 'active belligerency' and one of 'passive belligerency'.[4] The second incident was the conclusion of the Halibut Fisheries Treaty in 1923 between Canada and the United States, which carried the treaty-making powers of the Dominions a step further, for Canada had successfully asserted its right to negotiate and sign a separate treaty with a foreign country without the participation or even nominal control of Great Britain. The third incident was the refusal by Canada in 1924 to ratify the Treaty of Lausanne on the

---

[1] Articles of Agreement for a Treaty between Great Britain and Ireland, December 6, 1921: reprinted in A. B. Keith, *Speeches and Documents on the British Dominions*, 1918–31 (1948 ed.), p. 77.   [2] 149 H.C. Deb. 5 s., cols. 27–8.
[3] N. Mansergh, *Survey of British Commonwealth Affairs: Problems of External Policy*, 1931–9 (1952), p. 5.   [4] Toynbee, op. cit., pp. 2–3, 46–52.

pretext that she had not been represented at the Lausanne Conference and had taken no part in the negotiations leading up to the settlement. Canada thus declined to undertake responsibility for a British-made treaty and made clear that the self-governing units of the Empire were primarily concerned with their own foreign policies. 'Lausanne was', says Robert MacGregor Dawson, 'in a sense, complementary to Chanak. Chanak had drawn a distinction between a state of "active belligerency" and one of "passive belligerency", a state where one part of the Empire might be engaged in hostilities while another part abstained. Lausanne enunciated a companion doctrine of "active responsibility" and "passive responsibility". One part of the Empire might henceforth undertake certain active obligations, while another part, though acquiescing in the policy of the former, would recognize in the commitment no pledge for it to participate in enforcing the terms of the undertaking.'[1] The fourth event was the appointment by the Irish Free State of her separate Minister Plenipotentiary to Washington in 1924[2]—an act which, despite formal contemporaneous assertions to the contrary by the Imperial Government, marked a definite breach in the diplomatic unity of the Empire. The fifth incident was also occasioned by the Irish Free State when in 1924 she registered, despite British objections, the Anglo-Irish Articles of Agreement of 1921 with the League of Nations, thereby disregarding the *inter se* doctrine of the British Commonwealth, i.e. that the relations between the various parts of the Empire were in essentials not international owing to their partnership under the Crown. The sixth incident was the specific exemption of the Dominions and India from the obligations entered into by Great Britain in Europe through the Treaty of Locarno in 1925. The limitation of Dominion liability in the Locarno settlement not only led to a general acceptance by the Empire of the conception of passive responsibility, it also marked the final breakdown of the policy to secure a united foreign policy for the Empire. 'A tremendous blow had been struck', says A. G. Dewey, 'at the theory of the diplomatic unity of the Empire.'[3]

The task of readjustment and redefinition of intra-Commonwealth relations which had been envisaged in 1917 but later shelved was at

[1] Dawson, op. cit., p. 79.

[2] Ireland had in fact taken advantage of the right granted to Canada in 1920, as a special case, to send a diplomatic representative to the United States, but not exercised by the latter Dominion until February 1927. The Irish representation also went beyond the reservations contemplated in 1920. See ibid., pp. 36, 96–7, 202, 314–15.

[3] Dewey, op. cit., vol. ii, p. 252.

last taken in hand in 1926 under the combined pressure of Canada, the Irish Free State and South Africa.[1] The Inter-Imperial Relations Committee of the Imperial Conference of 1926, better known as the Balfour Committee, attempted to define Dominion Status in non-legal terms. Its report described the Dominions as 'autonomous Communities within the British Empire, equal in status, in no way subordinate one to another in any aspect of their domestic or external affairs, though united by a common allegiance to the Crown, and freely associated as members of *the British Commonwealth of Nations*'.[2] This general definition was open to, and was in fact subjected to, varying interpretations by constitutional lawyers and politicians, but it did lay down three indisputable essentials of Dominion Status. They were: allegiance to the King in common with Great Britain; equality of status to Great Britain; and free association with Great Britain. The Balfour Committee Report did not change the actual position of the Dominions; it only attempted an agreed general interpretation of existing facts. There still remained various rules of strict law and particular conventional rules regulating certain aspects of the relations of Great Britain and the Dominions which were inconsistent with the general declaration of equal status made in 1926. The Balfour Committee had looked into the 'existing administrative, legislative, and judicial forms' and found that they were 'admittedly not wholly in accord with the position as described in ... this Report'.[3] On some of these inequalities of status—those relating to the Title of His Majesty the King, the status of the Governor-General, the appeal to the Judicial Committee of the Privy Council, and the conduct of foreign relations—the Committee had arrived at agreed conclusions and made recommendations. Others—such as those relating to the reservation and disallowance of Dominion legislation, the Dominions' lack of power to legislate with extra-territorial effect, and the principles of Colonial Laws Validity Act, 1865—it suggested to be referred to a special conference of experts. This special conference—known as the Conference on the Operation of Dominion Legislation and Merchant Shipping Legisla-

---

[1] For the view that the role of South Africa was decisive see Mansergh, op. cit., pp. 10–11.

[2] Imperial Conference, 1926. *Summary of Proceedings*, Cmd. 2786 (1926), p. 14. 'The Declaration does not define "Dominion Status". It defines the status of a Member of the British Commonwealth of Nations, and it declares that this status is enjoyed by Great Britain and the Dominions. But it is possible from a study of the Declaration to discover what sort of status is conferred upon the Dominions.' K. C. Wheare, *The Statute of Westminster and Dominion Status* (1953 ed.), p. 29.   [3] Cmd. 2768, p. 15.

tion—met in London from October 8 to December 4, 1929, and recommended removal, so far as was thought necessary, of certain of these inequalities. Its recommendations were adopted in substance by the Imperial Conference of 1930, and in 1931 the Statute of Westminster was passed to give legal endorsement to some of them.

What did Dominion Status signify after 1926? It certainly meant—as it had come to mean even earlier—virtually complete self-government in the internal affairs of a Dominion. But Dominion Status in principle had, as Professor Coupland pointed out, 'nothing to do with the form or type of internal constitution in a Dominion'. It was, he wrote, 'only concerned with the external position'—'a matter, so to speak, of the "international" relations between the nations of the Commonwealth'.[1] Much confusion was caused because most people—both in India and England—failed to take into account this distinction. Dominion Status signified what the 1926 declaration had laid down: common allegiance to the Crown, equality of status, and free association. It included the right of a Dominion to conclude a treaty with a foreign power on any subject—technical or political—on its own initiative and through its own plenipotentiaries; the right of legation; the right of being represented in international conferences of every kind by its own separate delegations; the right to be bound by no international obligation to which it had not itself specifically agreed; and the right to conduct its own foreign relations subject to the conventional duty of consultation with other members of the Commonwealth.[2] Did the declaration of 1926 give the Dominions the right to secede from the Empire? General Hertzog maintained that it did. Others denied this. There was no authoritative pronouncement upon the point.

How did Indian nationalists react to this process of development and definition of Dominion Status? The Balfour Report put heart into the apologists for Dominion Status in India. 'Dominion Status has come to mean something indistinguishable from independence, except for the link with the Crown,'[3] they assured the young radicals within their ranks on the authority of that Report. And they quoted Hertzog's remarks to prove that 'the Empire's teeth had been drawn'. 'Between Britain and the Dominions there is a partnership at will on terms of equality and mutual benefit,' Gandhi told the 'Independence-wallahs'

[1] Coupland, *The Empire in These Days* (1935), pp. 275–6.
[2] P. J. Noel-Baker, *The Present Juridical Status of the British Dominions in International Law* (1929), pp. 204–5.
[3] *All-Parties Conference: Report of Committee* (1928), p. 21.

and he emphasized that Dominion Status implied 'a capacity to declare independence'.[1] But the thought that the Dominions had raced far ahead of them could not but make Indians impatient with their slow progress and feel more acutely their subordinate status. The passion for equality in the eyes of the world was the dominating force in India and the feeling of being left behind offended their pride. They wanted status. Those who still put their trust in evolving within the Empire wanted Dominion Status immediately. It did not matter, they said, what safeguards and reservations were imposed on that status. The more sensitive and sceptical spirits were impelled to seek the same equality of status even outside the Empire.

Lloyd George's misgivings in 1921 about defining Dominion Status did not prove altogether unfounded. After 1926 a certain element of rigidity seems to have entered into the concept of Dominion Status. Birkenhead wrote to Irwin in May 1928: 'You will remember that in dealing with the Indianization of the Indian Army[2] His Majesty's Government were averse from using the phrase "Dominion Status" to describe even the ultimate and remote goal of Indian political development, because it has been laid down that Dominion Status means "the right to decide their own destinies", and this right we were not prepared to accord to India at present, or in any way to prejudge the question whether it should ever be accorded.'[3] This would clearly indicate that after 1926 Dominion Status came to acquire—at least in the minds of certain British statesmen—a definite meaning, quite different from that of earlier years, and prompted second thoughts about the advisability of indicating the goal of India's advance by the use of that phrase. Lord Winterton,[4] a former Under-Secretary of State for India, made the following entry in his diary on October 25, 1929 after a luncheon with Peel and Birkenhead: '. . . a somewhat serious situation has arisen. Edward Irwin is anxious to make a declaration defining "Dominion Status" as the final goal. Now "Dominion Status" has a very special meaning (especially since the Imperial Conference of 1926), and use of the term would be in advance of any of the definitions hitherto attempted such as "self-government within the Empire" because of that meaning.'[5] During the debate in the Lords

[1] 'Independence', *Young India*, January 13, 1927.
[2] This refers to the *Report of the Indian Sandhurst Committee* (1927).
[3] Birkenhead, op. cit., pp. 258–9.
[4] Edward Turnour, sixth Earl of Winterton (1883–1962). MP 1904–51; Under-Secretary for India 1922–4 and 1924–9; Chancellor of the Duchy of Lancaster 1937–9.
[5] Winterton, *Orders of the Day* (1953), pp. 158–9.

on Irwin's announcement of October 31, 1929, Birkenhead asked: 'What does Dominion *status* mean? . . . Does Dominion *status* at this moment mean the same thing that it meant a month before the last Imperial Conference? Most plainly not.'[1] Would not these remarks of Birkenhead and Winterton themselves suggest that when they and their friends attacked Irwin and the Labour Government for having used a 'vague' and 'indeterminate' phrase their real objection to the announcement was on the ground that it had 'loosely and ignorantly employed'[2] a phrase which was no longer so vague and indeterminate. The storm that burst in England over Irwin's announcement proved that the Indian desire for a definite affirmation and indefeasible assurance of Dominion Status as the goal of British policy in India was no childish sentiment.

The recognition of India as potentially a Dominion, which was implied in her admission to the Imperial Conference and the announcement of August 20, 1917, was further confirmed by later developments. When at the Paris Peace Conference in 1919 special representation was given to the four chief Dominions in the British Empire delegation, the same treatment was accorded to India. Plenipotentiaries holding full powers in respect of India took part in the discussions at Paris and signed the Treaty of Versailles and the other Peace Treaties. India was treated formally in all respects on the same footing as the Dominions and like them she became a separate Member of the League of Nations. As Professor A. B. Keith wrote: ' . . . by securing admission of India to the League the British Government virtually, though not technically, bound itself to the task of creating a self-governing India which would be entitled on the same basis as the Dominions to vote freely on the business of the League.'[3] In fact, pleading for the inclusion of India in the League, Lord Robert Cecil[4] had remarked before the Commission drafting the Covenant: 'The British Government is trying just as

[1] 75 H.L. Deb. 5 s., col. 404.
[2] Ibid.
[3] Keith, *A Constitutional History of India* (1937), p. 468. See also Keith, *Letters on Imperial Relations, Indian Reform, Constitutional and International Law, 1916–35* (1935), pp. 201, 213, 348; *Letters and Essays on Current Imperial and International Problems, 1935–6* (1936), pp. 7, 124; and Cecil Hurst, *Great Britain and the Dominions* (1928), p. 7.
[4] Edgar Algernon Robert Gascoyne, Viscount Cecil of Chelwood (1864–1958), MP 1906–23; Under-Secretary for Foreign Affairs 1915–16; Minister of Blockade 1916–18; Assistant Secretary for Foreign Affairs 1918; Lord Privy Seal 1923–4; Chancellor of the Duchy of Lancaster 1924–7.

rapidly as possible to advance India into a self-governing colony.'¹ Referring to India's separate representation at the Peace Conference and the decision already made that she was to be an original Member of the League of Nations, Montagu observed in the Commons on May 22, 1919: 'I can only repeat that these things ... commit this House and Parliament to the view that this position is only justified if you can raise India to the position of a sister nation in the British Empire, and it is wholly inconsistent with the position of subordination.'[2]

The appointment in 1920 of a High Commissioner for India in London was another indication of India's coming Dominionhood. To him were transferred the agency functions, mainly economic, which had so far been performed by the India Office. India House presently took its place in London beside the national headquarters of the other Dominions. The first High Commissioner for India was an English Jew and an ex-member of the I.C.S., Sir William Meyer,[3] but a better guardian of India's economic interests could hardly be found.[4] On Meyer's death an Indian, D. M. Dalal,[5] was appointed to the office in 1923.

India's membership of the League, as the only non-self-governing country, was 'an anomaly among anomalies'.[6] Constitutionally India could not have a separate foreign policy, for her Government was a subordinate branch of His Majesty's Government in England. Indian delegates to the League were nominated by the Secretary of State in consultation with the Government of India and their briefs were prepared in London. Indian nationalists complained that their country's delegates to the League were not really representative[7] and that her membership of the League was a costly farce. What was the substance

[1] D. H. Miller, *The Drafting of the Covenant* (1928), vol. i, p. 164.

[2] 116 H.C. Deb. 5 s., col. 622. See also col. 2301.

[3] B. 1860; entered Indian Civil Service 1881; member of Viceroy's council 1913–18; High Commissioner for India in the United Kingdom 1920–2; d. 1922.

[4] For the tribute of an Indian nationalist see St Nihal Singh, 'India's First High Commissioner in London', *Modern Review*, December 1922, pp. 751–8.

[5] B. 1870; businessman; member of Secretary of State's council 1921; High Commissioner for India in the United Kingdom 1923–4; d. 1941.

[6] Miller, op. cit., vol. i, p. 493.

[7] The historian of the League makes the same complaint: 'The voice of India came, then and for too many years thereafter, not from the vast spaces of the sub-continent but from a dusty corridor in Whitehall.' F. F. Walters, *A History of the League of Nations* (1952), vol. i, p. 117. How easily is it forgotten that but for the occupants of that 'dusty corridor in Whitehall' the voice of India would not have been heard at all!.

of India's separate membership? The question is extremely controversial and not easy to answer in the present stage of our knowledge. It was claimed by the India Office in 1929 that it had been 'the deliberate object of the Secretary of State to make India's new status a reality for practical purposes within the widest possible limits'.[1] Indian delegates to the League sessions also testified to 'the reality of India's independence as a member of the League'.[2] It is not our purpose here to examine the truth of these assertions. But that India derived numerous advantages even from the quasi-independent character of her representation at the League is undeniable. India as a whole (both British India and the Indian states) was represented at the League. This not only meant a tacit recognition in international law and practice of the unity of India, it had also a marked effect on India's national position and on the growth of a sense of unity among her as yet somewhat loosely integrated populations. Membership of the League gave India prestige, collective self-esteem and moral influence. It stimulated her national self-consciousness and her interest in international affairs. It enabled her to know the world and to be known in turn. It gave a good many Indians the opportunity of familiarizing themselves with wider international problems and co-operating in their solution, and of establishing personal contacts with representatives of other countries. The knowledge and experience thus gained stood India in good stead when she became independent. Nor were her delegates to the League so unrepresentative. Few patriotic Indians would today regret the things said or done in India's name by such men as Srinivasa Sastri, Ramaswami Aiyer, Atul Chatterjee[3] and Muhammad Habibullah[4]—to mention only a few outstanding examples. Since 1929 the Indian delegation came to be headed by an Indian himself. It may well be said that the

[1] 'International Status of India', Memorandum presented to the Indian Statutory Commission by the India Office, *Report of the Indian Statutory Commission* (1930), vol. v, p. 1632.

[2] Report of the Indian Delegation to the session of the League Assembly, 1929, cited by C. A. W. Manning, 'India and the League of Nations', *India Analysed* (edited by F. M. Houlston and B. P. L. Bedi, 1933), vol. i, p. 34. See also J. C. Coyajee, *India and the League of Nations* (1932), pp. 23–6, and *Speeches and Writings of the Rt Hon V. S. Srinivasa Sastri*, pp. 401–25.

[3] B. 1874; entered Indian Civil Service 1897; member of Viceroy's council 1923–4; High Commissioner for India in the United Kingdom 1925–31; Indian delegate to the League of Nations Assembly 1925, 1946; President of the International Labour Conference 1927; member of Secretary of State's council 1931–6; Adviser to the Secretary of State 1942–7; d. 1955.

[4] B. 1869; member of Viceroy's council 1925–30; Leader of the Indian delegation to the League of Nations Assembly 1929; Dewan of Travancore 1934; d. 1948.

foundations of India's international status were firmly laid even while India was yet a dependency.

The defects and anomalies of India's membership of the League did not hold good as far as membership of the International Labour Organization was concerned, for in that body her independence was almost absolute and unquestioned.[1] As one of the eight leading industrial countries, India obtained a permanent seat on the governing body of the ILO, and in 1927 an Indian, Sir Atul Chatterjee, was elected President of the International Labour Conference.

Like the Dominions, India was represented at the various organizations and conferences of the League, and even at such international conferences outside the orbit of the League as those at Washington in 1921 and at Genoa in 1922. Like the Dominions, India was specifically exempted from incurring the liabilities of the Locarno settlement, and signed the Kellog-Briand Pact in her own right.

There was yet another recognition of India's coming nationhood. Fiscal autonomy had formed an important attribute of Dominion self-government. India was conceded the same autonomy in 1919. The Joint Select Committee had recommended: 'Whatever be the right fiscal policy for India... it is quite clear that she should have the same liberty to consider her interests as Great Britain, Australia, New Zealand, Canada and South Africa.'[2] This recommendation was accepted and took effect in what came to be known as the 'fiscal convention', i.e. that the Government of India in framing their tariff policy were to regard themselves as the guardian of Indian interests, responsible to Indian opinion, and that, if the Government of India and the Indian Legislature were in agreement, the Secretary of State was not to exercise his overriding power on behalf of any British interest. Successive Secretaries of State faithfully upheld the convention. No Secretary of State, said Wedgwood Benn,[3] in 1929, would 'attempt to lay a finger upon this principle of tariff autonomy which has been established in practice for ten years in Indian affairs. There is Dominion status in action. There is a Dominion attribute which has now become part and parcel of the rights of India.'[4]

Ordinarily commercial treaties between the United Kingdom and

[1] See Lanka Sundaram, 'India and the International Labour Organization' in *India Analysed*, vol. i, pp. 67–88.
[2] H.C. 203, vol. i, p. 11.
[3] William Wedgwood Benn, first Viscount Stansgate (1877–1961). MP 1906–1931, 1937–42; left Liberal for Labour Party 1927; Secretary of State for India 1929–31; created Viscount 1941; Secretary of State for Air 1945–6.
[4] 233 H.C. Deb. 5 s., col. 1552.

foreign countries contained a clause enabling India and other parts of the Empire to adhere to them at their option. But till 1929 India, unlike the Dominions, had not the right to conclude commercial treaties with foreign powers by direct negotiation without reference to the Government in London. Subject, however, to the reservations of the fiscal autonomy convention, the Government of India could, if they wished, advise the negotiation of separate commercial treaties to suit India's special requirements and such treaties could be concluded, signed and ratified in respect of India. Having no diplomatic representation abroad, she had necessarily to utilize the Foreign Office machinery for the purpose.[1] In September 1930 India entered into one such treaty with Turkey. India's position in all such matters was fast developing. In 1931 India appointed her Trade Commissioners to Hamburg, Alexandria and Zanzibar. In 1934 she negotiated a direct trade agreement with Japan.

The Government of India's right to negotiate directly with the other parts of the Empire regarding Indian nationals was recognized at the Imperial Conference of 1921. In 1922 Srinivasa Sastri, on behalf of the Government of India, visited Australia, New Zealand and Canada in order to discuss with the governments of those Dominions the problem of Indian settlers. A separate department of the Government of India dealt with this subject and was presided over by an Indian. Under section 7 of the Indian Emigration Act of 1922 the Governor-General in Council was empowered to appoint Agents in any place outside British India for the purpose of safeguarding the interests of Indian emigrants. In exercise of this power, Agents were appointed in Malaya and Ceylon. The Government of India entered into direct negotiation with the Government of the Union of South Africa regarding the treatment of Indian settlers in that country. After the successful termination of a round table conference with the Union Government, the Government of India appointed, at the request of the former, an Agent-General to South Africa in 1927 to watch over Indian interests.

Indian nationalists made light of all these significant preparatory steps and dismissed the status accorded to India in the intra-imperial and international spheres as a mere camouflage intended to disguise under forms the harsh fact of India's subordination to Britain. India's new status was, in truth, something more than a matter of form. It was

---

[1] 'Note on the Status and Position of India in the British Empire', Memorandum presented to the Indian Statutory Commission by the Government of India, *Report of the Indian Statutory Commission* (1930), vol. v, pp. 1337–8.

a striking testimony to the fact that the Government of India (including the Secretary of State) felt an Indian responsibility and not merely a British responsibility as to India. Moreover, it demonstrated clearly the sincerity of the British intention to raise India to the position of a self-governing Dominion. If that had not been the intention of British statesmen they would never have given India a footing and Indians a platform in the imperial and the international world. India's gratitude to those imperial statesmen who helped in creating a political personality out of a vast mass and gave her a recognized status in the world is great and real.

Long and close association had made India almost a permanent part of the very life and thought of Britain. The mention of India's name had for the British a multitude of associations, symbolical and sentimental as much as practical. Whether they thought of her as 'the grim Stepmother of our kind' 'in ancient tattered raiment'[1] or 'the brightest jewel in the British Crown', India evoked deep emotions in the hearts of Englishmen. 'India', wrote Charles Wentworth Dilke,[2] 'ought always to be first in our minds when we are thinking of Greater Britain.'[3] Curzon owned that he could 'scarcely avoid the language of emotion' when speaking about India.[4] He had no patience with the 'Colony-mad'[5] Joseph Chamberlain. 'I often wonder', he wrote to Lord Northbrook in 1903, 'what would have become of him and us, if he had ever visited India. He would have become the greatest Indian Imperialist of the time. The Colonies would have been dwarfed and forgotten; and the pivot of the Empire would have been Calcutta. Not having enjoyed this good fortune, we are now forgotten, and the Empire is to be bound together (or, as we are told, if the prescription is not taken, destroyed) without apparent reference to the requirements of its largest and most

---

[1] Hard her service, poor her payment—she in ancient, tattered raiment—
India, she the grim Stepmother of our kind.
Kipling, 'Christmas in India', *Rudyard Kipling's Verse*
(Definitive ed. 1940), p. 55.

[2] B. 1843; politician and author; MP 1868–86, 1892–1911; Under-Secretary to the Foreign Office 1880–2; President of the Local Government Board 1882–5; d. 1911.

[3] Dilke, *The British Empire* (1899), p. 17.

[4] Curzon, *Subjects of the Day* (1915), p. 27.

[5] 'Chamberlain always seems to me Colony-mad. He is much more concerned with the 10½ millions of white men (by no means the pick of the race) who inhabit those territories than with the 41 millions of the British Isles, or the 300 millions of our subjects in India.' Curzon to Hamilton, June 24, 1903, Curzon Papers, MSS. Eur. F.111/162, No. 44.

powerful unit.'[1] It pained Curzon that India, 'the only part of the British Empire which is an empire',[2] had no recognized place in the councils of the Empire. In a memorable address at Edinburgh in 1909, he reminded his countrymen that India had been the great determining influence in British foreign policy for more than a century and that the conquest and the government of India had given to England her place in the eyes of the world. India was, he said, the strategic centre of the defensive position of the Empire, the principal element in its fighting strength, the richest market for British manufactures, and the main field for the employment of British capital. But it was 'less in its material than its moral and educative aspects', remarked Curzon, that India had conferred 'so incomparable a boon upon the British race'; India had 'exalted and disciplined our character', developed in the British 'a sense of duty and a spirit of self-sacrifice, as well as faculties of administration and command'.[3] He ended by pleading that India should be placed 'at the "high table" in the banquet hall of the Empire States'.[4]

From Curzon, the 'imperialist', to Morley, the 'anti-imperialist', was a far cry. But even the great Radical, who felt bored with his Colonial kinsfolk,[5] felt the attraction of 'the most astonishing part of the Empire'.[6] To him, as to Curzon, India was 'the only real Empire',[7] and noticing the scant attention paid to that country in the proceedings of the Imperial Press Conference in 1909, he could not but feel that 'the part of Hamlet was rather omitted'.[8]

It may well be that the India which Curzon and Morley prized so highly was the ideal India—a magnificent pendant hanging from the

[1] Curzon to Northbrook, August 12, 1903, ibid., MSS. Eur. F.111/182, No. 199.
[2] Curzon, *The Place of India in the Empire* (1909), p. 10.
[3] Ibid., pp. 29–30.   [4] Ibid., p. 46.
[5] 'At this moment, people are going to be bored out of their lives (the boredom is already felt) by our Colonial kinsfolk, of whom you know something. Your Canadians are excellent, but some of the others are uncommonly rough diamonds. The feasting is to be on a terrific scale, and we shall listen to any amount of swagger on one side, and insincere platitude on the other.' Morley to Minto, April 12, 1907, Minto Papers, M. 1007, No. 21; 'The Colonial Conference is becoming the greatest bore that ever was known.' Morley to Minto, April 26, 1907, ibid., M. 1007, No. 25; 'I am not at all without sympathy for your kindly views about our young Colonial kinsfolk. But, say what you will, they are apt to be frightful bores, and if you had been condemned to eat between twenty meals day after day in their company, and to hear Deakin yarn away by the hour, I believe you would be as heartily glad to see their backs as I am.' Morley to Minto, May 24, 1907, ibid., M. 1007, No. 31.
[6] Morley to Minto, April 12, 1907, Minto Papers, M. 1007, No. 21.
[7] Morley, *Indian Speeches*, p. 134.   [8] Ibid., p. 135.

imperial collar—and what they resented was the lack of appreciation of their own exalted position as governors of that country. But even as such it was not without significance, for without the persistent advocacy of these ardent 'Indians',[1] India would have never secured her place in inter-imperial and international organizations while she was yet a dependency.

If Englishmen could not think of the Empire without India, they could not easily reconcile themselves to the idea of a self-governing India going out of the Empire. To Philip Kerr in 1912 the ideal goal was clear, that 'some day or other India should acquire the status of a self-governing Dominion', but 'she must for all time remain within the Empire'.[2] 'Commerce links us indissolubly', he wrote,' with India today and will continue to link us in the future. Strategy does so no less. We can never willingly acquiesce in the establishment of any foreign rule in India. We can never willingly see a regenerated India become an independent power. We should no more welcome Indian dreadnoughts in Indian waters, controlled by an independent Indian Government, than we should welcome the battleships of Russia or Japan. That is the cardinal feature of the future policy of Britain in India.'[3]

When in the Empire's greatest emergency, during the war, India proved herself to be not a cause of trouble, but a tower of strength, it was universally recognized that she had qualified for closer partnership on equal terms. Even the most conservative imperialist in England was converted to the long-cherished dream of Indian nationalists of a self-governing India on the Dominion model. It might well appear today that there was something wooden and unimaginative about applying the concept of Dominion Status to an ancient country like India, but anyone who tries to recapture the glow of those wartime years, both in England and India, would hesitate to pass such a judgement. After all, it was Indians who had demanded it, and Britain on her part had nothing else to offer but the fruits of her history. To have cherished any other ideal would have meant being false to the two hundred years of common history.[4]

---

[1] The word is Morley's. See Morley to Minto, March 26, 1908, Minto Papers, M. 1008, No. 18.

[2] 'India and the Empire', *Round Table*, September 1912, p. 623; Butler, op. cit., p. 175. The psychologist might detect an element of possessive love in this attitude.

[3] *Round Table*, September 1912, p. 622.

[4] It is significant that the concept of Dominion Status, though advocated by some, was not applied to Egypt. See *Report of the Special Mission to Egypt*, Cmd. 1131 (1921), p. 18.

The policy found the man. To Montagu 'the only imperialism that was worth having was a trusteeship which was intended to develop the country under the British flag into a partnership in the Commonwealth'.[1] India was the mastering passion of his life.[2] She played 'the same part in his political life that the great overseas Dominions did in the life and in the heart of Mr Joseph Chamberlain'.[3] When the Government of India Bill passed the Commons in December 1919, Montagu called it 'the proudest moment' of his life, for he had kept before him 'one ambition' and that was to have the privilege of commending to Parliament what he believed to be 'the only justification of Empire, a step of self-government for India'.[4] Among the makers of modern India and the Commonwealth his name must always rank high.

India, in a way, contributed to the widening of the concept of the Empire. In response to the challenge posed by her England realized that it was not enough to govern a people justly, the latter must be taught to govern themselves. And so the great experiment began in India: how to carry a part of the Empire, peopled by men of alien religions and races, by safe and ordered stages from autocracy to self-government—a transformation seldom achieved in human history without violent convulsions. India became the symbol and the test of the project of the Commonwealth. In a more fundamental sense than the Dominions, she held the key to the problem of *imperium et libertas*. If she could evolve to self-government within the Empire, it would not only provide a signal proof of the constructive genius of the British people, but also carry forward the evolution of the Empire into a true multi-racial Commonwealth.[5] Nor was the experience to be a gain to the Commonwealth alone. As Curtis wrote: 'In solving the problem of responsible government this vast and complex Oriental community will find she has solved it for the whole of Asia, and, in the fullness of

[1] 122 H.C. Deb. 5 s., col. 835.

[2] Montagu wrote in his *Indian Diary* (p. 363): 'I love this country; it is where I am happiest.' On March 15, 1922 he remarked in the Commons: '... the fascination of India's problems have obsessed me all my life. ...' 151 H.C. Deb. 5 s., cols. 2303–4.

[3] Remark made by Crewe in the Lords, December 12, 1919: 37 H.L. Deb. 5 s., col. 993.   [4] 122 H.C. Deb. 5 s., col. 835.

[5] That India was a test case was recognized even by foreign observers. An American historian of the Commonwealth wrote in 1929: 'If India becomes a Dominion, then will the balance swing toward the Commonwealth idea; if India continues subordinate to Great Britain, or becomes independent, then is the ideal of the Commonwealth but very partially attained.' W. P Hall, *Empire to Commonwealth* (1929), pp. 490–1.

time, for Africa as well. The greatest of all the services which one nation can render to another is example. For the greatest of problems are common to many: and solved by one, they are solved by many. Three continents are now living in the rays of a candle lighted by England centuries ago. India now has a candle which once kindled will never be put out till all the nations of Asia and Africa walk by its light.'[1]

The long-term common interests of Britain and India were too substantial to be wholly obscured from view by the dust-storm of Indian nationalist agitation. India occupied a strategic position along the lines of British communication between Australia, New Zealand, and the United Kingdom. She was the keystone of the Imperial defence system. She could be, as the First World War proved and the Second was to confirm, Britain's greatest military asset. The key to the security and continued stability of South-East Asia lay with the Indian subcontinent. From the Indian point of view, it was patent to all but the nationalist hotheads that India, with her comparatively undeveloped military and industrial resources, would need the continued cooperation of Great Britain for quite some time. In the defence of the Indian Ocean area and in the maintenance of a balance of power throughout the Eurasian continent, a future self-governing India and Britain were to have a common concern. It was a pity that Indian leaders wasted—and were allowed to waste—so much of their time and energy in demanding cuts in the army expenditure and the rapid Indianization of the army, for it precluded them from learning the basic realities and requirements of Indian defence.

The economic lives of India and Britain were almost inextricably interwoven. The United Kingdom was the biggest supplier of manufactured goods to India and the largest single consumer of her raw materials.[2] Till the end of the 'twenties India was still Britain's best

[1] Curtis, op. cit., p. lxi.
[2] A. Percentage division of India's imports on private account.

Year	UK	Empire	Foreign
1913–14	62·8	69·7	30·3
1918–19	56·5	65·4	34·6
1923–4	57·6	65·2	34·8
1928–9	44·7	54·1	45·9

B. Percentage division of India's exports on private account:

Year	UK	Empire	Foreign
1913–14	25·1	41·1	58·9
1918–19	31·1	51·7	48·3
1923–4	24·2	41·4	58·6
1928–9	21·4	40·1	59·9

customer, taking roughly 10 per cent of her total exports.[1] British shipping lines had a virtual control of transport for Indian trade. The total of British capital investments in India by 1929 was variously estimated to be between £500 million and £1,000 million.[2] With such a large stake in India, it was to be expected that British businessmen should view with disfavour the Indian demand for an immediate grant of *Swaraj* in the 'twenties. They feared that a precipitate withdrawal of British authority would plunge the country into anarchy and endanger their interests. They also feared discrimination at the hands of Indians. They were alarmed at the threat held out by some extreme nationalists that a self-governing India would expropriate 'British vested interests' and repudiate 'unjust financial liabilities' and sought

---

C. Value of India's sea-borne trade on private account with the UK in *lakhs* of rupees:

Year	Imports	Exports
1913–14	91,58	56,30
1918–19	83,56	69,62
1923–4	146,43	73,04
1928–9	113,24	72,37

Source: W. R. Rayner, *India's Fiscal Policy and Trade* (no date), pp. 224, 226, 293.

[1] Value (in £'000) and direction of UK exports: (including re-exports) during the years 1927, 1928 and 1929:

	1927	1928	1929
Canada	31,360	37,029	37,511
Australia	63,742	57,938	56,340
New Zealand	20,400	20,051	22,186
South Africa	31,843	33,107	34,109
Irish Free State	45,566	44,721	46,297
British India	86,337	85,068	79,372
Other British countries	69,446	72,533	71,698
Total British countries	348,694	350,447	347,513
United States	66,875	68,730	62,016
Europe	274,610	272,844	279,927
Other foreign countries	141,855	151,841	149,595
Total foreign countries	483,340	493,415	491,538
Total	832,034	843,862	839,051

Source: *Tables relating to the external trade of the UK, the Dominions and India with British and foreign countries*, Cmd. 3691 (1930), pp. 2–3.

[2] See the *Financial Times*, January 9, 1930; W. Y. Elliott, *The New British Empire* (1932), pp. 193–4; R. P. Dutt, *India Today* (1940), p. 147.

constitutional safeguards to fortify their position. But, by and large, they did not adopt an attitude of uncompromising hostility to Indian political aspirations as such. In fact, as British and Indian capital increasingly intermingled in great enterprises in India and mutual trust and confidence developed, many enlightened and intelligent British businessmen began to view the prospect of Indian self-government more hopefully. Lord Winterton, who was twice Under-Secretary of State for India, testifies that one of the most powerful reasons for the extension of self-government in India leading eventually to independence was the insistence of British businessmen that such an extension was advisable from their own point of view.[1] They pleaded, both in public and private, that opposition to Indian political aspirations would mean losing the goodwill of the consumers of British trade in India and they assured that 'the interaction and common interests of Anglo-Indian trade were such that, given goodwill on both sides, it would flourish after India attained independence; some prominent British businessmen in India went further, and told me that they thought it would increase, because the objection to buying British goods would disappear'.[2] 'It is not surprising', commented Winterton, 'that among the "Diehards" with Indian experience who opposed the advance of Indian self-government there were hardly any British businessmen of experience. The majority were former Civil Servants and officers in the Indian Army. . . .'[3] Similarly the Indian business community, with all its grievances against and jealousy of long-established British rivals, was practical-minded enough to appreciate the enormous advantages of Indo-British economic collaboration. It acted as a moderating influence on the nationalist agitation in India, through its hold on the Congress, and was a powerful factor working in favour of retaining the Commonwealth connection.

Sentimental, political, commercial and strategical considerations there were many—and they were often emphasized—which made Englishmen value the association of a future self-governing India with the British Commonwealth. But there was a more generous dream which appealed to liberal minds. The great peril to humanity in the 'twenties appeared to be the antagonism between the European and the non-European peoples. There could be no more effectual way of obviating the spectre of this tragic struggle haunting mankind than by fashioning a political system within the framework of which one of the greatest of Asiatic peoples and one of the greatest of European peoples lived together on a footing of equality, justice and mutual respect. Would

[1] Winterton, *Orders of the Day* (1953), pp. 190–1.   [2] Ibid., p. 191.   [3] Ibid.

not the Commonwealth, with India as its member, be an irrefutable demonstration in practice that a *modus vivendi* between Europeans and Asiatics could be found? Would it not provide a bridge between the two great sections of humanity, between the West and the East? 'If we manage to create in India', remarked Philip Kerr in 1912, 'a self-governing, responsible dominion, and if India, when it is responsible and self-governing, elects to remain within the British Empire, we shall have solved the greatest difficulty which presents itself to the world today.'[1] And the difficulty which Philip Kerr had in mind was no other than that of reconciling the East and the West, and the black and the white. 'A great ideal, a noble one, a fruitful one, partnership of the East and West in a great community of nations!'[2] said Lloyd George in 1929. 'The West needs the East', Benjamin Charles Spoor told the Indian National Congress in 1920, 'as much as the East needs the West. I pray to God that the day is not far distant when you people will secure real freedom, political, economic and spiritual. When you have secured that freedom it may be that we people in the West will also secure our freedom by your help when the time comes. And when that time comes I hope that we will get beyond the little cry of India for Indians and Britain for the British. I hope that day will reveal a new slogan—a worthier one, a better one—not India for the Indians, nor Britain for the British but the whole world for a free humanity.'[3]

This was an ideal that had long been cherished by Indian nationalists: India to provide the meeting-ground for the Occident and the Orient; her connection with Britain to be the symbol and the instrument of a larger union of mankind. It was for this reason that Gokhale considered the British connection to be 'providential'. He believed that his country was eminently equipped to act as an interpreter between Asia and Europe, for, as he wrote: 'In the case of other countries, the contact of the West with the East is largely external only; in India the West has, so to say, entered into the very bone and marrow of the East.'[4] This was also the burden of Rabindranath Tagore's[5] message. To

[1] 'Address delivered by Mr Philip Kerr at the Toronto Club, to the members of the Round Table Society—Tuesday, July 30, 1912', p. 12. Copy in the Curtis Papers.
[2] 231 H.C. Deb. 5s., col. 1316. For a similar remark made by Lloyd George at the Imperial Conference in 1921 see Cmd. 1474, pp. 15-16.
[3] *Report of the Thirty-Fifth Indian National Congress*, 1920, p. 69.
[4] Gokhale, 'East and West in India', *Hindustan Review*, July 1911, p. 2.
[5] B. 1861; poet and philosopher; awarded Nobel prize for literature 1913; sought synthesis of Eastern and Western cultures by founding at Santiniketan an international university called Visva-Bharati 1921; d. 1941.

Srinivasa Sastri the British Commonwealth stood unique in the world 'for the reconciliation of the East and the West'.[1] 'The British Empire', said Tilak, 'is already a League of Nations. Why should Indians—believers in a world polity—wish to separate from the British Commonwealth of Nations?'[2] The 'deep spiritual significance' of the Commonwealth idea appealed to C. R. Das and he believed that it was 'for the good of India, for the good of the world, that India should strive for freedom within the Commonwealth, and so serve the cause of humanity'.[3]

Two hundred years of common history and intimate contact had made England enter 'into the very bone and marrow' of India. It would be no exaggeration to say that Indian nationalists were more Anglo-Indian than Indian. However much they might have denounced the British *Raj* and even attempted to fly away from British civilization, they could not hide the fact that they were the products of that very *Raj* and civilization. Sapru and Sastri, Jinnah and Jayakar, Malaviya and Mohamed Ali—all lisped in English numbers. They were the living embodiments of all that was best in Indian culture, but profoundly influenced by the English. 'I owe everything that I have got to English education,'[4] frankly confessed Motilal Nehru before he became a non-co-operator. And his son—'the young Harrovian communist',[5] as *The Times* called him,—admitted later: 'Personally I owe too much to England in my mental make-up ever to feel wholly alien to her.'[6] Britain not only ruled India, she also claimed a portion of the Indian mind and the Indian heart. In this lay the secret of her imperial achievement in India.

The inevitable bitterness created by the nationalist movement and its periodical repression coloured Indian patriotism with a steadily increasing antipathy towards their rulers. It was intensified by a distrust in British intentions. In the minds of many Indians the sense of subjection bit so deep that they wanted to cut themselves away from their past by severing all relations with Britain. But there were many others, who, conscious of what they owed to England and of the close ties woven by a long connection, did not allow their patriotism to take an anti-British hue. 'With all our grievances against the English nation, I cannot help loving your country,' wrote Tagore to Andrews.[7]

[1] *Speeches and Writings of the Rt Hon V. S. Srinivasa Sastri*, p. 251.
[2] Karandikar, op. cit., p. 579.   [3] P. C. Ray, op. cit., pp. 248–9.
[4] Cited in Ranga Iyer, op. cit., p. 73.   [5] *The Times* January 2, 1930.
[6] J. Nehru, *An Autiobography*, p. 419.
[7] April 10, 1921: Andrews (ed.), *Letters to a Friend* (1928), p. 152.

Mohamed Ali told British statesmen at the Round Table Conference in 1930: 'We have a soft corner in our hearts for Great Britain. Let us retain it, I beseech you.'[1] Mrs Sarojini Naidu affirmed that it was 'impossible' for her 'to be unfriendly to England'.[2] 'My dreams for India', she remarked, 'have their roots deep down in my heart, but my friendships and associations with England have their roots intertwined with the roots of my dreams for India.'[3] And she hoped that British statesmanship would enable her to continue cherishing these 'twin loyalties'.[4] The 'twenties were rather clouded years in Anglo-Indian relations. But there were men on both sides who rose above the prevailing distrust, bitterness and hostility. Truly did Irwin remark in 1929 that if Indians and Englishmen were tempted to mistrust each other in the twentieth century, both India and Great Britain would be judged in the twenty-first by the degree to which they had 'refused to lose faith in one another'.[5] The time of judgement has come even earlier.

There was no greater friend of the English people in India than that so-called arch enemy of British rule, Gandhi. Chief amongst the services which he rendered to India and the Commonwealth was that he saved Indian nationalism from becoming narrow, violent, racial, or isolationist. 'I cannot, I will not hate Englishmen. Nor will I bear their yoke,'[6] he insisted. It was his firm and consistent belief that freedom in association with Britain was preferable to the one without that association. It sprang from his faith in human nature, his philosophy of non-violence and his ideal of human brotherhood. He did not allow Indian nationalism to get into the strait-jacket of secession or republicanism. He forced the fundamentalists and separatists in India to argue their case on a high moral level, free from distorting emotion and prejudice. He wanted the ability to be totally independent without asserting that independence. 'Any scheme that I would frame,' he said, 'while Britain declares her goal about India to be complete equality within the Empire, would be that of alliance and not of independence without alliance.'[7] His ambition was much higher than independence. Through the deliverance of India he sought to deliver the weaker races of the earth. He was anxious to convert Englishmen and witness the quiet transformation of the British Empire into a real Commonwealth of Nations. He aspired to be a citizen of such a

---

[1] Cmd. 3778, p. 103. [2] Cmd. 3997, p. 263. [3] Ibid.
[4] Ibid., p. 264. [5] *Speeches by Lord Irwin* (1930), vol. i, pp. 539–40.
[6] *Report of the Thirty-Ninth Indian National Congress*, 1924, p. 26.
[7] Ibid.

Commonwealth. He sought free and equal partnership for India with Great Britain 'not merely for the benefit of India, and not merely for mutual benefit . . . [but] in order that the great weight that is crushing the world to atoms may be lifted from its shoulders'.[1]

[1] Cmd. 3997, p. 394.

SOME CONCLUDING REFLECTIONS

Early Indian nationalists took British rule for granted as if, so to speak, it was the order of nature. They, however, desired that it should transform itself into a national government by identifying itself completely with the interests of the Indian people. They gloried in their membership of the Empire, but demanded that the rights and privileges of British citizenship be gradually extended to them and such modifications be made in the character of the British administration that in the fullness of time India might become self-governing like the Dominions.

British imperial thinking, until almost the coming of the First World War, was dominated by the concept of 'the two Empires'. Most Conservatives and Liberals shared the belief that Oriental communities were incapable of self-government. That the Indian Empire was artificial and could not last long—for a vast population could not be held down indefinitely by relays of Englishmen—was widely felt or feared, but nobody seemed to know how it would end. Conditions which had made the establishment of British rule possible in India were fast changing—mainly as a result of that rule itself—but there was little conscious effort to direct these changes to a preconceived and definite goal. That British policy in regard to Indian political aspirations was on the whole liberal and progressive cannot be doubted. But until 1917 it lacked a sense of direction and purpose. The reforms of 1892 and 1909 did not attempt to shift the foundations of British rule in India, but merely to adjust the machinery of British Government to the changed circumstances in the country. They aimed at associating Indians more closely with the administration and allowing them more opportunities to influence it, while maintaining intact its foreign and autocratic character.

Accidents of time and circumstance aided the rapid growth of Indian political aspirations. By the first decade of the twentieth century the ideal of self-government on the Dominion model came to be definitely adopted. It was dismissed as chimerical by responsible statesmen of the Empire. The more youthful radicals in India began to talk of secession as a combative response. Whereas Indian nationalists complained that their rulers lacked the will to promote their political advance on the lines of the Dominions, the latter pointed out that the will depended upon the way, which was so difficult to find. Perhaps both were right.

SOME CONCLUDING REFLECTIONS

The war brought about a change in the angle of vision. It was thought in England that India could develop on the lines of the self-governing Dominions. The concept of Dominion Status came to be applied to India by the declaration of August 1917. The period of doubt had culminated in an act of faith. By the Montagu-Chelmsford reforms of 1919 a certain measure of responsible government was introduced in the provinces and it was hoped that, if the experiment succeeded, it would be extended till India attained self-government like the Dominions.

The non-co-operation movement ruined the fair hopes of 1919. Indian impatience and intransigence hardened British opinion against further political advance and revived doubts about the capacity of Indians to work self-governing institutions. However justified the non-co-operation movement might have been as a moral protest and whatever its contribution towards building up a strong national movement in India, there can be little doubt that but for it the pace of constitutional advance in India would have been faster.

Early in the 'twenties Indian public opinion became unanimous on the point—and perhaps only on this point—that the time had come for a more or less final settlement of the Indian problem—a settlement by which the provinces would attain full responsible government and at the centre all subjects, except foreign affairs, defence and relations with Indian states, would be transferred to an Indian government responsible to an elected majority. It demanded that schemes should be framed which would ensure complete Indianization of the army and the civil services within a reasonable period of 25 or 30 years. By the end of that period it hoped to see the remaining subjects at the centre also to be transferred to a responsible Indian government. For any such quasi-final arrangement the British Government were not yet prepared; nor did they think that India was ripe for it. Indians wanted to have a definite vision of the goal with the milestones on the journey clearly marked out. The traditional dislike of the English for any such definite and explicit arrangement was reinforced by a vivid recognition of the immense difficulties and complexities of the Indian problem. It may even be doubted if many British statesmen had taken into account the full implications of the announcement of 1917 and the reforms of 1919. It was generally assumed that the introduction of responsible government in India would be a slow and long-drawn-out affair. Once this plan of slow-motion advance had been rudely disturbed by the march of events in India, there developed a tendency on the part of British statesmen to wait on events instead of thinking out and working out a bolder plan of campaign. There were second thoughts about the advisability of granting Dominion Status to an India instinct with hostility to British rule. The development and definition of Dominion Status after the war further encouraged the sceptics. The British attempted to deal with the Indian problem as political engineers rather than as psychologists. The dangers of going fast were realized but not those of delay.[1]

The question whether or not a future self-governing India should continue to remain within the British Commonwealth was a living political issue in India during the 'twenties. The words 'Empire' and 'Imperialism' had fallen into disrepute. They smacked of racialism, domination and exploitation. Imperial citizenship lost its halo to those who felt that they were being denied freedom within their own country and humiliated in other parts of the Empire because they were Indians. The policies of racial discrimination pursued in South Africa and Kenya acted as a constant irritant to Indian nationalists.

The older and moderate Congressmen would have been satisfied with Dominion Status if granted in time. They interpreted Dominion Status to mean perfect equality with Great Britain and freedom to secede at will. Like the Liberals, they demanded Dominion Status, with reservations for the transitional period, to be granted to India immediately. They desired to see the British Empire quietly transform itself into a real Commonwealth of Nations. They were anxious to preserve the British connection, for they valued the continued cooperation of the British people. Freedom within the Empire was to them preferable to freedom outside the Empire. It was not merely a matter of common material interests, but of sentiment and of principle. They cherished the ideal of the Commonwealth for the higher purposes it could serve—the promotion of international freedom, peace and brotherhood.

The younger and more radical elements within the Congress considered the British Commonwealth to be a mere euphemism for the

[1] It is significant that as late as December 1939 the Viceroy, Lord Linlithgow, believed that a slow pace was best calculated to hold India to the Empire: 'But there is also our own position in India to be taken into account. After all we framed the Constitution as it stands in the Act of 1935, because we thought that way the best way—given the political position in both countries—of maintaining British influence in India. It is no part of our policy, I take it, to expedite in India constitutional changes for their own sake, or gratuitously to hurry the handing over of controls to Indian hands at any pace faster than we regard as best calculated on a long view, to hold India to the Empire.' Linlithgow to Zetland, December 28, 1939: Zetland, op. cit., p. 277.

British Empire. They believed that India could never attain complete political and economic freedom unless she severed the British connection. To them the banner was as important as the forward march. Dominion Status was in their eyes a status of servitude. It was a wrong ideology, an uninspiring ideal. While frustration and racial hostility prompted some of them to desire a complete severance of the British connection, there were others who, under the influence of Marxism, imagined themselves to be engaged in a crusade against Imperialism. There were also many who entertained vague visions of an Asiatic Federation.

The Liberals interpreted Dominion Status in its widest possible sense. To them it meant 'independence plus'. They were anglophiles and convinced believers in the Commonwealth connection. The latter, in their view, was a guarantee of India's safe and ordered progress towards national freedom. They valued the Commonwealth as an association of the freest and most progressive nations in the world, and as an institution likely to serve the higher purpose of reconciling the East and the West.

The Muslims had their loyalists in the Aga Khan and Muhammad Shafi. They had their liberals in men like Jinnah and Ali Imam. Nor did they lack their quota of moderate and extreme nationalists. The Muslims had in Pan-Islamism a competing and far more compelling ideal. Many of their leaders cherished lively dreams of a Commonwealth of Islam.

What did the British Commonwealth mean to those Indians who did value it? To them it meant association with a country—Great Britain—for which, in spite of all the heat and passion of the nationalist struggle, they had a warm feeling. It signified the continuance of a long connection. They looked upon the Commonwealth as a minor League of Nations, an embryonic prototype for a wider international system. They valued it as a bridge between the East and the West, between diverse races, creeds and civilizations. They prized the Commonwealth not so much for the promotion of common material interests in trade and defence—the prevailing exaggerations and misconceptions of the nationalist era did not allow many Indians to gauge correctly their significance—as for the advancement of the higher ideals of justice, freedom, equality, peace and concord in the whole world.

SELECT BIBLIOGRAPHY

I. INDIA—CONSTITUTIONAL AND POLITICAL:
CONTEMPORARY AND LATER WORKS

Aga Khan, the	*India in Transition.* London, 1918.
Aiyer, P. S. S.	*Indian Constitutional Problems.* Bombay, 1928.
Ali, Mohamed	*Select Writings and Speeches of Maulana Mohamed Ali* (edited by A. Iqbal). Lahore, 1944.

All-India Muslim League: Proceedings of the Annual Meeting of the All-India Muslim League held at Nagpore, December 1910. Allahabad, 1911.
All-Parties Conference: Report of Committee. 2 pts. (Nehru Report). Allahabad, 1928.

Andrews, C. F.	*The Claim for Independence: Within or Without the Empire.* Madras, 1921.
Andrews, C. F.	*The Indian Problem.* Madras, 1921.
Andrews, C. F.	*How India Can be Free.* Madras, 1921.
Andrews, C. F.	*The Only Way to Swaraj.* Dacca, 1921.
Andrews, C. F.	*Indian Independence: The Immediate Need.* Madras, 1921.
Andrews, C. F., and Mukerji, G.	*The Rise and Growth of the Congress in India.* London, 1938.
Appadorai, A.	*Dyarchy in Practice.* London, 1937.
Archer, W.	*India and the Future.* London, 1917.
Banerjea, S. N.	*Speeches by Babu Surendranath Banerjea.* (edited by R. C. Palit and R. J. Mitter). 6 vols. Calcutta, 1891–1908.
Barker, E.	*The Future Government of India and the Civil Service.* London, 1919.
Beauchamp, J.	*British Imperialism in India.* London, 1934.
Beck, T.	*Essays on Indian Topics.* Allahabad, 1888.
Bernays, R.	*'Naked Fakir'.* London, 1931.
Besant, A.	*How India Wrought for Freedom.* Adyar, 1915.
Besant, A.	*India: Bond or Free?* Adyar, 1939.
Besant, A.	*Indian Problems.* Adyar, 1939.
Besant, A.	*The High Purpose of War.* Adyar, 1940.
Besant, A.	*The India That Shall Be.* Adyar, 1940.

SELECT BIBLIOGRAPHY

Bevan, E.	*Indian Nationalism.* London, 1913.
Bevan, E.	*Thoughts on Indian Discontents.* London, 1929.
Birkenhead, the Earl of	*Last Essays.* London, 1930.
Bose, S. C.	*The Indian Struggle, 1920–34.* London, 1935.
Brockway, A. F.	*India and Its Government.* Madras, 1921.
Brockway, A. F.	*The Indian Crisis.* London, 1930.
Bryant, J. F.	*Gandhi and the Indianization of the Empire.* Cambridge, 1924.
Buch, M. A.	*The Development of Contemporary Indian Political Thought.* 3 vols. Baroda, 1938.
Carpenter, E.	*India and the Empire.* Madras, 1922.
Carthill, A.	*The Lost Dominion.* Edinburgh, 1924.
Carthill, A.	*The Garden of Adonis.* Edinburgh, 1927.
Caveeshar, S. S.	*India's Fight for Freedom.* Lahore, 1936.
Chailley, J.	*Administrative Problems of British India.* London, 1910.
Chakrabarty, D., and Bhattacharya, C.	*Congress in Evolution.* Calcutta, 1935.
Chatterji, R.	*Towards Home Rule.* Calcutta, 1917.
Chaudhuri, B. M.	*Muslim Politics in India.* Calcutta, 1946.
Chelmsford, Lord	*Speeches by Lord Chelmsford.* 2 vols. Simla, 1919–21.
Chesney, G. M.	*India Under Experiment.* London, 1918.
Chintamani, C. Y.	*Indian Politics since the Mutiny.* London, 1940.
Chintamani, C. Y., and Masani, M. R.	*India's Constitution at Work.* Bombay, 1940.
Chirol, V.	*Indian Unrest.* London, 1910.
Chirol, V.	*India: Old and New.* London, 1921.
Chirol, V.	*India.* London, 1926.
Churchill, W. S.	*India: Speeches.* London, 1931.
Coatman, J.	*Years of Destiny: India, 1926–32.* London, 1932.
Coatman, J.	*The Indian Riddle.* London, 1932.
Coatman, J.	*India: The Road to Self-Government.* London, 1941.
Congress Memorandum	Submitted to the S.O.S. and the Viceroy at Delhi in November 1917. Adyar, 1918.
Congress Presidential Addresses	First Series, 1885–1910. Madras, 1935. Second Series, 1911–34. Madras, 1935.

259

Coomaraswamy, A. K.	*Essays in National Idealism.* Colombo, 1909.
Cotton, H. J. S.	*New India or India in Transition.* London, 1885.
Coupland, R.	*Britain and India, 1600–1941.* London, 1941.
Coupland, R.	*The Indian Problem, 1833–1935.* Oxford, 1942.
Coupland, R.	*India: A Restatement.* Oxford, 1945.
Coupland, R.	*The Goal of British Rule in India.* London, 1948.
Coyajee, J. C.	*India and the League of Nations.* Waltair, 1932.
Craddock, R.	*The Dilemma in India.* London, 1929.
Cumming, J. (ed.)	*Political India, 1832–1932.* Oxford, 1932.
Cumming, J. (ed.)	*Modern India.* Oxford, 1932.
Curtis, L.	*Dyarchy.* Oxford, 1920.
Curzon, Lord	*Speeches by Lord Curzon of Kedleston.* 4 vols. Calcutta, 1902–6.
Curzon, Lord	*Subjects of the Day.* London, 1915.
Das, C. R.	*India for Indians.* Madras, 1921.
Deakin, A.	*Irrigated India.* London, 1893.
De Mello, F. M.	*The Indian National Congress.* Oxford, 1934.
Desai, A. R.	*Social Background of Indian Nationalism.* Oxford, 1949.
Dutt, R. P.	*India Today.* London, 1940; Bombay, 1949.
Eminent Mussalmans.	Madras, 1926.
Fraser, A. L.	*India under Curzon and After.* London, 1911.
Gandhi, M. K.	*Hind Swaraj.* Madras, 1921.
Gandhi, M. K.	*Speeches and Writings of Mahatma Gandhi.* Madras, 1933.
Gandhi, M. K.	*Young India.* 3 vols. Madras, 1922–35.
Garratt, G. T.	*An Indian Commentary.* London, 1928.
Ghose, Aurobindo	*The Ideal of Human Unity.* Pondicherry, 1950.
Ghose, Aurobindo	*Speeches.* Pondicherry, 1952.
Ghose, Aurobindo	*The Doctrine of Passive Resistance.* Pondicherry, 1952.
Ghosh, P. C.	*The Development of the Indian National Congress, 1892–1909.* Calcutta, 1960.
Gokhale, G. K.	*Speeches of Gopal Krishna Gokhale.* Madras, 1920.
Gopal, Ram.	*Indian Muslims: A Political History.* London, 1959.
Gopal, S.	*The Viceroyalty of Lord Ripon.* Oxford, 1953.
Gopal, S.	*The Viceroyalty of Lord Irwin.* Oxford, 1957.

SELECT BIBLIOGRAPHY

Gour, H. S.	*The Future Constitution of India.* Nagpur, 1930.
Griffiths, P. J.	*The British Impact on India.* London, 1952.
Gwyer, M., and Appadorai, A.	*Speeches and Documents on the Indian Constitution, 1921–47.* 2 vols. Oxford, 1957.
Gwynn, J. T.	*Indian Politics.* London, 1924.
Hardinge, Lord	*Speeches of Lord Hardinge.* 2 vols. Madras, 1913–17.
Hill, C. H.	*India—Stepmother.* London, 1929.

(A) History of the Freedom Movement. 4 vols. Karachi, 1957–61.

Horne, E. A.	*The Political System of British India.* Oxford, 1922.
Houghton, B.	*The Psychology of Empire.* Madras, 1921.
Houghton, B.	*Reform or Revolution.* Madras, 1921.
Houghton, B.	*The Revolt of the East.* Madras, 1921.
Houlston, F. M., and Bedi, B. P. L. (eds.)	*India Analysed.* 3 vols. London, 1933–4.
Ilbert, C., and Meston, J.	*The New Constitution of India.* London, 1923.
Imam, Syed Ali	*Speech of Mr Syed Ali Imam, Bar-at-Law, President of the All-India Muslim League, Amritsar Session, 1908.* Bankipur, 1908.
Indian, An.	*Bridging the Gulf.* London, 1930.

(The) Indian Annual Register, 1919–23 (edited by H. N. Mitra). Calcutta.

Indian National Congress: Reports of the Annual Sessions, 1885–1928.

(The) Indian Quarterly Register, 1924–30 (edited by H. N. Mitra and N. N. Mitra). Calcutta.

Iqbal, M.	*Speeches and Statements of Iqbal* (edited by Shamloo). Lahore, 1948.
Iqbal, M.	*Islam as an Ethical and a Political Ideal.* Lahore, 1955.
Irwin, Lord	*Speeches by Lord Irwin.* 2 vols. Simla, 1930–1.
Irwin, Lord	*Indian Problems.* London, 1932.
Iyengar, S. S.	*Swaraj Constitution.* Madras, 1927.
Iyer, C. S. Ranga.	*India in the Crucible.* London, 1928.
Iyer, C. S. Ranga.	*How to Lose India?* Lahore, 1935.
Kamath, M. S.	*The Home Rule Leagues.* Madras, 1918.
Keith, A. B. (ed.)	*Speeches and Documents on Indian Policy, 1750–1921.* 2 vols. Oxford, 1937.

Keith, A. B.	*A Constitutional History of India.* Oxford, 1937.
Khan, M.	*An Apology for the 'New Light'.* Allahabad, 1891.
Khan, Syed Ahmed	*Sir Syed Ahmed on the Present State of Indian Politics.* Allahabad, 1888.
Khub Dekhta Age	*India Tomorrow.* Oxford, 1927.
Kidwai, M. H.	*Islam and Socialism.* London, 1913.
Kidwai, M. H.	*Swaraj and How to Obtain It.* Lucknow, 1924.
Kidwai, M. H.	*Pan-Islamism and Bolshevism.* London, 1937.
Kohn, H.	*A History of Nationalism in the East.* London, 1929.
Lal Bahadur	*The Muslim League.* Agra, 1954.
Lethbridge, R.	*India and Imperial Preference.* London, 1907.
Lethbridge, R.	*The Indian Offer of Imperial Preference.* London, 1913.
Lovett, V.	*The Importance of a Clear Understanding of Britain's Work in India.* Oxford, 1920.
Lovett, V.	*A History of the Indian Nationalist Movement.* London, 1921.
Low, S.	*A Vision of India.* London, 1906.
McCully, B. T.	*English Education and the Origins of Indian Nationalism.* New York, 1940.
MacDonald, R.	*The Awakening of India.* London, 1910.
MacDonald, R.	*The Government of India.* London, 1919.
Mahomedan, an Indian	*The Indian Moslems.* London, 1928.
Marriott, J. A. R.	*The English in India: A Problem of Politics.* Oxford, 1932.
Mason, Philip	*The Men Who Ruled India.* 2 vols. London, 1953–4.
Mazumdar, A. C.	*Indian National Evolution.* Madras, 1915.
Mehta, P. M.	*Speeches and Writings of the Honourable Sir Pherozeshah M. Mehta* (edited by C. Y. Chintamani). Allahabad, 1905.
Mehta, P. M.	*Some Unpublished and Later Speeches and Writings of the Hon Sir Pherozeshah Mehta.* Bombay, 1918.
Menon, V. P.	*The Transfer of Power in India.* Bombay, 1957.
Merewether, J. W. B., and Smith, F. E.	*The Indian Corps in France.* London, 1917.
Meston Lord	*India at the Crossways.* Cambridge, 1920.
Meston, Lord	*India and the Empire.* London, 1924.

SELECT BIBLIOGRAPHY

Meston, Lord	*Nationhood for India.* Oxford, 1931.
Milburn, R. G.	*England and India.* London, 1918.
Minto, Mary (Countess)	*India: Minto and Morley.* London, 1934.
Mirza, M. A.	*A Talk on Muslim Politics.* Lucknow, 1910.
Mitchell, K. L.	*India Without Fable.* New York, 1942.
Mitter, B. L.	*Extremists and Moderates: A Study.* Calcutta, 1918.
Mody, H. P.	*Ths Political Future of India.* London, 1908.
Montagu, E. S.	*Speeches on Indian Questions by the Rt Hon Mr Montagu.* Madras, 1917.
Montagu, E. S.	*An Indian Diary.* London. 1930.
Morison, T.	*Imperial Rule in India.* London, 1899.
Morley, J.	*Indian Speeches.* London, 1909.
Morris-Jones, W. H.	*Parliament in India.* London, 1957.
Mukherjee, H. and U.	*'Bande Mataram' and Indian Nationalism.* Calcutta, 1957.
Mukherjee, H. and U.	*Sri Aurobindo's Political Thought.* Calcutta, 1958.
Mukherjee, H. and U.	*India's Fight for Freedom.* Calcutta, 1958.
Naoroji, D.	*Speeches and Writings of Dadabhai Naoroji.* Madras, 1910.

National Liberal Federation of India: Reports of the Annual Sessions, 1920–9.

Nehru, J.	*Recent Essays and Writings.* Allahabad, 1934.
Nehru, J.	*Glimpses of World History,* 2 vols. Allahabad, 1934–5.
Nehru, J.	*India and the World.* London, 1936.
Nehru, J.	*The Unity of India.* London, 1941.
Nehru, J.	*The Discovery of India.* London, 1946.
Nehru, J.	*A Bunch of Old Letters.* Bombay, 1958.
Nevinson, H. W.	*The New Spirit in India.* London, 1908.
Noman, M.	*Muslim India: Rise and Growth of the All-India Muslim League.* Allahabad, 1942.
O'Donnell, C. J.	*The Causes of Present Discontents in India.* London, 1908.
O'Dwyer, M.	*India as I Knew It, 1885–1925.* London, 1925.
O'Malley, L. S. S.	*Modern India and the West.* Oxford, 1941.
Pal, B. C.	*The National Congress.* Lahore, 1887.
Pal, B. C.	*The Spirit of Indian Nationalism.* London, 1910.
Pal, B. C.	*Nationality and Empire.* Calcutta, 1916.

Pal, B. C.	*Responsible Government.* Calcutta, 1917.
Pal, B. C.	*Why I Advocate Home Rule for India.* Adyar, 1918.
Pal, B. C.	*Swaraj: The Goal and the Way.* Madras, 1921.
Pal, B. C.	*Swadeshi and Swaraj.* Calcutta, 1954.
Palande, M. R. (ed.)	*Source Material for a History of the Freedom Movement in India.* 2 vols. Bombay, 1957–8.
Panikkar, K. M.	*Indian Nationalism: Its Origin, History and Ideals.* London, 1920.
Panikkar, K. M.	*Imperialism in Practice and in Theory.* Madras, 1922.
Panikkar, K. M.	*The New Empire.* London, 1934.
Parkin, G. R.	*India Today.* New York, 1946.
Paul, K. T.	*The British Connection with India.* London, 1927.
Philips, C. H.	*India.* London, 1949.
Pole, D. G.	*India in Transition.* London, 1932.
Pradhan, R. G.	*Observations on Indian Home Rule.* Nasik, 1916.
Pradhan, R. G.	*Criticism upon Mr Lionel Curtis's Indian Studies No. 2.* Nasik, 1917.
Pradhan, R. G.	*India's Struggle for Swaraj.* Madras, 1930.
Rai, Lajpat	*Young India.* New York, 1917.
Rai, Lajpat	*The Political Future of India.* New York, 1919.
Raleigh, T.	*Lord Curzon in India.* London, 1906.
Reading, Lord	*Speeches by the Earl of Reading.* 2 vols. Simla, 1926.
Reed, S., and Cadell, P. R.	*India: The New Phase.* London, 1928.
Reed, S.	*The India I Knew, 1897–1947.* London, 1952.

Report of the Proceedings of the Second Session of the All-India Conference of the Moderate Party, 1919.

Roy, B. P. S.	*Parliamentary Government in India.* Calcutta, 1943.
Sapru, T. B.	*The Indian Constitution.* Madras, 1926.
Sastri, V. S. S.	*Self-Government for India under the British Flag.* Allahabad, 1916.
Sastri, V. S. S.	*Speeches and Writings of the Rt Hon V. S. Srinivasa Sastri.* Madras, 1924.
Satyamurti, S. (ed.)	*The Montagu-Chelmsford Reform Proposals.* Madras, 1918.

Sayeed, Khalid Bin	*Pakistan: The Formative Phase.* Karachi, 1960.
Schuster, G., and Wint, G.	*India and Democracy.* London, 1941.
Shafi, M.	*The Indian Constitutional Reforms.* Lahore, 1918.
Shafi, M.	*Some Important Indian Problems.* Lahore, 1930.
Sinha, S. P.	*Speeches and Writings of Lord Sinha.* Madras, 1922.
Sitaramayya, P.	*The History of the Indian National Congress.* 2 vols. Bombay, 1946.
Smith, V. A.	*Indian Constitutional Reform Viewed in the Light of History.* Oxford, 1919.
Smith, W. C.	*Modern Islam in India.* London, 1946.
Smith, W. C.	*Islam in Modern History.* Oxford, 1957.
Smith, W. R.	*Nationalism and Reform in India.* New Haven, 1938.
Stoddard, L.	*The New World of Islam.* London, 1921.
Stokes, S. E.	*The Failure of European Civilization as a World Culture.* Madras, 1921.
Stokes, S. E.	*Essays: Political and National.* Madras, 1921.
Stokes, S. E.	*National Self-realization.* Madras, 1921.
Strachey, J.	*India.* London, 1888.
Sundaram, L.	*India in World Politics.* Lahore, 1944.
Sunderland, J. T.	*India in Bondage.* New York, 1929.
Symonds, R.	*The Making of Pakistan.* London, 1950.
Thompson, E.	*The Reconstruction of India.* London, 1930.
Thompson, E. J., and Garratt, G. T.	*Rise and Fulfilment of British Rule in India.* London, 1934.
Tilak, B. G.	*Speeches of Srj B. G. Tilak delivered at Bellary.* Bellary, 1905.
Tilak, B. G.	*Speeches of Bal Gangadhar Tilak.* Madras, 1918.
Topa, I. N.	*The Growth and Development of National Thought in India.* Hamburg, 1930.
Townsend, M.	*Asia and Europe.* London, 1905.
Van Tyne, C. H.	*India in Ferment.* New York, 1923.
Wadia, B. P.	*The Sceptre of a World Empire.* Adyar, 1917.
Wallbank, T. W.	*India in the New Era.* Chicago, 1951.
Whyte, F.	*India, A Federation?* Calcutta, 1925.

Whyte, F. *India: A Bird's Eye View.* London, 1942.
Woolacott, J. E. *India on Trial.* London, 1929.
Zacharias, H. C. E. *Renascent India.* London, 1933.
Zetland, the Marquis of *Steps towards Indian Home Rule.* London, 1935.

II. THE EMPIRE-COMMONWEALTH: GENERAL WORKS

Amery, L. S. *Thoughts on the Constitution.* Oxford, 1947.
Barker, E. *Ideas and Ideals of the British Empire.* Cambridge, 1941.
Bennett, G. *The Concept of Empire from Burke to Attlee, 1774–1947.* London, 1953.
Bodelsen, C. A. *Studies in Mid-Victorian Imperialism.* Copenhagen, 1924.
Borden, R. *Canada in the Commonwealth.* Oxford, 1929.
Boyd, C. W. (ed.) *Mr Chamberlain's Speeches.* 2 vols. London, 1914.
Brady, A. *Democracy in the Dominions.* Oxford, 1958.
Carrington, C. E. *An Exposition of Empire.* Cambridge, 1947.
Carrington, C. E. *The British Overseas: Exploits of a Nation of Shopkeepers.* Cambridge, 1950.
Churchill, W. S. *The World Crisis: The Aftermath.* London, 1929.
Coatman, J. *Magna Britannia.* London, 1936.
Coatman, J. *The British Family of Nations.* London, 1950.
Cromer, Lord. *Ancient and Modern Imperialism.* London, 1910.
Cromer, Lord *Political and Literary Essays.* 3 vols. London, 1913–16.
Coupland, R. *The Empire in These Days.* London, 1935.
Curtis, L. *The Commonwealth of Nations.* London, 1916.
Curtis, L. *The Problem of the Commonwealth.* London, 1916.
Curzon, Lord *The Place of India in the Empire.* London, 1909.
Dawson, R. M. *The Development of Dominion Status, 1900–1936.* Oxford, 1937.
Dewey, A. G. *The Dominions and Diplomacy.* 2 vols. Toronto, 1929.
Dilke, C. W. *Greater Britain.* 2 vols. London, 1868.
Dilke, C. W. *Problems of Greater Britain.* London, 1890.

SELECT BIBLIOGRAPHY

Dilke, C. W.	*The British Empire*. London, 1899.
Egerton, H. E.	*British Colonial Policy in the Twentieth Century*. London, 1922.
Egerton, H. E.	*A Short History of British Colonial Policy*. London, 1924.
Elliott, W. Y.	*The New British Empire*. New York, 1932.
Ensor, R. C. K.	*England, 1870–1914*. Oxford, 1936.
Freeman, E. A.	*Greater Greece and Greater Britain*. London, 1886.
Furnival, J. S.	*Colonial Policy and Practice*. Cambridge, 1948.
Galbraith, J. S.	*The Establishment of Canadian Diplomatic Status at Washington*. Berkeley, 1951.
Goldman, C. S. (ed.)	*The Empire and the Century*. London, 1905.
Gooch, G. P., and others	*The Heart of Empire*. London, 1901.
Grigg, E. W. M.	*The Greatest Experiment in History*. New Haven, 1924.
Guthrie, E.	*Home Rule and Federation*. London, 1887.
Hailey, Lord	*The Position of Colonies in a British Commonweath of Nations*. Oxford, 1941.
Halévy, É.	*A History of the English People in the Nineteenth Century*. 6 vols. London, 1949.
Hall, H. D.	*The British Commonwealth of Nations*. London, 1920.
Hall, H. L.	*Australia and England*. London, 1934.
Hall, W. P.	*Empire to Commonwealth: Thirty Years of British Imperial History*. London, 1929.
Hancock, W. K.	*Survey of British Commonwealth Affairs*. 2 vols. Oxford, 1937–42.
Hancock, W. K.	*Argument of Empire*. Harmondsworth, 1943.
Harlow, V.	*The Character of British Imperialism*. London, 1939.
Herbertson, A. J., and Howarth, O. J. R. (eds.)	*Oxford Survey of the British Empire*. Vol. vi. Oxford, 1914.
Hirst, F. W., and Hammond, J. L.	*Liberalism and the Empire*. London 1900.
Hobson, J. A.	*Imperialism: A Study*. London, 1902.
Hodson, H. V.	*Twentieth-Century Empire*. London, 1948.

Hurst, C. J. B., and others	*Great Britain and the Dominions.* Chicago, 1928.
Hythe, Viscount	*Problems of Empire.* London, 1913.
Jebb, R.	*Studies in Colonial Nationalism.* London, 1905.
Jebb, R.	*The Imperial Conference.* 2 vols. London, 1911.
Jebb, R.	*The Empire in Eclipse.* London, 1926.
Jennings, I.	*The Commonwealth in Asia.* Oxford, 1951.
Keith, A. B.	*Imperial Unity and the Dominions.* Oxford, 1916.
Keith, A. B.	*Responsible Government in the Dominions.* Oxford, 1928.
Keith, A. B.	*Letters on Imperial Relations, Indian Reform, Constitutional and International Law, 1916–35.* Oxford, 1935.
Keith, A. B.	*Letters and Essays on Current Imperial and International Problems, 1935–6.* Oxford, 1936.
Keith, A. B.	*Speeches and Documents on the British Dominions, 1918–31.* Oxford, 1948.
Keith, A. B.	*Select Speeches and Documents on British Colonial Policy, 1763–1917.* Oxford, 1953.
Knaplund, P.	*The British Empire, 1815–1939.* New York, 1942.
Knaplund, P.	*Britain: Commonwealth and Empire, 1901–55.* New York, 1956.
De Labilliere, F. P.	*Federal Britain.* London, 1894.
Langer, W. L.	*The Diplomacy of Imperialism.* New York, 1951.
Lewis, G. C.	*An Essay on the Government of Dependencies* (edited by C. P. Lucas). Oxford, 1891.
Lloyd George, D.	*War Memoirs.* 6 vols. London, 1933–6.
Lowell, A. L., and Hall, H. D.	*The British Commonwealth of Nations.* Boston, 1927.
Lucas, C. P.	*Greater Rom and Greater Britain.* Oxford, 1912.
Lucas, C. P.	*The British Empire.* London, 1915.
Lucas, C. P., and others	*The Empire and the Future.* London, 1916.
MacDonald, J. R.	*Labour and the Empire.* London, 1907.
MacInnes, C. M.	*The British Commonwealth and Its Unsolved Problems.* London, 1925.

Mansergh, N.	*The Commonwealth and the Nations.* Oxford, 1948.
Mansergh, N.	*Survey of British Commonwealth Affairs: Problems of External Policy, 1931–9.* Oxford, 1952.
Mansergh, N.	*The Name and Nature of the British Commonwealth.* Cambridge, 1954.
Merriott, J. A. R.	*The Evolution of the British Empire and Commonwealth.* London, 1939.
Miller, D. H.	*The Drafting of the Covenant.* 2 vols. London, 1928.
Milner, A.	*The Nation and the Empire.* London, 1913.
Milner, Lord, and others	*Imperial Problems.* The Empire Parliamentary Association series. London, 1916.
Milner, A.	*The British Commonwealth.* London, 1919.
Morrison, D. M.	*India and Imperial Federation.* London, 1900.
Muir, Ramsay	*The Character of the British Empire.* Lahore, 1918.
Muir, Ramsay	*The British Empire.* London, 1940.
Mullett, C. F.	*The British Empire.* New York, 1938.
Neuendorff, G.	*Studies in the Evolution of Dominion Status.* London, 1942.
Newton, A. P.	*A Hundred Years of the British Empire.* London, 1942.
Noel-Baker, P. J.	*The Present Juridical Status of the British Dominions in International Law.* London, 1929.
Pakenham, F.	*Peace by Ordeal.* Cork, 1951.
Parkin, G. R.	*Imperial Federation.* London, 1892.
Ransome, C.	*Our Colonies and India.* London, 1895.
Rose, J. H., and others (eds.)	*The Cambridge History of the British Empire.* 8 vols. Cambridge, 1929–59.
Schuyler, R. L.	*The Fall of the Old Colonial System.* Oxford, 1945.
Seeley, J. R.	*The Expansion of England.* London, 1884.
Semmel, B.	*Imperialism and Social Reform.* London, 1960.
Silburn, P. A.	*The Governance of Empire.* London, 1910.
Smith, G.	*The Empire.* London, 1863.
Smith, G.	*Essays on Questions of the Day.* New York, 1893.

Smith, G.	*Commonwealth or Empire.* New York, 1902.
Spender, J. A.	*Great Britain—Empire and Commonwealth, 1886–1935.* London, 1936.
Stewart, R. B.	*Treaty Relations of the British Commonwealth of Nations.* New York, 1939.
Stokes, E.	*The English Utilitarians and India.* Oxford, 1959.
Stokes, E.	*The Political Ideas of English Imperialism.* Oxford, 1960.
Strachey, J.	*The End of Empire.* London, 1959.
Sydenham, Lord	*Studies of an Imperialist.* London, 1928.

The History of 'The Times'. Vol. iv. London, 1952.

Thornton, A. P.	*The Imperial Idea and Its Enemies.* London, 1959.
Toynbee, A. J.	*The Conduct of British Empire Foreign Relations since the Peace Settlement.* Oxford, 1928.
Trotter, R. G.	*The British Empire–Commonwealth.* Toronto, 1932.
Tyler, J. E.	*The Struggle for Imperial Unity.* London, 1938.
Underhill, F. H.	*The British Commonwealth.* Durham, 1956.
Wade, Mason	*The French Canadians.* London, 1955.
Walker, E. A.	*The British Empire: Its Structure and Spirit.* London, 1956.
Walker, P. G.	*The Commonwealth.* London, 1962.
Walters, F. F.	*A History of the League of Nations.* 2 vols. Oxford, 1952.
Wedgwood, J. C.	*The Future of the Indo-British Commonwealth.* Adyar, 1921.
Wheare, K. C.	*The Statute of Westminster and Dominion Status.* Oxford, 1953.
Williamson, J. A.	*A Short History of British Expansion.* 2 vols. London, 1954.
Winslow, E. M.	*The Pattern of Imperialism.* New York, 1948.
Worsfold, W. B.	*The Empire on the Anvil.* London, 1916.
Zimmern, A.	*The Third British Empire.* Oxford, 1934.

III. BIOGRAPHIES AND MEMOIRS

Adam, C. F.	*Life of Lord Lloyd.* London, 1948.
Albiruni, A. H.	*Makers of Pakistan and Modern Muslim India.* Lahore, 1950.
Ali, Mohamed	*My Life: A Fragment.* Lahore, 1942.
Amery, L. S.	*My Political Life.* 3 vols. London, 1953–5.
Andrews, C. F.	*Mahatma Gandhi's Ideas.* London, 1929.
Asquith, H. H.	*Fifty Years of Parliament.* London, 1926.
Asquith, H. H.	*Memories and Reflections, 1852–1927.* 2 vols. London, 1928.
Azad, A. K.	*India Wins Freedom.* Delhi, 1959.
Banerjea, S. N.	*A Nation in the Making.* Oxford, 1931.
Bapat, S. Y.	*Reminiscences of Lokamanya Tilak.* Poona, 1921.
Birkenhead, Earl of	*Frederick Edwin, Earl of Birkenhead: The Last Phase.* London, 1935.
Bolitho, H.	*Jinnah: Creator of Pakistan.* London, 1954.
Brecher, M.	*Nehru: A Political Biography.* Oxford, 1959.
Bromage, M. C.	*De Valera and the March of a Nation.* London, 1956.
Butler, J. R. M.	*Lord Lothian.* London, 1960.
Callwell, C. E.	*Field Marshall Sir Henry Wilson: His Life and Diaries.* 2 vols. London, 1927.
Campbell-Johnson, A.	*Viscount Halifax.* London, 1941.
Carmichael, M. H. E.	*Lord Carmichael of Skirling—A Memoir.* London, 1929.
Carrington, C. E.	*Rudyard Kipling: His Life and Work.* London, 1955.
Chamberlain, A.	*Down the Years.* London, 1935.
Chamberlain, A.	*Politics from Inside: An Epistolary Chronicle, 1906–14.* London, 1936.
Chaturvedi, B., and Sykes, M.	*Charles Freer Andrews.* London, 1949.
Chirol, V.	*Fifty Years in a Changing World.* London, 1927.
Cotton, H. J. S.	*Indian and Home Memories.* London, 1911.
Crankshaw, E.	*The Forsaken Idea: A Study of Viscount Milner.* London, 1952.

Dawson, R. M.	*William Lyon Mackenzie King: A Political Biography.* Vol. i, 1874–1923. London, 1958.
Desai, M.	*Maulana Abul Kalam Azad.* Agra, 1946.
Duff, M. E. G.	*Notes on an Indian Journey.* London, 1876.
Dugdale, B. E. C.	*Arthur James Balfour.* 2 vols. London, 1936.
Durand, M.	*Life of the Rt Hon Sir Alfred Comyn Lyall.* London, 1913.
Dwarkadas, K.	*Gandhiji through My Diary Leaves.* Bombay, 1950.
Dwivedi, R. (ed.)	*The Life and Speeches of Pandit Jawaharlal Nehru.* Allahabad, 1929.
Escott, T. H. S.	*Pillars of Empire.* London, 1879.
Esher, Viscount	*Journals and Letters of Reginald, Viscount Esher* (edited by Oliver, Viscount Esher). 4 vols. London, 1938.
Fowler, E. H.	*The Life of Lord Wolverhampton.* London, 1912.
Garvin, J. L., and Amery, J.	*The Life of Joseph Chamberlain.* 4 vols. London, 1932–51.
Graham, G. F. I.	*The Life and Work of Syed Ahmed Khan.* Edinburgh, 1885.
Halperin, V.	*Lord Milner and the Empire.* London, 1952.
Hancock, W. K.	*Smuts: The Sanguine Years, 1870–1919.* Cambridge, 1962.
Hardinge, Lord	*Old Diplomacy.* London, 1947.
Hardinge, Lord	*My Indian Years.* London, 1948.
Gandhi, M. K.	*An Autobiography.* London, 1949.
Ghose, Aurobindo	*On Himself and on the Mother.* Pondicherry, 1953.
Halifax, the Earl of	*Fulness of Days.* London, 1957.
Hamilton, G.	*Parliamentary Reminiscences and Reflections, 1886–1906.* London, 1922.
Hennessy, J. P.	*Lord Crewe.* London, 1955.
Hoyland, J. S.	*Gopal Krishna Gokhale.* Calcutta, 1933.
Hughes, W. M.	*The Splendid Adventure.* London, 1929.
Husain, A.	*Fazl-i-Husain.* Bombay, 1946.
Jayakar, M. R.	*The Story of My Life.* 2 vols. Bombay, 1958–9.
Kabir, H. (ed.)	*Maulana Abul Kalam Azad: A Memorial Volume.* Bombay, 1959.

Karandikar, S. L.   *Lokamanya Bal Gangadhar Tilak.* Poona, 1957.
Karve, D. G.   *Ranade—The Prophet of Liberated India.* Poona, 1942.
Lyall, A. C.   *The Life of the Marquis of Dufferin and Ava.* 2 vols. London, 1905.
MacManus, M. J.   *E. De Valera.* London, 1944.
Masani, R. P.   *Dadabhai Naoroji.* London, 1939.
Maurice, F.   *The Life of General Lord Rawlinson of Trent.* London, 1928.
Millin, S. G.   *General Smuts.* 2 vols. London, 1936.
Mody, H. P.   *Sir Pherozeshah Mehta.* 2 vols. Bombay, 1921.
Morley, J.   *Recollections.* 2 vols. London, 1917.
Murdoch, W.   *Alfred Deakin.* London, 1923.
Nanda, B. R.   *The Nehrus.* London, 1962.
Nehru, J.   *An Autobiography.* London, 1942.
Newton, Lord   *Lord Lansdowne: A Biography.* London, 1929.
Nicolson, H.   *Curzon: The Last Phase.* London, 1934.
Nicolson, H.   *King George the Fifth.* London, 1952.
Owen, F.   *Tempestuous Journey. Lloyd George, His Life and Times.* London, 1955.
Parvate, T. V.   *Bal Gangadhar Tilak.* Ahmedabad, 1958.
Parvate, T. V.   *Gopal Krishna Gokhale.* Ahmedabad, 1959.
Prasad, R.   *Autobiography.* Bombay, 1957.
Purani, A. B.   *Life of Sri Aurobindo.* Pondicherry, 1958.
Ratcliffe, S. K.   *Sir William Wedderburn and the Indian Reform Movement.* London, 1923.
Ray, P. C.   *Life and Times of C. R. Das.* Oxford, 1927.
Reading, the Marquess of   *Rufus Isaacs, First Marquess of Reading.* Vol. ii, 1914–35. London, 1945.
Riddell, Lord   *Lord Riddell's Intimate Diary of the Peace Conference and After, 1918–23.* London, 1933.
Ronaldshay, Earl of *The Life of Lord Curzon.* 3 vols. London, 1928.
Sacks, B.   *J. Ramsay MacDonald in Thought and Action.* Albuquerque, 1952.
Saiyid, M. H.   *Mohammad Ali Jinnah.* Lahore. 1945.
Sastri, V. S. S.   *Life of Gopal Krishna Gokhale.* Bangalore, 1937.
Setalvad, C. H.   *Recollections and Reflections.* Bombay, 1946.
Simon, Viscount   *Retrospect.* London, 1952.

Sinclair, M. A.	*Lord Pentland—A Memoir.* London, 1928.
Skelton, O. D.	*Life and Times of Sir Alexander Galt.* Oxford, 1920.
Skelton, O. D.	*Life and Letters of Sir Wilfrid Laurier.* 2 vols. Oxford, 1922.
Smuts, J. C.	*J. C. Smuts: A Biography.* London, 1952.
Spender, J. A.	*The Life of Sir Henry Campbell-Bannerman.* 2 vols. London, 1923.
Sydenham, Lord	*My Working Life.* London, 1927.
Tahmankar, D. V.	*Lokamanya Tilak.* London, 1956.
Templewood, Viscount	*Nine Troubled Years.* London, 1954.
Tendulkar, D. G.	*Mahatma: Life of Mohandas Karamchand Gandhi.* 8 vols. Bombay, 1951–4.
Tyabji, H. B.	*Badruddin Tyabji.* Bombay, 1952.
van den Heever, C. M.	*General J. B. M. Hertzog.* Johannesburg, 1946.
Webb, B.	*Beatrice Webb's Diaries, 1912–24* (edited by Margaret Cole). London, 1952.
Webb, B.	*Beatrice Webb's Diaries, 1924–32* (edited by Margaret Cole). London, 1956.
Wedderburn, W.	*Allan Octavian Hume.* London, 1913.
Whyte, W. F.	*William Morris Hughes: His Life and Times.* Sydney, 1957.
Winterton, Earl	*Orders of the Day.* London, 1953.
Winterton, Earl	*Fifty Tumultuous Years.* London, 1955.
Wolf, L.	*Life of the First Marquess of Ripon.* 2 vols. London, 1921.
Wolpert, S. A.	*Tilak and Gokhale: Revolution and Reform in the Making of Modern India.* Berkeley, 1962.
Wrench, J. E.	*Geoffrey Dawson and Our Times.* London, 1955.
Wrench, J. E.	*Alfred Lord Milner.* London, 1958.
Young, G. M.	*Stanley Baldwin.* London, 1952.
Zetland, Second Marquess of	*'Essayez'.* London, 1956.

SELECT BIBLIOGRAPHY

IV. UNPUBLISHED PAPERS AND RECORDS

(A) OFFICIAL

Report of a Conference between the Right Hon. Joseph Chamberlain and the Premiers of the Self-Governing Colonies of the Empire at the Colonial Office, in June and July 1897. September 1897. Miscellaneous No. 111. Confidential. Public Record Office, London.
Conference between the Secretary of State for the Colonies and the Premiers of Self-Governing Colonies. Minutes of Proceedings and Papers laid before the Conference. Colonial Office, October 1902. Miscellaneous No. 144. Confidential. Public Records Office, London.
C.O. 323. Correspondence, Original. Colonies (General). Vol. 475. Year 1902. Public Record Office, London.
C.O. 532. Correspondence, Original. Dominions. Vols. 2 and 3. Year 1907. Public Record Office, London.
Public Letters from India, 1888, vol. 9. India Office Library.
Political and Secret Letters and Enclosures from India, 1899, vol. 114. India Office Library.

(B) PRIVATE

Austen Chamberlain Papers.	University of Birmingham Library. A.C.
Cross Papers.	India Office Library. MSS. Eur. E.243.
Curtis Papers.	By kind permission of Mr Dermot Morrah.
Curzon Papers.	India Office Library. MSS. Eur. F.111.
Dufferin Papers.	India Office Library, Microfilm.
Elgin Papers.	India Office Library. MSS. Eur. F.84.
Hamilton Papers.	India Office Library. MSS. Eur. C.125 and 126; MSS. Eur. D.509 and 510.
Lansdowne Papers.	India Office Library. MSS. Eur. C.145.
Minto Papers.	National Library of Scotland, Edinburgh. M.
Morley Papers.	India Office Library. MSS. Eur. D.573.
Ripon Papers.	British Museum. I.S. 290.

V. OFFICIAL PUBLICATIONS

C. 5091, 1887.	*Proceedings of the Colonial Conference,* 1887.
C. 8596, 1897.	*Proceedings of a Conference between the Secretary of State for the Colonies and the Premiers of the Self-Governing Colonies,* 1897.
Cd. 1299, 1902.	*Papers relating to a Conference between the Secretary of State for the Colonies and the Prime Ministers of Self-Governing Colonies,* June–August 1902.
Cd. 1931, 1904.	*Views of the Government of India on the Question of Preferential Tariffs,* October 22, 1903.
Cd. 2785, 1905.	*Correspondence relating to the Future Organization of Colonial Conferences.*
Cd. 3404, 1907.	*Published Proceedings and Précis of the Colonial Conference,* April 15 to 26, 1907.
Cd. 3406, 1907.	*Published Proceedings and Précis of the Colonial Conference,* April 30 to May 14, 1907.
Cd. 3523, 1907.	*Minutes of Proceedings of the Colonial Conference,* 1907.
Cd. 3524, 1907.	*Papers laid before the Colonial Conference,* 1907.
Cd. 4426, 1908.	*Proposals of the Government of India and Dispatch of the Secretary of State.*
Cd. 5745, 1911.	*Minutes of Proceedings of the Imperial Conference,* 1911.
Cd. 5979, 1911.	*Announcements by and on behalf of His Majesty the King-Emperor at the Coronation Durbar held at Delhi on December* 12, 1911, *with the correspondence relating thereto.*
Cd. 8566, 1917.	*Extracts from Minutes of Proceedings and Papers Laid before the Conference.* Imperial War Conference, 1917.
Cd. 9109, 1918.	*Report on Indian Constitutional Reforms.* (Montagu-Chelmsford Report).
Cd. 9177, 1918.	Imperial War Conference, 1918. *Extracts from Minutes of Proceedings and Papers Laid before the Conference.*
Cd. 9190, 1918.	*Report of Committee appointed to investigate Revolutionary Conspiracies in India, with two Resolutions by the Government of India.* (Rowlatt Committee Report).

SELECT BIBLIOGRAPHY

Cmd. 123, 1919.	*Letter from the Government of India to the Secretary of State for India, dated March 5, 1919, and enclosures, on the questions raised in the Report on Indian Constitutional Reforms.*
Cmd. 141, 1919.	*Report of the Committee appointed by the Secretary of State for India to inquire into questions connected with the Franchise and other matters relating to Constitutional Reforms.*
H.C. 203, 1919.	*Report of the Joint Select Committee on the Government of India Bill.*
Cmd. 207, 1919.	*Report of the Committee appointed by the Secretary of State for India to inquire into the Home Administration of Indian Affairs.* (Crewe Committee Report.)
Cmd. 943, 1920.	*Report of the Committee appointed by the Secretary of State for India to inquire into the administration and organization of the Army in India.* (Esher Committee Report.)
Cmd. 1131, 1921.	*Report of the Special Mission to Egypt.*
Cmd. 1474, 1921.	Conference of Prime Ministers and Representatives of the United Kingdom, the Dominions, and India held in June, July and August, 1921. *Summary of Proceedings and Documents.*
Cmd. 1586, 1922.	Non-co-operation. *Telegraphic Correspondence regarding the Situation in India.*
Cmd. 1987, 1923.	Imperial Conference, 1923: *Summary of Proceedings.*
Cmd. 1988, 1923.	Imperial Conference, 1923: *Appendices to the Summary of Proceedings.*
	India's Contribution to the Great War (Government of India). Calcutta, 1923.
Cmd. 2128, 1924.	*Report of the Royal [Lee] Commission on the Superior Civil Services in India.*
Cmd. 2360, 1925.	*Report of the Reforms Inquiry Committee,* 1924. (Muddiman Committee Report).
Cmd. 2361, 1925.	*Views of Local Governments on the Working of the Reforms,* dated 1923.
Cmd. 2362, 1925.	*Views of Local Governments on the Working of the Reforms,* dated 1924.
Cmd. 2768, 1926.	Imperial Conference, 1926: *Summary of Proceedings.*

Cmd. 2769, 1927.	Imperial Conference, 1926: *Appendices to the Summary of Proceedings.*
	Report of the Indian Sandhurst Committee, 1927. (Skeen Committee Report).
Cmd. 3302, 1929.	*Report of the Indian States Committee.*
Cmd. 3451, 1929.	*Report of the Indian Central Committee, 1928–9.*
Cmd. 3479, 1930.	*Report of the Conference on the Operation of Dominion Legislation and Merchant Shipping Legislation,* 1929.
Cd. 3525, 1930.	*Supplementary Note by Dr A. Suhrawardy to the Report of the Indian Central Committee* (Cd. 3451, 1929).
Cmd. 3568, 1930.	*Report of the Indian Statutory Commission,* vol. i.—*Survey.*
Cmd. 3569, 1930.	*Report of the Indian Statutory Commission,* vol. ii.—*Recommendations.*
	Report of the Indian Statutory Commission, vols. iv-v. Memoranda submitted by the Government of India and the India Office.
Cmd. 3700, 1930.	*Government of India's Dispatch on Proposals for Constitutional Reform,* dated September 20, 1930.
Cmd. 3717, 1930.	Imperial Conference, 1930: *Summary of Proceedings.*
Cmd. 3718, 1930.	Imperial Conference, 1930: *Appendices to the Summary of Proceedings.*
Cmd. 3778, 1931.	Indian Round Table Conference, First Session, November 12, 1930–January 19, 1931. *Proceedings.*
Cmd. 3997, 1932.	Indian Round Table Conference, Second Session, September 7–December 1, 1931. *Proceedings.*
	Indian Round Table Conference, Second Session, September 7–December 1, 1931. *Proceedings of the Federal Structure Committee and Minorities Committee.* 1932.
	India in 1917/18–1934/5 (Government of India publication). 1919–37.
	Parliamentary Debates, 1900–30.
	Abstract of the Proceedings of the Council of

SELECT BIBLIOGRAPHY

the Governor-General of India, assembled for the purpose of making Laws and Regulations, 1885–1907.
Proceedings of the Council of the Governor-General of India, assembled for the purpose of making Laws and Regulations, 1907–16.
Proceedings of the Indian Legislative Council, assembled for the purpose of making Laws and Regulations, 1916–20.
Legislative Assembly Debates, 1921–30.
Council of State Debates, 1921–30.

VI. JOURNALS AND NEWSPAPERS

Amrita Bazar Patrika. Calcutta.
Bengalee. Calcutta.
Englishman. Calcutta.
Hindustan Review. Allahabad.
India. London.
Indian Review. Madras.
Journal and Proceedings of the Royal Colonial Institute. London.
Modern Review. Calcutta.
Nineteenth Century and After. London.
Pioneer. Allahabad.
Round Table. London.
Statesman. Calcutta.
The Times. London.
Times of India. Bombay.
United Empire. The Royal Colonial Institute Journal. London.
Young India. Ahmedabad.

INDEX

Abrahams, Sir Lionel, 84 and n.²
Africa, 138, 247
Aga Khan, the, 183 and n.², 187, 199, 203, 257
Agent-General to South Africa, 242
Ahmedabad, 122, 123, 196
Aiyer, C. P. Ramaswami, 167 and n.¹, 240
Aiyer, Sir P. S. Sivaswamy, 153 and n.⁴, 156, 174, 200
Alam, Dr Sheikh Mohammad, 200 and n.¹
Alekar, N. R., 115 and n.⁴
Alexandria, 242
Ali, Mohamed, 187 and n.², 189, 200, 201, 203, 207 and n.⁴, 251, 252, 257
Ali, Shaukat, 118 and n.³, 186, 189, 200, 201, 203, 204
Aligarh, 182
Aligarh College, 182
Allahabad, 42, 45
All-India Moderates' Conference: First, 151; Second, 152–3
All-India Muslim League, 12, 64, 76, 102, 180–205 *passim*
All-India Nationalist Muslim Party, 203
All-Parties Conference, 136, 137
All-Parties Convention, 202
All-Parties Muslim Conference, 203
Amrita Bazar Patrika, 30, 107
Amritsar incident, 110 and n.³, 111, 114, 152, 195
Andrews, Charles Freer, 119 and n.⁴, 122, 251
Anglo-Irish Treaty, 125, 139, 220, 233, 234
Anglo-Russian Convention, 185
Anjuman-i-Khuddam-i-Kaaba, 186
Announcement of August 20, 1917, 86, 103–6, 107, 150–1, 175, 177, 214, 222, 227, 238, 255

Ansari, M. A., 143 and n.³, 186, 200, 202
Arabia, 94, 123
Archbold, William A. J., 182 and n.⁵
Archer, William, 64 and n.²
Asia, 33, 63, 138, 246, 250
Asiatic Federation, 257
Asquith, Herbert Henry, 67 and n.², 89, 93
Assam, 198
Australia, 21, 31, 89, 90, 96, 120, 230, 233, 241, 242, 247
Austria, 186
Azad, Abul Kalam, 186 and n.⁴, 200, 202

Baldwin, Stanley, 229 and n.⁶
Balfour, Lord, 100 and n.⁴, 225–6
Balfour Committee, 235
Balfour Committee Report, 134 and n.⁴, 166, 167, 235, 236
Balkan War, 186–7
Bande Mataram, 45–6
Banerjea, Surendranath, 20 and n.⁶, 31, 32, 150, 151, 152
Barbados, 30
Basu, Bhupendranath, 20 and n.⁶, 68, 148
Belgaum, 133
Belgium, 153
Benares, 35
Bengal, 15, 150, 198, 199; partition of, 20, 35, 36, 37, 66, 181, 185
Bengal Chamber of Commerce, 87
Bengalee, 107
Benn, William Wedgwood, 241 and n.³
Besant, Mrs Annie, 68 and n.³, 70, 77, 99, 101, 113, 152, 165, 190
Bikaner, Maharaja of, 77 and n.², 97, 99
Birkenhead, Lord, 129 and n.³, 130, 135, 176, 216–18, 221, 224, 226, 227, 237, 238

INDEX

Blackett, Basil, 213 and n.⁵, 214–15
Boers, 33, 42, 135, 153, 166
Boer War. *See* South African War
Bolshevism, 195, 200
Bombay, 15, 34, 41, 70, 71, 72, 99, 102, 109, 151, 191, 198
Bonnerjee, W. C., 30 and n.⁵
Borden, Robert, 96, 97, 117 and n.¹¹
Bose, Subhas Chandra, 142 and n.¹, 143, 145, 200; cited, 118–19
Bosnia-Herzegovina, 186
Botha, General, 96
Boycott, 35, 38, 43, 44
Brelvi, Syed Abdulla, 200 and n.⁴
Bright, John, 22, 29
British capital investments in India, 248–9
British citizenship, 22, 23, 34, 41, 42, 153, 254
British Commonwealth, 11, 12, 13, 67, 80, 84, 98, 106, 108, 115, 116, 118, 119, 126, 138, 140, 142, 143, 144, 146, 158, 161, 167, 199, 205, 206–7, 215, 227, 232, 234, 235, 236, 246, 249–50, 251, 252–3, 256, 257. *See also* British Empire
British Commonwealth Labour Conference 1928, 140
British Crown, 21, 107, 137, 156, 157, 160, 184, 235, 236
British Empire, 11, 12, 13, 20, 21, 30, 34, 35, 40, 42, 44, 45, 47, 66–96 *passim*, 102, 105, 106, 108, 111, 112, 113, 116, 117, 118, 119, 120, 121, 122, 124, 126, 131, 132, 133, 138, 139, 144, 145, 150, 153, 155, 156, 157, 159, 160, 161, 168, 170, 175, 190, 191, 193, 194, 195, 199, 202, 204, 220, 227, 228, 230–8 *passim*, 239, 242–6 *passim*, 250, 251, 252, 254, 256, 257. *See also* British Commonwealth
British Empire League, 88
British Empire Review, 88
British Indian Association of Bengal, 30
British *Raj*, 16, 24, 29, 36, 44, 47, 51, 54, 59, 155, 156, 184, 194, 223, 234, 251
British Royalty, 21
British shipping, 248

British trade with India, 247–9
Bulgaria, 186
Burke, Edmund, 22, 53, 106

Calcutta, 20, 41, 42, 44, 109, 114–15, 139, 140, 143, 177, 191, 195, 200, 243,
Campbell-Bannerman, Sir Henry, 89 and n.⁵
Canada, 30, 31, 33, 42, 80, 89, 96, 117, 120, 230, 231, 233, 234, 235, 241, 242
Cavour, 66
Cecil, Lord Robert, 238 and n.⁴
Central Provinces, 53
Ceylon, 242
Chamberlain, Austen, 78 and n.⁵, 79, 91, 95, 96, 97, 98, 100, 102, 103
Chamberlain, Joseph, 87 and n.³, 88, 243 and n.⁵, 246
Chanak incident, 233, 234
Charter Act, 1833, 17 and n.², 22, 48
Chatterjee, Atul, 240 and n.³, 241
Chelmsford, Lord, 72 and n.⁷, 74, 76, 85, 94, 98, 113, 148
China, 138, 139
Chintamani, C. Y., 148 and n.², 155, 166
Chirol, Valentine, 56 and n.⁵, 57, 67, 82, 85, 227
Churchill, Winston, 229 and n.¹
Coatman, John, 12
Colonial Conference: 1887, 86; 1897, 86; 1902, 86, 87, 88; 1907, 89–91
Colonial Laws Validity Act, 235
Colonial model, 38, 45, 51, 181. *See also* Dominion model
Colonial self-government, 35, 39–40, 41, 62, 123, 189, 239. *See also* Dominion self-government
Colonial *Swaraj*, 57
Colonies, 16 and n.¹, 30, 31, 32, 35, 39, 40, 42, 51, 86, 88, 89, 90, 105, 159, 188, 239, 243. *See also* Dominions
Commonwealth; Commonwealth of Nations. *See* British Commonwealth
Commonwealth ideal, 11, 12, 129, 158, 178, 200, 204, 246 n.⁵
Commonwealth of Islam, 257
Commonwealth of Nations, the, 80, 84

281

INDEX

Complete independence, 12, 44, 116, 117, 118, 119–24, 132–5, 142–6, 166, 167, 176, 178, 196, 200, 202, 204, 205
Conference on the Operation of Dominion Legislation and Merchant Shipping Legislation, 235–6
Congress. *See* Indian National Congress
Congress Democratic Party, 119
Congress-Khilafat Swaraj Party, 127. *See also* Swarajists
Congress-League Scheme, 76, 77, 102, 109, 190
Congress Memorandum, 107–9
Congress Muslims, 188, 200, 202, 203
Connaught, Duke of, 228
Conservatives (British), 25, 26, 49, 101, 107, 216, 254
Constantinople, 187
Corn Laws, 222
Cotton, Sir Henry, 15 and n.[6], 31, 34, 89
Coupland, Sir Reginald, 12, 84 and n.[1], 105, 142, 236
Courtney, Lord, 57 and n.[6], 63
Craddock, Reginald, 57 and n.[2]
Craik, George Lillie, 82 and n.[2]
Crewe, Lord, 52 n.[2], 61 and n.[3], 62–4, 71, 91, 222
Crewe Committee Report, 228
Crimean War, 66
Cromer, Lord, 62 and n.[7]
Cross, Lord, 27 and n.[6], 29
Currimbhoy, Sir Fazalbhoy, 191 and n.[6]
Curtis, Lionel, 80 and n.[2], 82, 83, 84, 85–6, 105, 191, 224, 246
Curzon, Lord, 19 and n.[9], 21, 24, 26, 28, 30, 34, 35, 48, 56, 61, 62, 103, 104, 105, 107, 148, 195, 222, 227, 243–4

Dalal, D. M., 239 and n.[5]
Daoodi, Shafi, 200 and n.[5]
Das, C. R., 114 and n.[3], 127, 129, 130, 209 n.[3], 251
Dawson, Geoffrey, 131 and n.[4]
Dawson, R. M., 234
Dayanand, 36 and n.[1]

Deák, 51
Delhi, 20, 109, 127, 151, 193, 203, 209
Delhi Durbar, 20
De Valera, 147 and n.[1]
Dewey, A. G., 234
Digby, William, 34 and n.[1]
Dilke, C. W., 15 n.[7], 243 and n.[2]
Dominion model, 13, 56, 225, 245, 254. *See also* Colonial model
Dominions, 11, 65, 69, 70, 71, 75, 76, 77, 81, 82, 83, 84, 85, 90, 91, 93, 94, 95, 96, 97, 98, 105, 108, 109, 110, 117, 120, 135, 136, 142, 159, 160, 165, 166, 169, 170, 173, 190, 191, 219, 220, 225, 226, 227, 228, 230, 232, 237, 238, 241, 242, 245, 254, 255. *See also* Colonies
Dominion self-government, 57, 60, 63, 64, 162, 214, 216, 222. *See also* Colonial self-government
Dominion Status, 12, 105, 118, 125, 126, 127, 133, 136, 137, 138, 139, 140, 141, 143, 145, 163, 165, 166, 167, 168, 175, 176, 177, 178, 199, 200, 204, 205, 206, 211, 213, 214, 216, 227–30, 233–8, 241, 245, 255, 256, 257
Dominion Status-*versus*-Independence controversy, 136–9, 176, 203, 204
Downing Street, 96
Dufferin, Lord, 16 and n.[8], 18, 27, 29
Duke Memorandum, 85 and n.[1]
Duke, Sir William, 77 and n.[5], 84, 85
Dyarchy, 85, 109, 129, 130, 153, 164, 165, 209, 216, 221
Dyer, General, 110 n.[3], 112, 114

East Africa, 65
East India Company, 25, 41
Eden Commission, 171
Edinburgh, 244
Edward, King, 20
Egypt, 37, 119, 139, 182
Elgin, Lord, 19 and n.[2], 48
Elphinstone, Mountstuart, 22
Empire. *See* British Empire
Empire Parliamentary Association, 95
Esher Committee Report, 168, 169, 228
Europe, 16, 63, 68, 69, 80, 140, 234, 250

282

INDEX

Extremists, 37–45, 53, 57, 61, 65, 70, 76, 77, 113, 149, 150, 152, 183

Fazl-i-Husain, 184 and n.²
Fiscal autonomy, 109, 151, 241
Fiscal Convention, 241
Filipinos, 33
Fisher, H. A. L., 210 and n.⁸
France, 38, 66, 186
Fraser, Lovat, 59 and n.⁸, 64

Gandhi, Mohandas Karamchand, 112 and n.⁸, 113–46 *passim*, 176, 178, 193, 196, 236, 252–3
Gauhati, 134
Genoa Conference, 241
George V, King, 20, 144, 160
Germany, 16, 65, 70
Ghose, Aurobindo, 36 and n.⁴, 37, 38, 39, 44, 119, 183
Ghose, Motilal, 20 and n.⁷
Ghose, Rashbehary, 44 and n.¹, 45
Gladstone, William Ewart, 12, 14
Gokhale, Gopal Krishna, 21 and n.², 29, 35, 36, 40, 41, 42–3, 45, 52, 53, 58, 70, 113, 250
Government of India Act 1919, 105, 110, 127, 128, 129, 153, 161, 162, 164, 165, 175, 176, 197, 201, 208, 210, 211, 213, 214, 216, 217, 219–20, 225, 228
Greco-Turkish War, 182
Greece, 153
Gujerat, 114

Habibullah, Muhammad, 240 and n.⁴
Hailey, Sir Malcolm, 85 and n.³, 162, 175, 177, 206, 213–15
Halibut Fisheries Treaty, 233
Hamburg, 242
Hamilton, Lord George, 19 and n.⁷, 28, 29, 34
Hancock, Sir William Keith, 12, 98
Hardinge, Lord, 61 and n.⁴, 62, 65, 66, 73, 91–4
Hartington, Lord, 27 and n.¹
Hasan, Yakub, 192 and n.⁸
Hertzog, J. B. M., 135 and n.¹, 166, 236
High Commissioner for India, 239
Hijrat, 193

Hindoo Patriot, 30
Hind Swaraj, 112
Hindus, 179, 180, 181, 185, 187, 191, 197, 198, 199
Holderness, T. W., 87 and n.⁵, 90
Home Rule agitation: in India, 30–1, 69, 70, 77, 99, 113, 119, 190; in Ireland, 16
Hughes, William, 96, 232
Hume, Allan Octavian, 16 and n.², 17, 33, 52
Hunter Committee Report, 112, 114

Ilbert Bill, 49 and n.¹
Imam, Sir Syed Ali, 181 and n.⁴, 200, 201, 202
Imperial Conference, 86–98, 100, 106, 108, 166, 238; 1911, 91; 1921, 159, 161, 231, 242; 1923, 156, 160; 1926, 135, 237; 1930, 236
Imperial federation, 69, 70, 80, 119, 231
Imperialism, 21, 33, 138, 139, 257
Imperial Legislative Council. *See* Indian Legislative Council
Imperial Press Conference, 244
Imperial War Cabinet, 97, 98, 231
Imperial War Conference, 86, 97–8, 99, 100, 166, 231, 232
Inchape, Lord, 63 and n.¹, 90
Independence Leagues, 139
India House, 239
Indian Civil Service, 24–5, 28, 119, 224
Indian Councils Act 1892, 26, 27 n.⁹, 48, 50
Indian Councils Act 1909, 50, 53, 54
Indian Diary, 113, 119, 246 n.²
Indianization, 171–2, 224, 237, 255
Indian Legislative Assembly, 128, 130, 162, 163, 164, 169, 170, 171–2, 174, 206, 208, 210, 212
Indian Legislative Council, 36, 50, 69, 73, 76, 91, 92, 93, 151
Indian National Congress, 11, 12, 15, 16, 17, 18, 19, 28, 31–46 *passim*, 48, 52, 53, 56, 58, 65, 68, 71, 72, 76, 85, 101, 109–46 *passim*, 149, 150, 151, 154, 155, 161, 176, 177, 178, 179, 182, 183, 185, 187, 188, 189, 191, 192, 196,

283

INDEX

197, 200, 201, 202, 203, 206, 219, 249, 250, 256
Indian Ocean, 247
Indian princely states, 130 n.⁹, 141, 178, 214, 224, 240, 247, 255
Indu Prakash, 36
Inter-Imperial Relations Committee of the Imperial Conference 1926. *See* Balfour Committee
International Labour Organization, 241
Iqbal, Mohammad, 183 and n.⁵, 198 n.²
Iraq, 123
Ireland, 12, 37, 38, 119, 125, 129, 136, 139, 165, 166, 219, 221, 233; Irish Free State, 234, 235; Irish Home Rule Bill 1886, 33
Irwin, Lord, 131 and n.², 139, 141, 143, 168, 176, 218, 221, 237, 238, 252; announcement of October 31, 1929, 141, 142, 177, 206, 228, 229, 238; note on Dominion Status, 168
Islington, Lord, 95 and n.⁴, 96
Italy, 16, 38, 153, 185, 186
Iyer, Govindaraghava, 159 and n.¹

Jallianwalla Bagh, 201 and n.⁵
Japan, 33, 34, 37, 40, 242, 245
Jayakar, M. R., 134 and n.¹, 178 n.¹, 251
Jazirat-ul-Arab, 123, 193
Jihad, 193
Jinnah, Mohammed Ali, 113 and n.⁷, 116–17, 118, 127, 183, 187, 190, 191, 192, 195, 200, 201, 202, 203, 205–6, 217, 251, 257
Jinnah League, 200, 202, 203
Joint Select Committee on the Government of India Bill 1919, 151, 161, 192, 224, 241
Joynson–Hicks, Sir William, 226 and n.² and ³, 227

Karachi, 144, 146, 188, 189, 196
Kashmere, 198
Keith, A. B., 12, 223 and n.¹, 238
Kelkar, N. C., 134 and n.², 143
Kellog-Briand Pact, 241
Kemal Pasha, Mustafa, 196, 204
Kenworthy, J. M., 146 and n.⁶, 147

Kenya, 160, 161, 256
Kenya White Paper, 160
Kerr, Philip, 64 and n.⁵, 80, 81, 82, 84, 85, 86, 245, 250
Kesari, 40
Khan, Ajmal, 200 and n.¹
Khan, Sir Syed Ahmed, 179 and n.¹, 180, 181, 182, 183, 184
Khan, Zafar Ali, 186 and n.³, 189
Khilafat, 114, 115, 124, 152, 189, 190, 193, 194; Khilafat Conference, 193, 194, 195, 196, 202; Khilafatists, 200, 202, 205; Khilafat movement, 192–7, 204
Kimberley, Lord, 27 and n.⁴, 28
Kipling, Rudyard, 157, 243 n.¹
Kisch, C. H., 84 and n.⁴
Knight, Holford, 117 and n.⁷
Koran, 180, 202

Labour Government: 1924, 127, 129, 213, 216, 217; 1929–31, 141, 206, 217
Labour Party, 56, 117, 129, 210
Lahore, 142, 143, 198
Lansdowne, Lord, 18 and n.⁴, 24, 27, 28, 48, 61
Lausanne, Treaty of, 195, 233, 234
Law, Bonar, 62 and n.², 117 n.¹¹
League of Nations, 110, 158, 231, 234, 238, 239–41, 257
Lee Commission, 164 and n.⁴
Legislative councils, provincial, 27, 49–50, 52, 74, 75, 78, 89, 208
Letters to the People of India, 85
Liberal Federation. *See* National Liberal Federation of India
Liberal Government (1906–10), 36, 40, 61, 180
Liberal Party, Liberals (British), 25, 26, 49, 56, 117, 184, 254
Liberal Party, Liberals (Indian), 118, 127, 134, 137, 141, 154–78 *passim*, 197, 199, 204, 205, 212, 219, 256, 257
Linlithgow, Lord, 256 n.¹
Lloyd George, David, 86, 96 and n.⁵, 97, 98, 100, 105, 110, 193, 195, 220, 224, 233, 237, 250
Locarno, Treaty of, 234, 241
London, 84, 97, 135, 239

INDEX

London India Society, 34
Long, Walter, 97 and n.⁴
Low, Sidney, 20 and n.²
Lucknow, 76, 187, 190
Lyall, Sir Alfred, 63 and n.⁸
Lyttleton, Alfred, 88 and n.⁶, 89

Macaulay, Lord, 22, 29, 57
MacDonald, J. Ramsay, 140 and n.¹, 205, 208
Mackay, Sir James. *See* Inchape, Lord
Madras, 15, 65, 117, 135, 136, 139, 164, 176, 198, 211
Mahmudabad, Raja of, 191 and n.², 200, 202, 205
Malaviya, Madan Mohan, 45 and n.³, 115, 118, 134, 143, 251
Malaya, 242
Malcolm, Dougal Orme, 82 and n.³
Malcolm, Sir John, 22
Mansergh, P. N. S., 12, 233
Marris, William, 80 and n.¹, 81, 82
Mary, Queen, 20
Marxism, 257
Massey, William, 96
Mazhar-ul-Haq, 188 and n.², 189
Mecca, Sherif of, 190
Meherally, Yusuf, 200 and n.³
Mehta, Sir Pherozeshah, 19 and n.³, 29, 44, 45, 48, 53, 70, 84
Mesopotamia, 94
Mesopotamian Commission Report, 100 and n.⁶, 101; debate on, 101
Meston, Lord, 60 and n.², 81, 82, 85, 97, 99
Metcalfe, Sir Charles, 29
Meyer, Sir William, 239 and n.³
Middle East, 65, 138, 169, 170
Milner, Lord, 56 and n.², 86, 106 and n.², 107, 148, 227
Minto, Lord, 20 and n.⁵, 46–54, 56, 58, 89, 148, 182
Mitter, Sir B. C., 152 and n.⁴
Moderates, 40–5, 52, 62, 70, 71, 77, 111, 112, 118, 148, 149, 150, 151, 152, 154
Mohani, Maulana Hasrat, 122 and n.³, 123, 124, 183, 196, 197, 198 and n.², 200

Mohsin-ul-Mulk, Nawab, 182 and n.⁴, 184–5
Montagu, Edwin Samuel, 61 and n.⁶, 62, 86, 101, 102, 103 and n.⁴, 104, 107, 113, 119, 148, 149, 155, 163, 165, 171, 195, 197, 209, 210, 211, 222, 223, 224, 226, 228, 246
Montagu-Chelmsford reforms, 85, 111, 148, 151, 161, 209, 227, 255
Montagu-Chelmsford Report, 66, 86, 104, 109, 150, 151, 181, 191, 209, 210, 216, 218, 223, 224, 227
Morison, Theodore, 57 and n.⁴, 182
Morley, Lord, 35 and n.⁵, 36, 40, 46–55, 56, 57, 58, 71, 89, 148, 182, 244
Morley-Minto reforms, 46–55, 66, 84
Morocco, 186
Muddiman, Sir Alexander, 165 n.¹, 216
Muddiman Committee, 165 and n.¹, 216
Munro, Sir Thomas, 22
Muslim League. *See* All-India Muslim League
Muslims, 50, 52, 110, 179–206 *passim*, 257

Nagpur, 44, 115, 117, 118, 121
Naidu, Mrs Sarojini, 143 and n.², 187, 252
Nair, Sankaran, 22 and n.⁴, 32, 148
Naoroji, Dadabhai, 23 and n.¹, 34, 35, 41, 183
National Convention: 1908, 45–6; 1922–5, 165 and n.², 173
National Liberal Federation of India, 11, 12, 159, 163, 165, 166, 172, 174
Nationalists. *See* Extremists
National Liberal League, 150
Near East, 169, 170
Nehru, Jawaharlal, 121 and n.¹, 135, 137–9, 140, 141, 145, 146, 154, 200, 251
Nehru, Motilal, 127 and n.¹, 128, 130, 131–2, 136, 137, 140, 143, 145, 176, 215, 217, 251
Nehru Report, 136, 137, 138, 140, 142, 176, 198 n.², 202, 203
Newfoundland, 30
New India or India in Transition, 15, 31

285

INDEX

New Party, 37, 38, 40. *See also* Extremists
New South Wales, 30
New Zealand, 30, 96, 120, 233, 241, 242, 247
Nomani, Shibli, 186 and n.[1]
Non-co-operation movement, 114, 119, 122, 124, 126, 161–2, 194, 195, 196, 197, 209, 211, 255
Northbrook, Lord, 243
North-West Frontier Province, 199

Olivier, Lord, 213 and n.[5], 225
Orange River Colony, 37

Pakistan, idea of, 198 n.[2]
Pal, Bipin Chandra, 32 and n.[1], 39–40, 62, 65, 119
Pal, Kristo Das, 30 and n.[8]
Pan-Islamism, Pan-Islamists, 181–2, 189, 196, 197, 199, 200, 257
Parliament, 25, 26, 33, 52, 61, 89, 108, 110, 111, 112, 125, 128, 135, 141, 149, 162, 173, 174, 175, 199, 201, 213, 214, 222, 230, 239
Parliamentary sovereignty, 173, 219, 220, 222
Passfield, Lord, 229 and n.[4]
Passive resistance, 38, 43, 102
Patel, Vallabhbhai, 140 and n.[3], 146
Peace Conference, 231, 238, 239
Peel Commission, 171
Peel, Lord, 164 and n.[1], 237
Peel, Sir Robert, 222
Persia, 37, 94, 182, 186
Philippines, 34, 37
Philips, C. H., 53
Pollock, Sir Frederick, 88 and n.[2]
Pradhan, R. G., 59 and n.[2]
Prince Edward Island, 30
Punjab, 15, 52, 114, 198, 199

Queen's Proclamation 1858, 17 and n.[5], 22, 28, 42, 157
Quoran. *See* Koran

Rai, Lajpat, 116 and n.[2], 198 n.[2]
Raj. See British *Raj*
Ranade, Mahadev Govind, 22 and n.[2]

Rasul, Abdul, 183 and n.[4]
Ray, Prithwis Chandra, 150 and n.[3]
Reading, Lord, 131 and n.[3], 211, 213, 216, 217, 218, 225, 228 and n.[16]
Reed, Sir Stanley, 158 and n.[1]
Reforms Inquiry Committee 1924. *See* Muddiman Committee
Reichstag, 70
Rhodes, Cecil, 157
Ripon, Lord, 26 and n.[2], 29, 31
Risley, Sir Herbert, 91 and n.[5]
Roberts, Charles, 67 and n.[5], 103
Round Table, 79 and n.[4]—86
Round Table, 64, 66, 86, 93, 212–13
Round Table Conference, 127, 128, 141, 144, 173, 174, 177, 178, 206, 214, 252
Rowlatt Act, 113 and n.[9], 152, 195
Royal Proclamation 1919, 110, 111, 152
Russia, 33, 37, 139, 185, 186, 195, 245
Russian revolution: 1905, 47; 1917, 99

St Christopher's Island, 30
Sapru, T. B., 148 and n.[1], 156, 157, 158, 160, 167, 173, 174, 175, 178, 251
Sastri, V. S. Srinivasa, 66 and n.[5], 148, 149, 154 n.[3], 159, 161, 165, 240, 242, 251
Satyamurti, S., 117 and n.[10]
Seeley, John, 25 n.[1], 121
Selborne, Lord, 86 and n.[2], 105
Separate electorates, 52, 181, 191, 192, 199, 201–2, 203
Servant of India, 149
Servants of India Society, 158
Setalvad, C. H., 148 and n.[3], 167, 200
Seton, M. C., 84 and n.[3]
Sèvres, Treaty of, 112 and n.[1], 114, 192, 193, 194, 195
Shafi, Sir Muhammad, 92 and n.[2], 187, 188, 189, 199, 200, 202, 203, 206, 257
Shuckburgh, J. E., 84 and n.[5]
Simla, 26, 73, 164
Simon Commission, 175, 176, 200, 201, 202, 205, 206, 210–11, 219, 221–2, 224 and n.[6]
Simon, Sir John, 220 and n.[2], 221 and n.[4]

INDEX

Sind, 198
Sinha, Sir Satyendra Prasanno, 71 and n.[2], 72, 97, 99, 148
Sinn Féin, 37, 38, 44; Sinn Féinism, 195
Skeen Committee, 172 and n.[3]
Smuts, General, 160, 232
Sobhani, Azad, 196 and n.[7], 200, 202
Socialism, 200
South Africa, 21, 33, 42, 96, 112, 125, 135, 160, 161, 165, 232, 233, 235, 241, 242, 256
South African War, 19, 112
Southampton, Bishop of, 59 and n.[5]
Soviet Union. *See* Russia
Spoor, Benjamin Charles, 117 and n.[6], 250
Statute of Westminster, 12, 236
Statutory Commission, 130, 173, 174, 199, 210, 213, 217–22. *See also* Simon Commission
Strachey, Sir John, 15 and n.[1]
Surat, 45
Surat split, 44
Swadeshi, 38
Swaraj, 38, 39, 41, 44, 62, 114–17, 119, 123–7, 130, 132, 133, 136, 142, 166, 181, 185, 196, 197, 198, 204, 205, 209, 211, 216, 217, 228, 248
Swarajists, 126–7, 129–34, 173, 199, 204, 212–14, 217, 218
Sydenham, Lord, 227 and n.[7]
Syed Mahomed, Nawab, 188 and n.[8]

Tagore, Rabindranath, 250 and n.[5], 251; cited, 22
Tilak, Bal Gangadhar, 21 and n.[4], 40, 41, 65, 77, 99, 114, 119, 126, 183, 251
Times, The, 40, 67, 85, 99, 101, 152, 222, 227, 229, 251
Times of India, 77
Tories. *See* Conservatives
Toynbee, A. J., 222
Trade Commissioners, 242
Trade, Indo-British, 247–9
Transvaal, 37

Tripoli, 185, 186
Trusteeship, doctrine of, 157, 219, 246
Turkey, 110, 114, 139, 152, 182, 184, 185, 186, 187, 189, 192, 193, 194, 209, 233, 242; Sultan of, 182, 184, 190, 196, 204

United Provinces, 52, 69, 198
United States of America, 33, 34, 38, 196, 198, 226, 233

Victoria, Queen, 20
Vincent, Sir William, 162 and n.[4], 171
Viqar-ul-Mulk, Nawab, 181 and n.[2], 185
Vivekanand, 36 and n.[2]

Wacha, D. E., 45 and n.[2]
War, First World, 64, 67, 91, 113, 189, 230–1, 247, 254; India's contribution to, 65
War Cabinet, 96, 100
War Office, 168, 169
Washington, 234
Washington Conference, 241
Wazir Hasan, Sir Syed, 188 and n.[4]
Wedderburn, Sir William, 17 and n.[7], 152
Wedgwood, Josiah, 60 and n.[4], 117
Wellington, Duke of, 222
Whitehall, 26, 164, 212, 213
Whyte, Sir Alexander Frederick, 210 and n.[10], 223
Willingdon, Lord, 70 and n.[1], 85, 99, 211
Wilson, President, 110
Wint, Guy, 23
Winterton, Lord, 237 and n.[4], 238, 249

Young India, 121–2, 124, 135
Young Turk revolt, 37, 182

Zanzibar, 242
Zimmern, A. E., 106
Zulu rebellion, 112

For Product Safety Concerns and Information please contact our EU representative GPSR@taylorandfrancis.com
Taylor & Francis Verlag GmbH, Kaufingerstraße 24, 80331 München, Germany

www.ingramcontent.com/pod-product-compliance
Lightning Source LLC
Chambersburg PA
CBHW070555300426
44113CB00010B/1264